THE CHARTER D

The Special Joint Committee on the Constitution, 1980–81, and the Making of the Canadian Charter of Rights and Freedoms

The Canadian Charter of Rights and Freedoms is an important document for all Canadians. Few today, however, are aware of the extensive work and tumultuous debates that occurred behind the scenes to make it a reality.

In *The Charter Debates*, Adam M. Dodek tells the story of the Special Joint Committee of the Senate and the House of Commons on the Constitution, whose members were instrumental in drafting the Charter. Dodek places the work of the Joint Committee against the backdrop of the decades-long process of patriation and takes readers inside the committee room, giving them access to Cabinet discussions about constitutional reform. The volume offers a textual exploration of the edited proceedings concerning major Charter subjects such as fundamental freedoms, democratic rights, equality rights, language rights, and the limitations clause.

Presenting key moments from the transcripts, carefully selected and contextualized, *The Charter Debates* is a one-of-a-kind resource for scholars, students, and general readers interested in the Charter and its impact on constitutional politics in Canada.

ADAM M. DODEK is a professor and Dean of the Faculty of Law at the University of Ottawa. He is one of the founders of the university's Public Law Group, and in 2014 *Canadian Lawyer* named him as one of the top 25 most influential lawyers in Canada. In 2015 he was awarded the Law Society Medal by the Law Society of Upper Canada.

# The Charter Debates

*The Special Joint Committee on the Constitution, 1980–81, and the Making of the Canadian Charter of Rights and Freedoms*

EDITED BY ADAM M. DODEK

UNIVERSITY OF TORONTO PRESS
Toronto Buffalo London

© University of Toronto Press 2018
Toronto Buffalo London
utorontopress.com
Printed in Canada

ISBN 978-1-4426-5050-3 (cloth)     ISBN 978-1-4426-2848-9 (paper)

♾ Printed on acid-free, 100% post-consumer recycled paper with
vegetable-based inks.

---

**Library and Archives Canada Cataloguing in Publication**

The Charter debates : the Special Joint Committee on the Constitution,
1980–81, and the making of the Canadian charter of rights and freedoms /
edited by Adam M. Dodek.

Includes bibliographical references and index.
ISBN 978-1-4426-5050-3 (cloth). – ISBN 978-1-4426-2848-9 (paper)

1. Canada. Canadian Charter of Rights and Freedoms.  2. Canada.
Parliament. Special Joint Committee on the Constitution of Canada
(1980–1981).  3. Debates and debating – Canada.  I. Dodek, Adam, editor

KE4381.5.C48 2018              342.7108′5              C2017-907381-8
KF4483.C519C48 2018

---

This book has been published with the help of a grant from the Federation
for the Humanities and Social Sciences, through the Awards to Scholarly
Publications Program, using funds provided by the Social Sciences and
Humanities Research Council of Canada.

University of Toronto Press acknowledges the financial assistance to its
publishing program of the Canada Council for the Arts and the Ontario
Arts Council, an agency of the Government of Ontario.

Canada Council    Conseil des Arts
for the Arts      du Canada

ONTARIO ARTS COUNCIL
CONSEIL DES ARTS DE L'ONTARIO
an Ontario government agency
un organisme du gouvernement de l'Ontario

Funded by the    Financé par le
Government       gouvernement
of Canada        du Canada

*To the women and men who contributed to the making of our Canadian Charter of Rights and Freedoms – Founding Mothers and Fathers of Re-Confederation, each of them.*

# Contents

# Acknowledgments

This book was inspired by the publication of *Canada's Founding Debates* (2000) by Janet Ajzenstat, Ian Gentles, Paul Romney, and William Gairdner. It is only a slight exaggeration to say that I have been working on this book since then. Many people have helped turn what was a germ of an idea into a reality. Thank you to the Honourable Claire L'Heureux-Dubé and to the Honourable Roy McMurtry for their support for this project in its early stages. Excellent research assistance was provided by former University of Ottawa law students and now graduates Emily Alderson, Carolyne Burkholder-James, Tanya Carlton, Pinar Cil, Joel Reinhardt, and Lee Sela.

I would not have been able to undertake, let alone complete, this project without the generosity of my colleague and friend Peter Oliver of the University of Ottawa's Faculty of Law. In the great spirit of collegiality that permeates our relationship, Peter lent me his six volumes of the proceedings of the Joint Committee for eight years as I slowly worked on this project. He trusted me to take these prized possessions on sabbatical to Israel in 2014–15, where I completed most of the work on this book. How strange I must have looked sitting in cafés in Jerusalem leafing through the large red volumes. Several wonderful colleagues read earlier drafts of chapters and provided helpful comments. Thank you to Stephen Bindman, Vanessa MacDonnell, and Rosemary Cairns Way.

Thanks to participants in the events of the time and in the Joint Committee process who shared some of their memories with me: David Collenette, Irwin Cotler, Graham Fraser, Eddie Goldenberg, Serge Joyal, Joseph Magnet, Lorne Nystrom, Svend Robinson, Barry Strayer, Tamra Thomson, and Victor Rabinovitch. Others who provided help or encouragement along the way included Irving Abella, Jamie Benidickson, Andrew Cohen, Penny Collenette, Pina D'Agostino, Kerri Froc, Martha Jackman, David Lepofsky, Maureen Appel Molot, Henry Molot, Len Rudner, Douglas Sanderson, Beth Symes, and Charlotte Wolters. A special thanks to my colleague Constance Backhouse for her constant enthusiasm and encouragement over the duration of this project.

Special thanks to Daniel Quinlan at University of Toronto Press for his unwavering support for this project over a long haul. Two anonymous reviewers provided valuable suggestions, which strengthened the manuscript. As always, thanks to Nicky and Ben for their support and their patience. A good portion of this manuscript was written during the summer of 2015, in between practices and games as members of the Ottawa West Little League Intermediate Twins went on the run of their baseball careers, winning the district and provincial championships and earning the right to represent Ontario in the national championships in Saint John, New Brunswick. Try as I might, I could not find a reference to baseball in the debates of the Joint Committee. There is, however, a reference to *Hockey Night in Canada*.* It might surprise readers, and, like much of the debates, I think it is worth reading.

Finally, thank you to the Senate of Canada and the House of Commons for giving me permission to reproduce the proceedings of the Special Joint Committee of the Senate and the House of Commons on the Constitution, 1980–81 (co-chairs: the Honourable Harry Hays and Serge Joyal, member of the House of Commons). The reproductions of those proceedings contained in this book are not the official version of those proceedings. Readers are encouraged to consult the official versions, published by the Parliament of Canada.

---

* See Canada, Parliament, Special Joint Committee on the Constitution of Canada, *Minutes of Proceedings and Evidence*, 32nd Parliament, 1st Session, issue 18: 28–9.

# THE CHARTER DEBATES

The Special Joint Committee on the Constitution, 1980–81, and the Making of the Canadian Charter of Rights and Freedoms

# Introduction

A constitution is not only a document [for] lawyers, but also a document [for] people, poets and others ... at least I hope it is.

– Gordon Fairweather, Chief Commissioner, Canadian Human Rights Commission, Special Joint Committee on the Constitution, 14 November 1980

Most Canadians have some knowledge of the Canadian Charter of Rights and Freedoms. However, few are likely to have heard of the Special Joint Committee of the Senate and the House of Commons on the Constitution, 1980–81, known simply as the "Joint Committee." This is unfortunate because this committee is an "important part of the patriation story."[1] It served in large part as the forge that produced the Charter that Canadians cherish today. Moreover, what happened at the Joint Committee fundamentally changed the nature of constitutional politics in Canada by making public participation a critical part of constitutional reform. More than three decades after the Joint Committee completed its work, Canadians continue to feel its influence, even if they are not aware of it.

The Joint Committee that operated from November 1980 to February 1981 was neither the first nor the last "special joint committee" of Parliament on the Constitution. However, it was arguably the most successful and the most influential one. In comparison to the making of Canada's original Constitution in the 1860s, having a joint committee was a far more democratic and inclusive exercise in constitution making. Backbench and opposition MPs made important contributions to the most important political issue of the day, perhaps of the century.

The Joint Committee had a dynamism – others might call it chaos – that differs from the more stage-managed affairs in recent parliaments. While there was no shortage of barbs tossed by MPs against each other, the proceedings of the Joint Committee lacked the fundamentalism that has come to characterize politics at the federal level in recent years. To the governing Liberals, the holy triumvirate of patriation, a domestic amending formula, and a Charter of Rights was non-negotiable; however, some of the contents of the Charter and the language of specific provisions were certainly open for discussion. Moreover, citizens influenced the debate at the Joint Committee in a manner that we have not been accustomed to for some time.

It must be acknowledged that the Joint Committee was indeed a highly flawed process. Despite the large number of participants, they could hardly be considered representative of Canadian society. The groups and individuals who appeared before the committee were selected by the committee members behind closed doors and often reflected the affiliations or the interests of the committee members themselves, hardly a representative group. The committee did not travel, so witnesses had to go to Ottawa, making it easier for central Canadian groups to participate than those from elsewhere in the country. This was especially important because, often, groups were given only forty-eight to seventy-two hours' notice to appear before the committee. The presentations were, not surprisingly, uneven.

However, the Joint Committee marked the first time that ordinary Canadians became participants in constitutional change rather than mere observers or silent subjects of it.[2] As constitutional lawyer and feminist activist Mary Eberts wrote in 1981, discussions about constitutional change had to that point largely been the exclusive domain of governments and of specialists within them; few ordinary Canadians likely believed that this process was relevant in their lives.[3] The proceedings of the Joint Committee changed all that. The joint committee process facilitated significant public participation, which had at least three critical consequences.

First, the testimony of certain groups – not all of them – unquestionably influenced the final text of the Charter. Some claim that the work of the Joint Committee had little impact: "It is remarkable how little substantive change occurred in the patriation package between 2 October 1980 and early February 1981."[4] Such assertions are difficult to sustain. While it is an exaggeration to say that the Joint Committee completely "overhauled" the text of the Charter as initially proposed,[5] it did make significant changes to the document.[6] As the following chapters reveal, changes made at the Joint Committee were not merely "cosmetic";[7] they were substantive. A direct line can be drawn between changes to the text of the Charter and the testimony of various groups at the Joint Committee.[8]

Second, the joint committee process ignited and mobilized wide-spread public support for the Charter, which significantly strengthened the federal government's bargaining position vis-à-vis the provinces.[9] The Joint Committee was the grand public stage for Prime Minister Pierre Trudeau's "people's package," which "developed a legitimacy it had not enjoyed before. By demonstrating the popularity of the Charter, the joint committee process abetted the federal strategy in another way. It took the issue out from under the control of the provincial premiers."[10] However, the Joint Committee could have easily backfired. It could have become bogged down in procedural arguments instead of substantive discussions about provisions of the proposed Charter, or it could have created a public backlash against the governing Liberals for failing to listen to the public. None of these events happened, although, as we shall see, the first almost did.

One of the main criticisms that emerged from the witness testimony at the Joint Committee was that the October 1980 draft of the Charter was not strong enough. As Chaviva Hošek wrote, "The government had underestimated the intensity and extent of popular concern with the proposed Charter."[11] The Liberal government quickly harnessed this popular political energy by being open to proposed amendments to strengthen the Charter. In comparison with the strength of their support for a constitutionally entrenched Charter of Rights and Freedoms, Canadians cared far less about process or about the rules for further constitutional change. In short, the federal-provincial disagreements over the mechanics of patriation and the amending formula failed to engage Canadians. The popularity of the Charter allowed the federal government to leverage support for the Charter to advance its broader agenda for constitutional reform.[12]

The third critical consequence of the joint committee process was that it fundamentally altered constitutional culture and constitutional politics in Canada. The Joint Committee was a significant exercise in citizen engagement, made all the more impressive given the tight time constraints under which the groups had to operate. The work of the Joint Committee is an important, but neglected, part of the story of patriation.[13] As Alan Cairns has written, the process of making the Charter transformed Canada's constitutional culture, with the result that Canadians took ownership of their Constitution for the first time and asserted their right to participate in constitution making (and constitutional amendment).[14] The joint committee process produced a new set of actors in the constitutional process – the groups that sought and/or gained constitutional recognition through the Charter and would subsequently be known as "Charter Canadians."[15] The Charter's entrenchment as part of the Canadian Constitution "has resulted in a renegotiation of the rules of engagement between the state and its citizens."[16] The centrality of these groups and the Joint Committee in the patriation process "created a new public expectation about popular participation in constitution making – an expectation that the architects of the Meech Lake Accord would ignore to their peril."[17]

No one could have anticipated that the Joint Committee would produce such results.

While the Joint Committee turned out to be a dynamic entity, it was certainly not intended as such. Pierre Trudeau's government sought to use it as an outlet to release some of the pressures of an overheated House of Commons, which had become the primary forum for expressing opposition to Pierre Trudeau's unilateral plan. The whole point of Trudeau's patriation plan was to come up with a mechanism to convert the British North America Act – an act of the UK Parliament – into a wholly *Canadian* Constitution. To do this, the Canadian Parliament would have to ask its UK counterpart to enact one final statute for Canada.[18] It would do so by way of a "joint resolution" of the Senate and the House of Commons, asking the UK Parliament to enact a statute that would contain the elements of an agreed-upon Canadian Constitution.

By sending the proposed resolution to the Joint Committee, the Trudeau government intended to move debate (and opposition) out of the bright lights of the cameras and away from media interest since committee proceedings were not televised and not covered as closely as debates in the House of Commons. The government also planned to use the Joint Committee to channel public support for the Charter and for its patriation plans. As is often the case, the government was only partially aware of the depth of public sentiments. Chaviva Hošek has written that "in those early days the government was not aware of the strength of feeling in the country about the Charter. And certainly the demand for wider public participation in the process of constitutional change was to become far stronger than Ottawa had expected."[19] In retrospect, the federal government benefited as much from good luck as from deft strategic planning.

The Joint Committee's work was far more extensive that originally intended. Instead of reporting back to Parliament on 9 December 1980, as set out in the original resolutions establishing it,[20] the Joint Committee was twice extended, finally reporting on 13 February 1981 (tripling the length of its original mandate). Instead of sitting for one month, as originally planned, the Joint Committee sat for three, holding 106 meetings over 56 sitting days for a total of 267 sitting hours between November 1980 and February 1981. The fact that it did not travel limited its exposure to groups from many parts of Canada. The committee spent 276.5 hours hearing witnesses who were able to travel to Ottawa and 90.5 hours debating amendments clause by clause.[21] Minister of Justice Jean Chrétien participated in thirty-nine meetings with the Joint Committee. Robert Kaplan, the solicitor general, stood in for Chrétien as acting minister of justice during nine sessions,[22] mostly in January 1981, when Chrétien was hospitalized for a week for a suspected heart attack, which turned out to be a combination of stress and indigestion.[23]

The Joint Committee was intended to be an obscure, technical proceeding taking place out of the public glare. Instead, as discussed in chapter 3, it was the first parliamentary committee ever to have its proceedings televised; many Canadians watched them, and the media followed the committee's progress closely.

No one in federal or provincial politics at the time predicted the level of demand for public participation that would ensue. Certainly, it is evident from the Joint Committee's first sessions, when chaos and reversals triumphed over order and consistency, that there was no coordinated plan to deal with the massive requests for citizen participation. In the end, the Joint Committee reported that over 1,200 Canadians from coast to coast to coast had sent it letters, telegrams, and briefs: 914 individuals and 294 groups representing untold thousands of members, congregants, and constituents.[24] These numbers do not appear significant compared to the population of more than twenty-four million Canadians in 1980; however, they demonstrate far greater public engagement in the joint committee process than in ordinary parliamentary or constitutional proceedings. The committee heard from 104 groups and individuals, and representatives of six provincial and territorial governments. A complete list of witnesses is included in appendix B.

This public engagement elevated the role of what we would today call "civil society" in the constitutional process. One of the most powerful images of the Joint Committee was the parity that it created between governments and civil society. Thus, while the premiers of Prince

Edward Island (PEI), Nova Scotia, Saskatchewan, and New Brunswick appeared before the committee, they were treated on a par with Chief James Gosnell of the Nishga Tribal Council, twenty-two-year-old Tamra Thomson of the National Association of Women and the Law, Dr Art Shimizu of the National Association of Japanese Canadians, Doris Anderson of the Advisory Council on the Status of Women, Dr Wilson Head of the National Black Coalition, and Professor Max Cohen of McGill University and the Canadian Jewish Congress. But that is not quite true. The premiers were predictable: political and partisan. To them, the Joint Committee was simply another forum for politics. For the others, the true stars of the process, the Joint Committee was the only opportunity to make their voices heard. Most of them made the most of this unique opportunity.

The Joint Committee was a high-water mark for the influence of civil society (at the time, such participants were considered "special interest groups"). The list of groups that were actually allowed to appear before the Joint Committee was not necessarily logical, coherent, or representative; they were selected by a subcommittee of the Joint Committee that operated in secret. There is a limit to the claim that can be made about the diversity of these groups. Far more wanted to participate than were selected to do so. The groups that did participate came from a cross-section of Canadian society. Business and professional groups participated, including the Canadian Chamber of Commerce, the Canada West Foundation, the Business Council on National Issues, and the Canadian Life Insurance Association. Many minority language groups participated. There were eleven minority or ethnic groups: the National Black Coalition of Canada, the Canadian Jewish Congress, the National Association of Japanese Canadians, the Mennonite Central Committee, the Ukrainian Canadian Committee, the Afro-Asian Foundation of Canada, the Canadian Consultative Council on Multiculturalism, the Canadian Polish Congress, the Council of National Ethnocultural Organizations of Canada, the German-Canadian Committee on the Constitution, and the Italian-Canadians National Congress (Quebec Region). Human rights groups included the Canadian Human Rights Commission, the Canadian Bar Association (CBA), the Canadian Civil Liberties Association (CCLA), the Canadian Federation of Civil Liberties and Human Rights Associations, the Newfoundland Branch of the CBA, the Vancouver People's Law School Society, the Saskatchewan Human Rights Commission, the New Brunswick Human Rights Commission, and the British Columbia Civil Liberties Association. Religious groups included the United Church of Canada, the Church of Jesus Christ of Latter-day Saints, and the Ontario Conference of Catholic Bishops.

The opportunity to participate in the Joint Committee was a critical experience for many, especially for women's groups, as discussed in chapter 2. Although only four women's groups were able to testify – the Advisory Council on the Status of Women, the National Action Committee on the Status of Women (NAC), the National Association of Women and the Law, and the Canadian Committee on Learning Opportunities for Women – women exerted a strong influence on the process. Moreover, the process influenced many Canadians. "The hearings raised the political consciousness of many people, and revealed the range and vitality of the opposition to the wording of the Charter and its approaches to human rights."[25]

Three groups representing persons with disabilities appeared (the Coalition of Provincial Organizations of the Handicapped, the Canadian Association of the Mentally Retarded, and the Canadian National Institute for the Blind). Three right-to-life and one abortion rights group participated and two law enforcement groups (Canadian Association of Chiefs of Police, Canadian Association of Crown Counsels). For the first time ever, a gay and lesbian group appeared before a parliamentary committee. Of the ninety-five groups that appeared before the Joint Committee, seventeen of them were Aboriginal; this is a remarkable number for a community that had been historically excluded from the political process.[26] Many of these organizations had created special committees on the Constitution.

Unfortunately, the work of the Joint Committee has largely been forgotten.[27] Most accounts of patriation give little acknowledgment, let alone credit, to the Joint Committee. They tend to focus on Trudeau, the premiers, and especially the November 1981 accord that produced both agreement on patriation and the notwithstanding clause. As (now Senator) Marilou McPhedran wrote on the 25th anniversary of patriation, the stories of the women and men who contributed to the making of the Charter have largely been overlooked; they are not honoured at anniversaries or invited to speak at conferences.[28]

The work of the Joint Committee has also been given short shrift by the Supreme Court of Canada. Justice Lamer (as he then was) effectively sounded the death knell for the committee just three years after the Charter came into effect in the *B.C. Motor Vehicle Reference* (1985).[29] In a case considering the interpretation of the term "principles of fundamental justice" under section 7, the government led evidence regarding the intentions of those who had drafted the Charter, including the Joint Committee testimony of Minister of Justice Chrétien, Deputy Minister Roger Tassé, and Assistant Deputy Minister Barry Strayer (later Strayer J.). Justice Lamer sharply dismissed this evidence, stating, "Were this Court to accord any significant weight to this testimony, it would in effect be assuming a fact which is nearly impossible of proof, *i.e.*, the intention of the legislative bodies which adopted the Charter. In view of the indeterminate nature of the data, it would in my view be erroneous to give these materials anything but minimal weight."[30] Justice Lamer's conclusion had an immediate and lasting impact on Charter interpretation.

The Supreme Court's dismissal of our Charter history reflects and contributes to a general Canadian malaise about our history in general,[31] especially our constitutional history. In contrast, Americans are obsessed with their constitutional history. There is an endless stream of biographies on the founding fathers, Supreme Court justices, attorneys general, solicitors general, and other relevant constitutional actors. In Canada, not so. This neglect of constitutional history has a debilitating effect on Canadian constitutional culture. It promotes a negative vision of the separation of powers – the isolation of powers – that views the courts, the legislature, and the executive as separate constitutional silos. Rather than viewing constitutionalism as a dynamic and shared enterprise, it promotes a vision of constitutionalism that is static and linear: Parliament enacts the Charter, the courts interpret it, and the executive or the legislature responds. Moreover, because of the constitutional pre-eminence of the Supreme Court of Canada as constitutional interpreter and arbiter, ignoring the contributions of the other branches degrades their importance as constitutional actors – precisely at a time when public trust in those branches is already at a low level.

Justice Lamer's statements in the *B.C. Motor Vehicle Reference* came at a time when the American debate on originalism was on the rise. Elsewhere I have explained how "originalism is a dirty word in Canadian constitutional law" and how it is either "ignored or denigrated in Canada."[32] Justice Lamer's statements about the framers' intent have been equated with all forms of originalism, and his conclusion in the *B.C. Motor Vehicle Reference* has had the effect of silencing consideration of the contributions of those involved in the making of the Charter. This is both unfortunate and ill-conceived.

Justice Lamer's conclusion is problematic in a number of respects. First, he conflated the problem of the indeterminacy of the views of the

framers with its relevance. He correctly identified the problem of indeterminacy in attempting to divine a collective "framers' intent" for the
Charter. As this book shows, the Charter was the product of the work
and the opinions of many. But this fact itself does not render their contributions legally irrelevant. Even if a collective framers' intent could
be divined, whether it should be determinative is a wholly separate
question.

Indeterminacy is not a barrier for relevance, let alone persuasiveness,
in constitutional interpretation under the Charter. The Supreme Court
of Canada often considers competing social science evidence, differing historical interpretations, divergent academic writings, and various
types of foreign jurisprudence. In each case, the process of interpretation does not involve a search for determinacy on a particular issue but
one for persuasiveness in its application to the issue before the Court.
The question should not be whether the so-called framers had a unified identifiable position regarding the meaning of a right, but whether
those who contributed to the creation of the Charter had relevant opinions and assertions concerning the meaning of rights and freedoms
that the Court should consider and address. Phrased in these terms, it
becomes difficult to justify how their views are less relevant than those
of foreign courts, academics, or social scientists.

Second, Justice Lamer and others have set up a false dichotomy
between considering the views of those who contributed to the Charter and the living tree doctrine of constitutional interpretation.[33] They
falsely equate the view of those who contributed to the text with the
widely discredited "frozen rights theory" of interpretation under the
Canadian Bill of Rights.[34] But this equivalency is unfair because, again,
it conflates two elements: the views or the meanings of the words at
the time they are enacted and their interpretative force. Moreover, it is
entirely possible that, on certain issues, the views of those who contributed to the Charter may be more progressive that the position adopted
by some judges. As we will see below, this is indeed the case when it
comes to certain issues under section 1.

Third, paradoxically, those who argue for the living tree, or progressive, approach to constitutional interpretation often explicitly invoke
originalist arguments regarding the intentions of the so-called framers
of the Charter. Thus, for example, Justice Binnie wrote in 2007 that "if
you ask where the court gets its mandate to give an interpretation of
the Constitution other than its 'original meaning,' I say it comes from
a shared understanding of the framers and judges that this would be

the role of the courts."[35] As will be seen in chapter 12, Justice Binnie was absolutely correct. However, it is a problematic leap of logic to go from the assertion that the views of those involved in the making of the Charter are relevant to determining who should be chiefly responsible for interpreting Charter rights to the position that the views of those same participants should be irrelevant when it comes to the actual interpretation of specific rights. To be clear, this is not the position that Justice Binnie articulated. However, it is a fair reading of the Supreme Court's approach to Charter interpretation since 1982.[36]

My position is a simple one: the views of those who contributed to the enactment of the Charter matter; they matter in terms of constitutional history, and they should be acknowledged as legitimate sources in the interpretation of the Charter. By no means should their views necessarily prevail, but neither should they be completely dismissed as illegitimate. Simply put, the views expressed by those who contributed to the making of the Charter should be considered along with other interpretative sources.

In this group of "Charter Makers," I include the government officials who drafted the Charter; the witnesses who appeared before the Joint Committee; and the members of the Joint Committee, who debated the draft, made amendments, and recommended it to the House of Commons and the Senate as well as participated in the debates in Parliament.

Moreover, prevailing theories of interpretation at the Supreme Court support the consideration of the historical debates surrounding the Charter's enactment. Under "purposive interpretation," rights should be interpreted in accordance with their purpose.[37] It seems strange, to say the least, that in determining the purpose of an enumerated right, the Court examines philosophers, foreign court decisions, and social science evidence, but yet steadfastly refuses to examine the discussions and debates by those who actually enacted the language that the Court is interpreting. Similarly, contextual interpretation would seem to invite active engagement with the context in which the Charter was enacted. As Shalin Sugunasiri explained in *R. v. Big M Drug Mart Ltd.*,[38] "the Supreme Court manifested a significant methodological commitment to taking broader social and philosophical contexts into consideration in elucidating fundamental legal principles."[39] Again, how broader social and philosophical contexts can be relevant, while the more specific drafting context is not, is unclear.

This judicial denigration of the constitutional process that produced the Charter is also at odds with Hogg and Bushell's dialogue theory,[40] which the Supreme Court has endorsed in a number of cases.[41] The

Court has spoken about mutual respect among the different branches of government and asserted that the Charter has given rise "to a more dynamic interaction" among these branches.[42] Ignoring the work of one branch of government and of citizens relating to our fundamental law is not conducive to mutual respect.[43]

This book attempts to tell the story of the Joint Committee and the debates that occurred therein over provisions of the Charter that are now part of the Canadian Constitution. It is divided into two parts. In part one, I place the work of the Joint Committee in the political context of the constitutional negotiations of the period. Chapter 1, entitled "Prelude: The Long Road to the Joint Committee," takes the reader back to 1966, with Pierre Trudeau's involvement in the federal constitutional file as parliamentary secretary to Prime Minister Lester Pearson. It moves through the next decade and a half leading up to the creation of the Joint Committee in October 1980. Chapter 2 picks up in the fall of 1980 and describes the cast of characters at the Joint Committee: the senators and MPs who sat on the committee, the government witnesses, and some of the 104 groups and individuals that appeared before the committee. Chapter 3 focuses squarely on the Joint Committee, describing the major issues and events that occurred between November 1980 and the delivery of the committee's report in February 1981. Chapter 4 completes the story by taking the reader through the events culminating in the successful patriation of the Canadian Constitution and its proclamation on 17 April 1982.

In part two, I let the Joint Committee's participants speak for themselves. Each chapter in this part follows a similar format. Individual chapters focus on particular parts of the Charter or issues that captured the Joint Committee's attention in a sustained way. Thus, chapters address fundamental freedoms, democratic rights, mobility rights, legal rights, equality rights, official language rights, minority-language-education rights, Aboriginal rights, and the limitations clause. Each of these chapters begins with the text of the provisions under discussion, showing a marked-up version of the text that was referred to the Joint Committee to indicate the amendments it had agreed upon. In all but three instances (changes to section 6 and the addition of sections 28 and 33), the version that came out of the Joint Committee was the final draft in the eventual Charter. Where this is not the case, I have so noted. The text is followed by my short analysis and then the words of the members of the Joint Committee and the witnesses who appeared before them. Because there are many typos in the verbatim transcript, I have made non-substantive corrections without denoting [sic] so as not to distract the reader. In all cases, I have provided references to the issue number and the page from which the excerpt was taken so that curious readers can look up the debates in their entirety should they wish to do so.

In a book like this, there will be obvious omissions given that the transcripts of the proceedings run to thousands of pages. In choosing to focus on specific sections of the Charter, there are only sporadic references to several subjects that concerned many witnesses and committee members, such as abortion and God.

There is one more important caveat that must be offered, and that is regarding the treatment of Aboriginal issues. Aboriginal groups played an important role, both symbolically and substantively, in the work of the Joint Committee. They made up a remarkable seventeen of the ninety-five groups that appeared before the Joint Committee, or roughly 18 per cent of all witnesses. Consequently, there was much discussion of Aboriginal issues before the Joint Committee. Aboriginal interventions within and outside the committee led to two major changes to the draft resolution: (1) the addition of section 25, which provides, "The guarantee in this Charter of certain rights and freedoms shall not be construed so as to abrogate or derogate from any aboriginal, treaty or other rights or freedoms that pertain to the aboriginal peoples of Canada including (a) any rights or freedoms that have been recognized by the Royal Proclamation of October 7, 1763; and (b) any rights or freedoms that now exist by way of land claims agreements or may be so acquired"; and (2) the addition of section 35 – a self-standing provision relating to the rights of the Aboriginal peoples of Canada. Section 35 was seen as the provision with by far the greater potential and, indeed, it has turned out to have much more wide-ranging impact than section 25. Section 35 was seen as the beginning, rather than the end, of the constitutional entrenchment of Aboriginal rights. For this reason, it was placed outside the Charter in a separate section of the Constitution Act, 1982 entitled "Rights of the Aboriginal Peoples of Canada." While technically outside the Charter, Aboriginal rights are a critical part of the discussion about rights under our Constitution. I have therefore devoted a chapter to their analysis, but I am unable to do justice to the breadth and depth of the discussion of these issues. It is hoped that others will take up this mandate.

# PART ONE

## Chapter One

# Prelude: The Long Road to the Joint Committee

## A Very Long Prelude

In 1867, the Dominion of Canada was created by the British North America Act (BNA Act). It was a constitutional arrangement that became known as Confederation, which was intended to continue existing relations with Great Britain rather than sever them. The BNA Act, therefore, was an act of the British Parliament, which declared that Canada wished to have "a Constitution similar in principle to that of the United Kingdom" – i.e., largely unwritten. When the Fathers of Confederation met at Charlottetown in 1864 and then later at Quebec that same year, at no time did they discuss – let alone propose – how the legislation that would become the BNA Act would be amended.[1] It was simply assumed that the British Parliament would amend it as necessary. This is precisely what occurred over the course of the first fifty years of Canada's existence as the BNA Act was amended by Westminster numerous times.

However, as Canada came of age over the course of those fifty years, and especially through the experience of battlefield sacrifices in the trenches of the First World War, the existing constitutional arrangement became increasingly unacceptable. In 1926, the British Balfour Report acknowledged the independent status within the British Empire of the six dominions: Canada, New Zealand, Australia, the Irish Free State, Newfoundland, and South Africa.[2] This led to formal recognition of this fact in the Statute of Westminster in 1931. Under this act, Westminster forswore legislating for each of the dominions without their consent. The Statute of Westminster laid the foundation for *patriation* of the BNA Act – the legal act of converting a British statute into a domestic

Canadian constitution,[3] a process that became known colloquially as "bringing the Constitution home" to Canada. To do this, however, agreement had to be found on a process to amend the eventual Canadian Constitution. The first attempt by the prime minister and the provincial premiers to reach an agreement on patriation and an amending formula occurred in 1927, after the Balfour Report;[4] it was the first of thirteen unsuccessful attempts over the next five decades.[5] Success was finally achieved on the fourteenth attempt in 1981–82.

The quest for patriation and a domestic amending formula thus became either a national pastime or a national pathology, depending on one's perspective. Perhaps the thirteen failures were due to a lack of urgency. As Peter Russell wrote in 2004, "No liberal democratic state has accomplished comprehensive constitutional change outside the context of some cataclysmic situation such as revolution, world war, the withdrawal of empire, civil war, or the threat of imminent breakup. A country must have a sense that its back is to the wall for its leaders and its people to have the will to accommodate their differences."[6] This may have also explained the lack of success in constitutional reform in Canada until 1982; however, it does not explain why the efforts of 1980–81 succeeded where so many prior attempts had failed. For that explanation, we must go back to 1966.

The modern story of Canadian constitutional reform begins a half-century ago with the election in Quebec of Union Nationale Premier Daniel Johnson, Sr in 1966. He put constitutional reform squarely on the national agenda. Between 1960 and 1966, when Liberal Premier Jean Lesage led Quebec, there appeared to be an unspoken agreement between Quebec City and Ottawa not to raise the constitutional issues of patriation and an amending formula directly lest it be revealed to be unsolvable and damage relations between the two governments.[7] However, Premier Johnson, whose 1965 eponymous manifesto *Égalité ou indépendance* ("Equality or Independence") had captured the essence of his demands, threw down the constitutional gauntlet in the December 1966 Throne Speech with a demand for "a new constitutional order" to achieve "a true alliance between two co-equal peoples."[8] The federal government could no longer avoid the constitutional issue.

Prime Minister Lester Pearson had recruited the "three wise men" of Quebec to the Liberal Party in 1965. Labour leader Jean Marchand was clearly "the catch," but he insisted on bringing along two colleagues: journalist and editor of *Le Devoir* Gérard Pelletier and the Université de Montréal law professor and public intellectual Pierre Elliott Trudeau.

The latter was largely unknown outside Quebec. Soon after his election to the House of Commons in November 1965, Pierre Trudeau was made parliamentary secretary to Prime Minister Pearson, rapidly ascending to Cabinet as Minister of Justice and Attorney General of Canada on 4 April 1967. In these positions, Trudeau was at the centre of developing the federal government's constitutional strategy. He became prime minister in April 1968, with barely a year's experience as a Cabinet minister.

By this time, Canada's constitutional journey had been characterized by four decades of futility. It is entirely possible that the quest would have continued for another four decades and perhaps decades after that if not for Pierre Trudeau's dogged determination and the longevity of his term of office (1968–84, with the nine-month hiatus from June 1979 to March 1980, when Joe Clark was prime minister). As Lorraine Weinrib has written, "Until his final term as Prime Minister, Trudeau's rendezvous with the B.N.A. Act remained beyond his grasp."[9] If Joe Clark had not lost the vote in the House of Commons in December 1979 and gone immediately to the governor general to request a dissolution of Parliament and a new election, Pierre Trudeau would likely never have returned to politics. Instead, he returned to lead the Liberal Party back to victory in the February 1980 election. As Weinrib states, "It is likely that any other politician would have put the project aside, as previous prime ministers had done in the 1940s and 1950s."[10] But Trudeau was not any other politician.

For Trudeau, the constitution was his "magnificent obsession."[11] If history is a guide, the Constitution should have become Pierre Trudeau's "white whale" instead of his crowning achievement; it should have defeated him instead of ensuring his legacy. Trudeau would, in fact, fail several times before successfully patriating the Canadian Constitution in 1982. The Charter of Rights and Freedoms was the central component, giving Trudeau's patriation efforts a public profile and public support that previous patriation efforts had lacked.

But when Trudeau began his constitutional efforts, all this lay many years ahead.

## Pierre Trudeau's Quest Begins

The occasion of Canada's centennial year provided Pierre Trudeau with the opportunity to convince his Cabinet colleagues to jump into the constitutional fray.[12] He launched his public quest for constitutional reform on 4 September 1967, as minister of justice at the annual meeting of the CBA in Quebec City. (There is a lengthy tradition of federal ministers of justice speaking at the CBA's annual meeting. However, it has been some time since a minister has been invited to be the keynote speaker;[13] instead, over the past decade, the CBA has paid handsomely for notable speakers like Arianna Huffington, Rex Murphy, Maya Angelou, and Robert Kennedy Jr to appear.) In September 1967, Trudeau was enough of an attraction for the national legal association.[14] His star would soon cross over into the political mainstream as Trudeaumania took off just a few months later.

Trudeau's constitutional vision was clear, coherent, and compelling. He advocated entrenching a constitutional bill of rights as the first order of constitutional business. In so doing, he aimed to put Canadians at the centre of his constitutional reforms. Until Trudeau, constitutional reforms had essentially been about governments; but Trudeau served notice that federal and provincial governments would have to subordinate their interests and the conflicts between them to the greater interests of Canadians. At the CBA annual meeting, Trudeau declared, "I am thinking of a Bill of Rights that will be so designed to limit the exercise of all governmental power, federal and provincial. It will not involve any gain by one jurisdiction at the expense of the other. There would be no transfer of power from the federal Parliament to the provincial Legislatures, or from the provincial Legislatures to the federal Parliament. Instead, the power of both the federal government and the provincial governments would be restrained in favour of the Canadian citizen who would, in consequence, be better protected in the exercise of his fundamental rights and freedoms."[15]

In February 1968, Prime Minister Lester Pearson convened the "Federalism for the Future" conference. In preparation for this conference, Minister of Justice Pierre Trudeau released a policy paper entitled *A Canadian Charter of Human Rights*.[16] This "hastily-drafted" discussion paper[17] framed the debate for a constitutionally entrenched charter of rights over the next decade and a half, eventually leading to the Canadian Charter of Rights and Freedoms fourteen years later after many meetings, drafts, and failures. While *A Canadian Charter of Human Rights* did not set out the text of a proposed constitutionally entrenched bill of rights, it strongly influenced the drafting of the text of the Charter that would eventually be adopted in 1982.

The Canadian Charter of Human Rights contained five parts: (1) political rights (freedom of expression, freedom of conscience and religion, freedom of assembly and association), (2) legal rights, (3) egalitarian rights, (4) linguistic rights, and (5) economic rights.[18] The last category – what we would call today "social and economic rights" – listed the right to work, the right to protection against unemployment, the right to form and join trade unions, the right to social security, the right to rest and leisure, the right to an adequate standard of living, the right to education, and the right to participate in the cultural life of the community. Such rights were characterized as "desirable" but ultimately dismissed as not practical to pursue in a constitutional bill of rights at the time,[19] leaving the first four categories.

Trudeau's 1968 charter had the unintended consequence of creating "blocks of rights" whose structure would be carried over into subsequent draft charters and over whose rights the federal and provincial governments would come to negotiate.[20] Other blocks were added (notably, democratic rights, mobility rights, and minority-language-education rights), but the core four blocks can be found in the sections on Fundamental Freedoms (2), Legal Rights (7–14), Equality Rights (15), and Official Languages of Canada (16–22) in the modern-day Charter.

Given the many draft constitutional proposals that had gone nowhere in the preceding decades, Trudeau's Canadian Charter of Human Rights was unlikely to have provided the blueprint for the eventual Charter of Rights and Freedoms. By October 1968, after winning the Liberal leadership and a majority government, Trudeau's idea of altering the BNA Act "could have easily died from inertia."[21] The Opposition was stalled in Quebec. There was a lack of interest in constitutional reform in English Canada. But Trudeau persevered.

## The Rise of Executive Federalism

The February 1968 federal-provincial conference convened by Pearson became the template that Trudeau would use many times over the next decade and a half. As Peter Russell explains, "The formal set pieces remained thoroughly elitist: first ministers, attorneys-general, and government experts negotiating through the procedures of what Richard Simeon aptly termed 'federal-provincial diplomacy.'"[22] This process has also become known as *executive federalism*, denoting negotiations over federal-provincial affairs taking place among first ministers and their advisers. Whereas in his CBA speech and in other public appearances Trudeau talked about the rights of Canadians, the process that he set up did not permit public participation. Executive federalism did not allow a role for public participation; it was thoroughly elitist, often secretive, and rarely public.[23]

The period between 1968 and 1971 has been termed the "apex of executive federalism."[24] It featured no fewer than four first ministers' conferences on the Constitution, supported by numerous working sessions by officials.[25] However, the beginning of parliamentary and public involvement can also be traced to this period.

In January 1970, the Special Joint Committee of the Senate and the House of Commons on the Constitution of Canada was established, co-chaired by Senator Gildas Molgat of Manitoba and MP Mark MacGuigan of Ontario (later to become minister of external affairs and then Trudeau's last minister of justice and attorney general, 1982–84). In terms of democratic participation, the Molgat-MacGuigan Committee far exceeded the work of the Joint Committee in 1980–81. It held public hearings and meetings in forty-seven cities and towns across the country, hearing from 1,486 witnesses at meetings attended by 13,000 Canadians. The evidence totalled 8,000 pages. But in a sense, it was too much and too soon; the committee was considered "slightly ahead of its time."[26] Canada was not ready for a new constitutionalism that actually involved Canadians. However, the larger problem with the committee was its complete detachment from the main track of constitutional negotiations taking place between the federal government and the provinces.[27]

While the Molgat-MacGuigan Committee was touring the country hearing from Canadians, Trudeau, the premiers, and their officials continued to try to hammer out a deal. In June 1971, they seemingly reached an agreement at Victoria. The Victoria Charter – now considered a "mini–Charter of Rights"[28] – was a scaled-down version of Trudeau's 1968 proposal. It included only two of the four blocks of rights: (1) political rights (expanded to include what would later be called "democratic rights" – i.e., sections 3 to 5 of the Canadian Charter of Rights and Freedoms) and (2) language rights. There were no "egalitarian" or "equality" rights and no legal rights. There was agreement on constitutionalizing the Supreme Court, equalization, and a domestic amending formula – making them subject to provisions of the Constitution.[29] However, the agreement collapsed within a week as Quebec Premier Robert Bourassa returned to Quebec and withdrew his support in the face of internal opposition. Nearly a decade later, "Victoria" would continue to cast a shadow over the proceedings of the Joint Committee in 1980–81.

With the collapse of the Victoria accord, constitutional reform was placed on the back burner for several years. Thus, when the Molgat-MacGuigan Committee finally delivered its wide-ranging report in March 1972, there was no active group to "receive" it. Its recommendations far exceeded those agreed upon, then reneged upon, at Victoria.[30] After the failure of Victoria, "The provinces were generally bored with the subject [of constitutional reform] and the federal government had many other priorities in what were difficult economic times."[31]

However, things heated up again after the election of the Parti Québécois (PQ) in November 1976. Earlier in the year, Trudeau had written to the premiers, seeking their feedback on a proposed draft proclamation by the Senate and the House of Commons to jointly call on the British Parliament to patriate the Canadian Constitution. The premiers responded coolly several months later. In the words of Romanow, Whyte, and Leeson, the "quest" had begun anew.[32] But something was different this time.

**The Public Awakens**

The election of the PQ led to much more popular interest in constitution making through conferences, meetings, etc.[33] As Peter Russell wrote, "The people were to be involved as more than voyeurs in constitution making."[34] "But the politicians had other ideas. Constitution making was too important to be left to the people. By 1977, government task forces and commissions were working away on constitutional proposals."[35] There was thus a continued disjuncture between the process of constitution making and the popular interest and participation. "In the 1970s, constitutional politics was still highly elitist, and it was the aspirations of governments, not people, that really counted."[36]

Just after Canada Day in 1977, the federal government appointed the Task Force on Canadian Unity, known as "Pépin-Robarts" after its co-chairs, former Quebec Liberal MP Jean-Luc Pépin and former Conservative Ontario premier John Robarts. According to federal constitutional adviser Barry Strayer, it seemed "to have been designed more to provide an outlet for public concerns than as a source of inspiration for constitutional reform."[37] Indeed, Trudeau interrupted Pépin-Robarts with the release of a white paper on constitutional reform entitled *A Time for Action* in June 1978.[38]

*A Time for Action* laid out a two-stage approach to constitutional reform. First, the federal government would proceed to amend the

Constitution regarding matters for which it did not need provincial approval. Chief among these was a complete overhaul of the Senate and its replacement with a new House of the Federation. Second, the federal government and the provinces would work to reach an agreement on matters that required legislation by the UK Parliament.

The federal government converted *A Time for Action* into Bill C-60, the Constitutional Amendment Bill, which was introduced in the House of Commons for first reading on 20 June 1978.[39] Bill C-60 would have replaced most of the BNA Act and added to it; it would have created a new act, to be titled the Constitution of Canada Act. Bill C-60 was comprehensive and ambitious. It was also highly contentious. In addition to containing a proposed charter of rights and freedoms, it would have constitutionalized the Supreme Court of Canada, replaced the Senate with a new House of the Federation, and added a host of new measures.[40] Bill C-60 unleashed a deluge of constitutional proposals from private sector and public interest groups.[41]

After Bill C-60 was introduced, Parliament created another Special Joint Committee of the Senate and the House of Commons on the Constitution, co-chaired by Senator Maurice Lamontagne and MP Mark MacGuigan (who had previously co-chaired the Molgat-MacGuigan Committee). Public participation was seen as an "unusual but welcomed development, heralding a temporary change in the venue of constitutional deliberations from closed rooms to public forums."[42] The committee reported to Parliament at the end of October 1978; however, it had failed to galvanize public interest, let alone support, for constitutional reform beyond those who had directly participated in its proceedings.

### The End of Bill C-60 and Potentially of Trudeau's Constitutional Quest

Meanwhile, under pressure from the provinces and the Opposition, the Trudeau government agreed in November 1978 to refer the question of the constitutionality of its proposed unilateral changes to the Senate, included in Bill C-60, to the Supreme Court. The Court heard two days of arguments in March 1979 and issued its decision just before Christmas that year, sinking Trudeau's plans to overhaul the Senate.[43] In the meantime, the federal election of 22 May 1979 ousted Trudeau from power and gave Progressive Conservative (PC) Party leader Joe Clark a minority government. Trudeau announced his intention to resign as Liberal leader.

Clark had no interest in pursuing constitutional reform. Writing about the pulse of the business community and English Canada in 1979, Trudeau's biographers opined that these groups thought that "the constitution had become a bizarre obsession with Trudeau, a form of self-defeating madness that had done the country far more harm than good."[44] For Trudeau, the 1970s were characterized as his decade of "futile constitutional negotiations."[45]

That may very well have been how things ended for Trudeau and for Canada if Joe Clark's minority government had found a way to stay in office for longer than seven months. Instead, Clark sought to dissolve Parliament after losing a budget vote in the House of Commons in December 1979. This thrust Canada back into an election campaign and led Trudeau to "unresign" and lead the Liberal Party back to power after the February 1980 general election. As Graham Fraser wrote in 1984, comparing the 1979 and 1980 elections, "In the campaign that Trudeau was bound to lose, he talked constantly about national unity and the constitution. Ten months later, in an election he was likely to win, he talked about it very little."[46] And win Trudeau did. On 18 February 1980, Canadians returned the reins of power to Pierre Trudeau and his Liberal Party with a solid majority government.

### The Return of Pierre Trudeau: "The Quest Begins Anew"

Pierre Trudeau returned to 24 Sussex Drive in time to battle PQ Premier René Lévesque in the first Quebec referendum in May 1980. Before the referendum, Trudeau had pledged a "renewed federalism" if the No side won. After the proposal for sovereignty-association was defeated on 20 May 1980, he immediately launched back into the constitutional battle, leaving reform of the upper chamber aside after his defeat in the *Upper House Reference*.[47] The proposed charter of rights and freedoms quickly became the centrepiece of the federal government's plan for constitutional renewal[48] during 1980, in what has been called "the year of confrontation"[49] because of the battles between the federal and provincial governments over the patriation of the Constitution.

After the referendum, Trudeau's Minister of Justice Jean Chrétien took off on a lightning tour of the provincial capitals in advance of a first ministers' meeting scheduled for 9 June 1980. Trudeau shared with the premiers his "Priorities for a New Canadian Constitution," which was tabled in the House of Commons the next day.[50] Dubbed the "people's package,"[51] the federal government's constitutional proposal included patriation, a charter of rights and freedoms, and an amending formula. It was meant to contrast with the "governments' package," indicating the provinces' desire for greater legislative powers.[52]

Over the summer, officials and ministers met under the auspices of the Continuing Committee of Ministers on the Constitution, which had been established in 1978. Different drafts of the charter were tabled over the course of the summer. Jean Chrétien briefed the Cabinet on 3 July 1980 and kept it up to date over the course of July and August.[53] This draft differed significantly from previous versions, which had contained rights guarantees that would apply to the provinces only once they individually opted in to the charter. The federal government's July 1980 draft charter would apply immediately to Parliament and to all provincial and territorial legislatures.[54]

During the summer of 1980, the ministers and officials who were charged with and debating constitutional reforms gave the charter "remarkably little attention" because their efforts focused on other subjects, most notably entrenching it in the Constitution.[55] The focus on entrenchment and later on the amending formula continued through the fall of 1980. As a result, the primary work for the resulting charter defaulted to the federal government and the Joint Committee. At the end of August, the *Ottawa Citizen* reported on a leaked document prepared by Michael Kirby, head of the Federal-Provincial Relations Office for the prime minister and Cabinet, which set out a strategy for unilateral federal patriation in the face of continued provincial opposition.[56] To put it mildly, the release of the Kirby Memorandum did not create a positive atmosphere for the first ministers' meeting scheduled for 8 to 12 September 1980. That meeting could very well have marked the end for Trudeau's constitutional quest.

It is important to recognize the context of the continuing constitutional negotiations. In advance of the September 1980 first ministers' conference, a discussion at Cabinet had identified three major priorities for the Trudeau government: the Constitution, energy, and the economy.[57] Strategies for dealing with the Constitution were at times linked to the other two priorities. The September 1980 first ministers' meeting failed to make progress on any of these files; it was considered "one of the most acrimonious on record,"[58] and a formal dinner on the eve of the meeting almost turned into a constitutional wake. Chroniclers of that period wrote that the events of 7 September 1980, "illustrate[d] why more than a half century of failed attempts" had preceded that evening.[59] For one thing, the leak of the Kirby Memorandum had the desired effect of poisoning the atmosphere; the premiers ganged up against Trudeau. Jean Chrétien said that he had never been to a worse gathering.[60] Another event related to the fact that the day marked the fifty-fifth birthday of Saskatchewan Premier Allan Blakeney. A cake had been prepared for him, but it was served in order of precedence: to the governor general first, then the prime minister, then to the premiers of the provinces in the order in which they had joined Confederation[61] (the same order in which the provinces address the Supreme Court in references such as the *Patriation Reference* nearly half a year later). Trudeau barked at the governor general to eat his cake so that he could leave.[62]

If form could triumph over substance even in matters so mundane as a birthday cake, what hope was there for Canada's first ministers to find agreement on constitutional reform? Instead of the end of the constitutional quest itself, the September 1980 first ministers' meeting marked the end of a long phase: the end of the quest for unanimity and the end of the exclusivity of executive federalism.

## The Genesis of the Joint Committee

The Kirby Memorandum had set out a full plan for how to deal with the draft resolution of Parliament requesting the UK Parliament to patriate the Canadian Constitution with the Charter of Rights, the amending formula, and other provisions. It included sending the draft resolution for study by a special joint parliamentary committee. Kirby predicted that the House would not welcome (but would accept) such a committee but that the Senate would probably be pleased by such a move.[63] He counselled the government not to mention or suggest the committee but allow the Opposition to "demand" it. One advantage he identified was that "a highly contentious measure may be best contained in a Committee where it is more readily managed by the House Leader and his officers, and where easier and more effective relations can be maintained with the Press Gallery, since relatively few reporters will follow the proceedings." Kirby went on to suggest that "interested individuals and groups can participate directly in constitutional renewal." He also foresaw the difficulty of "managing" the committee process, stating that "careful choice of government members would be essential, and careful orchestration of hearings would be needed to ensure effective presentation of the government's position."[64]

After the failed first ministers' conference, the Liberal caucus met on 17 September 1980 to discuss the constitutional strategy.

Contemporaneous reports asserted that only some caucus members were nervous about proceeding unilaterally.[65] However, minutes from the Cabinet meeting the day after the caucus discussion reported that the Liberal caucus was split almost evenly on whether to impose the charter on the provinces or allow them to either opt in or opt out.[66] At caucus, MP Bryce Mackasey, a veteran of the debate over adopting the Maple Leaf as the Canadian flag in 1964, reassured his colleagues that that process had worked out in the end. On the decision to proceed unilaterally, a Quebec backbencher shouted out, "Allons-y en Cadillac! Let's go first-class."[67] At Cabinet, ministers more strongly supported imposing the charter on the provinces on the grounds that opting in was too weak.[68] Cabinet then debated the proposed charter clause by clause over several meetings.[69]

The Liberals clearly thought they had a winning political strategy. In the summer of 1980, Jean Chrétien was reported to have bragged to the premiers, "You come out against the rights of Indians and women and the handicapped, and I'm going to cut you into little pieces."[70] That bravado was muted by his acknowledgment that perhaps the government's charter wasn't quite the Cadillac they had claimed it to be. In his first appearance before the Joint Committee, Chrétien invited proposed amendments to the "first class" charter.[71] Indeed, his words would be visited upon him: the Liberals themselves were eventually forced to strengthen rights guarantees for Aboriginal peoples, women, and persons with disabilities. But all that would come later.

Pierre Trudeau's government was confident in proceeding unilaterally because it had the support of the PC government in Ontario. Cabinet records from the time reveal close communication between federal and Ontario officials as well as the Trudeau government's desire not to upset Ontario, especially in regard to language issues.[72] Ontario Premier Bill Davis and his government were able to support the charter because it believed that a traditionally conservative Canadian judiciary would not duplicate the excesses of an activist judiciary south of the border.[73] Given the track record of Canadian judges – especially regarding the Canadian Bill of Rights – Davis's position was understandable. The members of the Joint Committee clearly understood that the charter would transfer significant power to the judges; the concern – widely expressed both at the Joint Committee and in the academic literature[74] – was whether the judiciary would have the capacity to take the charter seriously after entrenchment.

As set out in the Kirby Memorandum, the federal government's plan was to introduce the proposed resolution in the House and then have both the House and the Senate refer it to a joint committee for a quick review out of the limelight. Both chambers of Parliament would pass the resolution by January 1981 so that it could be sent to London for enactment and proclamation in time for Canada Day that year. The timetable was overly ambitious and based on numerous political miscalculations by the Trudeau government; the belief that the Joint Committee would be a short, controlled, relatively dull process was just one of them.

Trudeau announced his plan to the people of Canada in a nationally televised address on 2 October 1980, after a special Cabinet meeting earlier that day had approved the plan.[75] The National Hockey League season would not open for another week, but that night, Trudeau competed against *Mork and Mindy*, *The Waltons*, and *Games People Play*.[76] Meanwhile, another prizefighter was in action: Muhammad Ali was making his fourth comeback, fighting Larry Holmes. The parallel was noted by Trudeau's biographer.[77] While Ali lost the fight that night on a technical knockout, in his own comeback Trudeau would ultimately succeed.

The proposed joint resolution was introduced in the House of Commons on 6 October 1980. Motions to refer the draft to a Joint Committee of the Senate and the House of Commons were passed by the House on 23 October and by the Senate on 3 November. They set a deadline of 9 December 1980 for the Joint Committee to report back to the respective parliamentary chambers.[78] At least, that was the plan.

## Chapter Two

# The Cast

## The Chairs: Contrasting Mavericks

As joint chairs, Senator Harry Hays and MP Serge Joyal were a study in contrasts. Harry Hays was a farmer, rancher, businessman, and politician who was considered "a loquacious and old-fashioned bag-man from Alberta."[1] Serge Joyal was a cultured, intellectual lawyer from Montreal, a man devoted to the arts who collected antique clothing. Hays was seventy-one; at thirty-five, Joyal was half his age. As would become apparent at the Joint Committee proceedings, Hays represented the past, while Joyal represented the future. They were, however, both considered mavericks within the Liberal Party. Joyal, in particular, was called the "black sheep boy" of the Liberal caucus.[2] According to Trudeau's biographers Stephen Clarkson and Christina McCall, the choice of these two nonconformists was meant "to signal that the process was being run not by Trudeau puppets but by patriotic, independent-minded Liberals."[3] But then, when Hays and Joyal were selected, the Joint Committee was meant to be a short and controlled affair, lasting only a month.

Hays and Joyal were thus not obvious choices to chair what would become a critical part of the constitutional patriation process. However, they were not even the prime minister's first choices; Senator Maurice Lamontagne, who had co-chaired two previous joint committees on the Constitution (in 1971 and 1978), and MP Bryce Mackasey were. But Lamontagne reportedly clashed with Trudeau over his methods and refused to be co-chair with Mackasey, his old rival from the Pearson Cabinet.[4] In a classless gesture, Jean Chrétien called Mackasey at his mother's funeral days before the Joint Committee was to begin to tell him the news that he was being dumped because Lamontagne had withdrawn.[5] So instead of two Quebec warhorses in Lamontagne and Mackasey, there would be an old-time western Canadian in Hays and a brash young bilingual Quebecker in Joyal.

Hays had a colourful Canadian past before entering politics. He had led the Canadian Swine Breeders during WWII and initiated the "Bacon for Britain" campaign to increase pork production as part of the war effort.[6] He was considered a "master breeder," developing the first pure breed of Canadian cattle, and it bears his name in tribute: the Hays Converter.[7] Hays had moved from running the farm to running the city of Calgary in 1959. He had served as mayor of Calgary until 1963, when he was elected to the House of Commons. Prime Minister Lester Pearson had made Hays – the only Liberal MP elected in Alberta or Saskatchewan – minister of agriculture from 1963 to 1965 and appointed him to the Senate in 1966 after he had failed in his re-election bid.

The well-liked Hays was considered reliable, if somewhat old-fashioned.[8] Loquacious and with a sense of humour, his tongue landed him in serious trouble on one infamous occasion at the Joint Committee, discussed herein. This appointment would be his last political hurrah; he died a few weeks after the Charter came into force. Whereas for Hays, the Joint Committee marked the end of his political career, for Joyal, it marked the beginning of his transformation from rebel to statesman, from outsider to a member of the Ottawa establishment.

Joyal had been first elected as an MP in 1974 at the age of twenty-nine, after working for three years as a special assistant to the Honourable Jean Marchand, the senior of the "three wise men" from Quebec who went to Ottawa in 1965 (the others were journalist Gérard Pelletier and Pierre Trudeau). Joyal was a Liberal Party activist but a thorn in the side of the party establishment. He had served as the vice-president of the Liberal Party of Canada (Quebec) while in his late twenties, and he had become a hero in Quebec in 1976, when he and three other members of caucus had broken publicly with the Trudeau government in support of a group of Quebec pilots and air-traffic controllers in a bitter dispute over the use of French in the skies. Joyal had represented the breakaway union against the federal government in a lawsuit against Air Canada.[9] In 1978, while still an MP, he had run unsuccessfully for mayor of Montreal as head of the Groupe d'action municipale. Joyal had been so rebellious in advocating for provincial rights for Quebec that Quebec caucus leader and Trudeau loyalist Marc Lalonde had sought to expel him from the Liberal caucus.[10]

According to Joyal, Lamontagne had suggested his name to Trudeau, who responded, "Es-tu fou? Serge Joyal, on ne le contrôle pas." ("Are you crazy? Serge Joyal, he can't be controlled.")[11] Joyal was considered the Liberals' "most talented pariah,"[12] and his appointment to co-chair the Joint Committee caused heads to turn within the Liberal Party and around Ottawa. "In Liberal Ottawa, where conformity and party discipline are prized above all, Serge Joyal's elevation to the co-chairmanship was an important signal to other potential mavericks that there could be life after Elba."[13]

The offer to co-chair the Joint Committee forced Joyal to make a stark choice between continuing to advocate for Quebec's rights against Ottawa and becoming an architect for the constitutional rights of all Canadians. He chose the latter, "grasping the opportunity to be a latter-day founding father, knowing that the act would have personal costs."[14]

Unlike Hays, Joyal was hailed for his role in chairing the Joint Committee. At thirty-five, he appeared more youthful than young as he sat at the helm of the committee. Often it was Joyal and not Hays who seemed like the senior statesman. After the Joint Committee got off to a rocky start, Joyal succeeded in earning the respect of his own caucus members and the other committee members. He celebrated his thirty-sixth birthday with the Joint Committee on a rare Saturday session on 31 January 1981. Tory James McGrath read out the horoscope that he had clipped from the morning's newspaper. "Those born on this date are independent, creative and highly tolerant of the foibles of others." Ever the showman, McGrath stated, "I am not kidding, Mr. Chairman, and it goes on to say, 'A somewhat aloof exterior covers a warm and friendly heart.'"[15] It was a nice touch that reflected the esprit de corps that had developed among members of the Joint Committee after three months of long days and nights of hearings.

Those long days and nights in the glare of the cameras over the previous three months had not so much aged Joyal as they had matured him. His performance did not go unnoticed by Prime Minister Trudeau, who appointed him a minister of state without portfolio in September 1981 and then a year later promoted him to secretary of state for Canada, an office that he held for the remainder of the Trudeau government and for the duration of the short-lived ministry of Prime Minister John Turner. Like many Liberals, Joyal was swept out of office in the Tory wave of 1984. For thirteen years, he worked in the private sector until Jean Chrétien appointed him to the Senate in 1997, where he became one of the most passionate and articulate defenders of the Red Chamber.[16]

## The Committee Members: No Portrait, No Glory

A contemporaneous account dubbed the members of the Joint Committee "the unsung Fathers of Re-Confederation"[17] because, as a group, they had already largely been forgotten. There is certainly no portrait of them convening in the West Block's Confederation Room.

The committee members were called "an unusual lot,"[18] but demographically, they reflected the largely white-male-dominated Parliament of the time. Of the twenty-five members, only one was a woman: lawyer Coline Campbell of Nova Scotia. The official roster (ten senators, fifteen MPs) included nine lawyers, seven businesspeople, five professors/teachers, one member of the clergy (MP Stanley Knowles), two farmers (Senator Harry Hays of Alberta and MP George Henderson of PEI), one advertising executive (MP James McGrath of Newfoundland), and a customs broker for fish exporters (Senator William Petten of Newfoundland). In point of fact, Stanley Knowles attended only one meeting, and his place on the committee was filled by the very active Svend Robinson, another lawyer – bringing the percentage of jurists up to 40 per cent.

They were an accomplished group: eleven out of twenty-four (44 per cent) had served in federal or provincial Cabinets, including a former premier (Senator Duff Roblin of Manitoba) and four former mayors (Senator Paul Lucier, Whitehorse; Senator Harry Hays, Calgary; MP Ron Irwin, Sault Ste. Marie; MP David Crombie, Toronto). Four of the members already had the Order of Canada, and seven others would receive it after their service, for a total of eleven of the twenty-five committee members, a remarkable 44 per cent. (None received the Order for their work on the Joint Committee.)

There was a clear generation gap between the senators (average age sixty-two years) and the MPs (average age forty-two years). At seventy-four, Senator John Connolly (Ontario) was the oldest member of the Joint Committee; he had been appointed to the Senate in 1953 by Prime Minister Louis St. Laurent. Senator Carl Goldenberg was only a year younger. At twenty-four, MP Jean Lapierre (Quebec) was the youngest member of the Joint Committee, with MP Svend Robinson (British Columbia) a few years older at twenty-eight. Of the ten senators, three were in their seventies, three in their sixties, three in their fifties, and one in his forties. In contrast, of the fifteen MPs, two were in their fifties, eight in their forties, three in their thirties, and Lapierre and Robinson the only ones in their twenties.

## The Government Members (Liberals)

The Liberal government representatives would have likely been chosen by the Prime Minister's Office (PMO) in consultation with the caucus leadership. As always, considerations of regional representation and language were paramount. There were seven Liberal senators: Harry Hays, joint chair; Jack Austin; John Connolly; Carl Goldenberg; Maurice Lamontagne; Paul Lucier; and William Petten. They represented Alberta, British Columbia (BC), Ontario, Quebec (two), Newfoundland, and Yukon. Connolly was the oldest of the group, but it was the youngest, Jack Austin, who often functioned as its leader because he had the strongest ties to the PMO.

The governing Liberals had eight of the fifteen MPs on the Joint Committee: Serge Joyal, joint chair; Robert Bockstael; Coline Campbell; Eymard Corbin; George Henderson; Ron Irwin; Jean Lapierre; and Bryce Mackasey. Two and a half hailed from Quebec (Joyal, Lapierre, and Mackasey, who was originally from Quebec but had moved to southern Ontario), two from Ontario (Irwin and the transplanted Quebecker Mackasey), and the others from Manitoba (Bockstael), Nova Scotia (Campbell), New Brunswick (Corbin), and PEI (Henderson). The governing Liberals could afford for Ontario to be somewhat "under-represented" since they had garnered the support of the Tory government of that province for their patriation plan.

Of the Liberal senators on the committee, Jack Austin was the clear leader. Austin, a forty-eight-year-old lawyer from Vancouver, had gone to Ottawa in the 1960s as an executive assistant to Minister Arthur Laing. He had run unsuccessfully for the Liberals in 1965 and returned to Ottawa in 1970 to become the federal deputy minister of energy. As such, he was part of the first Canadian trade mission to the People's Republic of China. In 1974, Trudeau had tapped him to run his office as chief of staff. Austin's stint heading up the PMO was short-lived; the next year, Trudeau appointed him to the Senate at the age of forty-three, where he had served for three decades until his mandatory retirement at age seventy-five. Senator Austin was often the PMO's designated "point man" on the committee, arguing against televising the committee proceedings until Cabinet reversed this decision.

Although not the oldest member of the Joint Committee, at seventy-three Senator Carl Goldenberg clearly functioned as its elder statesman and intellectual powerhouse. For Goldenberg, serving on the Joint Committee was merely another episode in six decades of constitutional advising: he had served as a constitutional adviser to prime ministers Mackenzie King and Pierre Trudeau and later to Jean Chrétien. In his speech on the Constitution to the CBA in 1967 as minister of justice, Trudeau boasted that he had appointed Goldenberg as his special counsel on the Constitution.[19] In fact, Goldenberg had written most of that speech.[20] More than a decade later, he was still in the middle of the constitutional fray, although he no longer exerted the same influence. His son Eddie was working for Minister of Justice Jean Chrétien, providing critical advice to the influential minister of justice behind the scenes. Goldenberg father and son no doubt discussed the committee proceedings outside the Confederation Room, where the proceedings were held.

Senator Maurice Lamontagne was a sixty-three-year-old professor of economics at Laval who had taught many future leaders of Quebec, including PQ Cabinet minister Claude Morin, who, more than anyone else, was associated with the first Quebec referendum in 1980.[21] Lamontagne had gone to Ottawa in 1954, first as an assistant deputy minister, then as faculty member of the University of Ottawa, where he had also served as an adviser to Lester Pearson. He had been an MP from 1963 to 1967 and a member of Pearson's Cabinet from 1963 to 1965. In 1967, he had resigned from the House to accept an appointment by Pearson to the Senate. In the 1970s, Lamontagne had twice co-chaired earlier joint committees on the Constitution, which had come to naught. In the fall of 1980, he had turned down the opportunity to co-chair the one that actually led to constitutional reform. Instead, he was content to play a supporting role on this Joint Committee.

Similarly, at seventy-four, Senator John Connolly was nearing the end of his tenure in the Senate. A law professor and former Liberal Party president, Connolly had served as government leader in the Senate from 1964 to 1968 under Prime Minister Pearson. A real party man, Connolly had long passed on the leadership in the Liberal party to younger men. He retired from the Senate in 1981, six months after the Joint Committee completed its work. Connolly died the next year, a few months after the Charter he and his colleagues had helped draft came into effect.

At fifty, Senator Paul Lucier, together with Senator William Petten, represented the Upper Chamber's youth brigade on the Joint Committee. Lucier had been appointed by Prime Minister Trudeau to the Senate in 1975 as the first-ever senator from Yukon, an appointment made possible by an amendment to the BNA Act, made the same year.[22]

He had previously served as mayor of Whitehorse.[23] The curmudgeonly William Petten, fifty-seven, hailed from St. John's, Newfoundland, and had served as the chief fundraiser for Joey Smallwood's Confederate Association. He had been appointed to the Senate in 1968 by Pearson and served as government whip in the Senate from 1974 to 1979 and 1980 to 1984, during the Joint Committee proceedings. Petten was tough and respected by Trudeau.

In their account of patriation, Robert Sheppard and Michael Valpy state that "no woman was invited to play more than a minor role."[24] While this is true in respect of the primary political actors, women did play an important role in the making of the Charter, primarily through their participation in the work of the Joint Committee and their continued mobilization afterwards, as discussed below. At the Joint Committee, Coline Campbell was notable as the only woman. A lawyer and teacher by profession, in 1974 she had become the first woman from Nova Scotia elected to the House of Commons.[25]

Robert Bockstael was a businessperson from Saint Boniface, Manitoba, when he was elected to the House of Commons in 1979, re-elected in 1980. He had served as a school board trustee for a decade and a half and as a city councillor in Winnipeg for six years immediately before being elected to the House of Commons.[26] Affable and well-liked, Bockstael was not one to "rock the boat."

However, other Liberal MPs on the Joint Committee were willing to do so – in particular, Jean Lapierre and Eymard Corbin.[27] A teacher and journalist, Corbin had first been elected as an MP from New Brunswick in 1968. He had never served in Cabinet or done much of anything of note. He maintained a low political profile generally but was prepared to agitate for language rights at the Joint Committee. He had been appointed to the Senate by John Turner in 1984 as part of the outgoing spate of controversial appointments at the behest of Trudeau.

At twenty-four, Jean Lapierre was the youngest member of the Joint Committee. He was considered "a hardworking street-smart lawyer from Quebec's Eastern Townships,"[28] and he spoke his mind at the Joint Committee. Sitting as a Liberal on the committee was the beginning of what would be a peripatetic political career for Lapierre. He left the Liberal Party after the failure of the Meech Lake Accord, sat as an Independent for six months, and then became one of the founders of the Bloc Québécois in 1990. He left the Bloc in 1992 and went back to law and broadcasting. In 2004, he returned to the Liberal fold as Prime Minister Paul Martin's minister of transport and his Quebec lieutenant.

He was re-elected in 2006 when Prime Minister Harper came to power, but Opposition was not for him, and he resigned his seat in 2007 to again return to broadcasting.

Liberal Bryce Mackasey might be considered the "silver-tongued" MP on the Joint Committee. A Liberal originally from Quebec but then representing the Ontario riding of Lincoln, he had also served in the Quebec legislature and for a brief time was president of Air Canada. He had been a minister under both Pearson and Trudeau. At the Joint Committee, he revelled in sparring with Tory James McGrath. But Mackasey's bluster concealed a genuine concern for the rights of the underdog, and Pierre Trudeau had a soft spot for the old Liberal warrior. Unfortunately for him, Mackasey achieved political notoriety for a comment that Brian Mulroney – then the leader of the Opposition – made in 1984 after incoming Liberal leader and Prime Minister John Turner had made a spate of patronage appointments at the request of outgoing Prime Minister Pierre Trudeau. These included the appointment of Mackasey as Canada's ambassador to Portugal. Mulroney savaged these appointments – publicly, in the televised debate against Turner, and privately, where he remarked of Mackasey, "There's no whore like an old whore."[29] After he became prime minister, Mulroney cancelled Mackasey's ambassadorship.

As parliamentary secretary to Minister of Justice Jean Chrétien, MP Ron Irwin was the formal link between the Liberal members on the committee and the government. The former mayor of Sault Ste. Marie had been made a member of the Order of Canada in 1975 at the age of thirty-nine for his work in improving that city. He had been first elected to the House of Commons in 1980.

George Henderson fit the stereotype of the friendly Islander. The shellfish technician, farmer, electrical engineer, and businessman was liked by all, but the MP from PEI exerted minimal influence.

Two other Liberals should be considered at least "honorary members" of the Joint Committee: Warren Allmand and Brian Tobin. The parties had the ability to substitute members of the committee who were not available, and they frequently did so. Tobin, however, was not a mere substitute. He had originally been appointed to the Joint Committee and attended most of its first meetings. He was later replaced by George Henderson, and his name was left off the list of committee members in the committee's final report. His name is buried near the end of the list of more than 140 "Other Senators and Members who served on the Committee."[30] That does not do justice to Tobin's contribution.

At twenty-six, Tobin attended nearly one-third of the Joint Committee's meetings. As a newly elected MP, he deferred to his caucus and gave little indication of his future as a founding member of the Liberal "Rat Pack," which would attack the huge Mulroney majority that had toppled the Liberals in the 1984 election. Tobin wrote that he had "a wonderful sense of participating with Canadians in a historical event as wide ranging in its implications as anything that our government had achieved since Confederation."[31] For Tobin, participating in the Joint Committee changed his perception of Canada; he came to realize that Canada "was and is a nation of tremendous complexity and diversity, unlike any in the world. If these qualities bring unique tensions and concerns with them – and without question they do – we should take pride in our ability to recognize and address them with patience and tolerance, if not with perfection."[32]

Warren Allmand, an anglophone MP from Montreal and former Cabinet minister under Trudeau in the 1970s, attended many of the Joint Committee's sessions. It was said that he hung around the Joint Committee "as an unwanted spare"[33] to speak out on native rights and minority-language rights in Quebec for anglophones. He was one of the few MPs and even fewer Liberals to vote against the eventual joint resolution in December 1981.

### The Opposition: Active and Effective Forces

The Opposition may have been outnumbered on the Joint Committee – but to a man (and all the Opposition members were men), each of the eight Tory and two New Democratic Party (NDP) members were active players on the Joint Committee and contributed to the changes to the Charter it produced.

### The Tories: Opposing Unilateral Patriation while Strengthening the Charter

The Official Opposition PC Party (Tories) was knowledgeable, vocal, and effective on the Joint Committee. In part, this was because all its representatives had served on the federal-provincial relations committee of the Tory caucus chaired by MP Jake Epp, which had been established in April 1980, after Trudeau had returned to power and the Tories to the Opposition benches.[34] Sheppard and Valpy wrote at the time that "the Conservatives turned out their best political performers for the committee fight; six of their eight regulars had been ministers in the Clark government. But they could not always see eye to eye on tactics and concocted much of their daily strategy on the run, occasionally after virulent disagreements behind the scenes."[35]

These strong disagreements may have resulted from the Tories' attempt to walk two paths at the same time: opposing unilateral patriation, while not opposing the idea of a charter and supporting various proposals to strengthen various provisions. They were undermined in the first mandate by two key factors: first, the Tory government in Ontario supported Trudeau's patriation plan; and second, very few witnesses who appeared before the Joint Committee were interested in the legalities of the patriation plan. Attempts by the Tories to engage witnesses in discussion on this subject generally fell flat. As a result, the Tories' interventions focused more on debating specific provisions of the Charter (or on the amending formula). Tory Senator Nathan Nurgitz and future senator Hugh Segal argued in 1983 that the federal Tories had "worked far more effectively to improve the Charter of Rights at the [Joint] committee than the Liberal sponsors of the resolution."[36] They are right to a point, but the Tories opposed the government partly by trying to stop it and partly by trying to strengthen the Charter.

But as other more neutral commentators wrote at the time, "The [PC] party had one objective – to delay Trudeau's constitutional juggernaut until the provinces could stop it, either through the courts or by way of a counter-offer. But, at the same time, they did not want to be on the wrong side of history, and so became swept up in an impulsive drive to create more rights."[37] While (like Nurgitz and Segal) most of the Tory members of the Joint Committee were so-called Red Tories (socially progressive and fiscally conservative),[38] their work to expand the rights contained in the Charter was partially pragmatic as well as philosophical. Often they were "sucking and blowing" at the same time: opposing entrenchment of rights, while also arguing that some rights should be expanded.

The Official Opposition succeeded in forcing the government to expand the work of the Joint Committee and to televise its proceedings.[39] Among the Tory members, there was division about the desired outcome of the committee: their leader, Jake Epp, understood the pull of the Charter to the Canadian people, but at least one of his fellow Tory committee members "actively wanted the committee to fail."[40] The committee accepted many of the Tories' proposed amendments to the Charter; consequently, they were able to emerge from the Joint Committee more as Charter champions than as Charter obstructionists. Despite their important contributions to the making of the Charter, after patriation the Tories were usurped by the Liberals in taking credit for the Charter, and during Stephen Harper's tenure as prime minister, the re-formed Conservative Party of Canada distanced itself as much as it could from the Charter.[41]

The Tories had eight of the twenty-five members of the Joint Committee: three of the ten senators – Martial Asselin, Duff Roblin, and Arthur Tremblay – and five of the fifteen MPs – Perrin Beatty, David Crombie, Jake Epp, John Fraser, and James McGrath.

The Conservative Opposition had a clear leader on the Joint Committee in forty-one-year-old MP Jake Epp. As the chief federal-provincial relations critic and chair of the caucus committee on the Constitution, Epp was the Tories' "platoon commander" on the constitutional file[42] and their "general" at the Joint Committee. Epp had been a high school history teacher in rural Manitoba before entering politics in 1972. Like five of his other Tory colleagues on the committee, Epp had served as a minister in the short-lived government of Joe Clark. He was "the son of a Mennonite clergyman – betokening a small-town, unassuming, decent, thoroughly nice, teetotalling, deeply religious man."[43]

The three Tory senators – Asselin (fifty-six), Roblin (sixty-three), and Tremblay (sixty-three) – were experienced and effective. Senator Martial Asselin was a lawyer from La Malbaie, Quebec. A former MNA, he was a rare pre-1984 political species: a PC from Quebec. He had been first elected under Diefenbaker in 1958, lost his seat in 1962 and again in 1963, but recovered it in 1965 and re-elected in 1968. He had been appointed to the Senate in 1972 by Trudeau, and he resigned in 1990 when Prime Minister Brian Mulroney recommended him for appointment as lieutenant governor of Quebec.

The patrician Senator Duff Roblin was highly respected. He was considered "the most significant premier of Manitoba in the 20th century" and "a pragmatic visionary."[44] A veteran of the Second World War who had fought in Normandy, Roblin had been appointed to the Senate by Trudeau in 1978. At the time of the Joint Committee, he was serving as Joe Clark's deputy leader. Mulroney later made him his government leader in the Senate.

Senator Arthur Tremblay was the only one of the three Tory senators actually appointed by a Tory prime minister. Joe Clark had appointed Tremblay to the Senate in 1979. The former author, educator, and professor had served as deputy minister of intergovernmental affairs in Quebec and, as such, was well versed in constitutional issues.[45] Tremblay also maintained an understanding of the issues and the interests of other provinces. It was said that "he talked of Quebec and the West as having the same problems with Trudeau."[46]

The five Tory MPs were equally effective; none lacked for experience, either. At thirty, Perrin Beatty was the youngest of the group. The year before the Joint Committee, Clark had made him the youngest person ever appointed to Cabinet, where he had served as minister of state. Despite his youth, Beatty was no political novice on the committee: he had first been elected to the House of Commons in 1972, and thus, by the time the committee began, he had eight full years of parliamentary experience. Beatty was completely loyal to Clark and strongly partisan.

Like Beatty, David Crombie (forty-four) represented Ontario, although he was thought of more as representing Toronto, the city he had served as mayor from 1972 to 1978. Crombie was forever known as Toronto's "tiny, perfect mayor." He had moved from city hall to the House of Commons in 1978 and served as minister of health and welfare in Joe Clark's short-lived government. He had spent ten years as an MP and had also served as a minister in Brian Mulroney's government, resigning in 1988. At the Joint Committee, Crombie particularly championed the rights of the disabled and succeeded in pressing the Liberal government to add disability to the list of enumerated grounds in section 15. Not a lawyer, Crombie carried with him a US guide to the Bill of Rights, from which he frequently quoted.

The long-time MP for Vancouver South, John Fraser (forty-eight), had also served as a minister in the Clark government. He was born in 1931 in Japan, where his father was selling BC lumber. His family had returned to Vancouver when he was three years old, and he had gone on to law school and law practice before entering politics.[47] At the time of the Joint Committee, Fraser had been an MP for eight years; he frequently quoted from *Black's Law Dictionary* when particular terminology was being debated. Not surprisingly, Fraser demonstrated a special interest in the testimony of the National Association of Japanese Canadians and spoke passionately about his family's connection to Japan and to Japanese Canadians.[48]

Like many of his peers on the Joint Committee, Fraser would go on to an illustrious career afterwards, including serving as a minister in the Mulroney government. He was well liked and respected across party lines, as demonstrated by his being the first Speaker of the House to be elected by his peers in 1986. In that first election, Fraser topped a field of thirty-nine candidates and was elected after eleven ballots and eleven hours. Two years later, he was re-elected on the first ballot in a field of twelve candidates, a testament to the confidence and popularity that he had earned from his peers.[49] He served as Speaker until 1994.

James Aloysius McGrath (forty-eight) had represented St. John's, Newfoundland, since 1957. He had also served as a minister in Joe Clark's government. He was active and engaged, biting but humorous. He was later appointed by Prime Minister Brian Mulroney as lieutenant governor of Newfoundland, a post in which he served from 1986 to 1991.

A notable frequent Tory substitute on the committee was Jim Hawkes, MP for Calgary West from 1979 to 1993. He was Prime Minister Stephen Harper's first political boss, but when Harper became one of the founders of the Reform Party, he ran against Hawkes in 1988. Harper lost but then beat him in 1993 to succeed him as the MP for Calgary West.

### The NDP: The Expanders

The NDP had only two members on the Joint Committee, both MPs as the party had no seats in the Senate. Lorne Nystrom (Saskatchewan) and Svend Robinson (BC) played active and important roles on the Joint Committee. But Robinson was not leader Ed Broadbent's choice; Stanley Knowles was. Broadbent told Robinson's biographer that he chose Robinson "as a young smart guy. Intellectually able. He would be careful on that file."[50] But that appears to be revisionist history in light of the fact that Knowles and Nystrom were officially appointed as the NDP representatives on the committee. Broadbent tried to keep his twenty-eight-year-old justice critic off the committee, but his caucus revolted and forced him to replace Knowles with Robinson.[51] Knowles's name appears on the Joint Committee report, but it is Robinson whose voice comes through in the proceedings.

The young Robinson had first been elected to Parliament in 1979 at the age of twenty-seven, a year after being called to the bar in BC. He still looked very much the university graduate student. "With his prominent glasses and shaggy haircut, at first glance he appeared better suited to a university chess club than the bright lights of television, but on camera, Robinson shone. ... As he articulated difficult principles, Robinson projected nothing but passion, competence and confidence."[52]

Over the course of his career, Robinson always pushed the envelope, and his work at the Joint Committee was perhaps the first indication of his persistence as well as his intelligence. He advocated for the inclusion of sexual orientation in section 15, for the protection of the right to strike, and for the constitutional right to access to information. Robinson crossed swords with the party leadership at times, on issues such as recognizing the supremacy of God in a preamble to the Charter. Michael Valpy, who later ran unsuccessfully as a candidate for the NDP in Ontario, wrote at the time of Robinson, "He, perhaps more than any other opposition MP, has been the architect of the Charter of Rights. ... No MP worked harder or more effectively to improve the constitutional proposals."[53] That assessment is perhaps a bit of exaggeration; Robinson was hard working and assertive but uncompromising and often bombastic and sarcastic. He often lauded his legal knowledge over others on the committee and quoted from obscure legal sources. In terms of energy and engagement, no other MP compared with Robinson. However, in terms of efficacy, he ranks low on the committee: the committee accepted only two of the forty-three amendments proposed by the NDP, while in contrast, it approved seven of the twenty-two amendments put forward by the Tories.[54] It is interesting to ponder whether Robinson could have been more effective if he had been willing to be more compromising and less doctrinaire. He seemed to prefer showboating and pontificating to achieving results. Ironically, considering the credit he is given for his work in improving the Charter, Robinson voted against the final text of the resolution because he thought the inclusion of the notwithstanding clause in November 1981 had made it fundamentally flawed.[55]

First elected as an MP from Saskatchewan in 1968, Lorne Nystrom had been the NDP critic for federal-provincial relations from 1980 to 1981. He took the lead for his party on those issues at the Joint Committee, while Robinson focused more on rights issues. Nystrom was also active on the language rights issue and those involving Saskatchewan.

Robinson and Nystrom took up the cause of many of the witnesses and pushed the committee to adopt amendments that would further expand the rights protected in the Charter. As discussed in chapter 3, the NDP proposed more than forty amendments on subjects ranging from access to information, expansion of grounds of discrimination, and labour rights.

### Government Officials

In considering the government officials, we must, of course, begin with Minister of Justice and Attorney General Jean Chrétien, who was responsible for its work and who also spent more time with the Joint Committee than any other non-member: he attended 39 of the 106 sessions.[56] But if he had had his way, Chrétien would not have been there at all.

The man who more than any other person except Trudeau is associated with patriation and the Charter of Rights sought to avoid responsibility for this file. When Trudeau returned to power in 1980, Jean Chrétien did not want the job of minister of justice or the responsibility for the referendum and constitutional files that went with it. The swearing-in ceremonies for Trudeau's new Cabinet had to be held up for days as Chrétien held out for appointment to Finance; his second choice was External Affairs.[57]

Justice was traditionally reserved for Quebec politicians with names like Dorion, Fournier, Laflamme, Gouin, Lapointe, Patenaude, Michaud, St. Laurent, Chevrier, Favreau, Cardin, and, of course, Trudeau.[58] For most of these, the Justice portfolio was a dead end, a political ghetto of sorts. St. Laurent and Trudeau were the exceptions. According to his biographer, Chrétien was also nervous about the impending referendum battle with René Lévesque.[59] The happy warrior who called himself "Trudeau's firefighter"[60] would later ascend to the Liberal leadership and become prime minister, in part on the strength of his accomplishments on the constitutional file. In the spring of 1980, there was no way to know that the attempt at patriation would succeed where all others had failed.

At times, Chrétien shone at the Joint Committee, and at times, he did not. His biographer is critical of his performance, saying that Chrétien often appeared unprepared.[61] At the same time, he credits Chrétien for his political skills throughout the patriation process, especially in reaching the final deal in November 1981, where there was no one except Chrétien who could have mediated between the federal government and the provinces. "In the final days, [Chrétien became] the father of re-Confederation."[62]

Always more prose than poetry, Chrétien facilitated the success of the Joint Committee in two ways. First, his pragmatic approach enabled him to accept and propose a broad list of amendments to the Charter. Second, his work in November 1981 ensured that there would be a charter: without that "deal," it is very possible that all the work of the committee would have been for naught.

Whereas Chrétien relished sparring with members of the Joint Committee, Solicitor General Robert Kaplan did not. He appeared as acting minister of justice in Chrétien's stead on nine occasions, mostly in January 1981, when Chrétien was hospitalized. Kaplan was impatient with committee members and appeared testy at times. He was embarrassed when he committed to support an amendment on property rights, only to have it reversed the next day, when Chrétien returned.

Two Department of Justice officials were front and centre with Chrétien during his appearances before the Joint Committee. Deputy Minister of Justice Roger Tassé and Assistant Deputy Minister of Justice for Public Law Barry Strayer flanked the minister at the witness table during his testimony (and during the appearances of Solicitor General Robert Kaplan when he stood in for Chrétien). Chrétien did not hear as well with his right ear, so the anglophone Strayer sat to his left (his good ear) and the francophone Tassé to his right (his bad ear).[63]

Tassé oversaw a group of extremely talented lawyers on the Department of Justice's constitutional team. These included Barry Strayer, Fred Jordan, Barbara Reid, Edith MacDonald, Louis Reynolds, and Eugene Ewaschuk.[64] Strayer, MacDonald, and Ewaschuk would all later be appointed to the bench. Tassé took pride in hiring future Supreme Court justice Ian Binnie into the department from the private sector as associate deputy minister of justice in 1982.[65]

Tassé is one of several people who have been given the appellation "the father of the Charter of Rights."[66] While that may be a bit of an exaggeration, he certainly deserves significant credit for his role in overseeing the drafting, redrafting, and amending of the Charter. In particular, Tassé himself was one of the architects of the "new" and vastly improved limitations clause; he is credited with adding "demonstrably justified" to the text of section 1.[67] He established a good enough relationship with his boss Chrétien that when Chrétien left politics in 1984 after losing the Liberal leadership to John Turner, Tassé joined him and adviser Eddie Goldenberg to work for the Ottawa office of the Toronto-based law firm Lang Michener.[68]

Constitutional adviser Barry Strayer had worked on the constitutional file since the late 1960s. In fact, he takes credit for drafting *A Canadian Charter of Human Rights* in 1968.[69] Flanking his boss Chrétien during the committee proceedings, he was frequently called upon to explain various provisions in the draft resolution. According to Strayer, one member of the committee thought he looked like a "young Henry Fonda."[70] Somewhat less charitably, another member referred to him as "God," as in "There but for the grace of God goes God."[71] By his own account, relations between the committee members and Justice advisers became more strained as the proceedings wore on because the committee members grew frustrated with the government's responses about why it opposed certain suggested amendments.[72]

Strayer is perhaps most notable for the Supreme Court's rejection of his testimony before the Joint Committee explaining the meaning of the "principles of fundamental justice" under section 7 of the Charter. In the *B.C. Motor Vehicle Act Reference*,[73] the Supreme Court stated that such testimony was entitled to "minimal weight,"[74] planting a supreme kiss of death on the proceedings of the Joint Committee. Strayer has expended significant energy over the succeeding three decades attempting to demonstrate the folly of the Supreme Court's statement.

## The Witnesses

Most of the one hundred witnesses who appeared before the Joint Committee appeared only once. Cumulatively, they made an impact by forcing changes to the Charter and demonstrating the widespread support for a constitutionally entrenched charter of rights and freedoms on the one hand and the popular disinterest in the legalities of patriation or the bickering among governments over the amending formula. They wanted a charter, and they wanted a much stronger charter than had been tabled in the House of Commons on 6 October 1980 and referred to the Joint Committee.

My colleague Joseph Magnet of the University of Ottawa holds the record for the most appearances by any non-governmental witness before the Joint Committee. He appeared three times: as special adviser to the delegation of the Canadian Jewish Congress, as legal counsel to the Société franco-manitobaine, and as legal counsel to the Ontario Conference of Catholic Bishops.

Only a few witnesses were specifically invited by the committee: Max Yalden, Commissioner of Official Languages; Gordon Fairweather, Chief Commissioner, Canadian Human Rights Commission; and experts who were brokered among the three parties: Maxwell Cohen, Faculty of Law, McGill University (who had already testified on behalf of the Canadian Jewish Congress); Peter Russell, Department of Political Science, University of Toronto; Gérard La Forest, Faculty of Law, University of Ottawa; and Gil Rémillard, Faculty of Law, Laval University.

Many luminaries of the day appeared before the committee: Doris Anderson (president, Advisory Council on the Status of Women); Alan

Borovoy (CCLA); Ottawa mayor and future MP Marion Dewar (Cana-
dian Connection); Dr John Humphrey (president, Canadian Human
Rights Foundation; appeared with the New Brunswick Human Rights
Commission), who had been involved in drafting the UN's Universal
Declaration of Human Rights; lawyer John Nelligan (CBA); and Profes-
sor Walter Tarnopolsky (CCLA), the foremost expert on the Canadian
Bill of Rights.

Others who would achieve professional prominence after their
appearance before the committee were Irwin Cotler (Canadian Jewish Congress), who was already a respected human rights activist and
McGill law professor but who would go on to a second career as a politician, achieving prominence as a minister of justice and as an Opposition MP; feminist lawyers and activists Mary Eberts (Advisory Council
on the Status of Women) and Marilou McPhedran (NAC), who was
appointed by Prime Minister Justin Trudeau as an independent senator
in 2016; lawyer, CBA president (1982–83), and future Canadian ambassador to the United Nations (1988–92) Yves Fortier (CBA); human rights
lawyer David Matas (CBA); and Inuit leader Mary Simon (Inuit Committee on National Issues).

The Canadian Association of Lesbians and Gay Men was the first
same-sex group to appear before a parliamentary committee. Among
that group was George Hislop, who more than twenty-five years later
would win a landmark victory at the Supreme Court of Canada for
same-sex partners challenging survivorship benefits under the Canada
Pension Plan.[75]

Perhaps no one debunked the fallacy that one person cannot make a
difference in public life more than David Lepofsky. In the fall of 1980,
the blind Lepofsky had recently graduated from law school and was
studying for the bar exam. He appeared before the Joint Committee on
behalf of the Canadian National Institute for the Blind, passionately
and persuasively advocating for the inclusion of disability in section
15. He so impressed the committee members that they encouraged him
to run for political office. Lepofsky did not take that advice but became
one of the country's most prolific and effective disability rights advocates, receiving the Order of Canada for his work.

There were other witnesses who captured the attention of the committee members through their persuasion, their passion, or both. Elder
Lena Nottaway of the Algonkians of northwestern Quebec represented
the only one of seventeen Aboriginal groups to come to Ottawa without their lawyer.[76] She performed quite well in the absence of legal

counsel. Diana Davidson, president of the Vancouver People's Law School, impressed with the depth and breadth of her knowledge. She had undertaken broad-based consultations and came prepared to press numerous positions with the members of the Joint Committee.[77]

Other groups clearly missed an opportunity. The Media Club of Canada repeatedly frustrated the committee by not having a position on important freedom-of-expression questions that committee members put to it. It asked for a year's time to consult and return to the committee.[78] That request was both unrealistic and ironic given that it came from the representative of the one group most used to working to a deadline. The Canadian Labour Congress was noticeably absent from the entire joint committee process, having chosen to boycott the entire affair and refuse entreaties from the government to participate – despite suggestions that the government might look favourably on a request to include the right to bargain collectively in the Charter.[79]

One of the earliest and most memorable groups to testify was the National Association of Japanese Canadians: Gordon Kadota (Vancouver), the president; Roger Obata (Toronto); and Dr Art Shimizu (Hamilton), the Constitution Committee chair. Their testimony was a key point in the Joint Committee's proceedings. They spoke emotionally about the need to protect rights and freedoms in light of the experience of the Japanese Canadians, but their words applied to many other groups in Canada as well.

As president of the National Black Coalition of Canada, Wilson Head was one of those groups. He spoke about the experience of discrimination against blacks in Canada for hundreds of years.[80] James Gosnell, president of the Nishga Tribal Council, noted that this was the first time that Aboriginal people had been consulted on constitutional change and given an opportunity to express their opinions.[81]

Until the Joint Committee, Aboriginal groups had struggled to obtain a constitutional audience, let alone constitutional recognition. They had achieved significant legal victories at the Supreme Court of Canada with the 1973 *Calder*[82] decision recognizing the existence of Aboriginal title, but they had only recently succeeded in attaining recognition as relevant constitutional players.

Aboriginal rights were never part of Trudeau's proposed Charter; from the 1968 Charter of Human Rights to the people's package released on 6 October 1980, Aboriginal peoples had been meant to wait. Aboriginal rights would be addressed in "the next stage" of constitutional reform,[83] whenever that would be. But Aboriginal groups were not willing to wait, and they launched a mass action campaign in the fall of 1980. As the Joint Committee hearings were under way, five hundred Aboriginal people arrived in Ottawa as part of the Constitution Express, a protest train that had travelled from Vancouver to Ottawa. The Joint Committee was prepared to alter its schedule to hear from leaders of the Constitution Express and the National Indian Brotherhood, but at the last moment, the leaders of both backed out.[84] Many other Aboriginal groups did testify before the Joint Committee.

In fact, Aboriginal groups were by far the most numerous of the classes of groups that appeared before the Joint Committee. The effect of this was that a significant portion of the time at the Joint Committee was devoted to debate and discussion over "Native issues" or "Native rights." As discussed in the Introduction, that story and the eventual inclusion of section 35 in the Constitution Act, 1982 (but not in the Charter) remains to be told.

In terms of process, Aboriginal groups gained recognition as relevant constitutional actors. The Joint Committee recommended including a provision in the Constitution mandating the convening of several first ministers' conferences with the participation of representatives of Aboriginal peoples in discussions of agenda items that directly related to Aboriginal peoples.[85] Moreover, the constitutional provisions provided that the agenda for these constitutional conferences had to include "constitutional matters that directly affect Aboriginal peoples."[86]

### The Influence of Women's Groups

All Canadians have a stake in their Constitution. Canadian women, however, have a particularly special one. Making up half the population, women cannot be considered a minority or a special interest group. In fact, women have the dubious distinction of having the Supreme Court of Canada declare them constitutional non-entities. In the aptly titled Person's Case, five notable and accomplished women challenged the notion that women were not qualified to be appointed to the Senate. Section 24 of the Constitution Act, 1867 (then known as the BNA Act) provided that only qualified "persons" could be appointed to the Senate of Canada. There was a strong body of precedent that held that woman were not qualified to hold public office, that they were not persons under the law. In 1928, the Supreme Court unanimously confirmed this view, holding that the common law incapacity of women to hold public office was continued under the BNA Act and thus women could not be considered "qualified persons" fit to be appointed to the Senate.[87]

Until 1949, Canadians could appeal decisions of the Supreme Court to the Judicial Committee of the Privy Council in London, and the "Famous Five," as they came to be known, did. The British law lords held that "the exclusion of women from all public offices is a relic of days more barbarous than ours" and recognized that women were indeed persons under the Canadian Constitution.[88] The case not only held that women could be appointed to the Senate (which occurred one year later, in 1930) but altered the status of Canadian women from objects of the Constitution to potential participants.

I say "potential participants" because, as constitutional lawyer and feminist activist Mary Eberts wrote in 1981, discussions about constitutional change had been the exclusive sphere of governments and of specialists within them; few ordinary Canadians likely believed that this process had much relevance to their lives.[89] Governments – and especially first ministers – dominated discussions about constitutional reforms until 1980. However, since there was no female first minister in Canada until 1991 (Premier Rita Johnson of BC) and no woman had ever been prime minister until Kim Campbell in 1993 (for just over four months), women did not participate in these discussions. Moreover, they were almost entirely absent from the delegations supporting the first ministers in their discussions.[90] The proceedings before the Joint Committee changed the equation and the conversation.

The most disappointing and notorious Bill of Rights cases had involved women. For example, in *Lavell and Bedard* (1974),[91] the Supreme Court had upheld a law that provided that an Indian woman who married a non-Indian man lost her status, whereas the same did not occur if an Indian man married a non-Indian woman. The high court held that the law did not infringe the bill's protection of "equality before the law" because that provision protected only equality in the administration of the law, not equality in the law itself. Similarly, in *Bliss v. Canada* (1979),[92] Stella Bliss had been dismissed from her job because she was pregnant. She had not worked long enough to qualify for maternity benefits under the Employment Insurance Act, and when she applied for regular unemployment benefits, she was rejected because she had not worked long enough. The Court upheld a provision of the Employment Insurance Act on the grounds that it treated all pregnant persons the same and refused to consider the fact that only women could become pregnant.

*Lavell and Bedard* and *Bliss* became emblematic of the failure of the Canadian Bill of Rights and of the need for a new constitutionally entrenched Charter of Rights and Freedoms. To this was added the case of *Sandra Lovelace v. Canada*: Ms Lovelace, finding herself in the same position as Lavell and Bedard, had petitioned the United Nations in 1979, challenging the impugned provision of the Indian Act that had stripped her and her children of their status when she married a non-Indian man. In an act of powerful symbolism, Ms Lovelace appeared before the Joint Committee as part of the delegation of the New Brunswick Human Rights Commission.[93] The names Lavell, Bedard, Bliss, and Lovelace pepper the transcripts of the proceedings. In 1980–81, these cases were so well known, so infamous, that no explanation was usually required; witnesses and committee members were well versed in the cases. These names had entered the political, legal, and constitutional lexicon of the day.

Given their past experience, it is not surprising that women's groups approached the patriation process tentatively and apprehensively. As Chaviva Hošek wrote, "The proposed Charter was not attractive enough or liberal enough to seduce people into supporting entrenchment without misgivings. On the contrary, the Charter had so many flaws that it frightened people and mobilized women and many other interest groups into action."[94]

For women's groups, their appearance before the Joint Committee was just part of a much larger and much more sustained political engagement. As part of this strategy, women's groups focused on several issues in the draft resolution: (1) the limitations clause; (2) the need for a statement of purpose guaranteeing equal rights to men and women; (3) the use of the word "person" throughout; (4) section 15(1); (5) the draft of section 15(2), which did not guarantee that women would qualify for affirmative action programs; (6) the use of the phrase "existing rights and freedoms" for native rights; (7) the three-year moratorium on equality rights; (8) the potential conflict between multiculturalism and equality (specifically, provisions of the Indian Act that discriminated against women); and (9) representation on the Supreme Court of Canada (at that time, no women had ever been appointed to that court).[95]

Four women's groups appeared before the committee: the Advisory Council on the Status of Women, the National Action Committee on the Status of Women (NAC), the National Association of Women and the Law, and the Canadian Committee on Learning Opportunities for

Women. Numerous others submitted written briefs. The appearance of the NAC provided one of the most memorable moments at the Joint Committee, described in the next chapter.

Women's groups exerted a significant impact on the Joint Committee proceedings, especially regarding section 15, as will be seen in chapter 10. But the proceedings also had an impact on them. "The deliberations of the Joint Committee afforded a crucial experience for women's groups, as it did for many other groups of concerned citizens. The hearings raised the political consciousness of many people, and revealed the range and vitality of the opposition to the wording of the Charter and its approaches to human rights."[96]

## Chapter Three

# At the Joint Committee

## An Auspicious Room but an Inauspicious Beginning

The committee proceedings took place in Room 200 of the West Block, known appropriately as the Confederation Room. The room had served as the site of numerous federal-provincial conferences and of state dinners for Queen Elizabeth II in 1977 and 1982. The largest room on Parliament Hill was ornately decorated with six crystal chandeliers;[1] it was a fitting venue for the task before the Joint Committee. The Confederation Room will likely never host another conference, committee, or state dinner. It and the entire West Block are under renovation and not accessible to the public.[2]

Despite its august surroundings, the Joint Committee got off to an inauspicious start. Its opening sessions were characterized by procedural wrangling and partisan bickering – in other words, politics as usual. The joint chairs struggled to maintain control of the proceedings. These first sessions of the Joint Committee gave no indication that this body would produce anything constructive, let alone historic.

The first session opened on 6 November 1980. Some senators did not even receive notice of the meeting. It was clear that there was no agreed-upon plan as to how to proceed. There were arguments about quorum, whether the committee should split into panels to hear witnesses, how many witnesses should be heard, whether written submissions should be received before the committee heard from witnesses, etc. There was even disagreement about the configuration of the table, and one member complained about his chair. This sounded more like the Vietnam War peace negotiations than the making of a country's constitution. NDP MP Lorne Nystrom had to remind his colleagues,

"We are discussing something here that is the essence of the country, it is the essence of the future of Canada."[3]

And amid all this squabbling, PC MP Perrin Beatty made a plea for his fellow members of the Joint Committee to maintain perspective about what they were doing. "This is not a constitution which belongs to us or to the politicians of Canada, it belongs to the people of Canada: and the issue here is not our convenience, the issue is how we ensure that Canadians be heard about their constitution."[4]

No committee proceedings had ever been televised before in Canada. At the inaugural meeting, committee members initially rejected the suggestion that the Joint Committee's proceedings be the first.[5] To be clear, the Liberals used their majority to block such an attempt as Cabinet had opposed televising the proceedings at a meeting in September.[6] Led by Trudeau-loyalist Senator Jack Austin, several Liberal members spoke strongly, but not particularly convincingly, of the dangers of letting television cameras into the Joint Committee.[7] However, within ten days, after pressure from the Opposition in the House, Cabinet reversed itself and instructed the Liberal members of the Joint Committee to support the Opposition motion to televise the proceedings (although Cabinet was concerned about televising the clause-by-clause review because it would slow down the process).[8] The decision was a critical one for the Joint Committee. Radio and television coverage began on 17 November 1980.[9]

However, the committee members did have a healthy belief that others would be interested in their work. They ordered the publication of 5,000 copies of the transcripts of their proceedings, five times the usual number for committee proceedings and more than three times the number ordered when the Joint Committee had studied Bill C-60 in 1978. Even then, the committee members were not sure that this number would be enough; they reserved the right to revisit the issue if demand warranted it.[10] They never did reconsider the issue. What happened to most of those copies is a mystery. Copies of the six volumes of proceedings are very scarce and can usually be found only in selected libraries. None can be found for sale on the Internet. It is likely that most of the 5,000 copies – if that many were actually printed – were discarded or destroyed.

The second day of committee meetings was only slightly better than the first. The committee agreed to invite Gordon Fairweather, chief commissioner of the Canadian Human Rights Commission, and Max Yalden, commissioner of official languages, to testify before it. Justice

Minister Jean Chrétien also appeared before the committee for the first of his thirty-nine appearances.[11]

The first question put to a witness was highly symbolic of the disjuncture between the politicians and the public. PC Senator Arthur Tremblay used the opportunity to question Chrétien about the amending formula.[12] Senator Tremblay was also interested in the language rights in the proposed Charter, but the bulk of his questions to Chrétien focused on unilateral patriation and the amending formula.[13] This line of questioning would set a pattern for the proceedings. The Opposition members of the committee tried to use the proceedings to attack the government's plans for unilateral patriation and the proposed amending formula. While as Minister of Justice Chrétien had no choice but to engage in such discussions, most of the 104 witnesses had no interest in these subjects; they came to the committee to testify about what concerned them most: the Charter and Aboriginal rights.

Chrétien testified for more than thirteen hours over the course of three sitting days in the first two weeks of the Joint Committee. When the members of the committee did engage in substantive discussions rather than procedural wrangling, they mostly focused on the legality of patriation and the amending formula. The Charter was hardly the centre of discussion. In fact, in reading the proceedings from these first sessions, one could be excused for coming away with the impression that the Charter was merely a minor aspect of the constitutional proposal rather than the centrepiece of the so-called people's package.

In the end, the debate about the legality of patriation was resolved by the Supreme Court's September 1981 decision. Similarly, the federal government's proposed amending formula was eventually abandoned in favour of one agreed upon first by the premiers of the "Gang of Eight" in the April 1981 accord and then by all the first ministers except René Lévesque in the November 1981 accord that led to patriation. Thus, the most important legacies of the Joint Committee were its discussions about the Charter and Aboriginal rights.

The substantive discussions about the Charter in these early sessions with Chrétien focused on the language rights provisions. The committee occasionally asked him a question or more about other specific provisions of the Charter: about the strange phrase "principles of fundamental justice" or the scope of "freedom of expression" or the application of the War Measures Act to the Charter. But these provisions made only cameo appearances in the early sessions of the Joint Committee, where executive federalism and "the old Constitution" were still front and centre.

All this changed on Friday, 14 November 1980, when Gordon Fairweather began to testify. The morning had the feeling of winter as temperatures were still below freezing, with fog, when he took his seat at the same committee table whose configuration had been the subject of deliberation the week before. As the fog lifted outside, Fairweather's testimony seemed to lift the fog that had so far enveloped the committee proceedings.

## The Fog Lifts, and the People's Package Emerges

Fairweather may have been appearing as a representative of the Canadian Human Rights Commission – one of many such organizations that would appear before the committee – but he was decidedly part of the parliamentary "club" that was running the proceedings. He had been a PC MP from 1962 until he resigned in 1977 to serve as the first chief commissioner of the new Canadian Human Rights Commission. He had served in the House of Commons with many of the members of the Joint Committee. Moreover, the committee had invited Fairweather to appear before it. He did not disappoint.

Fairweather was not interested in the federal-provincial struggles over patriation and the amending formula. He was there – and he intimated that the Joint Committee was there – for a higher purpose. He explained, "The Canadian Human Rights Commission approaches this appearance with a great deal of exhilaration and, in a personal way, with envy for the task that is before this Committee and this Parliament because the task, I suggest, is a noble one."[14] Asked whether he was in favour of entrenchment, Fairweather responded, "Of course we are in favour of entrenching human rights. We are part of the world, it is a world-wide movement. What I hope is that we can get on with it."[15] He then proceeded to instruct the committee:

Our thesis is that the Charter of Rights of Freedoms [is] there to protect the weak against the strong, to protect those who have no power from those who have, and that in any contest the Parliament of Canada would expect the Canadian Human Rights Commission to be on the side of the downs, and after three years experience we know that there are many in Canadian society who have no power.[16]

This was a clarion call to the committee members to focus on the issues that mattered to Canadians.

If the government thought that Fairweather would commend it and perhaps offer some minor suggestions to tweak its so-called Cadillac Charter, they were decidedly wrong. Fairweather lectured, "While urging the entrenchment of the Charter of Rights, we believe it to be our duty to suggest that worthy as the goal may be, the instrument you have before you as a means of accomplishing this goal is seriously flawed."[17] He then proceeded to take aim at the limitations clause, the equality provision, and the lack of an explicit reference to the rights of women. He found the draft's protection of legal rights "seriously deficient."[18]

In many ways, Fairweather's testimony set the tone for what the Joint Committee would hear after him. The committee's first witness would turn out to be one of its most important. Fairweather became one of the leading critics of the draft Charter and one of the most influential in forcing changes to it. Other groups would find common cause with him. The government consulted with him and relied upon him in drafting its amendment to the much-reviled limitations clause, which would become the section 1 of the Charter we have today (see the text of the government's proposal and revisions in chapter 5).

Fairweather also took aim at the Canadian Bill of Rights as the courts had interpreted it, stating that he was "appalled by some of the judicial interpretations which have flown in the face of what most of us believe should be the rights of women in society." He said he could "reel off" decisions "like [Lavell] and Bliss and others which are saddening to those who had hoped that the Supreme Court of Canada could do better."[19] He stated that it was "because of these decisions that we must have an entrenched Bill of Rights in this country to remind the judiciary that there have been changes in Canadian society."[20]

Fairweather championed the rights of women, proposing the language that would become the template for section 28 of the Charter: "The Charter of rights should contain an explicit reference to the rights of women. We suggest adding the following [unequivocal] principle: this Charter guarantees the equal right of men and women to the enjoyment of the rights and freedoms set out in it."[21]

## The Assault on Section 1 (the Limitations Clause)

The 6 October 1980 draft of the limitations clause had been agreed upon by most of the provinces the previous summer, when governments were still attempting to achieve federal-provincial cooperation. It was very deferential to government, providing that "the Canadian Charter of Rights and Freedoms guarantees the rights and freedoms set out in it subject only to such reasonable limits as are generally accepted in a free and democratic society with a parliamentary system of government."[22]

Fairweather commenced the assault against the draft of the limitations clause on Friday, 14 November. When the Joint Committee returned after the weekend, it began its first full week of hearing from Canadians. It also started to allow its proceedings to be televised (and radio-broadcast). The proceedings began with some of the leading human rights organizations and luminaries in the country. On Monday, 17 November, it heard from Max Yalden, the commissioner of official languages. His testimony and the questioning predictably focused on the language rights provisions of the Charter.

After Yalden, the attack on section 1 continued. On Tuesday, 18 November, the CCLA appeared before the Joint Committee, represented by its president, Professor Walter Tarnopolsky, the leading expert on the Canadian Bill of Rights; its past president, Mr. J.S. Midanik, QC; and its indefatigable general counsel, Alan Borovoy. Never one to mince words, Borovoy told the committee straight out that it needed more time. "We are very concerned that Canadian history, looking back upon these proceedings, might be somewhat upset by the disquieting paradox of a mere three weeks of hearings being devoted to enshrining the most enduring values in our society and our constitution."[23]

The government agreed to Opposition demands to extend the deadline for the committee's conclusion in exchange for cooperation on other matters before the House;[24] it was also concerned about needing to demonstrate to the British Parliament that its constitutional package was acceptable to most Canadians.[25] On 2 December, both the Senate and the House of Commons agreed to extend the deadline of the committee to 6 February 1981. That date was later further extended until 13 February 1981. What had begun as a one-month study was now becoming a longer, more serious, affair.

Tarnopolsky continued the battering of section 1 that Fairweather had begun several days before, characterizing it as the most important clause to change and stating that if it could not be changed sufficiently, it should be dropped altogether.[26] Group after group followed up the CCLA's criticism of section 1, including the Canadian Jewish Congress, the CBA, the NAC, other women's groups, the Canadian Federation of Civil Liberties and Human Rights Associations, and others. The limitations clause was dubbed the "Mack truck provision" because it was so wide open that you could drive a Mack truck through it.[27]

Within one month of the start of the hearings, it had become apparent to the Liberal members of the committee that the government's draft of section 1 was seriously problematic. The government members on the Joint Committee were clearly on the defensive. On 8 December, Liberal MP Bryce Mackasey opined that the representations of "virtually all the organizations on Section 1 have resulted ... in the Committee agreeing that Section 1 certainly needs revamping, to say the least, in its present form, and it would render all the good intentions of the Charter superfluous and null and void."[28] Behind the scenes, Minister of Justice Jean Chrétien was advising his Cabinet colleagues that a set of amendments to the draft resolution might change the situation.[29]

## The Parade Continues

The CBA appeared on 28 November with a cast of legal luminaries: William Cox, John Nelligan, Jacques Viau, Yves Fortier, Victor Paisley, and David Matas. The CBA had been an early and influential voice in constitutional reform discussions, releasing a discussion paper on the topic in 1978. At the Joint Committee, it made submissions on most sections of the Charter but focused particularly on section 1, fundamental freedoms, and the legal rights provisions.

The CBA was followed by the delegation from the Canadian Jewish Congress, which had historically found common cause with the CCLA. The Congress was represented by four of the most respected members of Canadian legal academe: Professor Maxwell Cohen of McGill University, Professor Martin Friedland of the University of Toronto, Professor Joseph Magnet of the University of Ottawa, and Professor Irwin Cotler of McGill University. At the time, Cotler was the president of the Canadian Jewish Congress; he would go on to an illustrious post-academic career. One of Canada's great orators, Cotler invoked the sense of the historic moment, telling committee members that their proceedings were "one of the most historic deliberations in the constitutional history of this country."[30] He stated that, since 1867, constitutional discussions had focused on the "continuing preoccupation with the powers of government at the expense of the rights of people." He worried that the committee was going down the same path and urged them to correct its course.[31] Professor Max Cohen was more direct about the focus of the work before the committee in drafting the Charter. "I do believe that a charter of rights of this [sic] historic proportions and dimensions should sound a trumpet, should be a Jericho, and by that I mean not some rather well worn cliché but we are stating a national system of values for a long time to come."[32]

The Canadian Jewish Congress was one of many organizations that had struck special constitutional committees to participate in the constitutional debates. Others included the CBA, the Canadian Federation of Civil Liberties and Human Rights Associations, the National Association of Japanese Canadians, and the NAC. The latter group provided important testimony but also one of the most memorable and notorious incidents at the Joint Committee.

### "Who Will Look After the Babies and Children?"

Jill Porter began the NAC's testimony with a very powerful and surprising opening statement, one that poured cold water on the contention that this was a Cadillac Charter. She asserted, "Women could be worse off if the proposed Charter of rights and freedoms is entrenched in Canada's constitution. Certainly the present wording will do nothing to protect women from discriminatory legislation, nor relieve inequities that have accumulated in judicial decisions."[33] The substantive contributions of the NAC were valuable, but they were not what was the most memorable aspect of its appearance before the Joint Committee.

After the NAC representatives had concluded their testimony, Joint Chair Senator Hays attempted to thank the organization. "We appreciate you coming and as a matter of fact we are honoured. However, your time is up and I was just wondering why we do not have a section in here for babies and children. All you girls are going to be working and we are not going to have anybody to look after them."[34] The comment shocked those in attendance and achieved instant infamy. A review of the video of the proceedings indicates that NAC President Lynn MacDonald could not believe what she had just heard. Joint Chair Serge Joyal looks mortified and unsure what to do.

Tory MP James McGrath responded immediately to Hays's comment. "You would have been better off, Mr. Chairman, if you had just used your gavel."[35] And the simple statement by the only woman on the committee, Coline Campbell, encapsulated the reason for the need for strong protection of women's rights in the Charter. She said to Hays, "It is a good thing the Charter is not passed,"[36] implying that his remarks were discriminatory if not unconstitutional. The comments reverberated outside the committee room. NDP MP Stanley Knowles demanded Hays's resignation and his replacement.

Hays's ill-conceived wisecrack acted as a catalyst for media attention on the insufficiency of the protection of women's rights under the draft Charter.[37] Feminist scholar Alexandra Dobrowolsky wrote that Hays's statement "may have done more than any brief to demonstrate to the Committee and to the country (through the wide media coverage of the quip) why women were mobilizing."[38] Feminist writer and activist Michelle Landsberg commented years later that Hays's statement was "so grossly ignorant and discriminatory" that it made the public understand the need to strongly protect women's rights.[39]

The statement would follow Hays for the remainder of his days and beyond. When he died a few weeks after the Charter was proclaimed, his quip was quoted verbatim in the press.[40] It even merits an entry in the index of the proceedings under "Women – Hays Remarks," as if that was self-explanatory.[41]

## A Painful and Shameful Legacy: The National Association of Japanese Canadians

Some of the most powerful, emotional, and persuasive testimony was provided by the National Association of Japanese Canadians. On 26 November 1980, its president, Gordon Kadota, told the Joint Committee members that his group had "requested this appearance because the Japanese Canadians have had a unique experience in Canada, an experience which more than ever must be told to contribute to the making of our future nation."[42] Mr Kadota continued, "Our history in Canada is a legacy of racism made legitimate by our political institutions, and we must somehow ensure that no group of Canadians will be subjected to the whims of political process as we were."[43] This was the reason for the group's support of entrenching the Charter of Rights in the Canadian Constitution. Roger Obata told of his experience growing up in Vancouver, having his family home confiscated, being interned in a concentration camp, and enlisting in the Canadian army during the Second World War.[44] Dr Art Shimizu implored the committee to strengthen the Charter, particularly section 1.[45]

In one of the most memorable moments before the Joint Committee, Mr Obata pleaded, "Ladies and gentlemen, we come to you today to plead for an inviolate entrenchment of the Charter of Rights because we are a people who were undermined, who were overridden, who were victims of a political process when such a basic and fundamental thing as rights were not guaranteed, and today they still are not."[46]

The emotional testimony of these three Canadians elicited a like response from committee members. MP John Fraser, who had been born in Japan, spoke of growing up in Vancouver with Japanese Canadians and of his father, who had fought alongside Japanese Canadians in the trenches of France during the First World War and had spoken out against the internment of Japanese Canadians.[47] The words of Mr Obata stuck in the heads of the committee members, who frequently mentioned the group's testimony long after they had departed from Parliament Hill. The group had made an impact, as would be seen later in the committee proceedings.

## Abortion and Capital Punishment

Two subjects took up an inordinate amount of discussion at the Joint Committee, given that they were not mentioned in the text of the draft Charter. These were abortion and capital punishment. The interest in abortion can be attributed to the preponderance of lawyers and Roman Catholics on the committee,[48] something that may also explain why a number of pro-life groups and the Ontario Conference of Catholic Bishops were invited to testify. At the clause-by-clause review, the Tories introduced an amendment to the Charter to add a provision to protect Parliament's right to legislate in these two areas.[49] It was opposed by both the Liberals and the NDP, and it was defeated. Jean Chrétien explained that such an amendment was not necessary because nothing in the Charter restricted Parliament's ability to legislate in respect of either abortion or capital punishment. He would be proved wrong on both issues.[50]

## The End of Phase 2

The hearings continued through the end of December. Cabinet had been following the proceedings during the fall, and by the end of November and into December, it was actively considering amendments to the draft Charter it had tabled with the Joint Committee.[51] Meanwhile, back in the committee room, the criticism continued to focus on section 1, section 15, and the legal-rights block of rights (sections 7 to 14).

The National Congress of Italian-Canadians, Quebec Region criticized the document as a whole as "sterile, dispassionate; as if Canada were not worthy of an identity, not worthy of accolades. We deplore the fact that a preamble was omitted from the Canada Act. Who are we, Canadians?" The representatives complained that it was "so dry it could have been drafted by a computer," and it was in need of an inspiring general preamble.[52] Many inside and outside the Joint Committee agreed on the need for a preamble of some degree of inspiration. The comments of the National Congress of Italian-Canadians would presage battles to come over the preamble, both at the Joint Committee and in the House of Commons.

On Friday, 19 December, Premier Allan Blakeney of Saskatchewan appeared before the committee. A fervent opponent of the Charter, Blakeney's testimony was notable as the only time that the notwithstanding clause – not included in the draft of the Charter before the Joint Committee – was discussed.[53]

The Joint Committee recessed for two weeks at the end of December. It returned on Monday, 5 January 1981, with a busy schedule featuring the Algonquin Council, the Union of Ontario Indians, the Association of Iroquois and Allied Indians, the Indian Association of Alberta, and the Federation of Saskatchewan Indians – five of the seventeen Aboriginal groups to appear before it. In the fall of 1980, Aboriginal groups had succeeded in organizing and mobilizing support for the inclusion of Aboriginal rights in this round of constitutional negotiations. Pierre Trudeau's government had attempted to defer or avoid the issue. There was incredibly little discussion about Aboriginal issues in the constitutional discussions that took place at almost every Cabinet meeting from June to November 1980.[54] But on 27 November, Aboriginal peoples finally made it on to the agenda of the Cabinet meeting;[55] of course, they did not know that at the time. In December, they were organizing the Constitution Express, which would arrive in Ottawa in the new year and continue on to England.[56]

Thus, on 5 January 1981, Eugene Steinhauer of the Indian Association of Alberta raised a question that was perhaps on the minds of many. He essentially asked whether the committee would simply rubber-stamp the government. Or, in the words of MP Jim Hawkes, how "real" was the committee?[57] This question would soon be answered.

An extremely hectic week of afternoon and evening sessions continued as the Joint Committee heard from eleven more groups and the four designated or brokered experts: Gérard La Forest of the University of Ottawa's Faculty of Law, Maxwell Cohen of McGill University's Faculty of Law (who had previously testified as part of the delegation from the Canadian Jewish Congress), Peter Russell of the University of Toronto's Department of Political Science, and Gil Rémillard of Laval University's Faculty of Law.

The second phase of the committee's work ended on Friday, 9 January, 1981. Over the preceding two months, more than three hundred individuals had appeared before it, representing some one hundred groups or appearing in their individual capacities.[58] The committee had received 962 briefs, letters, and telegrams before 31 December 1980, the deadline for such submissions.[59] To this point, it had sat for thirty-five days, but on many of these occasions, it met twice or even three times, frequently holding evening sessions late into the night. At the conclusion of the witnesses that Friday afternoon, the members of the Joint Committee gushed in the spirit of camaraderie.

The loquacious Tory MP James McGrath reported that the committee had sat for 176 or 177 hours. He complimented the impartiality of the joint chairs and made a plea for greater public involvement in the process. McGrath stated that he was "touched by the degree of collegiality and the spirit of co-operation that has developed in this Committee." Working on the Joint Committee was "one of the outstanding experiences of my parliamentary career, the co-operation and the fellowship – I can use that word, the fellowship – that has developed here and the fact that we have been able to discipline ourselves by keeping out of our discussions narrow partisanship. We scored points procedurally. We scored points with witnesses, but that is the nature of the adversarial game we are involved in in the parliamentary system and I think that is the way it should be."[60] Senator Hays proudly asserted that there had never been a committee as serious as this one. MP Lorne Nystrom expressed the view that the members of the committee were not Liberals or NDP or Tories but Canadians.[61]

## Phase 3 Begins: Clause-by-Clause

With these expressions of goodwill and optimism, Phase 2 of the committee's work was completed. Phase 3 – the clause-by-clause debate over proposed amendments – would be much more adversarial and at times plodding. A total of 123 amendments were proposed, nearly half of which (fifty-eight) came from the government side, something that is highly unusual in committee. The Tories proposed twenty-two amendments, of which seven were approved; and the NDP proposed forty-three amendments, of which two were approved.[62] Many of the amendments were compound ones affecting more than one subclause in the proposed resolution. For example, one unsuccessful Tory amendment proposed amending section 7 to add protection of the right to property and change "principles of fundamental justice" to "natural justice." An NDP amendment proposed to add to section 2 the freedom to organize and bargain collectively.[63]

## Chrétien Returns to the Committee Bearing Amendments

On Monday, 12 January 1981, the answer was revealed to the question from the week before as to whether the committee was merely going to rubber-stamp the government. A remarkable thing happened. Minister of Justice Chrétien returned to the committee and told its members that he had "studied with great care both the written briefs and the oral testimony of all the witnesses and I have taken into account the points which have been made by all members of this Committee during your deliberations. … The Government has listened to the views of Canadians as expressed before this Committee."[64] The planned amendments had been in the works since the end of November.[65] Chrétien proceeded to table with the committee a "tracked-changes" version of the resolution, which showed the changes that the government was prepared to support at that stage.

It is worth quoting Minister Chrétien's remarks because they acknowledge the work of the Joint Committee and contributions of specific groups.

> You have been told over and over again that Canadians want a strong Charter of Rights and Freedoms. You have heard this from the Canadian Civil Liberties Association and other human rights and civil liberties groups, from the Canadian Bar Association, from the Advisory Council on the Status of Women, from the Canadian Consultative Council on Multiculturalism, from representatives of church groups, from the Canadian Jewish Congress, from representatives of official language minorities and from representatives of the many ethnic groups making our country.

> I was most impressed by the eloquent and moving testimony of the National Association of Japanese Canadians and of those who have experienced discrimination in Canada.

> The draft Charter which you have been studying was the result of compromises achieved last summer in negotiations between the federal

government and the provinces. You have been told by many witnesses that Canadians are not satisfied with the type of compromise which weakens the effectiveness of constitutional protection of human rights and freedoms.

[I] accept the legitimacy of that criticism.

Today I want to announce that the government is prepared to make major changes to the draft resolution so as to strengthen the protection of human rights and freedoms in the Charter.[66]

The amendments that Chrétien tabled were extensive and substantive, and they focused almost completely on the Charter. Sections 1 and 15 were completely overhauled, as described in chapters 5 and 10, respectively. As seen in chapter 9, the legal rights sections would be significantly altered, although the government stood firm on the wording of section 7 (which was enacted in its original form). New Brunswick had agreed to be recognized as officially bilingual. Section 23 on minority-language-education rights was altered. An enforcement clause – section 24 – was added. A new section 25 recognizing existing Aboriginal rights was added. There was also to be a new section 26, instructing that the Charter should be interpreted "in a manner consistent with the preservation and enhancement of the multicultural heritage of Canadians."

Many were pleased with the amendments, but women's groups and others were upset at Chrétien's failure to include a clause explicitly guaranteeing the equal application of Charter rights to women and men (what would ultimately become section 28). As well, Aboriginal groups and their allies were upset at the failure to explicitly recognize Aboriginal rights. They would continue to press for what would become section 35. Faced with this increased pressure, and when the NDP threatened to withdraw its support for the entire package over the issue, Chrétien retreated from his opposition to entrenching Aboriginal rights in the Constitution and agreed to what would ultimately become section 35.[67]

For the remainder of the week, Chrétien presented the proposed amendments and answered questions about them. On section 1, the government's proposed amendment took the wind out of the sails of opponents to the limitations clause. The government was so concerned about reaction to this proposed amendment that it was prepared to drop section 1 altogether from the Charter if its proposed amendments were not well received.[68] In fact, the proposed amendment dissipated the criticism, and this "backup plan" was not needed. Section 1 remained in the Charter.

Not surprisingly, the questioning focused on the reasons for choosing particular language in some amendments and for not proposing other amendments. Why were people with disabilities not included in the list of enumerated groups in section 15? Why had the government not gone further on Aboriginal rights? Over the weekend, Chrétien was hospitalized for a suspected heart attack, which turned out to be a combination of stress and indigestion;[69] Solicitor General Robert Kaplan stood in for him as acting minister of justice for the week of 19 January. It was a rocky and confrontational week. Kaplan lacked Chrétien's political skills and was unable to parry Opposition questions. Questions turned into testy skirmishes. On Thursday, 22 January, Kaplan agreed to a proposed Tory amendment to add property rights to section 7.[70] The NDP strongly opposed, and the next day, MPs Svend Robinson and Lorne Nystrom successfully stalled the proceedings to prevent a vote. Over the weekend, Saskatchewan and other provinces reaffirmed their opposition to including property rights in the Charter. While Saskatchewan was a member of the Gang of Eight opposing Trudeau's unilateral patriation efforts, with an NDP government it was viewed as the weakest member of the pack with whom Trudeau and his advisers were trying desperately to reach a deal to support the federal initiative. The NDP had pledged its support but over the weekend threatened to pull it if property rights were included.[71]

The Liberals backtracked. On Monday, 26 January, Chrétien returned to the Joint Committee. After being welcomed back warmly by committee members, he quickly showed that he was in fine fighting form. Chrétien reneged on the government's commitment from just four days before. The Tories were apoplectic and moved that the government's breach of its undertaking to the committee constituted a breach of parliamentary privilege. The motion was defeated, with the NDP supporting the Liberals in opposing it.[72]

Kaplan was embarrassed *in absentia*; the goodwill that had been expressed just over a week before had dissipated, and the hard slogging over clause-by-clause amendment continued. To Kaplan's likely relief, he never returned to appear before the Joint Committee.

The Tories' proposed twenty-two amendments included adding a preamble recognizing the supremacy of God and the dignity and worth of all individuals; creating a subsection under section 2 recognizing the freedom from unreasonable interference with privacy, family, home, correspondence, and enjoyment of property; adding a section under Democratic Rights recognizing the right to freedom of information; adding the right to property under section 7 and changing "principles of fundamental justice" to "principles of natural justice"; adding the right to legal aid to the right to counsel under section 10; adding the right to an interpreter for the deaf in section 14; making various other changes to the legal rights provisions; and adding a section that would provide that nothing in the Charter would affect the authority of Parliament to legislate regarding abortion or capital punishment.[73] The committee approved seven amendments, including adding disability to section 15 and adding the right to an interpreter for the deaf in section 14.

The NDP proposed forty-three amendments, of which only two were approved. The ratio did not accurately reflect the NDP's influence at the Joint Committee. Many of these amendments dealt with matters of form (such as separating out freedom of the press as a distinct right) or minor changes to language, which the government opposed simply because it preferred its language and structure. In other cases, the NDP pressed forward with attempting to strengthen the rights guarantees, as had been proposed by some of the witnesses before the committee. The NDP pushed for the rights protections to be as strong as those contained in international human rights documents such as the International Covenant on Civil and Political Rights. Two important substantive amendments to fundamental freedoms were rejected: (1) the right to organize and bargain collectively (as a continuation of freedom of association) and (2) the right to access to government information. The NDP also proposed broadening the protected grounds on section 15 to include sexual orientation, disability, political belief, and lack of means. This amendment was rejected, but a Tory amendment to add disability as a protected ground was adopted.

Until this point, the NDP's amendments were solidly in the civil libertarian rights stream, attempting to expand the protections of the individual from the state. Only in one case did it propose a positive obligation on the state: to provide state-funded counsel to those charged with a criminal offence who could not afford it.[74] This proposal was defeated, although supported by the Tories, who had made a similar amendment. All in all, the NDP's amendments showed that it accepted the basic structure of the Charter and the blocks of rights that had been part of the constitutional conversation in Canada since Pierre Trudeau had released *A Canadian Charter of Human Rights* in 1968. The NDP did not raise, let alone push, the cause of social and economic rights that had been mooted and dismissed in that document. It remained very much within the framing of the Charter of Rights that Pierre Trudeau had enunciated.

The last three weeks of January meant intense work for the members of the Joint Committee. On Saturday, 31 January, they celebrated Serge Joyal's 36th birthday; both Jean Chrétien and Tory James McGrath toasted him.[75] Meanwhile, outside the committee, support was wavering in Cabinet for Trudeau's unilateral patriation plan. Cabinet minutes from 29 January show concerns from attacks on both flanks: the Canadian Chamber of Commerce was thought to be undermining the patriation effort, and there was fear of losing the support of the NDP. Ministers expressed concern over the position of the British and suggested enlisting the support of the Right Hon. Paul Martin, Sr, former Canadian high commissioner to the United Kingdom. Some ministers had second thoughts about proceeding. Some ministers were looking for an out: a reference to the Supreme Court or a referendum. They were dressed down in private by the prime minister, who told them that it was "too late to become nervous now because there could be no turning back. If the government were to be foiled in its plans to repatriate the Constitution, a general election would seem inevitable and a favourable outcome of such an election could not be a foregone conclusion."[76] In other words, soldier on.

As the month of January 1981 ended, the Joint Committee was running out of time: it had to report back to the Senate and the House by Friday, 13 February. Only a week remained for the rest of the clause-by-clause deliberations. During this week, the committee reverted to the "old Constitution": executive federalism, constitutional conferences, and the amending formula. The committee had tried to start its deliberations with the old Constitution, but these had quickly been usurped by the Charter, which took up most of the time. Because these issues came after the Charter in the proposed joint resolution, they were left for last when there was little time left and declining strength to deal with them. On Monday, 9 February, there was an argument over the title of the resolution.[77] By this time, the committee members appeared tired and disagreeable.

At the end of the proceedings, Joint Chair Serge Joyal gave perhaps his longest speech. He thanked the media, the staff of Parliament who had worked overnight on transcription, the witnesses, the public who had watched on television, and, of course, the members of the committee.[78] The other joint chair, Senator Harry Hays, had the last word. He boasted that the committee had held 103 meetings and had sat for 270 hours and that the minister had been in attendance for thirty-six sessions. Additionally, he stated that "one factor that has amazed me is that every chair has been filled at every meeting. 51 Senators out of the 102 have sat at this table, and 132 Members of Parliament have sat at this table – almost half of all the Senators and nearly half of all the Members of Parliament at some sessions or another."[79] The Joint Committee had been the work of many parliamentarians and many Canadians. And, with that, the public proceedings of the committee came to an end. The committee drafted its report *in camera*, as was and still is the usual practice. It presented its report to Parliament on Friday, 13 February 1981. In its report, which was ultimately adopted by Parliament, the committee recommended significant changes to the 6 October 1980 draft resolution that had been referred to it.

The draft of the Charter that emerged from the Joint Committee differed substantially from the one that had been originally referred to it. In most respects, it is the Charter that Canadians have today. Of its thirty-four sections, thirty-one were essentially chiselled into constitutional stone at the committee. As discussed in the next chapter, two significant additions still to come were sections 28 (equality of male and female persons) and 33 (the notwithstanding clause). The first clause had been advocated at the Joint Committee and was added soon after the committee reported back to Parliament, building on the momentum established at the committee. The second clause was (in)famously added by the first ministers in the November 1981 accord and came as a shock to many of the committee participants because certainly no one had advocated during the proceedings for the inclusion of a notwithstanding clause; indeed, the idea had been mentioned only a single time – by Saskatchewan Premier Allan Blakeney, in passing, during his appearance.[80]

The work of the Joint Committee was completed. In its report to the Senate and the House of Commons, the committee had proposed substantial changes to the proposed joint resolution of both Houses of Parliament. That proposed joint resolution would call on the UK Parliament to enact legislation to patriate the Canadian Constitution with an amending formula, a Charter of Rights and Freedoms, and nascent Aboriginal rights provisions. Now all that remained was for the Parliament of Canada to pass the joint resolution, if it indeed had the power to do so without the provinces' approval – that was the issue that the provinces were challenging in court. Then the British Parliament would have to act on that resolution and enact legislation. In short, in February 1981, when the committee delivered its report, it was by no means clear that anything would actually come of it.

## Chapter Four

# From the Joint Committee to Patriation

## Return to the House: Road Block and Compromise

The changes proposed by the Joint Committee led to a greatly strengthened charter in terms of the document's protections of rights and freedoms. Consequently, the final Charter helped make patriation of the Constitution a much more "saleable" package to the Canadian public.[1] Indeed, as members of the committee and the House would have been well aware, polls showed overwhelmingly strong support for the idea of a charter.[2] The Tories had noticed this groundswell of support and decided that they would oppose the Charter only on procedural grounds, confronting Trudeau's plan for unilateral patriation.[3]

And oppose it they did. When the Joint Committee's draft resolution was referred back to the House of Commons in mid-February 1981, the debate was testy. The Official Opposition was able to occupy the time of the House with debate on a single proposed amendment for more than a month.[4] At Cabinet, Prime Minister Trudeau asked his ministers to restrict out-of-country travel during the constitutional debate and encouraged them to travel within the country to speak about the Constitution.[5] In March, he privately expressed his concerns at Cabinet regarding growing opposition from the clergy to the government's constitutional proposal, mainly to the specific reference to women's rights, which the clergy feared could strengthen "the pro-abortionist position."[6]

The government was being continuously challenged to submit its plan for unilateral patriation to the Supreme Court for a ruling on its validity. On 12 March, it was reported at Cabinet that the public was growing tired of the constitutional debate and the sooner it concluded, the better. The Conservative filibuster was now in its fifth week, and the Liberals thought it was becoming "dull and repetitive."[7] On 19 March, the Liberals attempted to limit debate, and the Tories responded aggressively by using procedural mechanisms to slow all proceedings in the House to a crawl.[8] As the leader of the Official Opposition, Joe Clark demanded that Trudeau refer the matter to the Supreme Court for a ruling; three provinces (Manitoba, Quebec, and Newfoundland) had already referred the question to their highest courts. The matter came to a head on 31 March, when the Newfoundland Court of Appeal ruled against unilateral patriation. This meant that the federal government now had to appeal the decision to the Supreme Court; politically, it could not proceed in the face of this ruling that it lacked the legal authority to patriate the Constitution on its own. But the Newfoundland court decision facilitated a compromise: Parliament would vote on the proposed resolution, and the government would agree to update it and then submit the updated draft resolution to the Supreme Court, where appeals from judgments in the references from the three provinces were already pending.[9]

On 23 April, the House of Commons voted to accept amendments to the proposed resolution. It made two changes, both in the Charter. First, by a vote of 268–0, MPs voted to add section 28, which guaranteed the rights in the Charter equally to male and female persons.[10] It was added at the behest of women's groups and others and had been the subject of much advocacy, both at the Joint Committee and afterwards.[11] Second, the Liberals agreed to add a preamble that affirmed "the supremacy of God," something that it had refused to do at the Joint Committee. The preamble to the Charter now provides, "Whereas Canada is founded upon principles that recognize the supremacy of God and the rule of law."[12] A broader preamble proposed by the Tories was defeated, but the narrower preamble passed by a vote of 173–94.[13] For so much effort, argument, and hair splitting over these two provisions, both the preamble and section 28 have had virtually no juridical impact in the Charter's first thirty-five years.

The agreement to submit the amended resolution to the Supreme Court for a ruling allowed the House to vote, and it ended the tension and testiness that had consumed it over the preceding months. The vote itself served as a catharsis. Afterwards, Speaker Jeanne Sauvé invited all the MPs to join her for a drink at a reception for the Speakers of the parliaments from other Commonwealth countries, who were visiting Ottawa that day and had happened to attend the session for the important vote.[14] It was almost 11:00 p.m. on a Thursday evening, but the House was adjourning for two weeks, and it was too late for most members to catch a flight back to their constituencies. While some no doubt went back to their homes and hotel rooms to collapse into bed and grab some well-deserved sleep, others accepted the Speaker's invitation and had a drink or two "to the Constitution." After being delayed by the Opposition for over two months, the proposed resolution was moving forward to receive the blessing of the Supreme Court, where the federal government anticipated a speedy settlement of the issue.

### Waiting for the Supreme Court; Taking Stock

By the end of April 1981, the final terms of the Charter were virtually complete. Of course, given the history of constitutional attempts in Canada, the participants had no way of knowing that at the time. In any event, the Charter that was before Parliament that spring went far beyond anything envisioned by John Diefenbaker in the 1950s or agreed to by Prime Minister Trudeau and the premiers at Victoria in 1971.[15] Almost a decade and a half had passed since Trudeau had presented his constitutional vision to the CBA in September 1967 and released his proposed Canadian Charter of Human Rights.

Much had transpired during those years, and several important changes had occurred. Constitutional reform was no longer an obscure intergovernmental file or one man's vanity project. The Charter had awakened Canadians' interest in patriation, and broadcasting the Joint Committee's work to the nation had further popularized it. In the meantime, the provinces had finally come up with a united position on constitutional reform. On 16 April 1981, the premiers of the Gang of Eight – the eight provinces that opposed the federal government's patriation plan – put their signatures on a counter-plan for patriation, which included an amending formula. Variously known as the April Accord or the Chateau Consensus (it was signed at the Château Laurier hotel in Ottawa), the provinces agreed to patriate the Canadian Constitution "rapidly," adopt a new amending formula, enter into intensive constitutional negotiations during a three-year period based on the new amending formula, and discontinue all outstanding court actions regarding patriation.[16] Notably, the plan did not include the Charter – mention of it was conspicuously absent in the news release that accompanied the announcement of the accord.[17] Under the plan, the Charter would be included in the list of subjects to be negotiated under the new amending formula. The Gang of Eight invited Ontario and New Brunswick to sign the accord and called on the prime minister to call a constitutional conference. Neither happened. Instead, the federal government reached a détente with the Opposition parties in Parliament and confidently proceeded to the Supreme Court.

## The Supreme Court's Decision

The Supreme Court agreed to schedule the appeals from the three provincial references (from Manitoba, Quebec, and Newfoundland) on an extremely abbreviated timetable. The hearing took place over five days during the last week of April and the first week of May 1981. For reasons that remain unclear, the federal government expected a quick decision by the Court, certainly before the summer (in comparison, the unanimous decision of the high court in the 1979 *Upper House Reference* had been delivered eight months after the reference was heard). The Trudeau government planned to send the joint resolution to Westminster to be passed as soon as it received the Supreme Court's blessing; the government was concerned that it would lose critical time because the British Parliament planned to adjourn in advance of the wedding of Prince Charles and Lady Diana at the end of July 1981.[18]

But Canada Day came and went without a judgment from the high court, dashing the federal government's hopes of a quick patriation. As it waited, Cabinet wrestled with the impact of a postal strike and the Royal Wedding.[19] Finally, during the last week of September, the Supreme Court gave notice that the decision was ready. Prime Minister Trudeau was scheduled to travel to Australia to attend the Commonwealth Heads of Government meeting, and Cabinet actually debated whether he should cancel his trip and stay for the Supreme Court's decision or attend the meeting. The consensus was that Canada's economic problems were more important than its constitutional ones and that it was imperative for the prime minister to attend the Commonwealth meeting and promote Canadian commercial exports and Commonwealth interests.[20]

Supreme Court judgments are released to the parties, the media, and the public. Today, they are simply posted on the Court's website, and the Court sends out an email informing interested parties of the decision and tweets the release of the decision. In 1981, printed copies of judgments were all that was available; the fax was not even in widespread use. But the *Patriation Reference* was no ordinary judgment. Chief Justice Bora Laskin made the unusual decision for the judges to publicly announce the judgment in open court and also to allow live television coverage of the pronouncement. (This was years before the Supreme Court allowed the Cable Public Affairs Channel to televise tape-delayed coverage of its hearings.) Confusion reigned when the Supreme Court announced its judgment because as the judges entered the courtroom, one of them tripped over the cable and unplugged the live microphone; the announcement of the judgment was thus impossible to hear.[21]

The judgment was one of the Court's lengthiest, filling over 150 pages of the Supreme Court Reports.[22] Much more has been written elsewhere, parsing and critiquing the decision.[23] The Court was divided on the principal two issues before it. By a vote of 7–2, a majority held that, as a matter of constitutional law, the federal government was legally empowered to make a unilateral request to the British Parliament to amend and, indeed, patriate the Canadian Constitution without the consent of the provinces. However, a different majority of 6–3 held that, as a matter of constitutional convention, the federal government was required to obtain a "substantial degree of consent" to amend the Canadian Constitution. Neither side had obtained the outright victory that it had hoped for.

The Supreme Court came to be praised for its statecraft (while often criticized for its method)[24] because its decision effectively forced the federal government and the provinces back to the negotiating table. While British Prime Minister Margaret Thatcher had indicated to Pierre Trudeau that she preferred that the provinces approve of his patriation package, Trudeau had responded that as far as he was concerned, the British should simply "hold their noses" and pass his patriation package. In short, having proceeded down the unilateral road, Trudeau was not afraid to return to that route if he could not obtain a satisfactory deal with the provinces. The stage was thus set for one last attempt at achieving consensus on patriation.

**The November Accord**

A first ministers' meeting was scheduled for the first week of November 1981 in Ottawa as the "last chance conference."[25] Much has been written about that conference and the accord that it produced.[26] The official proceedings took place behind closed doors, while drama and deals occurred in the hallways, hotel suites, and in a famous kitchen at the Château Laurier. The conference was described as "the most sophisticated constitutional poker game since Confederation"[27] and a "fascinating madhouse."[28] Perhaps that is an exaggeration, but the drama produced a deal between the federal government and all the provinces except Quebec, and it both smoothed the way for patriation and produced political enmity with Quebec that survives to this day.

The "deal" struck between the premiers of all but one of the provinces and the federal government contained the following key elements: (1) patriation with an amending formula, as contained in the April Accord; (2) the Charter of Rights, as then contained in the draft resolution, with a "tweaking" of section 6 to allow for preferential hiring for provinces with unemployment rates above the national average; and (3) a notwithstanding clause, which would apply to fundamental freedoms, legal rights, and equality rights. Protection for Aboriginal rights (section 35) was dropped from the "package" to be patriated.[29] Here the blocks of rights that had been put in place in Trudeau's 1968 Charter played a critical role. Democratic Rights (sections 3 to 5), Mobility Rights (section 6), Language Rights (sections 16 to 22), and Minority Language Educational Rights (section 23) were not made subject to the notwithstanding clause. Although it was not clear at first, section 28 (equality of male and female persons) was to be subject to the override.

The federal government issued a fact sheet accompanying the release of the accord to "explain" how the notwithstanding clause would work.[30] It had not been the subject of public discussion at the Joint Committee; only Saskatchewan Premier Allan Blakeney had suggested the idea of a "non-obstante clause" in passing during his testimony.[31] The notwithstanding clause – this "peculiarly, perhaps embarrassingly, Canadian device"[32] – came to haunt the November Accord and Canadian constitutional politics.[33]

The November 1981 first ministers' meeting was the antithesis of the Joint Committee proceedings: it was closed, exclusive, and secretive. It succeeded in obtaining a deal that Peter Russell termed "an achievement in elite accommodation,"[34] but the response of many of those who had participated in the committee proceedings was one of disbelief. Women and Aboriginal people who had obtained so much through the joint committee process and in its immediate aftermath found that ten white men (Trudeau and all the premiers except for René Lévesque) had tossed out their gains with the stroke of a pen. The November Accord had jettisoned the section 35 protection for

Aboriginal rights and added a notwithstanding clause (what would become section 33), which not only could override sections 2 and 7 to 14 of the Charter but appeared to subject the hard-fought section 28 to the override as well.

It was not that Trudeau had traded away the long, hard-fought protection of the rights of women and Aboriginal persons to receive something in return. Their rights had been sacrificed "almost by neglect."[35] Unlike the proceedings before the Joint Committee, the voices of women and Aboriginal people were not heard because there were no women or Aboriginal people engaged in the process and there was no one to champion their interests. No first minister stood up for Aboriginal rights because they were not on anyone's "must list."[36]

So little discussion had occurred at the first ministers' meeting about applying the notwithstanding clause to section 28 that there was confusion in the aftermath about whether it would apply. When the prime minister was asked about it in the House of Commons on 6 November 1981, his answer was unclear.[37] Three days later, he clarified that the override would indeed apply to section 28.[38] The federal strategy was to blame the provinces both for the override and for the application of the override to equality rights and section 28.[39] By 18 November, when the government unveiled the final resolution to be approved by Parliament, it was clear: the clauses explicitly protecting the rights of women and Aboriginal Canadians had been abandoned.[40] Federal NDP leader Ed Broadbent withdrew his party's support for the package.

### The Charter Canadians Rise Up

However, something novel happened in November 1981. In the best tradition of democratic activism, the people rose up against their leaders. Public opinion turned strongly against the federal government and the provincial leaders. Women's groups leaped back into action and engaged in intense lobbying.[41] Canadians saw, "for the first time, a dazzling demonstration of the organizing skills and political clout of women's groups."[42] Provincial leaders were caught unawares and appeared stunned. The usual political strategies – inviting in the leadership of an organization and aweing it with access to, and an audience with, political leaders, or countering opposition groups with the messages of supportive groups – did not work this time. Under the intense and uncomfortable pressure, "the provincial governments folded like omelettes."[43]

On 24 November, the House removed section 28 from the application of the notwithstanding clause by a vote of 222–0.[44] Two days later, it restored section 35 Aboriginal rights by the same vote.[45]

The reaction to the November Accord "presaged significant changes in constitutional decision-making in Canada. The vigorous interest groups and pressure groups swept away the reluctant premiers in their path."[46] Many noted that this marked an important change in constitutional politics and constitutional law. No longer would they be the exclusive domain of first ministers and officials. In a sense, the federal government was a victim of its own success. The contents of the Charter had sparked considerable interest in the Constitution among ordinary Canadians, and the federal government's communications plan around the people's package had succeeded in popularizing the Charter. The Joint Committee had opened up a Pandora's box of popular participation that could not be shut afterwards, as reaction to the November Accord showed.

The resolution with the new Canadian Charter of Rights and Freedoms passed the House of Commons with all-party agreement on 2 December 1981, by a vote of 246 in favour and 24 against.[47] The only member of the Joint Committee to vote against the resolution was NDP MP Svend Robinson, who voted against it specifically because of the override.[48] Mercurial MP and shadow Joint Committee member Warren Allmand also voted against it because of his opposition to the Charter's failure to protect language rights across the country.[49] But by this time, public interest in the Constitution was waning; the government was focused on other matters – high interest rates, a perceived housing and rental crisis, increased concerns about urea formaldehyde foam insulation, and criticism of its recent budget.[50]

### History in the Making

Hansard indicates that, after the vote, "the members of the House rose and sang 'O Canada.'"[51] The record does not reflect the fact that MPs left their seats and congratulated Pierre Trudeau, Joe Clark, and Ed Broadbent.[52] The Senate passed the resolution on 8 December 1981, by a vote of 59–23. Not to be outdone, the honourable senators also rose to sing "O Canada."[53]

The MPs knew they were making history. After the resolutions had been approved by the Senate, they were transmitted to Government House for the governor general's approval. Normally this is a private, solitary, bureaucratic affair – the governor general has many official documents to sign and does not hold signing ceremonies the way that the president of the United States does. There are no souvenir pens given to sponsors of legislation. But this event was different. As described by chroniclers of the time, on hand were most of those who were considered the "Fathers of Re-Confederation": "Joe Clark and about thirty members of his caucus; Ed Broadbent and some of his MPs; senior staff members from the Federal-Provincial Relations Office and the Department of Justice, and, of course, Prime Minister Trudeau, his Cabinet, and many Liberal MPs."[54] Purposely excluded were any representatives of the provinces who had caused Trudeau so much trouble throughout the negotiations. The women and men who had contributed to the making of the Charter, both as members of the Joint Committee and as witnesses before it, were also not invited. They were not so much excluded as simply overlooked.

In retrospect, it may appear that it was smooth sailing from the December vote to the proclamation of the Charter by the Queen on a rainy day in April 1982. That would be misleading. Just before Christmas 1981, the Canada Bill was tabled for first reading in the British House of Commons, and Canadian opponents of the patriation package took their battle to London. Canadian Tories lobbied their British counterparts, especially in the House of Lords; representatives of Quebec's PQ government tried to block patriation; and Aboriginal groups who opposed the accord lobbied politically and also brought a court challenge to try to halt the deal. The Canadian government launched a diplomatic full-court press, sending former high commissioner Paul Martin Sr back to London with Cabinet ministers John Roberts, Mark MacGuigan, and Serge Joyal – the former joint chair of the Joint Committee who had since moved up from the backbenches into Trudeau's Cabinet. Working with Canadian High Commissioner Jean Casselman Wadds, they wined and dined British parliamentarians and public servants to overcome political uncertainty and opposition to the Canadian deal. They were successful.

The Canada Bill received second reading on 17 February 1982, and third and final reading on 8 March. The next day, the bill was tabled in the House of Lords and passed on 25 March. Queen Elizabeth gave her assent to the Canada Act on 29 March. All that was left was for her to proclaim the act that would make the Constitution Act, 1982 and with it the Canadian Charter of Rights and Freedoms enter into force. For this, Trudeau wanted the Queen to come to Ottawa. The date was set for 17 April 1982.

On 16 April – the eve of the official proclamation of the new Constitution by the Queen – Jean Chrétien hosted a gala dinner in the Parliament Buildings for all those who had participated in the constitutional reform process. Politicians and government officials toasted and good-naturedly joked about each other. While the members of the Joint Committee were invited to the celebration, they may as well not have been because any mention of their contribution, barely over a year old, was completely ignored that evening; already, they had become "forgotten men."[55] To say the least, none of the women and men whom Chrétien had singled out for credit when he tabled amendments before the committee in January 1981 were invited. They had already been written out of the constitutional narrative. Not only were they forgotten, they had also been rendered invisible.

Meanwhile, Trudeau's grudge against the premiers had its limits. On 17 April 1982, the day that Queen Elizabeth II signed the proclamation that entered the Charter and the rest of the Constitution Act, 1982 into force, he made all the provincial premiers (except Quebec's René Lévesque) members of the Queen's Privy Council for Canada, entitling them to use the title "the Honourable" for life and the letters "PC" after their name. None of the Joint Committee members or individuals or groups that had appeared before the Joint Committee was so honoured.[56] They, along with the hundreds of Canadians who participated in the Joint Committee's work, remain the unsung Mothers and Fathers of Re-Confederation.

# PART TWO

## Chapter Five

# The Limitations Clause

Guarantee of Rights and Freedoms

Rights and freedoms in Canada

The *Canadian Charter of Rights and Freedoms* guarantees the rights and freedoms set out in it subject only to such reasonable limits prescribed by law as ~~are generally accepted~~ can be demonstrably justified in a free and democratic society ~~with a Parliamentary system of government~~.

**Commentary**

Section 1 – "the limitations clause" – attracted more commentary than any other clause at the Joint Committee. Almost all of it was negative; no fewer than nineteen groups attacked the clause that was dubbed "the Mack truck clause" because it was so broad that the government could drive a Mack truck through it. As discussed in chapter 3, many groups called for its removal altogether, while others called for its severe restriction. Critics attacked almost every aspect of the clause, asserting that it allowed almost any potential restriction on rights set out in the rest of the Charter. As the discussion shows, it was not clear to many witnesses whether the government intended the limitations clause to apply only in the case of war or emergencies. The government's responses indicated its intention for the clause to apply much more broadly.

The government realized quite quickly that its draft of section 1 was draining its support for the Charter as a whole. Even while groups continued to attack section 1, the government was preparing to amend it. Cabinet considered ditching the controversial limitations clause altogether but decided to amend it instead because it feared that dropping it would discredit entirely the government's previous arguments in favour of a limitations clause.[1] Thus, in January 1981, Minister of Justice Chrétien tabled the proposed amendment to section 1, which was ultimately adopted and produced the limitations clause that we have today.

### General Explanation

**Mr. Roger Tassé, Q.C. (Deputy Minister of Justice):** Section 1 is meant to bring forward the concept that these rights that are spelled out in the Charter ... are not absolute rights. If you just take, for example, the freedom of expression, there are limits to the freedom of expression that already are spelled out in the Criminal Code and that will continue and should continue when a Charter of Rights like this is entrenched.

What the Section is meant to do is to bring that concept not only to the legislatures but also to the judges because in effect the judges when they are faced with cases where government action or parliamentary action, legislative action is being tested and challenged, in effect they have to decide whether limits, restrictions, that may have been imposed, because again these rights are not absolute, are reasonable ones. That is only what Section 1 is intended to do, that in effect the judges, when there are challenges brought before them, where in effect people would claim that their rights have been unfairly or unreasonably restricted that in coming to a conclusion when they are so challenged that in effect the courts will have to take for granted that there are some limitations that may well be reasonable and legitimate in the kind of society in which we live. (3: 15)

### "Reasonable" Limits

**Mr. Roger Tassé, Q.C. (Deputy Minister of Justice):** That is the test that the Court would have to apply and that is the whole purpose of the Charter of Rights. In fact, when you entrench a charter of rights like this one you are saying that Parliament and the legislature will constrain themselves when they legislate. (3: 15)

**The Hon. Jean Chrétien (Minister of Justice):** ... We have a Charter of Rights but this text is a limit; it is an indication to the court how to interpret the charter in relation to the different legislation because if you do not put those words there it could lead to all sorts of change by the courts that will not give them any limits of interpretation. As said by my Deputy Minister there is some legislation that has been well established in the Canadian society that are recognized, and we have to make sure that the courts do not destroy all the previous work of the evolution of our society. Otherwise we will be in great legal difficulty, so they will have to apply the test of reasonableness in their decision. I do think the Charter of Rights has its own limits, as you will find out when you are studying it, section by section. (3: 15)

## Who Will Decide What Is Reasonable?

**Mr. Svend Robinson, MP (NDP, BC):** ... I want to ask the Minister in particular about clause one of this proposed Charter of Rights and Freedoms because I suggest that in its present wording it is a gaping hole in the Charter which really makes the alleged rights and freedoms which are supposed to be protected completely illusory; and in fact if this section one is permitted in its present form that in many ways we will be in a worse position in this country than had this particular Charter not been implemented.

Mr. Minister, first of all with respect to clause one I would like to ask you who would determine what is generally accepted as a limitation on these rights and freedoms and what test would they apply? Would it be a numerical test?

**The Hon. Jean Chrétien (Minister of Justice):** It will be the court who will decide. The way I understand the courts to operate, the precedents will determine the next move. It will be the court because we are not giving them other tests than these.

**Mr. Robinson:** How will it be determined what is generally accepted? Will that be in terms of numbers, if the majority of Canadians accept particular limitation? Would this be your understanding of that provision?

**Mr. Chrétien:** I do not want to pass judgment for what the court will say but I do think there is some, as I explained earlier, there is some historical situation, trends in society, that they can measure; whether it be in terms of numbers and so on. Of course, we are putting a charter there for one reason, to protect the minorities against the abuses of the majority. ... I do not see them turning back the clock; it will be in terms of progress and in terms of protection. (3: 27)

## Emergency and Non-derogable Rights

**Ms. Mary Eberts (Legal Counsel, Advisory Council on the Status of Women):** We surmise that Section 1, at least in part, was included to give Parliament the chance to limit our civil liberties when it is necessary in times of war, apprehended insurrection or other civil emergencies and we suggest that it is in keeping with the democratic traditions of the western world if the limitations that can be placed on our liberties are explicitly spelled out in the charter of rights and not left to something like Section 1.

We suggest that Section 1 be reduced to a simple preamble explaining what the charter of rights is intended to accomplish and that Section 29 include a limitation that will come into effect only in times of war or other times of public emergency and that this section ensure a number of aspects. In time of public emergency which threatens the life of the nation so that it is a serious emergency and the existence of which is officially proclaimed, Parliament may authorize that temporary restriction of certain rights and freedoms to the extent strictly required by the exigencies of the situation but in a manner that the other rights and freedoms set out in this charter will be preserved. We also stipulate that there are some freedoms and rights set out in the charter that need never be interfered with no matter how grave the emergency.

We recommend that the non-discrimination rights never be tampered with and that there never be any derogation from freedom of conscience and religion, the right to vote and hold office, because there are already protections allowing for the suspension of elections which are found in Section 4.

The right to life, liberty and security of the person except when denied by a law duly enacted; the right to being safe from cruel and unusual treatment and punishment; the right to a translator in judicial proceedings should in our view never be suspended because of war or apprehended insurrection, and all the language rights in Sections 16 to 23 need in our view never be suspended because of any kind of civil or martial disability. (9: 130, 131)

**Ms. Monique Charlebois (Member of the Steering Committee, National Association of Women and the Law):** ... Our next item deals with Section 1 which we call the Mack Truck clause because a person could drive one right through it. We do not intend to dwell at length on this section which creates such loopholes in the legislation. Suffice it to say that we join with the comments of the Canadian Advisory Council on the Status of Women, the National Action Committee on the Status of Women, and the Canadian Civil Liberties Association and other groups in condemning Section 1.

I would just like to summarize a few of our objections. There are two main points. First, Section 1 applies at all times, it is not limited to emergency situations. Secondly, the standards of reasonable limits that are generally accepted in a democratic society appears [sic] to us to allow virtually any legislation passed by a majority in Parliament or a legislature.

Apart from concerns regarding the basic rights and freedoms which we share with other groups, we are concerned that this clause may have the effect of completely negating the protection provided by Section 15 on equality of rights. (22: 53)

**Mr. David Lepofsky (Member, Ontario Division Board of Management, Canadian National Institute for the Blind):** ... Section 1 should not govern either Section 14 or Section 15. It is our view that there should be no circumstances where the right to an interpreter, which a deaf, blind or just a deaf person may require in court, should ever be taken away. Why is it either in war or emergency that a deaf-blind person on trial should be denied an interpreter to know what the case is against them. It is too basic and a denial of natural justice.

Moreover when should unwarranted discrimination be permitted? At wartime? At peacetime? In the case of an emergency? It is hard to imagine a situation where it is justifiable, and therefore we have recommended, as have other groups, that Section 14 and Section 15 be absolute rights, rights not subject to Section 1.

Alternatively, if that point of view is not acceptable to the Committee, it is our submission that the wording in Section 1 is far, far too broad. You have heard all the arguments before, we can only reiterate them, that Section 1 – labelled by some as the Mack truck provision – will in fact make the rest of the Charter of Rights a virtually worthless and impotent means of protecting civil liberties.

In particular, the generally accepted view of the public with respect to handicapped persons is that they are often not capable of taking care of themselves, not capable of maintaining a job, not capable of self-sufficiency, and therefore the kinds of laws that I have discussed previously that are discriminatory would be under Section 1 generally accepted in a free and democratic society, passed by these kinds of Parliaments. And accordingly, if Section 1 remains, and if Section 15 is still subject to it, it is our view that Section 1 must be very narrowly constrained to protect minority rights and in particular, handicapped rights. (25: 13)

## Criticism of Draft of Section 1

**Senator Arthur Tremblay (PC, Quebec):** ... Are the limits mentioned in Section 1 whatever may be the individual linguistic rights mentioned elsewhere in the Charter, embarrassing for you as Commissioner of Official Languages.

**Mr. Max Yalden (Commissioner of Official Languages):** Mr. Chairman, broadly speaking this part of the first section embarrasses me a little, not necessarily as Commissioner of Languages, but as a citizen reading the text, I do not understand it very well. I find it so broad that whatever it says does not represent in my view a requirement for a legislature who should guide the courts very clearly, very explicitly. If it is the case, it seems to me that this section should be more specific, not stricter than it is.

As for the linguistic aspect, would the linguistic rights mentioned in Sections 16 to 23 be affected by this short paragraph? I really could not give you an answer, precisely, because I find these words ... so vague that I do not know what they mean. If I knew, I would answer you. (6: 28)

**The Hon. Jake Epp, MP (PC, Manitoba):** Mr. Fairweather, what I would like to do from looking at materials that you have provided earlier, is take you to your concern of Section 1 of the proposed resolution. At the bottom of your presentation as well as in the accompanying documents you stress your concern about Section 1. I would like to ask you from your perspective if the clause remains essentially in the form it now appears what are the technical consequences of that clause in relation to the protection of rights and freedoms?

**Mr. Gordon Fairweather (Canadian Human Rights Commission):** They are so serious that I could not imagine this Committee letting Section 1 go unamended. That section as drafted would challenge, in my opinion, the rest of the charter, and I suspect somebody is going to be getting an amendment.

It is, as I said, turning our backs on the international and national jurisprudence, and it is very broadly drafted. Why we do not use the language that is well accepted now and has been ratified by Canada, for the life of me I have no idea. This is a strong statement but I have strong feelings. I am absolutely committed to the entrenchment and the patriation and the goals. They are wonderful goals for this country at last but why not go for something better. (5: 11)

**Mr. Epp:** From your experience as a Commissioner of the Human Rights Commission, could you give us examples of if this proposed resolution had in fact been in effect with the prohibitions in Section 1, can you give us some specific examples of the restrictions it would have given or caused both to rights and freedoms and also to the Commission?

**Mr. Fairweather:** Yes. One was given last night, if I know correctly, by the Minister of Justice for Canada. It might be that generally accepted standards in this country for mandatory retirement, the anti-discrimination part having to do with age, could be challenged and rendered meaningless as a reform mechanism, because the generally accepted standards now are quite illiberal, if I may use that word in this place.

The generally accepted standards for Canada are to push people out at certain ages. I greeted this charter with excitement when I saw that the Government of Canada had included age, but when I see the language of Section 1, I wonder.

Another message that surely cannot be forgotten is that the generally accepted standards in Canada in 1940 and 1941 were to [intern] Canadians whose offence was that they were of Japanese origin.

In the Wellington Street Archives last night while you were doing something else I went to the festival of the 100th anniversary of the Chinese in Canada. They came to build the railway and I am as shocked as I know senators and members are to remember that people are enshrined and rightly, in our history were perpetrators of the Chinese Exclusion Act, the Chinese $50 a head tax act. The Chinese people in this country were not allowed to vote in a province I think until after the Second World War. It was Mr. Diefenbaker who gave the Native peoples the right to vote in the late 1950s.

I am not saying that a government that follows this one would, but it could, because those were I guess until reform came the accepted standards. ...

**Mr. Epp:** Do I understand you correctly, sir, that if the document before us were to be enshrined, entrenched, that an incident like Canadians of Japanese origin and the removal of these people from various parts of Canada, their prohibition of freedoms at that time, that in fact that kind of action would still be possible under the charter in its present form.

**Mr. Fairweather:** I think, Mr. Epp, my duty is to warn you, and I have given some examples, age and these other offensive matters could be put in jeopardy. I am not saying they will but they could. I think most of this charter is really a superb piece of work, but I cannot see why Canada wants to turn its back on accepted international standards and language that has been adjudicated. That is why I am being a bit fussy. It clouds the rest of a noble document. (5: 11–12)

**Mr. Svend Robinson, MP (NDP, BC):** I would also like to ask you with respect to the question that was touched upon by Mr. Epp and also initially raised by yourself, and that is the actions that were taken during and immediately after World War II with respect to Canadians of Japanese origin. Would you indeed confirm that it is at least very possible that under the charter as it is presently worded in view of the fact that it could be argued that action was "generally accepted" at that time, that that kind of action would indeed be permitted under Section 1 as it is now worded.

**Mr. Fairweather:** Section 1 raises that danger. (5: 14)

**The Hon. David Crombie, MP (PC, Ontario):** My second question relates to Section 1, which I understood at the outset from your remarks to be of considerable concern to you, and I have forgotten your words, but I think you regard the Charter of Rights as seriously flawed, those are the words I recall, in relation to Section 1. ...

**Mr. Fairweather:** It is seriously flawed, and I just cannot believe it is going to be the final enunciation of the principle.

...

**Mr. Fairweather:** I am basically not a very good lawyer but I think Section 1 means what it says. It is up to you ladies and gentlemen not to let this bill into Parliament with Section 1 in its present form. You have an obligation to us. We are trying to serve you. (5: 23–4)

**The Hon. David Crombie, MP (PC, Ontario):** In that particular section, you seem to be recommending to the Committee that unless we change Section 1, then in a sense the game was not worth the candle, that the rights that are promised are not delivered. I want to make sure that that is clear to the Committee. Are you suggesting that unless we change Section 1, then the resolution with respect to civil rights that is before us is either useless or dangerous or both?

**Mr. J.S. Midanik (Q.C., Canadian Civil Liberties Association):** Yes, that is our position. Not only that you change Section 1, but that the rest of the charter be changed along the lines we have indicated because we feel that the rest of the charter is also defective in many respects. But the major problem deals with Section 1 and if any form of Section 1 is kept so that there be some limitation at all, our position is that it should apply only to Section 2 and not to the rest of the charter. ...

So, what we are saying again is that if what you are going to give us is what we have now, what is before us, our position is thanks, but no thanks, we would rather take our chances with what we have. (7: 24)

...

**Mr. Ron Irwin, MP (LIB, Ontario):** Now, you have serious difficulty and a great deal of criticism with Section 1. ... I suggest that if an abuse occurs, then the person who is abused could apply to the courts to see if Parliament has abused that person by legislation and if the courts decide that such abuse has occurred in legislation, and it does not fit in within reasonable limits as are generally accepted in a free and democratic society, then that legislation will be struck down.

**Mr. Alan Borovoy (General Counsel, Canadian Civil Liberties Association):** The answer to that is yes but the difficulty is the test. If you are talking about that which is generally accepted in a free and democratic society with a parliamentary form of government, you may well be talking about everything that Parliament or the legislatures have said is acceptable and to the extent that you are doing that, then it renders the entire charter a verbal illusion. (7: 25–6)

...

**Mr. Ron Irwin, MP (LIB, Ontario):** Is that not the whole raison d'être of this discussion, how much power are we as legislators going to give up by way of entrenched rights to the courts, to not be touched forever.

**Professor Tarnopolsky (Canadian Civil Liberties Association):** I think our position is that you should either fish or cut bait. If you are going to have a bill of rights, make it a bill of rights which cannot be just over-ridden any time that a court is convinced, which we are suggesting would be relatively easy, that the limits are those which are generally acceptable. It would not just be in legislation, because, again, if I could use the Hogan case, I think that it would not be very difficult to convince a court that the practice of the police, namely, how can a lawyer help the chap, let him take the breathalyzer, it is probably generally accepted. So that I think the fear of those of our members who support a bill of rights would be that it would be disillusioning, that it would be disappointing for the populace to think that they have a bill of rights which really over-rode inconsistent legislative administrative action to find out it is not. We think that rather than promoting that kind of cynicism, the Parliament should face up to either creating a bill of rights which over-rides or stay with the one which we now have, which we have got some jurisprudence on and there are more cases than just a *Drybones* case which have been applied to some effect. (7: 26–7)

**The Hon. Bryce Mackasey, MP (LIB, Ontario)** [*in reference to the presentation by the National Association of Japanese Canadians*]: Mr. Chairman, I would hope in light of the grave concerns that our witnesses have today about Section 1, that the minister be requested to come back to this committee before December 8, preferably the fifth or sixth or so, earlier in any event, so that we can find out in an objective and non-partisan way what he intends to do about Section 1, whether it is to be left in its present form. The present form reflects not communication and dialogue with groups such as your own; it reflects the views of the provincial premiers of this country. It reflects the findings of the minister in his deliberations across Canada this summer as well as the selfishness of many provincial premiers. I think Section 1 is defective and has to be improved. I cannot presume to be talking for my party, but certainly I am speaking for myself. So I am very pleased with the forcefulness with which you have made your points. (13: 18)

**Mr. Ron Irwin, MP (LIB, Ontario):** Now, I put to you that no right is absolute; even the right of free speech is qualified in that perhaps for instance, under the Criminal Code you cannot cause a disturbance in a public place, for example, there are many restrictions to keep our society together without having it turn into anarchy or chaos. I suggest to you, because you are critical of the wording later on in general, that rather than deleting Section 1, we might come back with a better worded Section 1 that meets the requirements of more inspiring wording, and meets the requirements that rights in here are more enshrined and less susceptible to court interpretation.

**Mr. Victor Paisley (Canadian Bar Association):** Our concern with Section 1 as written is that it would, in our opinion, completely override the rest of the Charter. Without examining the given Section 1 which is envisaged, it is impossible to say whether our concern would be satisfied or not. We simply take the position that if it remains with the rest of the Charter, it would probably be of no effect at all.

**Mr. Irwin:** Many groups have expressed the view which you are expressing, and some have come back and said that it should be made stronger and not so intrusive. I appreciate the difficulty in not having that here now.

**Mr. Paisley:** May I add to what I have said further. We feel that even if there is no Section 1, it does not mean to say that there are going to be unqualified or absolute rights. Experience elsewhere with unqualified rights shows that they are in fact qualified by the courts. There is a statement of the courts in the United States to the effect that the right of freedom of speech does not give a person the right to call "fire!" in a crowded theatre. We believe that if you have the right stated in an unqualified fashion it would be interpreted in a reasonable way by the court. That is the reason why we suggest it is unnecessary to have this sort of introductory limitation clause as proposed. (15: 22–3)

...

**Mr. Norman Whalen (Vice-Chairman, Canadian Federation of Civil Liberties and Human Rights Associations):** Mr. Chairman, the serious structural limitations which occur repeatedly through this bill find first expression in Section 1 of the Charter. The limiting provision of this section is so general as to permit, if not cause, the certain failure of everything which the Charter sets out to achieve. If this is poor drafting, then it must be improved. If, however, it is the clear expression of the will of its creators, then they have a view of entrenchment which we will submit does not find reflection in the popular will of Canadians. If the rights set out in the Charter are subject to the limits stipulated in Section 1 then Parliament acting alone will always have supremacy over the Charter, effectively denying what the Charter proposes to create – entrenchment. (21: 6–7)

**Mr. Philip Cooper (Vice-President, Coalition for the Protection of Human Life):** Section 1 of the proposed Charter has come under strong attack and quite deservedly so. At a previous hearing, someone called it the Mack Truck Section. We call it the bathtub section because it makes it much too easy for our leaders and lawmakers to pull the plug on human rights and freedoms and if it is included in the Charter the Charter itself will be worth very little. ...

It will be hard to think of any statement more dangerously vague than this. What is meant by reasonable limits and how is this decided and which democratic society and Parliamentary system are we talking about. Such language opens the door to entrenched present injustices merely because they are widely accepted in supposedly free and democratic societies, and moreover ties Canadian law to the laws and customs of other countries over which Canadians have no control; and to me this is most ironic. We are talking about patriating our constitution and while we are doing this we are proposing to be tied to precedents, set in other countries. It is hard to see what this has to do with producing a Canadian constitution or a Canadian Charter. (22: 32)

**Mr. David Copp (Vice-President, British Columbia Civil Liberties Association):** Now, it is obvious there can be circumstances in which the rights listed in the Charter would have to give way. In times of serious crisis threatening the existence of the nation, such as invasion, insurrection, large scale natural disaster, a temporary emergency limitation on our fundamental rights might be necessary. This is obvious. In fact, it is so obvious and so widely agreed, that, given the difficulties in drafting an acceptable limitation clause, it might well be wiser to leave one out.

We cannot now foresee all the situations that might justify temporary emergency limitations. It might therefore be best to let the courts decide in particular cases when the facts of an emergency are known.

However, if there is to be a limitation clause, it must indicate clearly that most contingencies that face the nation are to be dealt with by ordinary means which respect the rights guaranteed in the Charter. It must indicate clearly that limitations are justified only in times of "public emergency which threatens the life of the nation," and then only "to the extent strictly required by the exigencies of the situation." Here we use the language of the International Covenant on Civil and Political Rights, Article 4, Section 1, to which Canada is a signatory. We recommend this language to you for your consideration.

Further, if there is to be a limitation clause, it must clearly indicate that limitations on the Charter justified by public emergency are temporary. We would argue for the inclusion in a general limitation clause of four subsections, the first requiring prompt Parliamentary authorization of the invocation of special powers under emergency legislation, such as the War Measures Act; Second, requiring regular renewal of this authorization if the powers are not to lapse; Third, allowing a small number of members of either House to force review of this authorization; And fourth, allowing any innocent person damaged under the special powers to seek compensation in a special tribunal. (22: 105, 106)

**Mr. Svend Robinson, MP (NDP, BC):** You have referred, as other witnesses have, to Section 1, which has been pointed out would permit the proclamation of the War Measures Act in the same terms as in 1970, and will permit the internment of Canadians of Japanese origin and the confiscation of their property. Would it be fair to say you would agree with the suggestion of the Canadian Civil Liberties Association that if Section 1 is not rewritten and perhaps if there is not a remedies section – I believe those are the sections you have pointed out as having perhaps the greatest weaknesses in the proposed charter – and indeed, we would perhaps be better off not giving the Canadian people the illusion that they have certain rights, but rather that we would be better off without this Charter, if those sections are not in fact amended?

**Mr. William Black (Member of Executive Committee, British Columbia Civil Liberties Association):** The other way in which, perhaps, you could put it, is that if we do not amend the section, Section 1, we would not have an entrenched charter, even if we were to enact this document. Section 1 imposes such severe limitations on the whole concept of an entrenched charter of rights that it has to be removed to give any effective force of entrenchment. (22: 115)

**Mr. Nick Schultz (Associate General Counsel, Public Interest Advocacy Centre):** Section 1, which preserves the existing constitutional tradition, must be deleted to fully entrench the Charter. Its meaningless vagueness opens the door to the very abuse to the supremacy of Parliament which the Charter is intended to check. Moreover, special provisions are necessary to instruct judges in the Charter's interpretation. By deleting Section 1 of the Charter, there will be removed an obvious peg for argument designed to thwart the Charter's purposes. (29: 20)

**Mr. Svend Robinson, MP (NDP, BC):** ... You have mentioned in your recommendations on Section 1, that you do not believe that the rights and freedoms should be subject to the kinds of limits which are generally accepted in a free and democratic society. Certainly we share the concerns about the sweeping nature of that exemption clause. I would assume that the specific reason you would want that deleted is that there might be an argument that, because abortion and the right of women to choose on abortion, is presently permitted in Canadian society, that that would continue to be permitted under that particular wording. Would that be your reason for wanting that changed?

**Mr. Philip Cooper (Vice-President, Coalition for the Protection of Human Life):** If I may answer that, we are, of course, concerned with how this would affect the unborn child. But as we say, we are appearing before you, not as some people would like to suggest, as a single-issue organization; we are a human rights organization concerned with the whole spectrum of human rights. It is important to put the question of abortion in a total human rights context. We are opposed to Section 1 precisely because it puts all human rights in jeopardy. That is the reason for our objection to that. (32: 38)

**Mrs. Gwen Landolt (Legal Counsel, Campaign Life – Canada):** However, we understand from practical points of view it may well be that Parliament may subsequently decide that is its final decision in spite of a very strong and ardent protest that the charter of rights be entrenched in the constitution. If that is the case then it is absolutely necessary to the profile people in Canada that the present proposed charter of rights must be amended for us to provide protection for the unborn child. It is our view that the present charter is inadequate to provide this protection. In particular we would like to draw attention to two sections of the proposed charter which give us grave concern.

The first is Section 1 of the charter. ... That is a wide opening and it is our view that that section would give the Supreme Court of Canada unprecedented wide and sweeping powers to make political decisions. The court need only to decide what in its opinion was generally accepted in a free and democratic society, and that would be that. It is tremendously wide and opens the door to all sorts of ramifications. Also that wording of Section 1 will have the effect of rendering the remaining sections of the charter meaningless since it would override any of the rights and freedoms including that of the right to life allegedly enshrined in the charter. ...

We would like Section 1 of the Charter of Rights and Freedoms to be eliminated. Section 1, as already mentioned, gives total and complete power to the Supreme Court of Canada to do what it likes, when it likes and how it likes. And no democracy can survive with a Supreme Court given the great power it has by Section 1 of the proposed Charter. (34: 122, 124, 125)

## "A Parliamentary System of Government"

**The Hon. James McGrath, MP (PC, Newfoundland):** Surely that makes everything that follows redundant because a free and democratic society would have within it in a parliamentary system freedom of conscience and religion. Ours does; it operates under the practices and conventions and traditions of the British Parliamentary System.

It seems to me that you have fallen into the same trap here as the Canadian Bill of Rights because you are going to exclude all the very commendable rights and freedoms that you have set out in Section 2 of Schedule B. It either means that they apply or they do not apply. What are the reasonable limits as are generally accepted in a free and democratic society. (3: 14)

...

**The Hon. James McGrath, MP (PC, Newfoundland):** ... your charter is meaningless in the light of what I said in Section 1 of Schedule B when you make it subject to the reasonable limits as are generally accepted in a free and democratic society with a parliamentary system of government. (3: 15)

**Emergency Powers**

**Professor Max Cohen (Chairman, Select Committee on the Constitution of Canada of the Canadian Jewish Congress):** Section 1 of the Charter is a very strange article. You have had a lot of comment on it. I do not wish to burden you with repetition. We made two points about it. ... We say that Section 1 tends to guarantee charter rights, and freedoms, and at the same time provides justification for the suspension of charter rights during an emergency.

I have a feeling that the draftsmen, when they drafted Section 1, were torn between two conflicting pressures on them intellectually and practically. The pressures were, how to maintain the theory of parliamentary supremacy when introducing a theory of a charter regime. It was an attempt to find some kind of practical, legal, political equilibrium between a charter regime system, on the one side, and a parliamentary supremacy regime on the other, that Section 1 represents.

But then, when you look at it, it is so great an invitation in language such as, "subject only to such reasonable limits as are generally accepted in a free and democratic society with a parliamentary system of government," that any aggressively minded lawyer with an aggressively minded government could ride through that series of gates with very little difficulty and find the charter heavily wrecked en route.

We feel that is not the way to begin a regime of a charter; it is not the way to start a new system of rights. We solemnly recommend the total elimination of Section 1, because when you go into Section 2 and the rest of the charter you are very specific there. You do not need Section 1.

To the extent that you need emergency powers, you will have them. We recommend that in a new article, Article 28(a) at the end of the brief. To the extent that you want to have an equilibrium between a charter regime and parliamentary supremacy, you must accept the fact that, once you introduce a charter regime, parliamentary supremacy is modified forever to that extent. That is a plain legal and political fact, and you cannot have the best of both worlds, except in an emergency and we provide for an emergency. (7: 85, 86)

**Conforming to International Standards and Treaties**

**Mr. Gordon Fairweather (Chief Commissioner, Canadian Human Rights Commission):** ... We are troubled by the language of Clause 1 which, in its present form, raises fundamental doubts about just how serious the commitment is to reform.... The language used departs from that to be found in domestic constitutions of many modern states but what is even more significant is it departs from the European Charter and the International Bill of Rights ratified by Canada, because the language in Clause 1 is unique, it has never been tested. On the other hand, jurisprudence is building up which explains the language of other domestic and international charters. It is in our opinion foolish to turn our backs on a useful body of jurisprudence. As well, the language seems to us to be dangerously broad. We know you will seriously consider recommendations for a more careful wording of Clause 1. (5: 8)

**Mr. Svend Robinson, MP (NDP, BC):** I wonder if you could confirm that unless this Section is indeed amended that we would in fact be in violation of our requirements under the International Covenant on Civil and Political Rights and indeed, because we have signed the optional protocol, that another state could indeed take us before a tribunal of the United Nations to complain of that violation.

**Mr. Fairweather:** Section 1, indeed that would be my opinion. You put it very well. (5: 14)

## Minority and Women's Rights

**Ms. Lynn McDonald (President, National Action Committee on the Status of Women):** The opening section under guarantee of rights and freedoms falls short of the statement of principle we would expect. Imprecise wording in the limitations clause could open the way to a variety of interpretations of permitted exceptions. Indeed, the potential for driving a truck through the clause led our participants at the conference to dub it the "Mack truck clause."

Failure to clarify the guaranteed rights and freedoms by removing the limiting clause would render useless subsequent sections. Therefore, NAC proposes that the general limiting clause be deleted.

If there have to be restrictions on rights and freedoms in time of war these should be specified as well as those rights and freedoms not to be abridged under any circumstances. NAC recommends that the rights and freedoms not to be abridged under any circumstances should include at least the right not to be subjected to any cruel and unusual treatment or punishment and the human right to equality in the law. (9: 58)

...

**Ms. Lynn McDonald:** I think for reasons similar to what Mr. Fairweather and other witnesses have raised regarding the treatment of Japanese Canadians. It was within my lifetime that married women were thrown out of the Public Service on marriage. The Stella Bliss case shows how unacceptable women in the labour force are if they are pregnant or if they have very young children. We cannot take as generally accepted all of the rights and freedoms that we would want to have. There are still people that would argue that women do not have a right to jobs on the same basis that men have that right. So we would certainly want that to be in there very strongly. (9: 63–4)

**Mr. Art Shimizu (Constitution Committee Chairman, National Association of Japanese Canadians):** The second point I wish to make is the very serious reservations we have with the manner in which Section 1 is presently framed. ... Its broadness and vagueness can be interpreted to give the government the licence to invoke, for instance, the War Measures Act or any future emergency powers act. It is our view that rather than limiting the rights of individuals and groups on certain occasions, there should be limits put on the definition of what constitutes an emergency. This principle should in some fashion find expression in the constitution. Also, unless the constitution guarantees that the Bill of Rights is to supersede all past, present and future legislation, then ladies and gentlemen, we believe that you are not only condoning the past, you are preparing the way for history to repeat itself. (13: 10)

**Professor Manoly Lupul (Director, The Institute of [Ukrainian] Studies):** ... We are opposed to the present wording of Section 1 of the Canadian Charter of Rights and Freedoms. ... In our view, this clause allows too much leeway in allowing the suspension of the charter. ...

The internment of Ukrainian Canadians during World War I was carried out by a government which apparently felt that it was acting in a manner consistent with the principles generally accepted by Canadian society at that time. This unjust and arbitrary treatment of Canadian citizens was repeated again during World War II in the case of the Japanese Canadians. Even the most fundamental principles of our justice system – the right of habeas corpus and the right to be presumed innocent until proven guilty – were arbitrarily suspended in the internment of Canadians who were allegedly dangerous enemy aliens. It is our view that the limitations clause in Section 1 of the Charter is so broad in its application that it would do nothing to prevent a repetition of this kind of systematic abuse of those fundamental rights which the proposed Constitution is supposed to protect, and we would therefore recommend that Section 1 of the Canadian Charter of Rights and Freedoms be deleted. (14: 54)

**Mr. Orest Rudzik (President, Ukrainian Canadian Committee, Toronto Branch):** As a practising lawyer, what concerns me is, first of all, as the provision stands now it comes pretty close to being a tautology. Obviously, in any parliamentary system Parliament is sovereign and fully capable at any one moment of over-riding any other previous enactments. We are not like the Americans who can enshrine a bill of rights and move it up into a kind of platonic heaven and then refer to it for refuge and security. We have to live with the institutions that we are very happy to live with.

So it strikes me that if we do not accept it as a tautology, then we are in fact enshrining a rather dangerous precedent that we, as an immigrant group, has [sic] experienced in World War I; that the Japanese have experienced in World War II; and as our French Canadian kin have experienced as recently as October 1970: the ease with which a government can, if it feels that an emergency is upon them, exercise their parliamentary society.

Our preference would be to see these rights enshrined absolutely; and then there would be, at least, an onus on the part of the government of the day to explain to its electorate why it feels the emergency is present. ... I think Professor Tarnopolsky and some of the other spokesmen expressed their anxiety that this be tacitly accepted as a kind of legitimization of the government, perhaps, being too willing to lean to the opinion of its own day at the time when an apprehended emergency occurs. As I say, we have a bit of historical experience to bear this out. (14: 59–60)

## The Government Amends the Limitations Clause

**The Hon. Jean Chrétien (Minister of Justice):** Many witnesses and most members of the Committee have expressed concerns about Section 1 of the Charter of Rights and Freedoms. These concerns basically have to do with the argument that the clause as drafted leaves open the possibility that a great number of limits could be placed upon rights and freedoms in the Charter by the actions of Parliament or a legislature.

The purpose of the original draft was to ensure that the people, the legislatures and the courts would not look upon rights as absolute, but would recognize them as subject [to] reasonable limitations. While some believed no limitation clause was necessary, many witnesses agreed such a clause is desirable but argued that a more stringent formulation is necessary.

You have received a number of constructive suggestions. I am prepared on behalf of the government to accept an amendment similar to that suggested by Mr. Gordon Fairweather, Chief Commissioner of the Canadian Human Rights Commission and by Professor Walter Tarnopolsky, President of the Canadian Civil Liberties Association. The wording I am proposing is designed to make the limitation clause even more stringent than that recommended by Mr. Fairweather and Professor Tarnopolsky. I am proposing that Section 1 read as follows:

> The Canadian Charter of Rights and Freedoms guarantees the rights and freedoms set out in it subject only to such reasonable limits prescribed by law as can be demonstrably justified in a free and democratic society.

This will ensure that any limit on a right must be not only reasonable and prescribed by law, but must also be shown to be demonstrably justified. (36: 11)

...

**Senator Duff Roblin (PC, Manitoba):** Now, the point is that we heard testimony from some 19 different organizations, I will not name them all but some of their presentations stick in my memory, the Canadian Civil Rights Association, the Canadian Jewish Congress, the Canadian Human Rights Commission, the Canadian Advisory Council on the Status of Women, the National Association of Japanese Canadians, and a good many others, who were concerned about Section 1.

While I cannot attempt to summarize with any accuracy what each one said, some of them at least – and some of the important ones left me with the impression – that this Section 1, as it stood, was so limiting in its impact and force as to destroy – in fact some of them went so far as to say they would just as soon not have the whole thing if Section 1 was in there: that the limiting character of Section 1 was so severe as to destroy the effectiveness of the other guarantees in the Charter.

... I take it that the purpose of this change was to somewhat reduce the limiting direction to the courts of Canada that this section gives when they interpret the rest of the Charter.

I want to explore with you just how far it really goes in making that change in the rules; because "reasonable limits" is the same phrase we have in the previous one, and it is modified by "prescribed by law." That is number one. That can probably be married off with "parliamentary system of government" which you have in the first effort. Then it goes on to say, "as can be demonstrably justified." Well, if there is a law passed by Parliament, I think the initial assumption is that it is justified or Parliament would not have done it.

Whether the courts will take that view, I do not know. But it seems to me that there is a risk that they will. Then you go on to say: "as can be demonstrably justified in a free and democratic society." Well, if a free and democratic society passes a law, what is the difference between the situation that we have here and the one you had in the former one where you said: "generally accepted in a free and democratic society with a parliamentary system of government." My fear is that you have not moved very far in removing the objections of those 19 bodies which have appeared before us, and I would like to have your rationale.

**The Hon. Jean Chrétien (Minister of Justice):** I think we have moved quite far; and, in the case of those who were the main proponents of the change, Professor Tarnopolsky and Mr. Fairweather, it is the text which they have more or less suggested, and they have approved it and commended me on it.

This is to make sure that, even if the law were passed – it was a danger before that it was almost impossible for the court to go behind a decision of a Parliament or a legislative assembly; but here, even if the law is passed, there is another test, namely that it can be demonstrably justified in relation to this Charter.

So this limited clause narrows the limits of the courts. The first one – and you heard the testimony given here, where there was argument to the effect that it was so limiting in scope as to be almost useless, and we would be caught in the same position as we were in the case of the Bill of Rights of Mr. Diefenbaker which has not in fact been used in the courts. Why have we done it?

It was not my initial proposition. I have done it under pressure from the provincial governments. It is a good illustration of trying to get on the right keel and you end up with a situation where it was meaningless. So we went back to the original text. This will permit the courts to appreciate whether legislation passed by the different levels of Parliament and legislative assemblies are in conformity with the Charter. The intention of a Charter is to limit the scope of the legislature and Parliament in relation to the fundamental rights of Canadian citizens. ...

**Mr. Chrétien:** The idea is that we have to find the proper balance between the protection of individual rights and the legitimate power of any legislative body. You have to respect the fact that there are legislatures and people have been elected there and they should keep some power of legislation. (38: 40–4)

## Demonstrably Justified

**Miss Coline Campbell, MP (LIB, Nova Scotia):** ... I wonder if there is a difference in your view in onus between a reasonably justifiable onus on the person before the courts to show that their rights, let us say that the legislatures have not infringed upon the rights of the person, or demonstrably justifiable.

To me it seems there might be a heavier onus on the legislature to show they have not.

**The Hon. Jean Chrétien (Minister of Justice):** I have explained this morning the policy of why we have done it, and that it was to find an equilibrium, between the rights of the citizens to be protected by the courts and the power of the legislature or Parliament to pass law, and perhaps you are asking me a rather technical question and would you reply to that, Mr. Strayer, please.

**Mr. Barry Strayer (Assistant Deputy Minister, Public Law):** Mr. Chairman, it was the belief of the drafters that by going to these words demonstrably justified or can be demonstrably justified, it was making it clear that the onus would be on the government, or whoever is trying to justify the action that limited the rights set out in the charter, the onus would be on them to show that the limit which was being imposed not only was reasonable, which was in the first draft, but also that it was justifiable or justified, and in doing that they would have to show that in relation to the situation being dealt with, the limit was justifiable.

So whereas before there was no indications as to who had the onus of proving that the limit was reasonable or unreasonable, or whether it was generally accepted or not generally accepted. This seems to put the onus, appears to put the onus on the government that has to try to uphold some kind of limit to the rights set out in the charter. Uphold the legislation or administrative action or whatever it is in question.

I might add, Mr. Chairman, that this kind of language was recommended by the Canadian Human Rights Commission. They had two possible drafts, and one of them was very similar to the words in the present proposal, the new proposal. They used words such as prescribed by law as are reasonably justifiable in a free and democratic society. Professor Tarnopolsky, in appearing before the Committee, talked about using words such as restrictions as are prescribed by law and are necessary for the purposes of a free and democratic society, or he said you could use terms such as demonstrably necessary, but he said the onus has clearly to be on the one who argues in favour of restrictions, and that apparently is what he thought such language would do, it would put the onus on the person trying to justify the limitation. (38: 44–5)

## Application of Section 1

**Mr. Svend Robinson, MP (NDP, BC):** Mr. Minister, Section 1 as it stands now modifies everything that is contained in the Charter, and I appreciate that there can be difficulties in defining which particular rights should never be abrogated. Would you be prepared to look as a minimum at least at excluding those rights which are contained in the Covenant? If you look at the Covenant I am sure you would agree that it is not a very comprehensive listing, but at least excluding, for example, the right to protection from cruel and unusual punishment. Would you be prepared to look at those areas which this Committee as a whole could agree upon should be protected from trampling upon at any time?

**The Hon. Jean Chrétien (Minister of Justice):** If you ask me would I be willing to look upon, I can look into that but I do think that why we have proceeded in that way, the technical reason, I will ask my advisor to reply to [that] aspect.

**Mr. Barry Strayer (Assistant Deputy Minister, Public Law):** Well, any attempt to make a list is going to be arbitrary, I think, even if you look at the international covenant. It is somewhat arbitrary in the rights it says can never be derogated and those which it implies can be derogated.

For example, in time of emergency or war it forbids derogation from rights such as rights against discrimination, apparently, on the basis of national origin; and one can argue over what rights ought to be in theory derogable in times of emergency and ones which might not be, but the approach which we are taking here in the new Section 1 is to leave that as a matter of judgment in the situation and it is very hard to imagine any situation, for example, where a court would say that it was, in the words of the section, demonstrably justified in a free and democratic society to use cruel or unusual punishment. Even in time of emergency.

**Mr. Robinson:** Mr. Chairman, I understand the argument that was made, but just to conclude this question with respect to Section 1, I do hope that if the Committee can agree on certain restricted areas which, as you say, should never be, I assume you would agree, never be violated, that the government would be prepared to at least consider a possible amendment to that effect. (38: 46–8)

### "Prescribed by Law"

**Mr. Svend Robinson, MP (NDP, BC):** The second part of my question, Mr. Chairman, relates to the use of the word law in Section 1. Any limitations must be as the section states prescribed "by law." My reading of that, and I hope I am wrong, but my reading of that is a regulation of the government could limit in fact any of the rights or freedoms which are contained [in] this proposed Charter. I believe that the word law indeed does include a regulation as it has been defined in Canadian jurisprudence and, Mr. Minister I would hope ...

**Mr. Chrétien:** When you talk about regulations ...

**Mr. Robinson:** If I can just conclude my question, Mr. Minister, my understanding is that that is the way the law is interpreted, if that is the case then what this is saying is the government, the Cabinet can take away any of these rights, although there is still the recourse to the courts, and I would hope that you would be prepared to look seriously at an amendment which would make it very clear that it is only legislatures or Parliament which could abrogate these very fundamental rights of Canadian citizens?

**Mr. Chrétien:** Yes, but the regulation that when we vote any laws in Parliament we always make provisions for regulations, and the regulations that flow from law are part of the law that has been passed, a delegation of authority to the executive to proclaim some regulation that will make possible the law that we pass to be enforced, and I think that everything is part of the same law and it will be impossible to – I can look at your suggestion but the principles are the same and if any regulation passed by any government in relation to regulation based on the law, this same test will apply, and the citizens will have the same recourse and I do not see the point unless there are some regulations that could be made outside of the law, but there is not. When you pass an Order in Council, we always have to base our decision on some legal, we need a legal base.

**Mr. Robinson:** There is no debate in Parliament.

**Mr. Chrétien:** But there is a debate in Parliament to authorize the executive branch of the government to do this and do that, otherwise if we are not authorized by Parliament we cannot do that. Perhaps, I do not know, there might be some exception to that rule. Do you know any?

**Mr. Strayer:** No.

**Mr. Chrétien:** I do not. Because if we act without any authority from any law, our action is illegal. So I am not preoccupied with the problem you are raising. Of course, you can always argue in the House we should never give any delegated authority to any Order in Council.

**Mr. Robinson:** No, no.

**Mr. Chrétien:** No, but you could, and say everything has to be approved by Parliament on a daily basis. We could but it would be a hell of a mess.

**Mr. Robinson:** Mr. Minister, I am saying that where there are to be abrogations, that Parliament should discuss that at least. (38: 46–8)

...

**Senator John Connolly (LIB, Ontario):** Just on that last point, I wonder whether this should not be said, that if Parliament is discussing a piece of legislation which authorizes the making of regulations, it flows from the passing of that piece of legislation that the regulations must be within the four corners of the act, and I suppose the theory is that if Parliament is afraid that something is going to be done under the authority to make regulations which go beyond the act, then I suppose it is up to the parliamentarian at that time to make his objection. Now, you do say, and you did say, if a regulation violates the mother act under which it is made there is recourse to the courts. Your objection to that, I take it, is that it takes too much time and expense and everything else, and I think that is the risk we run in connection with giving the executive a regulation making authority.

**Mr. Chrétien:** And there is too, I would like to say there is, under statutory act procedures there is a revision of all the Orders in Council by Committees of the House and you remember that, but I do think that the principles are the same. We are giving the Canadians some rights and the limits are mentioned in Section 1 and the courts can intervene and if the rights of the citizens have not been respected in the piece of legislation or any regulation, they are illegal and the court will decide that they do not meet the test that they can be demonstrably justified in a free and democratic society. (38: 48)

...

**The Hon. John Fraser, MP (PC, BC):** ... what effect does this have on the law contained in the common law and has this been considered?

Specifically, and to make it easy, a contract, contracts in their very nature are discriminatory, and I am wondering if this problem has been addressed? ...

**Mr. Roger Tassé, QC (Deputy Minister of Justice):** I think that is an important question you have raised, Mr. Fraser. In effect when you look at the meaning of law, it may mean a number of things and in this context it could mean an Act of Parliament, for example, and we did not want it to be restricted to an Act of Parliament for some of the reasons that have been expressed, and also for another reason that has not been mentioned so far, and that is in effect we wanted also to cover rules of the common law.

For example, in the area of libel, defamation. And in many provinces this has not been clarified. There are rules that have just been expressed over time by the courts and we did not want to upset all of this legislation so that is why in effect in French we have used an expression that would embody as well rules of common law that have been established by courts and it could be in the civil law field or in the common law, most probably in the common law, but also would include the statute and include a regulation enacted under an appropriately passed or enacted legislation.

**Mr. Fraser:** So what you are saying, then, is that ...

**Mr. Tassé:** Perhaps if I may just expand on what I have just said.

For example, if you look at the freedom of expression, the law of defamation, the law of libel imposes some limits on that so we wanted these to continue to have application and we think that they would fit in effect the tests that are set out in Section 1.

**Mr. Fraser:** Well, then, by the same token, so does the law of master and servant, the law of contract and the law of partnership, and a number of other common law notions.

Could you foresee a situation where, on the basis of the rights set out in here, you could have a conflict between what are considered laws which stem from the body of case law that has come down over the centuries which could be in conflict with the right that has been set out in the Charter?

**Mr. Tassé:** Well, Mr. Fraser, we do not see these rights or these prescriptions of the Charter to have application in terms of a relationship between individuals. We see them as applying in terms of a relationship between the state and individuals, so I am not sure that in terms of contract laws, unless we were looking at the situation where in fact we are talking of contracts passed between the state, the government, and that might offend a constitutional limitation on some of these rights, then the Charter might be called upon for assistance but if we are just looking at in effect relationships, contractual relationships between individuals, I do not see how the Charter itself could be called upon to assist in resolution of conflicts that may arise.

**Mr. Fraser:** Well, I do not want to take this too far into the realm of theory but individual contracts are constantly formed as a result of discrimination between certain options and certain individuals, and that has always been, within some limitation, an accepted freedom to enter into contract unless there is a specific piece of legislation which forbids it. You can take, for instance, the codes in some of the provinces which now constrain absolute freedom of contract in hiring policies.

But I take it that what you are saying is that in the English version when you say "prescribed by law," that is not just statute law, but is also the common law?

**Mr. Tassé:** Yes.

**Mr. Fraser:** As decided by the cases?

**Mr. Tassé:** Yes.

**Mr. Fraser:** But they could still be challenged if somebody could take the issue to a court and say that law can no longer be demonstrably justified in a free and democratic society?

**Mr. Tassé:** That is correct.

**Mr. Fraser:** Thank you. (38: 48–50)

### Placement of the Limitations Clause

**Mr. Svend Robinson, MP:** I wonder, though, why it was thought that the appropriate location for a limitations clause was right at the very beginning of the proposed Charter of Fundamental Rights and Freedoms, and whether you would be prepared to look at the possibility of moving the limitations clause in whatever form we may finally end up with – and naturally, there may be complications, because if there is a preamble in it, it would be inappropriate to do this; but if there is no preamble, on the proposed Clause 1, moving the limitations clause to the end of the proposed Charter?

In other words, I believe it would be important symbolically, if nothing else, to start out with the list of fundamental freedoms, the mobility rights and a positive statement of what the rights are, and then at the conclusion of the proposed Charter to indicate what limitations might exist on those rights rather than starting out with limitations and then a statement of rights.

**The Hon. Robert Kaplan (Acting Minister of Justice):** Well, before directly answering the question, I would like to understand that you are suggesting that the difference is symbolic, and that it does not make any real difference.

**Mr. Robinson:** Certainly, I would not argue that there was any difference in substance in the way this will be interpreted, and I am sure your advisers could confirm that.

**Mr. Kaplan:** I do not think there any real difference either. I think it is purely a matter of style. Our view of the matter was that it was more realistic and useful to the reader to see at once that the rights were not absolute, but that they were constrained.

That would be made immediately clear to a person consulting the statute without having to read the first 30 sections to find that what was contained in the proposed Clause 1 was really not the whole story.

It seems to be more honest.

**Mr. Robinson:** Mr. Minister, if it is agreed that there is no difference in substance – and we are talking about a document, a Charter of Rights which, hopefully, would be widely distributed to school children, to Canadians right across the country, and I would suggest there is a certain symbolic value in setting out those rights and then at the conclusion of those rights indicating what the limitation, if any, may exist in respect of them, as is done in the Diefenbaker Bill of Rights, where the rights were enumerated and at the conclusion of the Bill of Rights, there are references, for example to the War Measures Act and to other limiting provisions. (42: 25–6)

## Application/Non-derogable Rights

**Mr. Robinson:** Mr. Minister, in view of the many representations by distinguished groups, Civil Liberties Association, Mr. Tarnopolsky, Mr. Fairweather and others, in view of their representation, what I found at least to be persuasive representations, that there were certain rights which should never be derogated from, who in fact did you listen to in arriving at your proposed Clause 1, which witnesses did you listen to, which witnesses made a recommendation in line with your proposed Clause 1 that there should be no derogable rights?

**The Hon. Robert Kaplan (Acting Minister of Justice):** Well, I think the government was influenced even by the witnesses with which it disagreed, and we have tried to reflect in the version the cutting edge that we want in the Charter of Rights, a Charter of Rights and Freedoms that will make a real difference to the Canadian people, and I would not want to indicate that any of the witnesses were ignored because that is not the case.

**Mr. Robinson:** Well, there were certainly a few that were not listened to. Thank you. (42: 30–1)

## Chapter Six

# Fundamental Freedoms

2. Everyone has the following fundamental freedoms:
    (a) freedom of conscience and religion;
    (b) freedom of thought, belief, opinion and expression, including freedom of the press and other media of information;
    (c) freedom of peaceful assembly; and
    (d) freedom of association.

## Commentary

Unlike other parts of the Charter, the "fundamental freedoms" heading was a normative rather than a descriptive term. There was a surprising degree of consensus about the content and the language of what would become section 2 of the Charter. This is probably because most of section 2 derived directly from the "fundamental freedoms" contained in the Canadian Bill of Rights, which was then incorporated into Trudeau's 1968 white paper, *A Canadian Charter of Human Rights*. Only one amendment to section 2 was made at the Joint Committee: the CBA asked that freedom of peaceful assembly and freedom of association be separated into two distinct rights for purposes of clarity. The government accepted that suggestion.

At the Joint Committee, discussion about freedom of religion focused on its impact on denominational schools and their rights under section 93 of the Constitution Act, 1867. Much of this discussion is contained in chapter 14 on section 29 of the Charter. There were interesting discussions about freedom of conscience and conscientious objectors to military service and to performing abortions. On freedom of expression, concerns were expressed about the boundaries or limits of the rights, specifically hate speech.

Given the recognized importance of freedom of the press, there was surprisingly little interest in this subject. This was due perhaps to the fact that only one media group appeared before the Joint Committee, and it was ill prepared. The Media Club of Canada requested a year's time to consult and formulate positions and return to the committee. It provided little of use to the committee's deliberations, but the questions posed to its members show the issues that were on the mind of committee members.

Freedom of peaceful assembly and freedom of association also attracted minimal discussion. MP Svend Robinson (NDP, BC) proposed amending the section on freedom of association to add the phrase "including the freedom to organize and bargain collectively." The proposed amendment was defeated. Some 25 years later, the Supreme Court of Canada would essentially read-in Robinson's proposed amendment to the meaning of "freedom of association" protected under the Charter.[1]

**Fundamental Freedoms Generally**

**Hon. Bryce Mackasey, MP (LIB, ON):** It is going to include a Charter of Human Rights which will not satisfy everybody, but I think our mistake is to presume that is the end of the process. I think [MP] Perrin Beatty made the point very clearly that we will be amending our constitution periodically for another century and centuries after, facing the reality of the future. What we are trying to do here is make it a little easier, and ironically closer to the views of the people. If we act a little faster we will be able to reflect consensus in, for instance, the Charter of Human Rights. At the present moment, we probably have consensus on very few things, fundamental rights, freedom of speech, freedom of religion, freedoms that this country has taken for granted. Those things must be enshrined in a constitution. I come from a province where I saw my fundamental rights wiped out by a piece of legislation called Bill 101. I am sorry to say it, but I feel that deeply about it, and perhaps for the first time I realize how fragile rights are, enshrined in provincial legislation. (32: 5)

...

**Mr. Bruce Smith (President of Toronto Ontario East Stake, Church of Jesus Christ of Latter Day Saints):** The Church of Jesus Christ of Latter Day Saints or the "Mormon Church," is a Christian organization with roots in Canada which go back to the early 1830s. There are at present approximately 85,000 members of the Church in Canada, with congregations in every province and the territories. ...

At the onset, we wish to make it clear that as a church we take no position on the purely political aspects of the proposed resolution; our members are totally free to think and act according to their own individual wishes on those matters. Believing as we do that churches have a responsibility to provide and safeguard a moral framework in which their members can exercise their beliefs, we wish, however, to address some of the possible moral implications of the resolution.

Our basic concerns relate to the potential impact of certain proposals within the resolution on the sanctity and strength of the family, on protection provided by society to women and children, on the relationships between courts and legislatures in making legal policy, and on the inviolability of fundamental freedoms. We can perhaps best illustrate these concerns by examining specific sections of the proposed resolution. In doing so, we wish only to point out concerns, not obvious and totally identifiable dangers. Indeed, it is in the vagueness of the wording of certain portions of the proposed resolution that the greatest dangers lie, because it is impossible to tell exactly what is meant or what was contemplated by the draftsmen.

Section 2 of the proposed resolution deals with fundamental freedoms. We applaud the apparent intention of the proposals, believing as we do that "no government can exist in peace, except such laws are framed and held inviolate as will secure to each individual the free exercise of conscience, the right and control of property and the protection of life." Yet we must admit to an uneasiness about the extent to which the proposed resolution actually safeguards the essential freedom it so laudably espouses.

Part V of the proposed resolution provides procedures for amending the constitution, either as a result of legislative resolutions or by referendum. These amending procedures apparently do not ensure that legislative action cannot sweep away those fundamental freedoms outlined in Section 2. We strongly believe that freedom of conscience, religion, thought, belief, opinion, expression, assembly and association must be very carefully safeguarded; subject only to the reasonable restraints commensurate with a democratic society, they must not be subject to the vagaries, no matter how well intentioned, of legislatures. Past history, our own and others, has taught us the need to place them above legislative action. Unless they are safeguarded, it would be possible, at some time in the future, for legislatures to deny them to one group or another in our society. The procedures for amending the constitution must, we submit, pay particular attention to the absolute need to protect those fundamental freedoms mentioned in Section 2 of the proposed resolution. ... (29: 7)

**Professor Peter Russell (University of Toronto):** I believe that a Charter of Rights only guarantees a change in the way in which certain decisions are made. It does not guarantee rights or freedoms, it guarantees a change in the way in which decisions are made about rights and freedoms.

Rights and freedoms raise, every case, difficult policy decisions. Take any right or freedom in your Charter, just start with the right of free expression, free speech. We can all immediately think of a whole range of policy issues as to what the limit of that freedom should be. Is it an abridgement of the right of freedom of expression to require broadcasters to have a certain amount of Canadian content? Is it a breach of free expression to prosecute people for violating the obscenity provisions of the Criminal Code and so on and so forth.

They are difficult decisions and those decisions will be made as the result of a Charter in a different way from the way in which they are made now.

The way will be different in this sense: the court will basically, and fundamentally it will be the Supreme Court, will essentially set down the basic guidelines on how far you can go in expressing those rights or enjoying them and how far government can go in limiting them.

Government will be in a sense given direction by the courts. The courts will say how far you can modify free broadcasting by having Canadian content. Both the courts and the legislatures will continue to be active, as they are in the United States, but there will be almost a transfer of functions. The court's function, instead of taking general standards set by the legislature and interpreting them and then the legislature, if it finds the court is going too far or not far enough, correcting the courts, it will be the reverse. It will be the courts, in a sense, correcting the legislature. (34: 148–9)

### Freedom of Conscience

**Chief John Ackroyd (Chief Metro Toronto Police, Canadian Association of Chiefs of Police):** The Association is of the opinion that the words "of conscience" are vague, and unnecessary, in that there is a real risk that the word "conscience" could be given so broad an interpretation by the courts as to make various sections of the criminal law inoperative, for example, those sections relating to morals and drug offences. We are also concerned with what these words may mean in relation to various cults that are operating in our country. ...

**The Hon. James McGrath, MP (PC, Newfoundland):** ... What would you put in the place of "conscience"?

**Chief Ackroyd:** Well, I would leave the word out. If not, then I would certainly feel it should be moved into Section 2(b). In fact, I am not even sure it is necessary there. Phrases like "freedom of thought" – and I do not have the constitution before me and I am speaking from memory – are expressed there, and that would cover it. My concern would be that in moral offences, whether one can argue before a court that certain sexual behaviour might be within one's rights of freedom of conscience; certain cults believe in the use of certain drugs as part of their conscience; and can they argue that, because it is part of their cult that the use of certain drugs and chemicals give them a right to argue that they have freedom of conscience? That is a type of concern we are raising.

**Mr. McGrath:** It can be argued, of course, that without freedom of conscience you will be subjected – this addresses a question, for example, of dictatorship and the problems of a police, fascist or communist state. A lot of them have freedom of conscience in their specific bills and charters. But we know that in states other than the western democracies there is no freedom of conscience.

I am afraid that what you are recommending here, notwithstanding my own reservations on entrenchment, goes a little bit too far.

**Chief Ackroyd:** May I respond to that? I notice that Section 2(b) speaks of freedom of thought, belief, opinion and expression, including freedom of the press and other media of information.

**Mr. McGrath:** But there is a big difference, with respect.

**Chief Ackroyd:** That is what concerns us. (14: 7, 13)

...

**Mr. Svend Robinson (NDP, BC):** The first question relates, again, referring to the brief of the Canadian Association of Chiefs of Police which was supported in this respect by the [A]ssociation of [Crown] Counsel, suggesting that we should not include a reference to freedom of conscience in a proposed charter of rights, because, as the police chiefs put it, our courts might strike down certain laws which would be rendered, or which they might view as inoperative as a result of the elimination of freedom of conscience. Do you believe that there is any validity to that criticism, and that we should maintain the concept of freedom of conscience in the charter of rights?

**Mr. William Black (Member of Executive Committee, British Columbia Civil Liberties Association):** It seems to me that the value of including freedom of conscience as well as freedom of religion is that it makes clear that people can have very deeply held beliefs that they might not call religious beliefs, but which are equally fundamental to them, and using the phrase "freedom of conscience" it gives them rights as well as people who deeply hold religious beliefs. It seems to me that the possibility that the Supreme Court of Canada or any other court would interpret that in a way which would hinder law enforcement is nonexistent. I cannot imagine the court giving it any such interpretation. (22: 117–18)

...

**Professor Peter Russell (University of Toronto):** "Freedom of conscience" is again a phrase which bothers me a great deal. My conscience often moves me to do some pretty funny things, and maybe yours does; but I do not see a place for that in the higher law of Canada. (34: 156)

### Freedom of Religion Generally

**Mr. David Lepofsky (Member, Ontario Division Board of Management, Canadian National Institute for the Blind)** [In the context of responding to the concern re defining *handicapped*]: Mr. Chairman, I would invite anyone to define what religion means in a comprehensive manner. I think that that term, while we know that certain religions, Judaism, Christianity, Buddhism are religions, there will be many borderline cases where we do not know if those groups are religions or not. But that has not precluded the drafters of this Charter from including religion. (25: 5)

...

**The Hon. Bryce Mackasey, MP (LIB, Ontario):** ... you mentioned I think, where you state the provinces have been too narrow in their thinking. I think that would exemplify to all Canadians who watched the last federal-provincial conference. Would you care to comment on that? ...

**Mrs. Diane Davidson (Vancouver People's Law School):** Yes. Again, I will say this that all the people at the conferences or who have seen that were equally embarrassed and irritated. I only saw a bit of it, fortunately. I turned it on and there was an actual provincial Premier saying that he was not in favour of freedom of religion on the grounds that when he spends his Christmas vacation in the States he is offended by the stores being open.

**Mr. Mackasey:** I think that was the Premier of Saskatchewan, if I am not mistaken. (32: 25)

**The Hon. James McGrath, MP (PC, Newfoundland):** If I may be permitted one more question, Mr. Chairman, perhaps it might be wise if I as a professed Papist, got my eye off the royal boudoir and go into the classroom.

What do you foresee, Professor, as the impact on the right of separate or denominational schools in Canada with respect to Section 2(a) of the proposed charter, given the experience of the U.S. Supreme Court, for example, where they ruled that the recitation of the Lord's Prayer was unconstitutional and that it violated the Constitution. Could that happen under Section 2(a) in Canada?

**Professor Peter Russell (University of Toronto):** Yes, it could. But you must remember that the first amendment of the American Constitution, the one to which you referred to, in addition to a guarantee of freedom of religion, has a freedom from an established church. There is an anti-establishment clause. The cases in the United States that deal with problems of constitutional validity of programs supporting denominational schools and the like often are ruled unconstitutional because of the non-establishment or anti-establishment clause of the American Bill of Rights, and not always the freedom of religion which cuts them down; but certainly the freedom of religion clause will raise questions like that, and the lawyers, again, in the first years of the Charter's existence would wish to test its limits, where their litigants have interests, and one could be those groups which dislike reciting the Lord's Prayer in school and may regard that as a violation of their freedom of religion.

Another likely area is Sunday closing, Sunday observance legislation, and certainly in the United States that has been a fertile source of litigation on the freedom of religion clause resulting in some limitation on Sunday observance legislation.

**Mr. McGrath:** Just in conclusion, Mr. Chairman, what you are saying is that freedom of religion means freedom from religion as well?

**Professor Russell:** Well, in the United States it means freedom from a state supported and sanctioned church. They cannot have an established church in the United States that is funded by the government and supported by the government, and then you get into difficulties when there are tax arrangements that are helpful to denominational schools or support of transportation systems for children who are using denominational schools and the funds come from the state. There is a whole set of problems that have to get sorted out in that area. Then there is the school prayers questions. (34: 156–7)

## Freedom of Religion: Taxes

**Mr. McGrath:** My question is, does Section 2 of the Charter in any way threaten the tax exempt privileges that you now enjoy as a church, in terms of any question that could be placed before the courts; because freedom of religion means freedom not be exposed to religion in certain circumstances, in other words, no religion in terms of interpretation can be construed as a religion, for the purposes of this section.

**Mr. Bruce Smith (President of Toronto Ontario East Stake, Church of Jesus Christ of Latter Day Saints):** Mr. Chairman, it had not occurred to us that this section would in any way threaten our tax exempt status, at least it had not occurred to me, and I do not see any inherent meaning in this. I think along with other sections of the Charter that the possibility for amendment could indeed threaten any of these sections and thereby affect the question before us. (29: 15)

## Freedom of Religion: Additional Protections

**Ms. Carole Christinson (Afro-Asian Foundation of Canada):** Historical incidents provide a number of cases of harassment and forcible deportation of Afro-Asians. ... In view of the above concerns we wish to make the following recommendations: ... 4. That a clause in the constitution provide for the protection of places of worship of Afro-Asian religious sects from vandalism and defamation; such acts encourage hatred and disdain for that which is different. ... We do not feel that with such very broad powers, as implied by the government, for example, having access to the CBC and nationwide media, we see far too little in this kind of medium which would sensitize and educate the average Joe Blow Canadian as to why some people worship in a temple which looks different from a synagogue or a Roman Catholic church.

**Mr. Ron Irwin, MP (LIB, ON):** On your recommendation number 4, you are concerned about worship, vandalism and defamation. By reading Sections 2 and 7 of the proposed Charter, it deals with freedom of religion, freedom of association and tying that into the sections of the Criminal Code relating to vandalism and to perhaps civil rights in defamation suggests that the wording is there, maybe the enforcement is lacking, but the wording is there.

**Mr. Sebastian Alakatusery (Chairman, Afro-Asian Foundation of Canada):** We are really looking for explicit wording for enforcement.

**Mr. Irwin:** More aggressive wording?

**Mr. Alakatusery:** More aggressive, yes. (32: 32–43)

## Freedom of Religion: Rules of Succession

**The Hon. James McGrath, MP (PC, Newfoundland):** I want to put this proposition to you, Professor. I had hoped to put it to Professor Cohen today, and I hope he is watching us tonight in the comfort of his living room, because I had a chance to consult with some of Mr. Mackasey's little people, and I came up with something which did concern me very much, and that has to do with the entrenchment of fundamental freedoms, specifically the potential impact of Section 2(a) on the Canadian monarchy.

If the Canadian monarchy is the English monarchy, and if the successors to the throne of Canada are determined by English statutes of succession – and you have identified the Act of Settlement – then I want to put this proposition to you, because I will read in part from the Act of Settlement:

> And it was thereby further enacted, That all and every person and persons that then were, or afterwards should be reconciled to or should hold Communion with the See or Church of Rome or should profess the Popish Religion, or marry a Papist, should be excluded, and are by that Act made for ever uncapable to inherit, possess, or enjoy Crown and Government of this Realm and Ireland and the Dominions thereunto belonging, or any Part of the same or to have or exercise any Regal Power, Authority, or Jurisdiction within the same.

And it goes on.

Very simply, Professor Russell, the next Canadian monarch will be Queen Elizabeth's successor. If Prince Charles were to fall in love with a Canadian who professed the Papish religion. ...

**The Hon. Bryce Mackasey, MP (LIB, Ontario):** I know just the girl!

**Mr. McGrath:** I seriously put this proposition to you. That there could very well be a challenge, and I ask for your learned opinion on this. There could be a challenge to the monarchy in terms of the provisions of the Charter of Rights as contained in Section 2(a) particularly (a) freedom of conscience and religion.

**Professor Peter Russell (University of Toronto):** It is a little far-fetched.

**Mr. McGrath:** It may not be as far-fetched as you may think.

**Professor Russell:** As I said at the beginning of this discussion, the one thing a Charter of Rights guarantees is that a certain number of policy questions get referred to the Courts.

The limits of those questions are really only set by the imaginations of lawyers in the pocket-books of their clients, and the imaginations of our lawyers are getting ever greater, and I do not know about the pocket-books of their clients, but people do put up money to go to court for odd reasons, and I suppose anything is possible.

But I must say I have never thought of that.

**Mr. McGrath:** I can assure you it is a serious proposition, because we are dealing here with the Head of State of Canada and the Head of State of Canada is determined by this ancient statute that I have just quoted from – the Act of Settlement.

**Professor Russell:** But I cannot see what the action would be about. I think the British would have a problem with their Act and their monarch, and I know this very issue is a matter of some debate and discussion in the United Kingdom, as you are probably aware. Now, I am not a betting man, but I have a hunch that we might see a change in that legislation in this generation – in England, and that bar on royal marriage to a Roman Catholic might be removed. I think that may happen. In Canada it would be a difficult issue for the courts. The plaintiff would have to argue, I guess, that the monarchy, as such, violated Section 2(a) of the Charter of Rights. That would be your point. We would hope for a ruling – if we ever get one, from the Supreme Court of Canada that the monarch is unconstitutional. (34: 155–6)

## Freedom of Religion: Conscientious Objectors

**Mr. Ross Nigh (Vice-Chairman, Mennonite Central Committee, Canada):** Our spiritual forefathers were the anabaptists of western Europe. Over 400 years ago they felt compelled to take a stand against the taking of human life in any form and to many of them it was contrary to their understanding of the teaching of scripture. For their beliefs and practice they suffered cruelly; many died. When our forefathers came to Canada around 200 years ago they appealed for and were promised exemption from military duty. ...

In World War I, the severe test of these provisions came. In the spring of 1918 the German forces made one last gigantic assault on the Western Front and for a while it looked as if the Allied front would break. It was under the stress and desperation of that time that exemptions which had been written through Order in Council by government were cancelled and the young men of our churches had their faith and their convictions severely tested; many served periods in jail.

I had hoped to bring along today a very close friend of mine who was my bishop for many years, Mr. B. J. Swalm who is 84 years of age, but he had other commitments and was not able to come. He could articulate his experiences during this war. One thing I remember, while he served as my bishop in the Niagara Area was that when he was visiting our area he would ask me to drive past St. Catharines Jail where he spent several months during World War I.

Bishop Swalm was one of the founders of this organization, the Mennonite Central Committee. The experience in World War II was different and here I can speak from personal experience, because I was of draft age at that time and young men of my age were being called into service. My spiritual training and upbringing, church teachings, taught me participation in war was wrong but I had to make a decision at that time that I had to know what I believed personally and I had to make a personal decision. I went through weeks of study and soul-searching which reinforced my teaching and brought me to the decision that I could not take a human life, or be part of a life-taking organization.

Now, in the Second World War, because of early representation to government by the leaders of our churches, an alternative service program was developed whereby our young men could serve in non-military forms of service such as reforestation, road-building, fire-fighting, agricultural work and some in ambulance and hospital work on the front lines.

As I came through those years and in perspective I have two strong feelings. First of all I have a deep respect for the boys, for the integrity of the boys who were my friends and are still my friends, who did not feel as I and went into military service, and we today wish to acknowledge our deep respect for those who disagree with us in this area.

The second was a great appreciation which I also hold today for a country where conscience is recognized and where opportunity was given for alternative forms of service of national value, and service that was helpful to society. I am thankful for a country where the right to be different is recognized; where a minority view does not endanger or dehumanize. So it is for this reason that we feel now in the formulation of a constitution in peaceful times apart from emotional pressures of a wartime society, that we include a clause in the constitution that would recognize the right of conscience that would lead one to abstain from the taking of human life. ...

We believe in light of past experience and differences of interpretation and application of past government decisions that a clear and brief, concise statement in the constitution would be helpful and we urge the inclusion of such in the Canadian Charter of Rights and Freedoms.

I might just call your attention to the statement that is written in the constitution of the Federal Republic of Germany: "No one may be compelled against his conscience to render war service involving the use of arms." (12: 45–8)

...

**Mr. W. Janzen (Director General, Ottawa Office, Mennonite Central Committee, Canada):** Thank you. This concern is somewhat different than the one which Mr. Nigh has explained. If that one could be covered with a clause like, "No one shall be compelled against his conscience to take human life," then the second one might be covered with a simple affirmation of freedom for religion without specifying that it be for individuals or for groups, thus leaving that question to be decided when problems in relation to that arise.

As it is worded at the present time in the proposal, it is cast in explicitly individual terms and we are concerned that that might create difficulties which perhaps are not foreseen at the present time or even considered desirable. The written brief refers to several such difficulties and I will not go over that material, but I would say that these difficulties can arise also in relation to communities other than the Amish or Old Order Mennonites or Hutterites which are referred to in the brief. We know that for generations and centuries the phenomenon of people going off unto themselves for religious reasons to live a bit more as a community unto themselves is an experience that has been present in our civilization and probably will be present, and we would like to have that freedom respected. We are a bit concerned that by casting the provision for freedom of religion in individual terms there might be some difficulties, as explained in the brief. ...

So what we are asking basically is two clauses: one is a clause that would say something to the effect that no one shall be compelled against his conscience to take human life, and the other one would be a simple affirmation of freedom for religion without specifying that it be for individuals or communities, thus leaving that to the wisdom of the legislatures or the courts to deal with those problems as they might arise. (12: 48–50)

## Freedom of Religion: Conscientious Objection and Abortion

**Mr. Ross Nigh (Vice-Chairman, Mennonite Central Committee, Canada):** A conscientious objector clause in the Charter might have implications for areas other than military service. People in police work or in medical work sometimes have to face the question of taking human life, too. The areas of euthanasia and abortion are examples but because of technological and other changes the number of areas may increase. In 1969, when the abortion issue was debated in Parliament, along with other amendments to the Criminal Code, it was emphasized that medical personnel would not be forced to be involved with them. Because of this, a conscientious objector clause, which was considered at the time, was viewed as unnecessary. However, the government's Badgley study of 1977 found that some strong pressures are brought to bear on medical workers.

We believe the right to abstain from the taking of human life should be extended in the area of abortion as well. (12: 48)

**The Hon. Jake Epp (PC, Manitoba):** ... you argue that the same rights should be extended to persons working in hospitals, people in the medical field, specifically people who because of conscience cannot accept the taking of life through abortion. Do you feel that the clause that you propose would in fact give them that protection they seek?

**Mr. W. Janzen (Director General, Ottawa Office, Mennonite Central Committee, Canada):** We are not sure about that. As it stands here we say it might have some implications for that concern, and I think it would suggest something in that direction but we are not sure of that and we have not sought a specific legal opinion. It is a concern to us that we recognize that that is not something on which we have complete clarity.

**Mr. Epp:** Do you have practical demonstration of members of your organization, adherents to your organization of churches that form your constituency, that people have been put into that position, namely of performing medical acts which contravene their conscience and specifically their position that they do not have the right to take life in that form?

**Mr. Janzen:** I do not know of specific personnel from our community. I do know that in the 1977 Badgley report there is some rather strong testimony from doctors and so on who were subject to considerable pressure and that is the reference for it here. (12: 50–1)

...

**Mr. Lorne Nystrom (NDP, SK):** My second and last question, Mr. Chairman, concerns another area where I have admired your organization – the whole question of the conscientious objector. You mentioned this morning, if I heard you correctly, two possibilities: one, enshrining in our constitution that no one should be compelled to take human life against one's conscience, and you also referred to another option, which is in Federal Republic of Germany, that basically you enshrine that it pertains only to military service. I gather that you prefer the first option, which is more sweeping, that one of you mentioned earlier, the possibility of problems concerning policemen in their work, and firefighters in their work, and getting into the whole abortion controversy and euthanasia and so on. You did mention, I believe, two options: that no one should be compelled to take human life against one's conscience, and the other option being what is enshrined in the German Republic which, I gather, says the same thing but as it pertains only to military service.

**Mr. Janzen:** We would prefer the more general one in regard to taking human life.

**Mr. Nystrom:** If the Committee or the government in its wisdom did not want to be as sweeping, the second would also cover a very important point, would it not?

**Mr. Janzen:** We would be grateful for what there is. (12: 53)

...

**Miss Coline Campbell, MP (LIB, Nova Scotia):** Do you think that in Section 2, taking Section 2(b), freedom of thought, belief, and opinion or Section 2(a) freedom of religion, will that protect parties in hospital who have been pressured into assisting an abortion if this is entrenched?

**Dr. DeVeber, M.D. (Head of Pediatrics at University of Western Ontario, Coalition for the Protection of Human Life):** I would hope not. I really cannot answer your question but I would think it is a genuine concern.

**Miss Campbell:** Perhaps you did not quite understand. I was looking for a clause in the Bill of Rights or in the proposal that would allow persons to refuse to assist, and you may have misinterpreted it.

**Dr. DeVeber:** I think that is an excellent idea. I would be in favour of putting that clause in.

**Miss Campbell:** Particularly if Section 1 over-rode any statute. So you could see that freedom of religion perhaps being, or belief that the ...

**Dr. DeVeber:** I think belief is more important because there are more and more doctors I know who are against abortion on demand, not on religious grounds, but just because they believe it is wrong. So it would be beliefs of any kind.

**Mr. Philip Cooper (Vice-President, Coalition for the Protection of Human Life):** May I make a comment here? When the present Criminal Code, the present abortion law was going through the Justice and Legal Affairs Committee there was an attempt made to insert a conscience clause. Now, the then Minister of Justice, Mr. John Turner, said that this would not be necessary. He could not conceive of any doctor or nurse being required to take part in an abortion. Experience has shown since then that he was dead wrong. ... (22: 41–2)

**Mr. Jim Hawkes, MP (PC, Alberta):** There is another conundrum inside your brief, and in contrast to the testimony we had the other day. They wanted to protect the rights of the fetus, your brief clearly says to us: protect the rights of the woman. There is another group involved in the abortion issue and that is medical personnel. Does your association have a position on their right to refuse to participate in any medical procedure, including the procedure of abortion?

**Dr. Wendell W. Watters (Honourary Director, Canadian Abortion Rights Action League):** As far as I know, I am just trying to search my memory now, I think the Canadian Medical Association does have a clause in its Code of Ethics that allows physicians to withhold these services in terms of abortion. I do not think any physician can be expected to perform any act that he finds repugnant, and I am quite sure that, again, I am speaking from memory, that the Canadian Medical Association does respect that.

**Ms. Eleanor Wright Pelrine (Honourary Director, Canadian Abortion Rights Action League):** That clause, however, goes on to say that should the physician, because of personal, moral, religious or ethical beliefs, be unable to perform a particular procedure, he or she is obligated to so inform the patient and to refer the patient to another physician who will perform the procedure. I am certainly prepared to accept that Code of the Canadian Medical Association.

**Mr. Hawkes:** Would the freedom of conscience, which is also contained in this charter, be relevant to that issue?

**Mr. J. Robert Kellermann (Legal Counsel, Canadian Abortion Rights Action League):** I think that a doctor might argue that he did not want to perform a particular operation or medical treatment of some kind on the basis of freedom of conscience, but that is fine, I do not think that in any way contradicts the position of CARAL. CARAL's concern is that there be doctors available for the women who want to choose to have an abortion, and as long as that is guaranteed we are not in any way interested in forcing other doctors to involve themselves in that process. They just do not want other doctors standing in the way of women having that right.

**Ms. Pelrine:** And who indeed would want to submit to any medical procedure performed by an unwilling physician? (24: 107)

### Freedom of Religion: Clash with Denominational Rights

**The Hon. James McGrath, MP (PC, Newfoundland):** Then how do we avoid getting into the kind of situation which has developed in the United States where, for example, in certain instances, the Lord's Prayer recited in the classroom has been ruled by the courts to be unconstitutional? I say that as one who comes from a province which has, by law, a denominational system of education which is publicly funded. That law is enshrined in the constitution of Canada by virtue of the terms of union between Newfoundland and Canada, and indeed, is threatened by the provisions of the bill now before us.

**Mr. Philip Hammel (President, Canadian Catholic School Trustees Association):** But what is the question?

**Mr. McGrath:** The question is: if we are to entrench a Charter of Human Rights in the constitution, how do we avoid the situation whereby the courts of this country will, in fact, be almost in a position of a parallel legislature in terms of defining new laws by the constitution; for example, you could be restricted as to your hiring practices; as to your conduct in the classroom. I have cited the instance in the United States where the recitation of the Lord's Prayer has, in certain circumstances, been declared unconstitutional. That is a dilemma I find myself in; I am very much in favour of fundamental human rights being protected by law, but I have this dilemma.

**Mr. Hammel:** I think whatever approach is taken, whether the statute approach or the Charter of Rights and Freedoms one, I think we simply have to recognize that there are individual rights, and then there are, in our case, organized group rights. In this case, we are dealing with denominational group rights, although, for example, as a Roman Catholic I do not in any way tend to judge anyone's right to freedom of conscience, I do feel that when he does not abide by what the Roman Catholic religion teaches, then he is no longer a Roman Catholic, and, therefore, does not have the rights of the group. So I think we have to approach it from that particular point of view, that there are certain group rights which are at least equal to, or, perhaps, supreme over some individual rights. I do not think we can simply make it sound as if the individual rights are total. (19: 9–11)

...

**Professor Joseph Magnet (Counsel, Conference of Catholic Bishops of Ontario):** But the jurisprudence in the United States to which you refer arises under a constitutional guarantee to nondiscrimination and also to a constitutional guarantee which prevents the establishment of religion. In this proposed resolution there is no anti-establishment clause, and therefore, it simply reflects the Canadian theory which has been true throughout the history of this country that the basic Confederation pact protects certain denominational reasons. Indeed, you might say establishes, but certainly we would not think an antiestablishment clause would be possible in Canada.

**The Hon. Bryce Mackasey, MP (LIB, Ontario):** One of the things that concerns me about our deliberation is our tendency to look to the American experience, both in discussing jurisprudence, and it concerns me a little because I think we are a unique country and our constitution has got to reflect our unique character. We have the built-in advantage, I think at this stage, as some members opposite have pointed out, of amending to some degree our constitution. We have the advantage of one hundred and some years of history, our own history not the American history, and it seems important to me that somehow we balance in this constitution the problems between individual rights and collective rights, such fundamental freedoms of association and religion. (3: 58)

### Freedom of the Press

**Senator Jack Austin (LIB, BC):** Under section 2, where you see Subparagraph (b), reference to freedom of thought, including freedom of the press and other media of information, Minister, is it the intention to in any way enlarge the present rights as they are so indistinctly understood of the press and other media in Canada? Is it, for example, now open to argue as to protection of sources in the hands of journalists and press and electronic media people?

**The Hon. Jean Chrétien (Minister of Justice):** I do not know how the Court will interpret that, but we are dealing here, we are formalizing the guarantee that exists traditionally in this society concerning the freedom of the press and other media. What will be the interpretation of the Court in terms of the sources of information and so on, it would not be for me, I do not know what the Court will decide or if there will be some different circumstances that will have to be analyzed by the Court before rendering a judgment.

**Senator Austin:** Your attempt here was to be neutral?

**Mr. Chrétien:** As much as possible. (3: 78–9)

...

**Mr. J.P. Nelligan (Chairman, Special Committee on the Constitution of Canada, Canadian Bar Association):** In Section 2(b), that section gives the impression that the freedom of the press and the media is an individual right. Well, in fact, as we have already pointed out in our report, the freedom of the press is merely a mode by which the general freedom of expression is exercised, it is not a right of an individual as such. (15: 12)

**Ms. Esther Crandall (President, Media Club of Canada):** Thank you, Mr. Joint Chairman, for giving the Media Club the opportunity to [appear] before this Special Joint Committee. As you will see from our submission, Media Club is concerned with the profession, therefore concern of members is with the proposed entrenchment in a charter of rights and freedoms of a new Canadian constitution, freedom of the press.

[Indicated that the Club thought it needed an additional year to prepare the kind of brief that it would like to prepare for the Joint Committee] ...

**Mr. Lorne Nystrom, MP:** I want to refer you to Section 2 of the resolution which is a Section on fundamental freedoms. ... What I want to ask you is, how do you think the word "everyone" would be interpreted as it pertains to everyone has the following freedoms, the freedom of the press, freedom of other media of information.

I want to take you back in this country about four of five years when the government across the way introduced legislation, which I supported, concerning *Time* magazine and *Reader's Digest*, to try and Canadianize the magazine industry in this country.

I am wondering whether or not if we were to enshrine Section 2 in the constitution as written, *Time* magazine or *Reader's Digest* could have gone to the courts and said: "We have a constitutional right in this country of freedom of expression and freedom of the press and freedom of information, freedom of the media; therefore, the government of Canada and the Parliament of Canada do not have the right to legislate restrictively against our two organizations."

Could it be interpreted in that way?

**Ms. Crandall:** Mr. Nystrom, I think that is the kind of question which an expert should be asked to answer. ...

**Mr. Nystrom:** I appreciate the answer. The reason why I ask the question is that the words "everyone" and "citizens of Canada" are used throughout the resolution. I am not a lawyer myself, but it would seem to imply that these could be given a fairly wide interpretation, and I am concerned that we might have in a constitution something that is restrictive where we could not increase Canadian content.

Let me ask you the same question again about the electronic media. There is growing concern that we Canadianize radio, television – and the CRTC is concerned about this, about television programs coming in from the United States. There is talk now about a second CBC network in this country.

Again, I want to ask you a similar question pertaining to the electronic media. If everybody has the freedom of expression and freedom of the press and other media of information, in your opinion, or perhaps in the opinion of your colleague, do you think we would be able to do this as a Parliament, where the constitution says we are denying a fundamental right to everyone, perhaps NBC, New York, or ABC somewhere in the United States?

**Ms. Alison Hardy (Historian, Media Club of Canada):** I think, Mr. Nystrom, that it is very important. I have served abroad for Canada in the Department of External Affairs, in the public affairs field, and I feel that it is very important that we develop a Canadian culture, that we develop an interest in things Canadian and a pride, and I grant that there are very good programs produced by the electronic media of other countries but I think we should be proud of our own heritage and be proud of what we can do.

I have just been at a briefing on plans for CBC 2, *Tele Deux*, and I am very pleased that this is what may be coming along shortly and I would hope that we would not refuse all foreign media offers to assist us in our cultural development, but I think we should certainly give ourselves the chance to be first in the field and to welcome the opportunity and the pride in our own country and in what we can develop ourselves.

This is a continuing subject of interest financially as well as culturally, naturally, and I would hope that the media club, which now covers the electronic media representatives as well as the press, would be in the forefront of assisting in developments if possible. Thank you.

**Mr. Nystrom:** ... I also wanted to ask your interpretation of a couple of other words in Section 2. I wanted to ask you what you think the interpretation in your opinion would be of other media of information. We have singled out here freedom of belief, opinion, expression, including the freedom of the press. I know what the press is, I think, but what would be the interpretation legally, in your opinion, of other media of information, what would that include?

**Ms. Hardy:** I would expect that that would include the electronic journalism. The press is usually referred to as print media. Media is a very broad term that has had to be used because you cannot just refer to the press now because it covers a number of other representatives who inform, through one source or another, and I think the electronic media has an important place now in our culture because communications in this country is aspect of helping unify the country, I think, by letting us get to know each other, not only through print but through electronic means. (24: 7–22)

...

**Senator Renaude Lapointe (LIB, Quebec):** ... I would like to ask you if you have considered, Ms. Hardy, the notion of freedom of the press as an individual right or collective right?

**Ms. Alison Hardy (Historian, Media Club of Canada):** It could be considered both because if you speak of freedom of the press for a newspaper, it includes the whole role of a newspaper in a community as well as the role of an individual reporter or columnist, so that I really feel that there would be no point in having freedom of the press for an individual if you did not have it for the publication for which the individual happened to be working, either perhaps in the electronic media or in the print media. So I would prefer to have it refer to both an individual and collective group.

**Senator Lapointe:** Do you think that editors of papers or radio stations would have to come here also to express their opinion on freedom of the press?

**Ms. Hardy:** We would include them as responsible leaders, presumably in the community, and the value of having responsible leadership is very noticeable now that the Royal Commission on Newspapers is sitting and I think that you have to have the leadership in order to develop followers and principles. (24: 15–17)

...

## Freedom of Expression: Generally

**Mr. Wilson Head (President, National Black Coalition of Canada):** We want to make it very clear, first of all, that in principle we support the entrenchment of a bill of rights in the constitution. We want to see the constitution patriated to Canada and we want to see in that constitution an entrenched bill of rights. However, we do have some concerns. We are not altogether happy with all of the bill of rights. In that connection we are, I suppose, in somewhat the same situation as a number of other groups who have appeared before you.

For example, we feel that some of the statements are too vague. Having been a part of the preparation of the brief of the Canadian Civil Liberties Association, I can say that I, personally, share some of the concerns that they have in terms of the vagueness of some of the language, and I speak particularly of such words as "fundamental freedoms," and those kinds of things in which we talk about "natural rights," et cetera.

We would like to see some of these things spelled out. On the question, for example, of freedom of speech, we believe very strongly in freedom of speech, while at the same time, of course, being against censorship. But we would like to see freedom of speech limited only in certain specific ways. In the brief we have indicated, for example, that to a large extent we believe in the doctrine of clear and present danger. We think that freedom of speech should be curtailed where the danger is clear. For example, we have no right to go into a crowded theatre and shout "Fire!" resulting in people being trampled to death as a result of fleeing from a fire which is nonexistent and where there is no danger at all. In a situation like that, obviously, we do not have absolute freedom. But we think this needs to be spelled out a lot more clearly than it is today. (22: 8)

...

## Freedom of Expression: Hate Propaganda

**Professor Max Cohen (Chairman, Select Committee on the Constitution of Canada of the Canadian Jewish Congress):** This Committee [of the Canadian Jewish Congress] did not have a parochial view; this Committee does not pretend that the human rights question belongs to any sector of the Canadian people. It belongs to them all. But ... there are two or three areas where the Jewish interest happens to be special, and in some cases very sensitive. One is the problem of war criminals, and how that relates to certain protections offered by a charter of rights in the criminal law field. Another is the problem of free speech, and how far that affects such things as hate propaganda. (7: 84)

...

**Professor Cohen:** ... Section 2 then begins the real ball game, namely everyone has the following fundamental freedoms. The one difficulty we had, as a committee, is with Section 2(*b*). What do we do with freedom of thought when you have got legislation dealing with [hate] propaganda? How far is it possible to retain such articles as Section 281(1) of the Criminal Code and Section 281(2)? Moreover, you will see we have quoted from Article 20 of the United [Nations] Covenant of Civil and Political Rights where propaganda of this kind is regarded as inconsistent with freedom of speech.

So we raised the question which seemed to me to be necessary to raise with you, that caution must be exercised, we hope, by the courts in due course, or by you, as draftsmen on how far you are prepared to push the concept of free speech consistent with our experience of hate propaganda.

One suggestion we make here – and I do not wish to do anything more than to drop it as a hint, but you may want to have some language that some of the modern constitutions have, which state very starkly and flatly that the advocacy of genocide or group libel is forbidden. But I had the honour to be the chairman of the special committee on hate propaganda in 1965. At that time we came to the flat conclusion that the advocacy of group hatred and genocide was totally inconsistent with the democratic process and no democratic state could tolerate it. Now, whether you want to put that flatly in a constitution is for you to consider; but I think it is for us to bring it to your attention, because it is of importance. (7: 86–7)

**Senator Carl Goldenberg (LIB, Quebec):** On Section 2 I was interested and have been concerned myself with the possible impact of freedom of speech, freedom of expression on hate propaganda legislation. Would Professor Cohen tell me whether or not there is a similar provision guaranteeing freedom of expression in the federal Bill of Rights and the various provincial legislation.

**Professor Max Cohen (Chairman, Select Committee on the Constitution of Canada of the Canadian Jewish Congress):** The Diefenbaker Bill of Rights says expressly freedom of speech. I think that the Saskatchewan Human Rights Code recently codified has similar language. I would be surprised if most of the human rights legislation of the provinces do not have parallel language, the Quebec Human Rights Code and so on. So that in general as a concept I think it is widely used as a phrase.

Curiously enough, Senator Goldenberg, the International Covenant has, under Article 20, language that will interest you, and that is, any propaganda for war shall be prohibited by law; Article 21. Article 20, Clause 2 says that any advocacy of national, racial or religious hatred that constitutes incitement, discrimination, hostility or violence shall be prohibited by law. And that is a covenant to which we are a party. (7: 111)

...

**Mr. Lorne Nystrom (NDP, Saskatchewan):** I would like to welcome Mr. Head and Mr. Mercury here this morning and to begin by picking up the answer to the second last question by Mr. Head when you were referring to the KKK, the Ku Klux Klan. I want to ask you a couple of questions about whether or not you think the Klan's activities would be affected by the Charter as the Charter is written and to what extent you think a Charter of Rights should curtail the activities of the Ku Klux Klan.

I want to say as a preamble that I, like you, am very concerned about the possibility of the Klan's growth in this country. It is a very reprehensible organization and it is one that is a very negative force in our society. I say as a member from Saskatchewan, because in my province back in the 1920's the Klan had a major influence on politics. I think the Province of Saskatchewan is the only province historically in our country where the Klan was well organized, where it had a major impact back in the 1920's. It had an impact in the 1929 election and succeeded in helping turf out the Liberal government of that day and electing in its place a more conservative alternative.

In those days of course in my province there were not any black people. The Klan's activities were directed mainly against Catholics and immigrants from Eastern European countries. I think of people that came in from Poland, the Ukraine, Czechoslovakia, from Russia and the like, so I have a really negative feeling of hostility against people like the Klan who base their whole raison d'être on racism and attacks on other people.

I would like to ask you whether or not you think the Charter as written would have any effect on an organization like the Klan, and secondly to what extent should a Charter of Rights curtail their activities in light of the fact that we also have enshrined here such things as freedom of assembly and freedom of speech.

**Mr. Wilson Head (President, National Black Coalition of Canada):** This is no doubt a very tricky question. In some of the organizations that I have been involved in, both in the United States and in Canada since I have been living here for the last 20 years, we have had to wrestle with the situation and you never get a unified opinion. You get differences of opinion across the board, and the whole concept of freedom of speech in terms of absolutes is one thing. As I indicated earlier, it has to have restrictions at a certain level. I think the tricky point of it is how do you define that balance. At what point do you draw the line?

The usual thing said is you draw the line at behaviour, and this is what our Attorney General says in Ontario. He says when the Klan takes some illegal action we will crack down on them just like we would on anybody else who takes illegal action. That does not get at the question though of what happens as they are building up to that illegal action. Are they permitted to do anything they want to, short of this.

The new Klan is more sophisticated than the old Klan was. I suspect they have legal advice because they seem to be avoiding taking action which will get them in conflict with the law as now written so in a sense then we have to look again at the way our laws are written and say how can we make this law a little more explicit.

I am not a lawyer and I am not sure even lawyers could do any better when they come down to drawing this out. One person said to me some time ago, if you really got into this I know what would happen, lawyers would have a great time because they would make a lot of money arguing the case.

But I feel that it is up to the government to make it very clear where it stands on this matter. Let me put it this way. I still feel a sense of pride when I hear the ringing words of the Declaration of Independence. All men are created free and equal. All men have certain inalienable rights. We know that those have not been lived up to fully but at least the statement is there that this is where the government is, this is where the government stands, and it will take all the legal methods it can to live up to those statements.

I am saying to a large extent this may merely be symbolical but I think in this case the symbolical act is important. The government has made a commitment in this situation. I will leave it to the lawyers to decide how far you can go in terms of drawing the line. I cannot do that myself, but I feel it is important for the government to state this in its new constitution. Whether it is in the body of the constitution or the preamble. I think this is extremely important and needs to be stated.

**Mr. Nystrom:** I wonder if Mr. Mercury could add something here, because you are saying you are not a lawyer, nor am I, and we are talking about their activities being in conflict with the law as written.

I ask this again because of a couple of comments you made earlier, Mr. Head, that you had the feeling that the KKK could grow from what one of their leaders has said. I refer back to Saskatchewan in the 1920s again; we were a province of fewer than a million people, and I believe the membership in the Klan in those days was nearly 30,000 people which is an amazingly high number of people for an activity of that sort. You also referred to the possibility that public opinion can change very quickly in a crisis or a major eruption of society and the eruption in our society in those days of course was the mass influx of immigrants from Eastern Europe. I am thinking particularly, as I said, of the Ukrainian people, and up until that time Saskatchewan was primarily an Anglo-Saxon settlement. The English people were the first to come, primarily from places such as Ontario and parts of the United States. So we had this great upheaval in society and because of that unfortunately a lot of people joined the Klan.

I, like you, do not want to rest on my laurels and say it can never happen again. I think history can repeat itself. So I want to ask Mr. Mercury whether or not he can add anything else to what we should be putting in our Charter to make sure the activities of reprehensible organizations such as this are curtailed, yet of course recognizing as you say we need to have freedom of assembly and freedom of speech.

**Mr. J.A. Mercury (Executive Secretary, National Black Coalition of Canada):** One of the things that I worry about, Mr. Nystrom, is the fact that when we are talking about prohibitive action towards any group, that same action can be utilized against other groups. Incidentally, if I may correct you, the membership of the Klan in the 1920s in Canada was upwards of 40,000 in actuality. One of the things we must not lose sight of is that there are other government institutions in place that have the tools to do the job right now if they would utilize the authority that they already have at their disposal.

For instance, one of the insidious things we have found about the Klan lately – and as Mr. Head has already indicated, they seem to be using modern day communicative methods – is that we find the Klan in all facets of the communications media, electronic, visual and audio.

Now, I think when an organization does a specific thing or comes into being that is news; but when it is exploited by various facets of the media to boost their circulation, which appears to be taking place with the Klan, particularly in the Province of Ontario, and latterly, we have been getting reports as recently as two weeks ago, for instance, in Nova Scotia, I question whether governmental bodies, such as the CRTC cannot step in and make some prohibitive ruling.

For example, if you were to make a group of people aware that such and such a group is in existence, fine; but when you find a group spewing the type of garbage this type of organization is doing on open line shows two and three hours at a stretch on consecutive nights, in consecutive weeks, I question whether that is really in the public interest.

I am saying it does not require action in a bill of rights; the tools are there to do the job now if we utilize those tools. (22: 15–18)

**Mr. Jean Lapierre (LIB, Quebec):** Now, under Section 2, you talk about free speech. I have a note to the effect that in a way you would like it to be limited. In Section 2(b) you are recommending the inclusion of the doctrine of "clear and present danger." I was wondering why.

**Mr. Wilson Head (President, National Black Coalition of Canada):** That is because we recognize that there can not be absolutism in free speech. As I have indicated earlier, there has to be some limit at some time, but we would like any to apply as rarely as possible.

For the most part, we feel unless there is a clear and present danger, free speech should be permitted at all times. That comes back to Mr. Nystrom's question, namely, to what extent should the KKK have freedom of speech? That is a very practical example. It causes some difficulty to some minds.

We would say, in general, the freedom of people to advocate the destruction of other people should be among the prohibited grounds. This is not a matter of free speech. It is saying, in effect, that the KKK is in favour of the destruction of black people, or the destruction of Jewish people, and they have been – and to some extent still are – advocates of the destruction of Catholic people, and it is in my view the kind of step which could, if carried out, lead to genocide; and I would be opposed to anybody advocating genocide; and I think the KKK skirts that issue very clearly, it gets very close to it. I think in this situation they ought to be looked at.

Certainly, already the Canadian Human Rights Commission has, in a case dealing with hate messages on the telephone, ruled against the Western Guard, which is a companion organization of the KKK. This is a case where the Western Guard was putting on messages on Toronto telephones, where you dial a number, 967–777.

**Some hon. Members:** Do not tell anybody.

**Mr. Head:** Are there any KKK members here? It is all cleared up right now, so it would not do you any good, folks.

But that ruling – and I happen to have it with me, and I was reading it on the plane on my way here – did condemn the Western Guard. That was a case which was brought before the Canadian Human Rights Commission recently. (22: 20–1)

## Limits on Freedom of Expression

**M. Jean Lapierre (LIB, Quebec):** Thank you, Mr. Chairman. Gentlemen, I read your brief with great interest.

… As for clause 2(b) on freedom of expression, I will say that I am from Quebec and I have lived under Mr. Duplessis' repression. Therefore, I believe that if we limit freedom of expression in Canada, we would be in a very difficult situation and I must admit that very few groups have asked us to limit that freedom because it is one of our greatest freedoms and it does contribute to the greatness of our country.

I looked at the examples that you are giving, to prove that, with or without a charter, the rights have not been well protected. But all the examples you have given referred to [war]time. You know as well as I do that a charter of rights is valid only in peaceful times and that in [war]time, during an insurrection, etc., the same yardsticks do not necessarily apply because those do not represent a normal situation. (26: 55)

**Mr. Dietrich Kiesewalter (Coordinating Chairman, German-Canadian Committee on the Constitution):** May I answer at least one part of the number of questions that you have had. At first you indicated that you cannot agree with our thoughts on freedom of speech and you have the right to say that it is very important to have freedom of the press and so on. You pointed out the example of the implementation of the War Measures Act.

**M. Lapierre:** No, Mr. Duplessis' repression.

**Mr. Kiesewalter:** Yes, I know. The point we are trying to make is that there should be some provision in the law and we are not arguing for the importance of freedom of speech, or freedom of expression because we value it as highly as anyone else. But there should be some provision that provides for accountability of the mass media towards groups that feel discriminated by films, newscasts, documentaries, whatever. This is the only thing we are trying to get across and I think you will agree that this is, especially in our case, a real problem; that we have no way of getting back at the mass media that has portrayed us in a rather negative way for generations.

**M. Lapierre:** Is it necessary that [that] section be included in the Constitution? Do you not think that ordinary statutes could allow protection against libel or such things? Such laws [existed before this Constitution here was written].

**Mr. Kiesewalter:** We understand that there are provisions in the human rights charter, especially in regard to freedom of expression that has a clause where it says that groups that feel unjustly treated by the media have the right to expect from the same media the possibility to present their own point of view. I think something like this would be quite acceptable. We know that in the Criminal Code there is provision for us to go to the courts and take radio stations or television stations to court but what we would rather have is provision made in the Bill of Rights that makes the media, do it the other way around, accountable for the position they have taken. (26: 55–6)

### Limits on Freedom of the Press: Negative Stereotyping

**Professor Gunther Bauer (Vice Chairman of German Speaking Alliance of Ottawa and Region, German-Canadian Committee on the Constitution):** Thank you, Mr. Chairman. Allow me, Mr. Chairman, to make a few introductory remarks in order to give you and the members of your Committee the proper background information. Many of the people represented by this Committee here at the table came from parts of Europe which belong today to other countries, such as Poland, Czechoslovakia, USSR, Romania and others. Most of the people who came to Canada after World War II had suffered greatly during and after the war. Half of my family and relatives, for example, perished during and after the last war. There are many families in Ottawa, whom I know of, that had similar losses. You may say of course, and many Canadians have said this to us, you started the war so do not blame us; and we accept this to a certain degree.

Let me refresh your memory about one important fact, namely that 2.5 million Germans from the eastern provinces of Germany lost their lives shortly after the war had ended. That is after the Potsdam Agreement had been signed. Many of those 2.5 million Germans who, by the way, were mostly children, women and elderly people were relatives of German Canadians. We fully realize that no human rights charter or Geneva Convention did or could have prevented this from happening.

We think this background information is necessary for you to understand why we feel so strongly about Section 2(b) and why we would like to see some means and ways incorporated in the proposed constitution to make the mass media accountable for negative stereotyping. In this country of ours everything bad and evil connected with war is German; every war criminal is German; every German alive or dead is or was a Nazi. I know, Mr. Chairman, these are very strong statements but they stem from our own life experiences.

We have appended to our submission of our brief to you a copy of an article from Maclean's October issue which we hope you have an opportunity to read. In this article, a third generation German Canadian who is now presently a member of the Manitoba Legislature describes his experiences of being discriminated against because of his German descent.

I do not wish to say more about this at this particular time but would rather, with your permission, Mr. Chairman, ask Mr. Grenke to share with you a few observations he has made regarding the problem of human rights as it relates to the German communities in North America. Thank you for your time. (26: 41)

...

**Mr. Ian Waddell (NDP, BC):** I see and I agree. I just wanted to ask you perhaps one last question. You make reference to hate propaganda in your brief, the difficulties of any community that is faced with that kind of evil. I understand that the Criminal Code has some protection against hate literature and I wonder if you think that is adequate or whether you would ask that there be some additional provisions in the constitution document.

Are you in a position to be able to comment on that? I know it is a tough one.

**Mr. Arthur Grenke (Historian, German-Canadian Committee on the Constitution):** May I first of all add in relation to World War II, during World War II the Germans were not treated as badly as the Japanese, the prime reason being that because of World War II. Germans tended to shed their identity to a great extent and the main people who suffered during the Second World War were the members of the Deutsch-Canadeschr Aabeiter and Famer Verbend, which was a leftist organization, and the members of the Bund. Now, these peoples, many of them were interned and so on and so forth, but generally the German community as a whole tended to be left alone.

Regarding hate propaganda, this is really a very difficult issue and it affects us not the same way as it affects many other communities. It affects us largely in such films as Holocaust, Hogan's Heroes and so on, so forth. Now, as I understand it, the Broadcasting Act does not allow or permit an ethnic community to challenge a certain program, the broadcaster can present what he wishes but at the same time he is required to, and I will read what I was told by Bill Howard of the Legal Branch of CRTC, that the station is obliged to provide the opportunity for expression of different views on matters of public concern. Now, this does not apply to drama as yet, it applies largely to public opinion programs.

Now, what we would like is if, somehow, in some way, if a program is presented which presents us in a negative view, that laws be passed which enable us to present our point of view on that particular television station which presents a program which stereotypes Germans in a negative way. (26: 48–9)

...

**Mr. Laurence Decore (Chairman, Canadian Consultative Council on Multiculturalism):** In dealing with fundamental freedoms, Section 2, the Council is concerned that organizations such as the Ku Klux Klan are again burning crosses in Canada, in my own provinces. We believe that the intended meaning of freedom of opinion and expression should not allow individuals or groups to infringe on the rights and freedoms of others. No group should be allowed to propagate hate messages at the expense of any other group.

The Council therefore recommends that Section 2(b) be strengthened in line with Article 19 of the International Bill of Human Rights to read:

Freedom of thought, belief, opinion and expression, including freedom of the press and other media of information subject to the rights or reputation of others. (29: 125–6)

## Limits on Fundamental Freedoms

**Mr. Roger Tassé, Q.C. (Deputy Minister of Justice):** In effect, Mr. Chairman, that Section 1 is meant to bring forward the concept that these rights that are spelled out in the Charter, those you have mentioned and the others, Mr. McGrath, are not absolute rights.

If you just take, for example, the freedom of expression, there are limits to the freedom of expression that already are spelled out in the Criminal Code and that will continue and should continue when a Charter of Rights like this is entrenched.

What the Section is meant to do is to bring that concept not only to the legislatures but also to the judges because in effect the judges when they are faced with cases where government action or parliamentary action, legislative action is being tested and being challenged, in effect they have to decide whether limits, restrictions, that may have been imposed, because again these rights are not absolute, are reasonable ones. That is only what Section 1 is intended to do, that in effect the judges, when there are challenges brought before them, where in effect people would claim that their rights have been unfairly or unreasonably restricted that in coming to a conclusion when they are so challenged that in effect the courts will have to take for granted that there are some imitations that may well be reasonable and legitimate in the kind of society in which we live. (3: 15)

...

**Mr. Roger Tassé, QC (Deputy Minister of Justice):** Perhaps if I may just expand on what I have just said.

For example, if you look at the freedom of expression, the law of defamation, the law of libel imposes some limits on that so we wanted these to continue to have application and we think that they would fit in effect the tests that are set out in Section 1. (38: 49)

## Freedom of Assembly

**Mrs. Diana Davidson (President, Vancouver People's Law School Society):** I should say, when I say "we," I am referring to the delegates at the conference in Vancouver, the conference at Naramata and the tiny seminars in Prince Rupert and Terrace and those groups that have gotten hold of us. So far as I am able, I believe that the recommendations I am bringing to you have been endorsed by those with whom we have been in contact and given the time limitations, we have made really our best effort and have been in a peculiarly good position to make that effort to get the opinion of as many people as we could. ...

With respect to Section 2, the fundamental freedoms section, freedom of the press and other media should be enumerated separately from thought, belief, opinion and expression and the phrase "of information" in Section 2(b) and the word "peaceful" in Section 2(c) should be deleted. (32: 10)

...

**Mr. J.P. Nelligan (Chairman, Special Committee on the Constitution, Canadian Bar Association):** In Section 2(c) the draftsmen should make certain, in light of reported cases, that the rights of assembly and of association are distinct and separate rights and are not a single right as has been found in the courts. (15: 12)

...

**The Honourable Jean Chrétien (Minister of Justice):** Section 2 – with respect to fundamental freedoms, the government is prepared to accept the recommendation of the Canadian Bar Association to separate in Section 2 freedom of peaceful assembly from freedom of association to ensure that they are looked upon as separate freedoms.

## Freedom of Association

**M. Jean Lapierre (LIB, Quebec) [Translation]:** Gentlemen, I found your presentation quite refreshing because you were the first group to really pinpoint the details of freedom of conscience and religion. ... In your recommendations, and I am referring to Section 2 of the draft resolution, you asked that community rights be respected. Do you not think that Section 2(a) which refers to freedom of conscience and religion, along with the freedom of association guaranteed in Section 2(c) offers sufficient protection for community rights since freedom of conscience coupled with freedom of association would seem to cover the concept of community.

**Mr. William Janzen (Director General, Ottawa Office, Mennonite Central Committee:** That is a possibility. The freedom to associate is a very valuable one. In the specific judgment of the Supreme Court to which we have already referred in our brief, there were several arguments on the side of the Hutterite community, and one of them was that the individuals had freely associated with that community and that there was a contract.

But we note too, that the dissenting judgment argued very strongly that, in view of the background of the individuals who had made that contract, they virtually had no choice, and that, therefore, it was in a sense a community which was being allowed to exercise quite a bit of power over individuals who had grown up within it.

While we respect the dissenting judgment, we think there might be better protection in leaving that issue somewhat vague so that it could be studied in relation to problems as they arise. (12: 53–4)

...

**Mr. Clarke MacDonald (Senior Secretary, Office of Church in Society, United Church of Canada):** Finally, we affirm that a Charter of Rights and Freedoms cannot serve its intended purpose unless it includes a section on the right of workers to join unions and to take collective economic action. The right to collective bargaining has been a position of the United Church since about the mid 1940s and was reaffirmed on a number of occasions as late as the early part of the past decade. (29: 81)

**Mrs. Diana Davidson (President, Vancouver People's Law School Society):** With respect to Section 2, the fundamental freedoms section. ... This section should include freedom to organize, freedom from economic deprivation and freedom to a clean environment.

The last three – freedom to organize, freedom from economic deprivation and freedom to a clean environment, are not traditional rights but are rights which history has shown to be necessary. While we may forgive early drafters of bills of rights for their failure to see that economic conditions can render one's rights ineffective and barren, surely this is inexcusable in our own time. ...

The absence of entrenched protection for union organizing is also disturbing. Interpretation of various doctrines of individual freedom can be used by the court to deprive workers of the right and power needed to organize. Such interpretation should be explicitly ruled out by a clear right to organize. (32: 10–11)

**Miss Coline Campbell (LIB, Nova Scotia):** I think I could probably direct my questions to the officials who are here from the Department, and I go to the Section 2, under the fundamental freedoms, and in particular, freedom of association. Does every province have the right at common law, or has it been abridged by legislation to freedom of association, in terms of unions? And if it is a term of common law then we are not really abridging them in this Act but I am just wondering if there is not some interpretation here.

For instance, in the maritime provinces, and I eliminate Newfoundland, fishermen cannot associate, cannot form an association, or at least they appear to be under that basic impression that they cannot form an association without legislation. I am glad if this is going to give them the right to associate or form a union, or am I looking at it too broadly or does this not imply collective bargaining being given to everybody across Canada, and in particular, let us say, the fishermen of the maritime provinces?

I will go further on that and just say perhaps you could tell me if the right to strike is a basic common law or would that have to be legislated? It seems to me that it can be abridged. Perhaps you would like to comment on that.

**Mr. Roger Tassé (Deputy Minister of Justice):** Yes, Mr. Chairman. Pursuant to Section 1 it would be possible for Parliament or the Legislature to impose limits or restrictions on the right of association or freedom of association.

As I pointed out yesterday to the Committee, these rights that are spelled out in the Charter are not absolute rights and they are susceptible to restrictions and limitations.

For example, in 1962, the Supreme Court held that at the time where we had a similar freedom set out in the Canadian Bill of Rights, the Supreme Court held that dissolving the SIU [Seafarers International Union] would not violate the right of association since the union was engaged in illegal acts infringing the rights of others, so it held that in that case it was a legitimate exercise on the part of parliament to restrict the freedom of association that the SIU, the union in that case, had claimed should be recognized.

**Miss Campbell:** I agree that there were illegal activities in that particular case, but going to a broader area where you have a group of fishermen, let us say, asking for a province to pass legislation so that they can organize and have collective bargaining, and one would assume that they did not have it at common law, and that this particular section will give it to them unless a province would strictly abridge it. Take it away.

**Mr. Tassé:** I think in effect this charter would not go as far as to require that there be federal or provincial legislation that would allow for recognition of the right, but the legislation that exists would have to be legislation that would allow for the expression of that right to take form and take place without undue limitation. So in effect if the objectives are of …

**Miss Campbell:** This would supersede any provincial legislation?

**Mr. Tassé:** Well, I am not sure that I am going that far. I think what I am saying, I think that provincial legislation and federal legislation would have to be read as against this freedom that the charter would recognize of two individuals to organize themselves and associate for that purpose.

As long as the purpose of the association is a legal one, is a legitimate one, the legislature or the parliament could not intervene to restrict them.

**Miss Campbell:** It comes from the common law, the common law that we have established from Great Britain?

**Mr. Tassé:** Well, under the common law, I suppose in effect it would be possible for parliament or the legislature to restrict the rights in whatever way, shape or form, but that is the purpose of a charter. It is to in effect entrench and constrain the exercise of legislative authority of the parliament and the legislatures so that they could not be taken away or unreasonably tampered with.

**Miss Campbell:** How far does this right at common law go? Does it give them the right to strike and the right to lock-out until it is taken away? Now, I am not sure, I think the right to strike is usually given.

**Mr. Jean Chrétien (Minister of Justice):** We can give you an answer on that.

**Miss Campbell:** Well, I am sure *I* can say that one more group of people at least in the east who would like to *see* this in order to have the right to go to freedom of association without having to ask to have legislation so that they can associate.

I mean, my understanding of the Maritime Fishermen's Union is that they would like to have the right to form a union. Even though they say Maritime Fishermen's Union, there is an element there of discrepancy.

But their provincial legislatures must give them the right. This gives them the right. If I take freedom of association, as given in common-law, the right to collective bargaining on the part of any group, they do not need to seek any further than this law, and then it would be up to the provincial governments to abridge that right.

**Mr. Tassé:** Well, I would doubt that they would be happy with just the possibility of their being in a position to exercise their common law right. I think we have seen that in almost all jurisdictions, there has been a need for the organization of relationships between the employers and the employees, so that, you know, there will be a framework within which these relationships will take place and this Charter here does not go that far as to provide for that, but it says that the right exists, but the implementation of it and the organization of relationship, for example, in the labour field is something that would be either the responsibility of Parliament or the Legislature, but they are the ones that will decide how these relationships could take place, and what happens if certain things happen. If there is a strike, for example, in the work condition, it could place that would be recognized as a legal act.

**Miss Campbell:** In other words, they would abridge it they will abridge the basic common law.

**Mr. Tassé:** Well, it would give a statutory constitutional basis for these rights, but it is not the full answer to all of the questions that may arise in the context of employer and employee relationships.

**Miss Campbell:** Well, then you go back to the Seafarer's case where it says the activities were illegal.

**Mr. Tassé:** And for that purpose, the Supreme Court in effect recognized that what Parliament had done in terms of restricting the rights of that association to exist was valid because of the purpose that the Union had set for itself, it was recognized as being in effect, unwarranted, if not illegal.

**Miss Campbell:** Yes. (4: 47–9)

## Proposed Amendments or Additions to Fundamental Freedoms

**Mr. Fred Pennington (Board Member, Canadian Council on Social Development):** We believe that the extent to which a society tolerates and encourages freedom of expression is an indicator of the stability of the nation, as well as an indicator of its receptivity to change, we suggest that the Committee consider wording in Section 2, particularly which would reflect the importance of freedom of expression for both individuals and organizations. ...

We would respectfully remind the Committee of the key recommendation of the Task Force on Government Information Policy that:

1. The right of Canadians to full, objective and timely information and the obligation of the state to provide such information about its programs and policies be publicly declared and stand as the foundation for new government policies in the field. This right might be comprehended within a new constitution in the context of freedom of expression. (19: 27–8)

...

**Senator Duff Roblin (PC, Manitoba):** I really have three points I would like to inquire about. The first relates to the type of freedom which is not mentioned in Section 2, but which, perhaps, deserves some consideration in a Bill of Rights, and that is freedom of information.

I believe you may be aware that bills have been introduced into the House of Commons of the federal legislature to provide for freedom of information. They have not yet become laws, but they are certainly being considered very carefully. It occurs to me that you might have some opinion as to whether or not the subject of freedom of information is a suitable one to include in a Bill of Rights which would have some priority over regular legislation and give status, as it is thought, to that aspect of freedom which would not be accorded to a regular bill of Parliament. Should freedom of information be considered by this Committee as one of the freedoms we should pay special attention to?

**Ms. Alison Hardy (Historian, Media Club of Canada):** I consider freedom of information to be an important subject, and I am glad that there has been a continuing development in this field, so that when we have all the freedom of information we need, it will be well and sensibly set up based upon experiences in other countries. It is important that if you are going to have an informed citizenry, that the government provide information to them to educate them. People look to the government now for so much in the line of information. It is a tremendous source of information. I think it is very valuable that there is an opportunity for citizens to get in touch with their member of Parliament or department of government, either at the federal, provincial or municipal level, and to obtain the required information. ...

**Senator Roblin:** So I take it you would like to see some protection for freedom of information in this bill. (24: 20–2)

## Chapter Seven

# Democratic Rights

Democratic rights of citizens

**3.** Every citizen of Canada has, ~~without unreasonable distinction or limitation~~, the right to vote in an election of members of the House of Commons or of a legislative assembly and to be qualified for membership therein.

Maximum duration of legislative bodies

**4.** (1) No House of Commons and no legislative assembly shall continue for longer than five years from the date fixed for the return of the writs at a general election of its members.

Continuation in special circumstances

(2) In time of real or apprehended war, invasion or insurrection, a House of Commons may be continued by Parliament and a legislative assembly may be continued by the legislature beyond five years if such continuation is not opposed by the votes of more than one-third of the members of the House of Commons or the legislative assembly, as the case may be.

Annual sitting of legislative bodies

**5.** There shall be a sitting of Parliament and of each legislature at least once every twelve months.

## Commentary

There was remarkably little discussion of the sections of the Charter given the title "Democratic Rights." Unlike other parts of the Charter, no witnesses or groups were interested in them; their constituency was, in effect, all Canadians.

Only one change was made to the Democratic Rights provisions of the Charter at the Joint Committee. The phrase "without unreasonable distinction or limitation" was excised from it given the application of the general limitations clause contained in section 1 of the Charter. The debate at the Joint Committee centred on this and four other issues. On section 3, in addition to their concern over the phrase "unreasonable distinction," Aboriginal groups were concerned about the clause's potential application to enable non-First Nations people to vote in First Nations government elections. Second, the NDP, the Canadian Jewish Congress, the Newfoundland Bar Association, the CCLA, and the Vancouver People's Law School expressed concern that the standard used in section 4(2) to "suspend" democracy was too subjective. Third, there was debate over the majority necessary to suspend the House under section 4(2). And fourth, both the CBA and the Canadian Council on Social Development wanted to enshrine a "right to information" in the Democratic Rights section. The government opposed recognizing such a right on the very unconvincing grounds set out within that it intended to enact legislation on the subject (which it eventually did by way of the Access to Information Act).[1] More likely, it opposed the inclusion of such a right because of the positive obligations that it would impose on government.

### The Right to Vote

**Professor Max Cohen (Canadian Jewish Congress):** ... We like that, but we think there is something missing there [in section 3]. What is missing is that the Section does not include the right to take office. It talks about being qualified, but it does not talk about the right to take office; you might have all the qualifications and have the right to vote. So you had better amend that to make it perfectly clear that if you have all those qualifications, then you equally have the right to take office, which is not there now. (7: 87)

...

**Ms. Mary Eberts (Legal Counsel, Advisory Council on the Status of Women):** Similar problems arise with the restrictions that might, according to this charter, be placed on the right to vote, to hold public office and to participate in referenda. At the moment the charter simply says that these are not to be subject to unreasonable limitations and we think that we have a list of unreasonable limitations in Section 15 that should be applied to those clauses. (9: 131)

...

**Mr. Jean Lapierre, MP (LIB, Quebec):** There are some other places where you make recommendations. Section 3, for instance, you say that the phrase "unreasonable distinction and limitation" is too vague and should be removed. I think it was put there to make sure that voters are more than 18 years old, and prisoners do not vote and things like that. If we were to remove it, then where will be the majority rule and so on?

**Mr. Wilson Head (President, National Black Coalition):** Well, all we are saying is that you should state it clearly. If you are talking about 18-year-olds. if you are saying 6-year-olds voting, or under 18s then state it. Because what is "unreasonable changes from one generation to another"? All we have to do is to look back over the last ten years and see how "reasonableness" has changed. (22: 21)

**Mr. Sykes Powderface (Vice-President, National Indian Brotherhood of Canada):** Section 3 provides that every citizen has the right to vote, without unreasonable distinction or limitation, in any election of members of the House of Commons or of a legislative assembly. The term "legislative assembly" is not defined. As a generic term, it could be interpreted to include an Indian band council. It must be clear that Section 3 cannot be used to enable non-Indians, who are resident on reserve lands, to vote in Indian government elections. It should also be clear that Section 3 cannot be used to invalidate the residency requirements in northern areas that have been proposed by the Dene and the Inuit, to ensure that the permanent native populations have political power, rather than the transient Euro-Canadian population. (27: 86)

### Continuation of Parliament in Times of Real or Apprehended War, Invasion, or Insurrection

**Professor Max Cohen (Canadian Jewish Congress):** Section 4 has that very important classical Canadian phrase with which we are so familiar in the War Measures Act – "real or apprehended," "in time of real or apprehended war, invasion or insurrection." Well, "real or apprehended" can now leave the Canadian scene. It makes no particular contribution to the understanding of the art of government or the nature of the emergency process. We think the emergency theory set out in [the Canadian Jewish Congress's brief] does not require the "real or apprehended" doctrine and we suggest its total elimination from the language of any Canadian legislation or any Canadian charter. (7: 87)

...

**Mr. Jean Lapierre, MP (LIB, Quebec):** On section 4(2) we have not had many representations, but you seem to be worried about the continuation of the House of Commons in special circumstances. But in practice I do not think anybody has to worry, because the practice has been that governments have lasted for less than four or five years. But you seem to be worried about the word "apprehended." I was a little surprised, because it is new for me.

**Mr. Wilson Head (President, National Black Coalition of Canada):** Well the word "apprehended" – and I looked it up in the dictionary to make sure I was right when I talked about it but that word to me is a very imprecise one. What is "apprehended"? Is it something that is going to happen, or something that you think is going to happen, or that there is evidence that it is going to happen, or how strong is the evidence? It seems to me that one has to be clear that it is going to happen, and then you should only restrict liberties to the extent that it is absolutely necessary, and as I have indicated in my comments to Mr. Nystrom that, in the case of discrimination, it is never necessary. (22: 21)

...

**Mrs. Diana Davidson (President, Vancouver People's Law School Society):** With respect now to the democratic rights section, the phrase "real or apprehended war, invasion or insurrection" should be deleted. Moreover, there is little support for the suspension of the right to vote contained in Section 4(2). The feeling is that once democracy is suspended temporarily, we run the risk of having lost it for good. Many have pointed out to me that at time of war the right to vote is even more important in order to provide a method by which we can signify our reactions to the way in which the war is being conducted. By way of example, I ask you only to consider the effect of suspending the right to vote in the United States during the Viet Nam War or in present day Israel's numerous apprehended and real emergencies. (32: 11–12)

...

[NDP MP Svend Robinson proposed three amendments: first, that the phrase "in time of real or apprehended war" be replaced by "in time of real or imminent war"; second, that the one-third requirement be changed to one-third "present or voting" – i.e., that in all cases a two-thirds majority of those present and voting would be required; third, that a new clause be added providing that "No continuation under Clause 4(2) of the House of Commons or a legislative assembly beyond five years shall last longer than six months but a continuation may be renewed under that subclause before it expires."]

**Mr. Svend Robinson, MP (NDP, BC):** The first proposal is that rather than the present wording in Clause 4(2), "in time of real or apprehended war, invasion or insurrection," that we should be using the word "imminent" to substitute for the word "apprehended." The reason for that is the word "apprehended" allows our courts virtually no jurisdiction whatsoever to go behind that declaration. These are the same words that are contained in the War Measures Act, Mr. Chairman, which has certainly been judicially determined in a very narrow fashion to be a subjective kind of test. Is it apprehended or is it not? It does not matter whether there are any objective grounds for that, the only thing that matters is whether or not the government believes, that could be without any reasonable grounds, believes that there is an impending war, invasion or insurrection.

This would substitute the word "imminent" which would give the courts an opportunity to review that declaration because, Mr. Chairman, what we are talking about is a suspension of democracy itself, and surely when we are talking about something that fundamental, the courts should have an opportunity to ensure that this declaration which is made of an apprehended war, invasion or insurrection indeed has some objective basis. I would point out that this particular amendment has been proposed by, among others, the Canadian Jewish Congress, the Newfoundland Bar Association, the Canadian Civil Liberties Association and the Vancouver People's Law School.

It may be argued by some that there is a safeguard of requiring a two thirds majority, however clearly that would not get around the concern which is raised with respect to the totally subjective nature of this test.

It may also be argued that there is a test of demonstrable justifiability; however, in response to that I would point out, Mr. Chairman, that all that has to be demonstrably justified is that there was an apprehension. It does not have to be demonstrably justified that there was any basis for that apprehension, merely that the apprehension itself existed.

So that is the purpose of the first proposed amendment, Mr. Chairman. ...

The purpose of the second proposed amendment, very briefly, is to clarify what majority is required, that we are talking about those persons who are indeed present and voting at the time the vote is taken and not one third of the total number of members who may in fact be eligible to vote.

The final section is perhaps the most important, Mr. Chairman, because what the proposed Clause 4(3) would indicate is that there cannot be an indefinite denial of the right of the citizens of Canada to decide for themselves who is to govern them. There cannot be an indefinite suspension of democracy.

As Clause 4(2) is now worded, once a decision is made by two thirds of the members of a federal Parliament or provincial legislature to extend their mandate beyond five years, that extension can be indefinite, and what this suggests is a very reasonable procedural safeguard. It suggests that there should be a review at least every six months to ensure that it is still the will of Parliament of the legislative assemblies that this state of emergency exists, that this suspension of democracy should be continued.

Now, again, there may be some who suggest that demonstrable justifiability should apply here, but surely there should be an option on the elected representatives of the people to determine for themselves at some point, at periodic intervals, whether the suspension of democracy should indeed continue.

So that is the purpose of that clause, Mr. Chairman. I would note that the ramifications of a declaration of emergency are very serious indeed because it has been held by the highest court of this land that when there has been a declaration of emergency, that the division of powers no longer exists. Under Section 91 and Section 92 the federal government can move in and encroach on any provincial powers.

So when we are talking about a suspension of democracy, when we are talking about a possible reallocation of powers in Canada, surely it is not unreasonable to suggest that elected members should have an opportunity to pass judgment on that at periodic intervals. (43: 90–2)

...

**The Hon. Jake Epp, MP (PC, Manitoba):** Mr. Chairman, regarding the amendment and the question, first of all, of real or apprehended war. If I understand correctly, the present regime that governs this area is the fact that we are at a situation where the government as such at the present time, and where governments in the past have been at a grave or probable danger and that the New Democratic Party amendment would move us toward a position of a clear and present danger.

I have difficulty with their amendment for this reason, that I believe it is the responsibility of government to govern and while all of us have seen the experience of 1970 and do not want to see that repeated,

I do feel on the other hand, on the other side of that balance well, so to speak, there is the need to govern, especially at that period of time.

For that reason I do not like the idea of "imminent" because who then determines what is imminent, and I think in this case it is the elected representatives of the people that must decide that rather than take it to court where the very delay of the action could cause grave difficulty and in fact danger to the country.

The second amendment, I believe that in view of the suspension of democratic rights it is not sufficient for those members who are present and voting, I believe it should be one third of the members in the House, in terms of membership, the people I believe have a right to know as to their representatives.

The last Clause, Clause 3, appeals to me. I believe that the government itself would want the reassurance of the House every six months in terms of approval of the position that they have taken.

**The Joint Chairman (Mr. Joyal):** Thank you very much, Honourable Jake Epp. Mr. Hawkes on the same point. (43: 92–3)

...

**Mr. Jim Hawkes, MP (PC, Alberta):** Mr. Minister, the quorum in the House of Commons is 20, and is it conceivable that the unanimous agreement of those 20 people in quorum would have the force in law to continue the Parliament of Canada beyond five years in the extreme case with that wording?

**The Hon. Robert Kaplan, MP (Acting Minister of Justice):** Yes.

**Mr. Hawkes:** And that is satisfactory to the Government?

**Mr. Kaplan:** Well, how many members of Parliament might have survived to that particular time given the kind of war or other incident that one could imagine?

**Mr. Hawkes:** Do we also with the wording have the situation where ...

**Mr. Kaplan:** I am making the point that it is reasonably flexible and it is tending to be balanced in favour of the emergency power, but the apprehension has to be bona fide and I do not think Mr. Robinson gave sufficient weight to that. The apprehension has to be a genuine bona fide apprehension and once it is, as Mr. Epp said, he wanted the government and the Parliament to have the authority to operate. (43: 93–5)

...

**Mr. Robert Bockstael (LIB, Manitoba):** Thank you, Mr. Chairman. The members of the Liberal party on the government side feel that the word "imminent" is not a suitable word. "Imminent" could mean a month, a week, a day, and we are convinced that the word "apprehended" is more apropos and we want to stick to the word that better describes the potential or the possibility of such a situation. So that is to the first amendment which the NDP have proposed and we hold to our original text which wants to use an apprehended situation.

In the second instance that the House would have to come together every six months to decide whether it is allowed to continue, this is unnecessary; it would depend on the nature of the urgency. The position taken by the government to continue beyond its normal term of office would have to be evaluated and justified and it does not make sense, if the Cabinet was maintaining the work of the government during a recess, to have to bring all the members back so that at least two thirds are in favour of continuing at the time of an emergency; it does not seem a sound proposal.

Calling an election in such a situation would place the country with executive management of the country while we are trying to decide whether we are going to have a new Minister of National Defence, and it is not consequential. So we oppose that amendment that they propose and we hold to our original text also which indicated that we would want two thirds of the members of the House in favour of continuing rather than two thirds of the members present. We, on this side, would vote against all three amendments.

**Mr. Epp:** May I ask Mr. Bockstael what about the third part of the amendment? Mr. Bockstael, would you address that? ...

**Mr. Bockstael:** The third one, no continuation unless the assembly is called together within six months automatically to renew or extend its mandate. ... We do not agree with that one because it would necessitate calling Parliament to see if it can keep on going in the middle of a war, if you use it in that context. (43: 96–8)

[Each of the three proposed amendments failed.]

## The "Right to Information"

**Mr. James McGrath (PC, Newfoundland):** Mr. Chairman, I move that Clause 5 of the proposed constitution act, 1980 be amended by ... and (b) adding thereto ... the following heading and Clause:

Right to Information
5. Everyone has the right to have reasonable access to information under the control of any institution of any government. (43: 101–2)

[The NDP proposed a sub-amendment to clarify that the Tories' amendment would apply to federal, provincial, and municipal governments. It was defeated.]

...

**The Hon. Robert Kaplan (Acting Minister of Justice):** ... I would like to indicate that the Government opposes this amendment to the Charter because of considering it a very serious abandonment by Parliament of a responsibility to deal with the question of access to information.

Our objection is not because we disagree that there should be a right of the citizen to have information. Far from it. On that subject, we are putting our legislation where our position is, and we have made it clear to Canadians and tabled in the House a very substantial document which is quite similar to the document and to the approach which was taken by the Conservatives when they formed the government, although I think ours goes further in giving information and access to information of the citizens.

We think this is the proper approach to take, the Parliament of Canada and the other legislatures taking their responsibilities to establish proper rules and proper procedures for giving citizens access to information. ... This is a new area. It is an area in which I think legislatures are far more capable, and governments are far more capable of designing proper rules than are judges. (43: 105)

**Mr. James McGrath (PC, Newfoundland):** The Minister suggested that in some way this amendment to entrench freedom of information in the Charter would somehow pre-empt or prejudice the right of the House of Commons to legislate in this area. The same can be said about the whole Charter of Rights. We had evidence presented to the Committee to indicate that many people felt that the best way to protect rights was by the statute route as opposed to the constitution entrenchment route, and so I say to the Minister, through you, Mr. Chairman, with great respect, that that argument just does not wash, because what we are proposing to do is to enshrine in the constitution the principle of freedom of information. It would then require legislation to put that into practice.

In other words, you cannot have one without the other, and what we are asking the Committee to do is to enshrine the principle, which has already been accepted by the government because it did propose to legislate in this area, and to me it just makes sense to have it enshrined in the constitution so that the legislation, which will be complementary to the principle which we would enshrine, would then spell out the parameters or the regulations under which freedom of information would operate.

Now, I do not think I can go any further than that without oversimplifying it.

Mr. Chairman, to conclude I want to point out to you that there were two groups that came before the Committee which strongly recommended that we enshrine the principle of freedom of information, The Canadian Council on Social Development, and they made the point that it would serve as a reminder to both governments and citizens that government exists only through and with the consent of the people.

The other group that appeared before us was the Canadian Bar Association, and they talked about the right to information being a twin right with the right to privacy.

We all know the extent of government in Canada, the growth of the bureaucracy and the threat that it imposes on the individual in terms of an individual's right to know what the government knows about him. Forget all about the workings of government as we see it day to day in Parliament, just take it to the level of the individual, an individual could have a bad report made with respect to an investigation concerning a security matter or a credit matter or any matter you could think of, and with the computerization of information and the use of the SIN number by the government and by institutions, that wrong information in some cases or information no longer relevant could plague that person for the rest of his life and he, surely, under those circumstances would be entitled to know just exactly what was in his social insurance number file and he would have that right under the freedom of information.

Of course, the other well known arguments with respect to freedom of information regarding the government investigations and the ongoing day to day workings of the government are so well known to members it is not necessary to bring them out here, but I would suggest to the Minister, in conclusion, Mr. Chairman, that by voting to enshrine freedom of information in the constitution in no way interferes with or prejudices the right of the government to legislate, indeed it imposes upon the government an obligation to legislate in order to put in place the regulations to implement the principle that we would be enshrining in the constitution.

**Mr. Perrin Beatty, MP (PC, Ontario):** What we are saying is that the constitution should recognize for the first time a very fundamental right and that is that if you look at the control of information as a property right, that information, either about ourselves as individuals or about the activities of our government which operates by consent of the people, that that property right belong not to the Government of Canada or the government of any province but to the people of Canada, and that the positive onus is put upon the government to justify either coercing private information about an individual from him or to justify withholding information from him in the name of the national interest or the provincial interest.

This is why, Mr. Chairman, I feel that when we are considering so many other rights for inclusion in the constitution, for example rights to vote, rights not to be discriminated against because of age, what we are asking the government to do, if they are determined to oppose the amendment that we are moving, is to tell us why these other rights are more compelling, are more important in a democracy to our citizens than the right to freedom of information, the right to control of information about ourselves, the right to access to information about how government conducts its activities.

We believe that this right is central in a democratic system of government, we believe that it in no way derogates from the government's responsibility to pass legislation to give access to information; indeed, it confers that positive obligation and we feel that it is a right which is on a level, which is equal at least to that of the various other rights conferred in the constitution, that consequently should be included in the Charter of Rights and that we should make this recognition of this very fundamental change in policy on the part of the government with this new constitution we are proposing for Canada. ... (43: 112–14).

**Mr. Robinson:** Mr. Chairman, Mr. Beatty referred to certain other rights and made specific reference to the right to vote and asked quite properly why the right to freedom of information should be considered any less important. I would like to look at it from a slightly different angle and to suggest that the right to vote is surely predicated on access to information, that an informed citizen is essential for the proper exercise of democracy, and that if a government can withdraw information at will, be that a federal or a provincial or municipal government, or choose what information that government wants to give to its citizens, then how can it be argued that they have all of the information that is required to make an informed decision as to who can best represent their interest in Parliament or legislative assemblies; or for that matter, when we talk about the freedom of the press, how can it be argued that the full freedom of the press can be exercised when the press, who have a unique responsibility in society, are regularly denied information, basic information which they may wish to pass on to the people of Canada.

I would suggest that as well as being an essential principle in its own right, that if we are to fully recognize the principles contained in other sections of this proposed Charter, that we must include the principle of freedom of information. ...

I would like to just conclude, Mr. Chairman, if I may by referring to a quote which I take from the excellent report of the Canadian Bar Association, *Towards a New Canada* and they indicate that they have for some time been championing the political right of freedom of information. They quote Ralph Nader as saying, and I quote: "A well informed citizenry is the lifeblood of democracy." The democratic process cannot function adequately without timely information about the activities of Parliament.

And that would apply equally to provincial legislatures. I would hope, Mr. Chairman, that this fundamental principle, this principle which is so essential in Canadian democracy would be recognized in this statement of what purports to be fundamental Rights and Freedoms. (43: 114–15).

## Chapter Eight

# Mobility Rights

**MOBILITY RIGHTS**

~~Rights of citizens to move~~ Mobility of citizens

**6.** (1) Every citizen of Canada has the right to enter, remain in and leave Canada.

Rights to move and gain livelihood

(2) Every citizen of Canada and every person who has the status of a permanent resident of Canada has the right

(a)  to move to and take up residence in any province; and
(b)  to pursue the gaining of a livelihood in any province

Limitation

(3) The rights specified in subsection (2) are subject to

(a)  any laws or practices of general application in force in a province other than those that discriminate among persons primarily on the basis of province of present or previous residence; and
(b)  any laws providing for reasonable residency requirements as a qualification for the receipt of publicly provided social services

Affirmative action programs

(4) Subsections (2) and (3) do not preclude any law, program or activity that has as its object the amelioration in a province of conditions of individuals in that province who are socially or economically disadvantaged if the rate of employment in that province is below the rate of employment in Canada.

## Commentary

Mobility rights were a key component of Trudeau's vision of the Charter as a nation-building instrument; they would ensure that residents of one province would be entitled to rights when they moved to other provinces. The discussion of mobility rights at the Joint Committee focused on several discrete issues: concerns in the North; the impact of pipeline construction in the Northwest Territories and Yukon, specifically the influx of people from the south and the impact on the Aboriginal population; preferential hiring generally; restricting land ownership to provincial residents; and eligibility periods for receipt of social services.

No amendments to section 6 were added at the Joint Committee. The addition of clause 4 allowing preferential programs for provinces that had an unemployment rate higher than the national average was added at the behest of Newfoundland in the November 1981 accord. There was much discussion about this general problem at the Joint Committee.

### General: Citizens and Permanent Residents

**Professor Max Cohen (Chairman, Select Committee on the Constitution of Canada of the Canadian Jewish Congress):** And now, Section 6 is a very important area of mobility rights. Here, we are concerned that the section begins, "Every citizen." We are not sure if you really want to confine that mobility right only to citizens. What about permanent residents? What about landed immigrants? What about refugees? – a whole category of people legally in Canada, one way or another! They ought to have total mobility rights. We ought not to have two, three, or four categories of mobile citizens in Canada.

In the same Section 6, we feel the words "permanent resident" has now become a term of art and should be regarded as such, and, therefore, they should have the full protection as well as the citizens of Section 6(1). Finally, because we are signatories to the Convention on Refugees of 1951, we feel that refugees also should have certain rights of mobility which this particular section of the charter would not give to them once they are admitted refugees in the classical definition of that term as defined in the Convention of 1951 itself. (7: 87–8)

**Mr. Jean Lapierre, MP (LIB, PQ):** When you refer to a person having the status of a permanent resident, does that include landed immigrants?

**The Hon. Jean Chrétien (Minister of Justice):** The answer is yes. ... They are landed immigrants. Those are the people whom we wished to cover as there is a certain period during which a person may be permanent in Canada but not yet a Canadian citizen. We would not want this charter to exclude legitimate residents of Canada who have not yet obtained their status as citizens.

**Mr. Lapierre:** Fine. Now, would this section effect the legislative provisions provided in the Public Service Act which requires that people be Canadian citizens before they are employed?

**Mr. Chrétien:** I do not know. I will check that out and reply later. (3: 47–9)

### General

**Miss Nicole Dumouchel (Board Member, Canadian Council on Social Development):** These clauses [Section 6(3)(a) and (b)] would well have the effect of limiting the mobility rights as specified in Section 6(2)(b) to the extent of reducing the nation to a series of sovereign states.

As we understand this section, it would allow provincial governments to prevent Canadian citizens and landed immigrants from moving between or within provinces, on whatever grounds the provinces might enact as law, except residency. Though the provinces would be subject to the general prohibition of discrimination on human rights grounds, such as age, race, sex, national origin, they could be allowed to prevent Canadians from moving into their province for any other legislated reason they choose. Though Provinces have this right now, under the British North America Act, they must bow to national interest when required. Section 6(3)(a) appears to extend provincial rights regarding migration, and to further limit federal jurisdiction. (19: 28–9)

**Mr. Jim Hawkes, MP (PC, Alberta):** ... we have been assured by ministers in the House of Commons and by lots of speeches by members on the opposite side, that the Government of Canada is intent on doing a wonderful thing in this new constitution of ensuring mobility rights for Canadians. Now, your brief, and it takes you almost two or three pages to point out to us that in your judgment what we would be doing by putting this wording in the constitution of Canada is two very important things: we would be opening the door in a legal sense to considerably more restriction of mobility than is currently the case today. That is the first point you make and I think you make it eloquently. Am I correct?

**Ms. Nicole Dumouchel (Board Member, Canadian Council on Social Development):** Yes, we are questioning the restriction on mobility quite definitely. And the creation of a series of sovereign states which would give more power for the final authority to the provinces and reduce the quality and strength of Canada.

**Mr. Hawkes:** In other words, what this section would do would give the constitutional approval to provincial governments to be more restrictive in terms of allowing people to come into their provinces?

**Ms. Dumouchel:** Yes, definitely. (19: 34)

## Concerns for the North

**Senator Paul Lucier (LIB, Yukon):** Mr. Minister, my questions really pertain to the Mobility Rights Clause ... as they relate to the North. I would like to start out by saying that northerners generally agree with the concept of mobility rights.

**Some hon. Members:** Hear, Hear.

**Senator Lucier:** In fact since only the natives were originally there, most of us are there enjoying the North because we had an opportunity to go there and to seek employment and to make our homes there. So we do agree generally with the concept of mobility rights. What we are concerned with is with the possibility of the northern gas pipeline with a very real probability of it being built now, there could be a very large influx of people into the North in a very short period of time, which could have a devastating effect on the people of the Yukon. I speak of the Yukon right now but I am sure that this will affect the Northwest Territories in later years.

I am wondering if something cannot be done in conjunction with Section 6 to protect the Yukon from the possibility of this influx of people coming in. The government of the Yukon Territory went to great lengths during the preparation for the pipeline to protect themselves against that type of thing happening. I am really very concerned that, for instance, the whole Yukon consists of 25,000 people, and it is not unlikely that the pipeline would bring in 25,000 people more. That does not sound like very large numbers to the people down here, maybe, but you could compare it to 8 million people dropping into Ontario for a couple of years. I think when you look at it in that light you will find that it could have a devastating effect and I am just wondering if something could not be put in or if in some way the people of the Yukon and the people of the North could be protected against that type of thing happening.

**The Hon. Jean Chrétien (Minister of Justice):** I do not know how Mr. Lucier, I am not in a position to tell you clearly how that can be done. Of course there is some limitation in terms of employment to outsiders in the construction of the pipeline in the North. I say that under this provision of mobility rights it will be possible to pass legislation that could provide for affirmative action. I think that affirmative action should not be based only on a criteria of the origin of the person. I think that would be against the law. We have to recognize the danger in the Yukon situation where there could be a huge influx of people coming and creating the same type of social disturbance that existed in Alaska at the time of the Alaska oil pipeline. We have some problems at this moment about this Charter of Rights and the affirmative action that exists in our own legislation. I think that we will have to study and try to find some solution. Among these solutions that were provided in this Bill was hiring for people coming from outside should be done outside, that the people will not just flock into Whitehorse and wait for a job there; and the question of training, and so on.

There are some areas there that ought to be looked into, I realize that the social impacts of short term projects like the construction of the pipeline will last only a few years; and the stability of the society in those areas after the construction occurs, or during the construction time. We are looking into that. I am aware of your concern. What we are seeking at this moment is to make sure that we do not limit the rights of Canadians to move across Canada, and in fact, in the Yukon most of the residents now who are not Indians have come from all parts of Canada including Windsor, Ontario. (3: 31–2)

**Mr. George Braden (M.L.A., Leader of the Elected Member of the Executive Committee, Government of the Northwest Territories):** The

Northwest Territories has a small population consisting largely of Native people, many of whom are only now beginning to develop the skills in the trades which will enable them to compete in the southern Canadian job market. Now with the probability of substantial activity in the oil and gas field in the Northwest Territories, there is every likelihood that a sizeable labour force will be required. In the absence of any legislation to give preference in hiring to northern residents, it is most probable that companies engaged in such economic activity in the territories will import labour from the south and may make little or no effort to train and employ northern residents.

The concept of mobility rights would be acceptable if there is indeed going to be an equal exchange of labour between various parts of Canada. I am afraid however, that in the north-south context, the traffic is going to move only one way, that is, southern labour coming north. There will be hardly any movement of labour going south. Economic conditions for northern residents are difficult at the best of times. In my view, the constitution should recognize the reality of the northern frontier with its delicate balances. In their present stage of development, the Native people of the Northwest Territories are simply not able to compete with an unrestricted flow of labour from the south, and I would urge you to find some means by which the territories could be exempted from the mobility rights provisions. (12: 60–1)

...

**Miss Mary Simon (Member, Inuit Committee on National Issues [ICNI]):** The main reason for including mobility rights in the Charter is to encourage the creation of a true economic union within Canada. ICNI supports this concept which is intended to strengthen the economy in all areas of Canada. However for cultural, economic, social as well as environmental reasons, an additional limitation is required in Section 6(3). Both the northern environment and Inuit communities are particularly susceptible to significant environmental and social impacts when faced with large-scale development. Laws or practices of federal application, as provided in Section 6(3)(a), may be sorely inadequate to meet the special needs of Canada's North and to protect Inuit culture.

The same is true in relation to our northern economy. The massive influx of a temporary workforce from southern parts of Canada when northern projects are announced, if unrestricted, may have severe consequences in the North. In such a situation, we would be unable to compete. Northern unemployment would not be reduced. Therefore, special protections are necessary in order to develop a viable northern economy and to establish a northern workforce. The principle of priority of contracts and employment for northern residents appears to be inconsistent with the mobility rights in the Charter. Therefore, benefits owed to Inuit under the James Bay and Northern Quebec agreement may never be realized. The loss of this benefit, which presently has the force of law, is unacceptable. (16: 11–12)

**Mr. David Joe (Legal Counsel, Council for Yukon Indians):** [It was previously expressed] that there would be no preferential hiring in the Yukon. That could be declared to be unconstitutional. At this point in time, with the Northern Pipeline Act in the regulations, there is allowance for preferential hiring for Yukoners, and that section could be struck out; that area concerns us. (18: 14–15)

**Mr. Ron Irwin, MP (LIB, Ontario):** Now, on mobility, you have indicated that you have serious reservations. You are opposed to having the mobility rights enshrined so that Southern Canadians can go north to work. How about the reverse? How would you feel if, say, Saskatchewan, Alberta, Ontario or any of the provinces said that you had to be a resident for two or three years in that province or you could not work there?

**Mr. Harry Allen (Chairman, Council for Yukon Indians):** Well, I guess a lot of it depends on the political situation. I think in the Yukon, the needs and aspirations of the Yukon Indian people in terms of making decisions, I think the Yukon Indian people have to play a major role. In terms of right now I think our people, around approximately 80 per cent of our people are unemployed. This lack of economic development in the Yukon Territory, the training in terms of our people is very low. So taking all these circumstances into account I think that we have some type of clause of residency in terms of the Yukon territory to ensure that the Yukon Indian people get some of the benefits of employment, the training and some of the benefits that come from development or whatever occurs in the Yukon.

**Mr. Irwin:** All right. You make an economic argument but I would like to deal with the cultural argument. I know that from a recent report, that by intrusion of television, basically from Southern Canada, and mostly American, it has changed significantly the culture of the North. For instance, Indians who are usually peaceful one to one, even though they are in a very hostile environment, are fighting more and the report I saw says there is a direct relationship to the violence they are seeing on the television that is coming in from the South, *Hockey Night in Canada, Starsky and Hutch* and this type of thing. Would you agree that there is a cultural intrusion into the north from the south? What is it doing to your own culture?

**Mr. David Joe (Legal Counsel, Council for Yukon Indians):** The answer to that is yes, there is a cultural impact. There would be a devastating cultural impact if you were to leave the mobility clause as is; and as I can recall, in our participation before the Lysyk Inquiry, which was an inquiry established to determine the social and economic impact which would accompany the construction of a pipeline with the capital costs of approximately six billion dollars, we were told there would be approximately 2,000 people on a daily basis during the construction period that would be coming to the Yukon. I cannot imagine – and I shudder to think what would be the cultural impact of those transients coming into the Yukon.

We can appreciate the sensitivity that different provinces have with respect to their own respective aspiration, whether or not they want a shifting workforce in this country or no. But we, as Yukon Indian people, do not feel that our cultural values should be left unprotected when there is an industrial onslaught through a transient workforce which would come for a very short period of time and make demands on the infrastructure up there which we are not, at this point in time, totally sure could secure and provide the kind of services that southerners generally desire.

**Mr. Irwin:** This makes more sense to me. I can understand the cultural onslaught. But it is very difficult to explain to someone in Alberta, Ontario or Newfoundland, why they cannot work out of their province. Canadians generally, I think, would accept the proposition that we are destroying a culture in the north, in fact several fragile cultures in the north. Perhaps a discrimination clause based on that type of proposition would be acceptable to Canadians at large, and, as has been said, you should not confuse unity with uniformity. It is important to all of us, as Canadians, that your culture should survive. ... (18: 28–9)

**Mr. Jim Hawkes, MP (PC, Alberta):** Just a couple of confirmatory questions. Your concern about mobility is on two sides, is that correct? You want to protect yourself against invasion, large influx of people, but to redress the disadvantage economic conditions there must be provision in the constitution for preferential hiring and training and programs of that kind and those should be clear and specific; those were the two major ...

**Mr. Harry Allen (Chairman, Council for Yukon Indians):** Yes. (18: 36)

...

**Mrs. Diana Davidson (President, Vancouver People's Law School Society):** Some compromise must be worked out between the interests of the residents of outlying areas and the interests of persons prepared to move to an area because of a particular job or because of a particular construction project. ... It can often create an impossible situation in which the people who are committed to an area are temporarily inundated with transient people who, when they leave, leave behind an upheaved economic situation and leave financial responsibilities for community projects which must be paid for by those remaining behind. I understand that Newfoundlanders are also very concerned about those mobility rights. (32: 13–14)

**The Hon. Jake Epp, MP (PC, Alberta):** There are serious concerns north of 60°, which is totally federal jurisdiction, so let us get away from the provinces for a bit; totally federal jurisdiction where your government itself through legislation such as the Northern Pipeline Agency have in fact passed laws which, under Clause 6, would in fact, discriminate. It would discriminate in favour of northern residents and especially, natives living north of 60°. I have no difficulty with that in terms of the resource development which is to take place in the north, which is to take place, that residents in those areas get first call on those jobs. I think that is also why Parliament passed the legislation relating to the Northern Pipeline.

Have you had any discussion with either the government of the Northwest Territories or of the Yukon? Or the National Indian Brotherhood, or the Council of Yukon Indians, for example, or the Minister of Northern Affairs asking that Minister how present federal legislation would be affected by Clause 6(2)?

**The Hon. Jean Chrétien (Minister of Justice):** Yes, we have had some discussion and I think some of the clauses of this pipeline legislation will have to be adjusted.

## On Restricting Land Ownership to Residents

**Mr. George Henderson, MP (LIB, PEI):** The Minister is probably aware of provincial legislation in the Province of Prince Edward Island and probably other provinces whereby the selling of land to non-residents, if you will, land over ten acres in acreage is prohibited to non-residents. Knowing Prince Edward Island of course has a limited amount of arable land to sort of head off the speculators from especially the U.S. but in other parts of the country, this legislation was put through and I believe challenged at the Supreme Court, and the Supreme Court upheld the provincial legislation.

I notice here also that there is a qualification of becoming a resident. Could I have clarification from the Minister that there is nothing within this legislation or this package that would supersede the provincial legislation of the Province of PEI in regards to land use?

**The Hon. Jean Chrétien (Minister of Justice):** Mr. Henderson, we discussed that during the summer at the conferences, and the possibility that this question of owning lands in the province could be affecting the legislation of PEI in terms of people who buy lands there, absentia ownership. The way I understand it, the mobility rights will not permit absentia ownership in the case of PEI.

We are not interfering, but the way I understand it, it will not supersede the provincial legislation in that matter. (3: 66)

## Preferential Hiring: Nova Scotia

**The Hon. John Buchanan (Premier of Nova Scotia):** There has been over the past number of months some comment, both political and editorial, that we have passed in Nova Scotia, or are proposing to pass, legislation which will restrict the movement of Canadians into our province and restrict people other than Nova Scotians in obtaining employment in our province.

I want to set the record very straight on that at the present time. That is completely incorrect. We have not on our books such legislation, nor do we contemplate such legislation. We believe Canadians should have a right to work in any part of this country, whether it is British Columbia, Nova Scotia, Newfoundland or in the Arctic or in the Northwest Territories or the Yukon. We believe Canadians have that right at the present time and it should continue.

But we have proposed and will propose in Nova Scotia that in matters maybe affecting off shore, if Nova Scotians are fully qualified, that these Nova Scotians be at least entitled to some form of preference to obtain a job, I repeat if they are fully qualified for that position.

I do not think anyone could really argue against that proposition, because it is a position which has been taken historically by the federal government and by the provincial governments throughout this country. I do believe that provinces should be able to continue to have a right of some form of determination of preferences within our provinces, contractual relationships, employment preferences of a qualified nature and that we should be very careful of entrenching in our constitution proposals which would absolutely do away with any form of provincial right on this kind of mobility right. (17: 46–7)

### Preferential Hiring: General

**Mr. Raymond J. Halley, Q.C. (President, Canadian Bar Association, Newfoundland Branch):** ...With regard to Section 6 dealing with mobility rights of Canadians, we certainly agree with this provision in principle. We are concerned in the province that despite the affirmative action provision of Section 15(2), the local employment preference provisions of our petroleum regulations may be ruled invalid by the courts. Particularly when reference is made to Section 6(3)(a). We feel that this Committee should give consideration to a designation of a province such as Newfoundland as a disadvantaged area. This would justify the province in enacting local employment preference provisions, on an interim basis hopefully, and of course these preferences would be eliminated when the economic benefit of the offshore resources put the province on an equal footing, not even with other Canadians but with the other members of the Atlantic Region. (9: 78)

**The Hon. Jake Epp, MP (PC, Manitoba):** I would like to get back from what you have been saying to the Northern Pipeline Agency Act. By what has now been euphemistically termed affirmative action, it need not only be for native people, it could be for other groups as well. Would the Chamber under the principle you have just enunciated, that is the delivery at the local level of certain goods and services, maybe we should leave it at services, at the local level, would that then confirm the validity of the hiring of native people, for example, in projects north of 60°, especially resource projects because those are the ones we are facing right now?

**Mr. Sam Hughes (President, Canadian Chamber of Commerce):** Our concern is with impediments to the free flow of labour in this particular case. If the hiring of local people did not mean that other people from other parts of Canada could apply for work and be logically hired at the same economic cost, then we would have some reason to question any law that excluded others. (8: 12–15)

**The Hon. James McGrath, MP (PC, Newfoundland):** The Minister, I was intrigued when the minister said that the government would have to change the northern pipeline legislation to conform with the provisions of this section of the bill. My question to the Minister is, there are two provinces that I know that have local hiring regulations, the Province of Newfoundland and the Province of Nova Scotia. There are other jurisdictions as well, for example, apart from the federal government itself with their hiring practices north of 60°, there are a number of municipalities that have local hiring practices.

My question to the Minister is: have you examined the local hiring practices and regulations of the Government of Newfoundland and the Government of Nova Scotia to determine whether or not they are inconsistent with the provision of Clause 6, because I think you can argue, and there were arguments from a number of witnesses, or at least one that I know of for sure, probably two, that there are certain circumstances where local hiring practices would not in fact be inconsistent with the right of free mobility. In other words, you can move where you want as long as you know that if you move to a certain area you are going to have to take your chances in terms of local people being given the first option to any jobs that may be open there. Now, I do not have any problem with that but my colleagues, I must confess, do seem to have a problem with it.

**Mr. Chrétien:** We debated that problem many, many times in front of this Committee. First I would like to say that Parliament has enacted some legislation, but not Nova Scotia. They have passed legislation but they have refrained from proclaiming the legislation and they have indicated that they do not have the intention of proclaiming it.

**Mr. McGrath:** They do not have the intention?

**Mr. Chrétien:** They have not given the intention of proclaiming it today, and I do not know what they will do in the future but it is not a problem at this time that is debated in the government. They have not decided to proclaim it. They might proclaim it tomorrow or 10 years from now, but it is not a hot issue, if I can use that term, at this moment.

I think that the problem, as we say, is that there can be some affirmative action by the provinces to create some opportunities, special opportunities for a special area of the province, but it cannot be discrimination based on the province of origin. The provincial government could decide that, for example, because of a social problem, say, quite easy in Newfoundland, in Labrador, for example, that they will give a priority for the resident of Labrador over the resident of Newfoundland and the rest of Canada. You will have to face the political responsibility of making that problem within your province, just like it might be that there might be an affirmative action in Quebec, say in the Gaspé area, if a discrimination, if I can use the term discrimination, applies to the resident of Quebec City and Montreal and Toronto on the same basis, then that is all right. What we do not want is the notion that based on the provincial residents and this is the concept that we are rejecting, because that way you are creating a concept of different citizenship across the land and we want the same rights to apply to all Canadians.

**Mr. McGrath:** In other words, if I understand you, it is all right to discriminate within a province, it is all right for a government by affirmative action to say that within a province only people who are resident within the set area may be eligible for employment on a project or an industry or a development that is taking place there, as long as you do not discriminate by province. You can discriminate by region, is that what you are saying? That is how I understand it.

**Mr. Chrétien:** Our problem, as I tried to explain to you, is discrimination based on the provincial barriers, the concept that you are a citizen of a province in relation to a citizen across the border to the next province. Within the province we do recognize that there is need for affirmative action and it can be done, and the provincial government will have to take the responsibility vis-à-vis its own electors, having to discriminate in terms of one as against the other.

**Mr. McGrath:** Let me put it to you another way. You have taken Labrador as an example and it is a very good example. The Province of Newfoundland could discriminate against people living on the island of Newfoundland but working in Labrador, but they could not discriminate against people living on the Quebec side of the boundary?

**Mr. Chrétien:** No. If there is a discrimination, it is for everybody outside of Labrador. Supposing someone becomes a resident of Labrador and Quebec is just joining, the discrimination will apply to the resident of St. John's, Newfoundland, of Corner Brook and to the citizen of Montreal. But if they go and reside there, that is another problem. He is a resident of Labrador.

**Mr. McGrath:** In the case of the Ontario government, let me just put it to you another way, the Ontario government may discriminate against people from southern Ontario working in northern Ontario, but they may not discriminate against people from Quebec working in Northern Ontario, is that what you are saying?

**Mr. Chrétien:** They can discriminate against both, but not only against the citizen of Quebec because he is a citizen of Quebec, or a citizen of Manitoba because he is a citizen of Manitoba. But if he puts a restriction on his own citizens, just like the rest of Canada, that is fine, to take his local responsibility that he wants to have an affirmative action in one area of the province. But the citizen of the other parts of the province, just like a citizen of the rest of Canada will be faced – we do not intervene in Parliament either. There is a right in the Charter that belongs to the citizen but not to the Parliament of Canada. (46: 82–4)

**Mr. Gordon Fairweather (Chief Commissioner, Canadian Human Rights Commission):** I am absolutely delighted to see that mobility rights are to be enshrined. I think most people in Canada, if you ask them, would think they had mobility rights. I think this is fine. I must say it is not only Newfoundland; the province of Quebec and the Construction Act also, and anyone living in this city knows the contretemps between Hull and Ottawa construction workers that exercised Premiers, First Ministers and everybody else. ...

If the Maritime Provinces, from where I come, had been restricted in mobility there would have been social revolution in this country and I think it is time that people remembered that. It is a very curious thing to think that now, when there is a little bit of change in prospect, barriers are to be put up. It sounds like medieval Europe. It is easier to get by in modern Europe, for people to have jobs, than it is in some provinces.

We are totally committed to this principle and I think 99 per cent of the people of Canada are. If Alberta had ever restricted Newfoundlanders or New Brunswickers, what kind of a country would we have had, or the great receiving province of Ontario. It is not the receiving province now, but it was. Look, do we not have anything in common as citizens? Surely we have. If we have not that, we are just wasting time here. (5: 19)

...

**Mr. Graeme T. Haig, Q.C. (Chairman of the Constitution Reform Committee, Canadian Chamber of Commerce):** Section 6 deals with but one of four elements that the Chamber regard as being very important to the economic development and job creation in Canada. Provincial laws favouring a specific business, the criteria being residency in that particular province, can, by definition, be at best, short-sighted, and at worst, coddling a business to the point that it is a weak business. It is not going up in an environment, tough, strong and competitive. The business of hiring preference from one province within a province to the exclusion of residences of other provinces, is to us abhorrent. It is a practice that exists in several of the ten provinces and something that we would regard with disfavour. We would regard, too, with a great deal of skepticism bordering on disfavour the practices of preferential purchasing from province to province. It breeds balkanization of what could otherwise be large world-scale companies enabling Canada to compete effectively internationally.

... I would add only that one area you did not touch on ... the free flow of capital. To us, one provincial premier saying: My province is not for sale; another provincial premier blocking the purchase from Atlantic Canada of a financial institute within his province is totally wrong and in both cases damaging to Canada. (8: 12)

## Economic Union

**Mr. Sam Hughes (President, Canadian Chamber of Commerce):** I would like to draw to your attention the concern of the business community of Canada to the subject known as economic union, that in our mind's eye is the free flow between the provinces of goods, services, capital and labour. We recognize that in the proposed statement under Section 6, that mobility of individuals has indeed been accepted. I would at this point like to question whether or not citizenship should be the test for mobility of people across Canada as it seems to be.

We have a concern that impediments exist between provincial jurisdictions that those impediments are creating economic hardships, not only with the jurisdictions but for Canada as a whole in the development of its export trade. We would be very pleased to discuss further with you the reason for the reduction of impediments in these four area, but I think at this time I will leave it as a simple statement of fact that we would like to have it happen and like to have it done within the constitution. (8: 6)

...

**Mr. Raymond J. Halley, Q.C. (President, Canadian Bar Association, Newfoundland Branch):** ... The commitment to an economic union as exemplified by the mobility of labour clause appears hollow when one province can be allowed to impede the development of resources in another province. Surely mobility rights should be extended to include mobility and free interprovincial access of goods, capital and services. (9: 82)

...

**Professor Max Cohen (Chairman, Select Committee on the Constitution of Canada of the Canadian Jewish Congress):** You may be interested to know how strange it is that we, as a united country of 113 years' experience of a great federal union, have less mobility than the recently born European Common Market. The Common Market has already worked out a system of total mobility for doctors and nurses, and the idea of Italian barristers in the Inns-of-Court frightens me. The very image of it as a picture; but there it is. The same is true of Italian nurses and of British nurses somewhere in south Germany; and the mobility now is to the point where it is supposed to be total. They are working on engineers, architects and others and I am told by students of the common market here that in due course, under the Treaty of Rome they expect to have total mobility in all professions. Well, we are nowhere near that after 113 years!

You try to become a member of the Law Society of Upper Canada when you come from a civilized place like Manitoba, without having the right amount of money, the right amount of qualification and the right amount of internship period, etc. etc. I am not saying this in anything but a semi-facetious way; let me say I am semi-serious and semi-facetious. (7: 87–8)

**Mr. Peter Gordon (Chairman, Business Council on National Issues):** ... We believe that the good of the Canadian economy requires broad protection of mobility of rights – not just the mobility of citizens in search of a livelihood but the right of persons to move goods, services, capital, entrepreneurship, freely within the territorial boundaries of Canada. We believe that economic efficiency requires that we distinguish between maximizing the size of the nation's economic pie and distributing that pie equitably among Canadians. We further believe that steps towards more equitable distribution should be carefully calculated so as to minimize the necessary trade-offs in terms of failing to achieve the maximum possible national output.

It cannot be stressed enough that Canada's domestic market is very small by comparison with that of the world's major trading blocs. In fact, with a population of less than 25 million people, it is one of the few advanced economies without free trade access to markets in excess of 100 million people. It needs to be as free as possible of internal barriers in order to permit Canadian firms the broadest possible base from which to compete internationally.

If large economies like the United States and the European economic community need free internal movement of economic factors in order to be competitive, how much more must a small economy like Canada need that exact freedom? And yet provinces have increasingly during the past several years taken measures designed to interfere with the economic free flow of goods, services, labour and capital in the hope of boosting the local economy and generating additional employment. This trend seems likely to continue. But this progressive fragmentation makes it more difficult for Canadian firms to develop in the most efficient manner, and as a result jeopardizes the very basis of our position as a high-income industrial nation.

Of course regional development can be a legitimate political objective. All we would argue is that where governments wish to interfere with the natural processes of regional economic change, they be required to reach specific agreements amongst themselves and treat such agreements as exceptions to the general constitutional rule. Even though such exceptions will occur, it still is our contention as representatives of the business community that the preservation of relatively free interprovincial trade within the Canadian federation is essential to the economic welfare of all Canadians. However, the common market can be protected in many ways, either by the constitution, by the courts or through co-ordination of both levels of government, as long as the economic system is acknowledged and protected. (33: 135–6)

## Intersection with Aboriginal Rights

**Ms. Rose Charlie (Western Vice-President, Indian Rights for Indian Women):** Section 6 deals with mobility rights. As things stand now, Indians have special hunting and fishing rights within their own treaty areas, but not outside them. Does this provision mean that a status Saskatchewan Indian who moves to Ontario carries with him/her those special rights, or not? This matter should be stated clearly; it should definitely not be a matter of unconstrained judicial interpretation. (17: 85)

**Mr. Delbert Riley (President, National Indian Brotherhood):** Section 6 provides for mobility rights. The reserve system involves a restriction on mobility. Indians are free to live on or off their reserves, but non-Indians are restricted in their access to reserve lands. It must be clear that Section 6 cannot be used to attack the reserve system. (27: 86)

## Relationship to Language Rights

**The Hon. David Crombie, MP (PC, Ontario):** Section 6(2)(b) ... allows every citizen of Canada and every person who has the status of a permanent resident of Canada the right – and this is Section 6(2)(b) to pursue the gaining of a livelihood in any province. The concern of – if I may use an example – many French speaking Quebekers in the past has been their inability to move about the country to gain a livelihood and the problem rested on the inability to find a home both in their culture and language and in their workplace, educationally and so on. I wonder if you felt that the provision, both in terms of the mobility rights and in relation to their language rights, that we would have improved the situation in any way by this resolution, and, if not, is there any other change you might make?

**Mr. M. F. Yalden (Commissioner of Official Languages):** On this specific point, Section 6(2)(b) I would suppose that would turn out to be useful to persons whose language is the French language, moving out of Quebec and into the nine other provinces, or vice versa, in the sense that someone might, for example, go to court on the educational question we were talking about earlier. If there were no educational facilities available, such a person might argue that he was being impeded from pursuing the gaining of a livelihood in the particular province.

How can you gain a livelihood in a province if you cannot educate your children or get any services from the government and are completely barred from living in your language? I would have thought that would provide a form of additional protection for the minority. I do not really know whether that is so in fact, because I think it is the kind of clause that lawyers are going to find to be of very intriguing effect if and when it comes before the court.

I do not have any change to propose in respect to that type of mobility right. I did argue in respect of Section 23(2) that, by giving a mobility right in respect of a language of education in Section 23(2) and by including the citizenship requirement in Section 23(1), you could create all sorts of confusion, both administrative and human, at the family level, by various people going through other provinces and having a right which their neighbours or relatives have not, because they went directly to a province.

I do not, in any sense, come out against a mobility right. I think the motivation to give a person who moves to a province unequivocally the right to continue his children's education in the language in which they began is a good idea. It is both humane and a sensible provision. I just do not like the way it combines itself with Section 23(1) and the possible consequences of it. (6: 35)

...

**Mrs. Lucille Roch (General Director, Société franco-manitobaine):** ...
We are asking you to be generous, to have a vision of Canada that will

allow all Canadians to feel at home anywhere in their country. Freedom of movement and the freedom to live anywhere in Canada will mean nothing if Canadians, particularly French-Canadians, cannot leave their home province for fear of losing their language and not being able to pass on their culture to their children. (10: 23)

### The Professions

**Mr. Jean Lapierre, MP (LIB, PQ):** I would ... like to have some clarification on the actual meaning of Section 6 and particularly on its impact on the provincial statutes, in particular, the professional statutes.

**The Hon. Jean Chrétien (Minister of Justice):** ... Section 6 does not intend to standardize the statutes which govern the professions. This is a provincial jurisdiction and it will continue to be; it means that any profession, whether it be legal, medical or other, will still be governed by provincial statutes; the terms of reference will be established by the provinces. The only thing that section 6 does is that people who want to enter any such profession, cannot be barred from it if they are not a resident of the province; suppose that in order to become a plumber in Quebec, you must satisfy 25 conditions, any Canadian citizen who will meet those 25 conditions will be able to become a plumber in Quebec or a physician in Quebec. There should not be a 26th condition saying: "You must also be a Quebec citizen."

The conditions will be established by the province based on the criteria which must be met within each specific profession. So, this section means that any Canadian citizen who meets those criteria may practise his career or profession in the province in question. (3: 47–8)

### Passports

**The Hon. Jake Epp, MP (PC, Alberta):** ... Have you checked with External Affairs on the matter of the ability to withhold or revoke passports? How would that ability which External Affairs now uses, how might it be affected if Clause 6(1) be passed?

**Mr. Chrétien:** I do not know. (46: 74)

### Social Programs

**The Hon. David Crombie, MP (PC, Ontario):** I have concern with respect to the great army of programmes, federal programs which go to provinces and I wonder if, in your own mind, that created difficulties and indeed it would inhibit mobility in relation to social programs such as the Canada Assistance Plan, et cetera?

**Mr. Gordon Fairweather (Chief Commissioner, Canadian Human Rights Commission):** Mr. Crombie, I would much prefer that [subsection 6(b)] was not in the act. I think that residency for the delivery of assistance in Canada and its provinces for those who need it is mean-spirited.

**Mr. Crombie:** Particularly in relation to federal programs?

**Mr. Fairweather:** Federal programmes are cost-shared and other formulas and my bit of an outburst, I am a little embarrassed by it except that I feel things passionately, on mobility was the movement of people. Through the last 20 years mean-spirited regions, provinces, states in the United States, have put up residency requirements for the receipt of what is an entitlement, that I think is a poor idea.

**Mr. Crombie:** I appreciate your point. ... I wanted to know whether or not you regarded Section 6(3)(b) as a barrier to mobility?

**Mr. Fairweather:** Yes. I suspect that was part of the bargain ...

**Mr. Crombie:** And ought to be changed?

**Mr. Fairweather:** ... that they tried to strike during the summer to get provincial acceptance. I do not know, that is what I suppose. I do not imagine that clause was put forward by Canada.

**Mr. Crombie:** Well, ought it to be changed in your view?

**Mr. Fairweather:** Of course it should be changed in my view. (5: 22–3)
...

**Miss Nicole Dumouchel (Board Member, Canadian Council on Social Development):** In addition to our general concern regarding mobility for all Canadians, we are specifically concerned with Section 6(3)(b) which would place severe restriction on access to social services. Access to public social services is already limited by defining eligibility. Benefits under the Old Age Security and Guaranteed Income Supplement programs are available only after 10 years' residence in Canada. Canadians face residency and restrictions at the provincial level for access to public housing and for discretionary income supplements and tax credits.

Regarding access to public social services, the Canada Assistance Plan has taken the lead in enforcing mobility rights by requiring provision of social assistance, without regard for residence.

Given CAP's recognition of the importance of portability of social benefits, we must ask about its future if Section 6(3)(b) is enacted.

It appears that the universal nature of the Canada Assistance Plan could be ruled invalid. What consequence will that have for people in need of social assistance? In a society as mobile as Canada's, it would be a tragedy if the new constitution allowed residency to become a criterion in the determination of eligibility for human services.

If our constitution is to truly reflect our hopes for the future, and is to serve as a statement of the principles to which this nation aspires, surely these sections which now reflect an insular attitude and lack of generosity must be stricken. One must ask what higher goal these restrictions would address? What national interest? To permanently enshrine barriers to social services is unacceptable. We recommend that Canada's constitution reflect mobility rights consistent with Article 12 of the International Covenant on Civil and Political Rights. (19: 28–9)

**Mr. Nick Schultz (Associate General Counsel, Public Interest Advocacy Centre):** With respect to mobility rights, the limitation proposed by Subsection (6) and Subsection (3) seriously discriminates against the poor. ... NAPO [National Anti-Poverty Organization] would ask that Subsection 3 be deleted in its entirety. (29: 22)

...

**Dr. Richard Splane (President, Canadian Association of Social Workers):** On Section 6 ... we have particularly strong feeling. We do not feel that the subsection of that act which makes the mobility principle, which we strongly endorse, subject to, and I quote, any laws providing for reasonable residency requirements as a qualification for the receipt of publicly provided social services.

We think that that is a dangerous provision. Some of us who have been in the social welfare field for many years remember what the situation was in the 1930s, not only in the 1930s but in the 1940s and 1950s, the situation was deplorable in terms of provincial barriers. A great deal of social work time was taken up in dealing with residency requirements and sending people back across borders and the like.

The action taken by the Unemployment Assistance Act in 1956, 1957, was the first measure which effectively began to outlaw that practice and it was followed up by the Canada Assistance Plan, which makes any province which signs the agreement under the Canada Assistance Plan must not make residency a condition for assistance. What we would fear is that if a constitution came back with this kind of provision in it, that that would weaken that piece of legislation.

We are at the same time very concerned about the fact that it now exists, that it takes 90 days for one to achieve entitlement under the medical care program and we deplore that and feel that that should be removed. So our suggestion about Section 6, Mr. Chairman, is that the section that I have just read should be struck out of legislation. (29: 149)

...

**Mr. Jim Hawkes, MP (PC, Alberta):** On Section 6, the mobility rights part, as I understand your brief, in terms of what is before us, that Section 6(3)(b) is what you would feel to be the most dangerous part of the resolution as you read it in terms of the populations that you have concerns about as a professional; that is the part of the Charter which could eliminate universality, universal access for people to social service. That is your concern with it. And in fact, you want to go the opposite way. Is that right?

**Mr. Splane:** No, that is not what we say. We see universality as the ultimate goal. I think social workers have been working for universal programs, income security programs and universal programs as soon as they can be mounted and staffed and financed in a wide range of social services. All we recognize – we do recognize, however, that it is some time before that goal will be achieved and, meanwhile, we would be concerned that a court might make it, might rule out the possibility of some special group – the aged, for example – being helped in a special way that was necessary in their interests. (29: 152)

...

**Mrs. Margaret Mitchell, MP (NDP, BC):** It seems to me that in your brief Section 6(3)(b) is particularly important, and I think it is particularly important to the Committee. I would imagine you are probably the only group that has really stressed this as strongly as you have and I would certainly hope that will draw attention to this.

Concerning the mobility, the limitations on mobility rights, you have mentioned that you are concerned that there would be abuses of the rights to social services and, I imagine, such things as transients being refused services as they move from province to province, might be one thing. Perhaps you have some other examples that would bring this clearer to the Committee and I wondered what changes you would propose from the present provincial eligibility for social assistance. Are you saying that there should be the same kind of eligibility right across Canada and there should be no restrictions at the provincial border based on residency?

**Mr. Splane:** Yes, Mr. Chairman. The most difficult case, the most difficult kind of residence requirement is that which relates to social assistance to persons coming into a province and being in need very soon after they arrive.

This right to refuse assistance and to send people back to their home province, in quotes, was so strongly felt in the thirties, and forties and fifties, that when the Unemployment Assistance Act was passed in 1956, one province stayed out for a full year fearing that if it signed an agreement which prohibited it from making residency a condition for assistance, that they would be flooded by persons coming into that province.

It did not happen. It has not happened with the Canada Assistance Plan. I see no reason why, if that most controversial aspect of social benefits, residency, can be removed in that case, why it cannot be removed for health services and for any other kind of social services that might be needed by a family or an individual moving from one province to another.

**Mrs. Mitchell:** Yes, I think another example that is very dramatic in our memories on the west coast and perhaps in other provinces, is the mass movement of young people some 10 years ago, when they moved, were hitchhiking across the country, and in many cases, were forcibly removed back home without due consideration to the particular needs. (29: 154–5)

**Mr. Chrétien:** Mr. Chairman, we studied this problem during the summer and we have had long discussions with the provinces. We came to the conclusion that giving an absolute mobility right in this matter could create considerable administrative problems. What we want in Clause 6(3)(b), is to allow citizens who move a reasonable residence period before being eligible to certain social benefits, to do so in such a way that the necessary control and the distribution of these benefits to these citizens could be made in an appropriate manner by the provinces.

So, in this matter, if the residence criteria imposed by a province is totally unreasonable in relation to the administrative need that we were told about during the summer, then the courts will judge that this residence requirement is unreasonable. To simplify the administrative problems of the provincial governments, we have accepted to have this condition of reasonable residency before having access to social services. Sometimes, with the mobility of population, close to retirement age or for other reasons, toward different provinces, we understand that different programs apply. For example, on Vancouver Island, the number of retired persons is a burden for the province. So, we must be satisfied that the person receiving these benefits is really a citizen of the province and is not there only for those benefits. So, it is in that context that we propose this amendment. It is to allow better administration on the provincial level where it would be permitted to impose a reasonable residency requirement as a qualification for the receipt of social services or benefits. (46: 78–9)

**Mr. Jim Hawkes, MP (PC, Alberta):** Can I direct your attention ... to the mobility rights, Section 6(3)(b). And in that Section, sir, you say that there is an exception, that people will not be entitled to public social services. You do not say "provincial social services," which might provide protection for budgets at one level, but you simply ask us to accept that the poor, the disadvantaged in this country who choose to move to better their position will not have the same right of access to public social services that those that are wealthy would have. It is those kinds of principles that are sprinkled throughout this Bill, that cause me considerable concern. We should never, never, sir, have a Constitution that is built on the principle that I do not know or that I do not understand.

**Mr. Chrétien:** I know very well what it is, sir. And I understand quite well, that is a provision that was put in the Bill of Rights at the request of provincial governments to ensure that the passage of people from one province to another does not create undue burden upon the government of the said province. It is at the request of provincial governments who are responsible for the administration of social programs in Canada that we have put in clause (b) to sub-clause 3 concerning the rights and freedom of circulation and settling in.

So it is to maintain the most reasonable administrative norm possible that we have allowed that to the provinces before being obliged to pay for social services out of public funds to make sure that there is a minimum period of residence inside a province. That is common practice and has been established in Canada for quite a while now and it is at the request of the provinces that we decided not to, through that mobility clause, create confusion in the administration of social programs at the provincial level.

**Mr. Hawkes:** Surely to God, Mr. Chairman, there is a difference between the word "public" and the word "province," and surely you put careful care and attention into this Bill before you used the loyalty to those members to foist it on the Canadian public. Surely you can understand that we are governed by words in law and the words that are in the Constitution are vitally important to that social contract?

**Mr. Chrétien:** I explained why we put those words in there. It was at the request of the provincial governments for the reasons I have just set out. (4: 119–21)

...

**Mr. Chrétien:** In our country it is the provinces who have the administrative and legislative responsibility for giving social services to our citizens. It is not the central government. So that is why when we use the word "public" it means that it applies to ...

**Mr. Beatty:** Family Allowance, Old Age Pension?

**Mr. Chrétien:** But insofar as the question of family allowances is concerned, there is no such thing as residency requirements in one or the other case, it applies generally to all Canadians. The question of residence is not a prerequisite concerning ...

**Mr. Beatty:** Unemployment Insurance?

**Mr. Chrétien:** It is the same thing. Federal programs apply to all Canadians.

**Mr. Crombie:** With differences from province to province. Two provinces on the family allowance ...

**Mr. Chrétien:** Yes, yes.

**Mr. Chrétien:** As for family allowances, that does not apply generally because it is the same level of family allowances for all Canadians. I believe that Mr. Crombie had a valid point when he said, concerning unemployment insurance, that there are situations which vary from one place to another in Canada depending upon the level of unemployment insurance. I recognize that point and Clause 6.3(b) would apply there. (4: 122)

...

**Mr. Crombie:** Mr. Chairman, through you to the Minister, there are three specific programs I would like to ask you about and will ask them briefly. I know we have some problem with time but they are three fundamentally important social programs in this country and I want to know your view of the effect of this legislation on them. First of all, the Canada Assistance Plan is truly the workhorse of social programs particularly dealing with those Canadians who are most in need, and indeed whose social existence is often at risk.

The Canadian Council on Social Development had this to say, given the Canada Assistance Plan's recognition of the importance of the portability of social programs, the most important thing about CAP is its portability and its universality, their worry with CAP is that this legislation could strike down or strike at the heart of the universal aspect of the Canada Assistance Plan and therefore reduce benefits for those Canadians most in need.

**Mr. Chrétien:** We are not worried about it because the agreement under CAP, one of the requirements is that there should be no residence test applied to benefits because it is a shared cost program with the federal treasury, and one of the tests, we say that they cannot apply a residence test because we know for some people it is basic, as you say, the core of the social programs, the residence test there cannot apply under the present agreement that we have with the provinces and we are completely in control of it because we are paying half the cost.

**Mr. Crombie:** Could you offer comment on two other programs that are not dealt with financially on a cost shared basis in the same way and therefore might have an entirely different impact, on medicare and pensions?

**Mr. Chrétien:** I will ask my advisor to give you the precise answer.

**Mr. Fred Jordan (Department of Justice):** Yes, Mr. Crombie, with regard to the Medical Services Act, my information is that it does provide for a three month waiting period when you move from one province to another, but of course the province to which you have moved is also party to it and will be paying that during the period so you do have a residency requirement there. On the hospital and services Diagnostic Services Act there is no residency requirement but you can exclude, and I think this is one of the important things that the provinces are concerned about, people such as tourists, transients and visitors from claiming their benefits. ...

**Mr. Crombie:** Would you agree, then, that this particular section will carve in stone that inability of the federal government to control the universal aspect of Medicare?

**Mr. Jordan:** Yes, it would enable the provinces as the clause provides to spell out what they believe to be reasonable residency requirements. Of course, the courts would be able to look at that and say it is or it is not in the circumstances of the case. (46: 80.)

## Chapter Nine

# Legal Rights

---

Life, liberty and security of person

7. Everyone has the right to life, liberty and security of the person and the right not to be deprived thereof except in accordance with the principles of fundamental justice.

Search or seizure

8. Everyone has the right ~~not to be subjected~~ <u>to</u> to be secure <u>against unreasonable</u> search ~~or~~ <u>and</u> seizure ~~except on grounds, and in accordance with procedures, established by law.~~

Detention or imprisonment

9. Everyone has the right not to be <u>arbitrarily</u> detained or imprisoned ~~except on grounds, and in accordance with procedures, established by law.~~

Arrest or detention

10. Everyone has the right on arrest or detention

(a) to be informed promptly of the reasons therefor;
(b) to retain and instruct counsel without delay <u>and to be informed of that right</u>; and

(c) to have the validity of the detention determined by way of *habeas corpus* and to be released if the detention is not lawful.

Proceedings in criminal and penal matters

11. ~~Anyone~~ Any person charged with an offence has the right

(a) to be informed ~~promptly~~ without unreasonable delay of the specific offence;
(b) to be tried within a reasonable time;
(c) not to be compelled to be a witness in proceedings against that person in respect of that offence;
~~(c)~~ (d) to be presumed innocent until proven guilty according to law in a fair and public hearing by an independent and impartial tribunal;
~~(d)~~ (e) not to be denied reasonable bail ~~except on grounds, and in accordance with procedures, established by law~~ without just cause;
(f) except in the case of an offence under military law tried before a military tribunal, to the benefit of a trial by jury where the maximum punishment for the offence is imprisonment for five years or a more severe punishsment;
~~(e)~~ (g) not to be found guilty on account of any act or omission, unless ~~that~~ at the time of the act or omission, ~~did not~~ it constituted an offence under Canadian or international law or was criminal according to the general principles of law recognized by the community of nations;
~~(f)~~ (h) if finally acquitted of the offence, not to be tried for it again and, if finally found guilty and punished for the offence, not to be tried or punished ~~more than once for an offence of which he or she has been finally convicted or acquitted~~ for it again; and
~~(g)~~ (i) if found guilty of the offence and if the punishsment for the offence has been varied between the time of commission and the time of sentencing, to the benefit of the lesser punishement ~~where the punishment for an offence of which he or she has been convicted has ben varied between the time of commission and the time of sentencing.~~

Treatment or punishment

12. Everyone has the right not to be subjected to any cruel and unusual treatment or punishment.

Self-crimination

13. A witness who testifies in any proceedings has the right when compelled to testify not to have any incriminating evidence so given used to incriminate him or her that witness in any other proceedings, except in a prosecution for perjury or for the giving of contradictory evidence.

Interpreter

14. A party or witness in any proceedings who does not understand or speak the language in which the proceedings are conducted or who is deaf has the right to the assistance of an interpreter.

## Commentary

The broad topic of legal rights gave rise to a varied, and at times heated, debate at the Joint Committee. During clause-by-clause, the members of the Joint Committee considered amendments to many of the eighteen sections and subsections that now make up sections 7 to 14 of the Charter.

Section 7 attracted significant criticism and questioning over the open-ended nature of its language and because of its obvious comparison with the due process clause of the US Bill of Rights, which provides that "No person ... shall be deprived of life, liberty, or property, without due process of law. ..." The controversial American doctrine of "substantive due process" loomed large in the minds of the drafters, witnesses, and committee members. It was the reason the government had chosen the language of "principles of fundamental justice" instead of "due process of law." There was thus much discussion about the meaning of "principles of fundamental justice" as well as a Tory proposal to add property rights to this provision, a proposal that was accepted and then opposed by the government. This section was also the focus of debate over some of the most controversial and divisive social issues such as abortion, capital punishment, and euthanasia.

There was also strong opposition to the original limiting language in sections 8, 9, and 11(e) (bail), which would have allowed restrictions on those rights "in accordance with procedures established by law." Many witnesses asserted that this phrase eviscerated the protections offered as Parliament or the provincial legislatures would still retain the right to pass any law – including laws seen as unfair or arbitrary. Only the Canadian Association of Chiefs of Police supported the sections as drafted. The government responded by introducing amendments removing these limitations on those rights.

The eight subsections contained in the draft of section 11 received detailed scrutiny during clause-by-clause, and several amendments were accepted, including adding two new subsections protecting the right against compelled self-incrimination (section 11(c)) and trial by jury (section 11(f)). The discussion of legal rights raised the issue of remedies for illegally obtained evidence; this is discussed in chapter 12 on remedies. In addition, witnesses and committee members spoke in favour of other legal rights that were ultimately not included in the Charter, such as due process protections in civil or administrative proceedings as well as in criminal ones, the right to legal-aid counsel for those unable to afford private legal assistance, the right to remain silent, and the right not to be deported.

Perhaps not surprisingly, there is next to no discussion in the debates about the rights of prisoners. There was no group to advocate on their behalf, and the focus of other groups was much more on the application of rights provisions earlier in the criminal justice process: investigation, interrogation, arrest, bail, and trial.

## Legal Rights – Generally

**Professor Max Cohen (Canadian Jewish Congress):** Let me put it to you in broad, practical-philosophical terms. One should see articles of this kind and others like it. In terms of the modern problems of the administration of criminal justice, how do you draw a balance between the police and the prosecutor in a world in which urban crime is rampant. How do you tilt the balance one way or the other to meet the exigencies of the situation. Well, the tilting process cannot be done every day by the legislature. Perhaps you ought to give discretion to the courts to work out the tilting process over time as they see the urgencies of the occasion day by day, case by case around them. (7: 90)

**Mrs. Diana Davidson (President, Vancouver People's Law School Society):** Section 7, the omnibus rights clause, leaves out many rights which have traditionally characterized our system, including the right to a fair hearing, the right to a public hearing, the right to a jury, the right to the use and enjoyment of private property or, in lieu of same, fair compensation for its loss. We are in favour of there being included in this section rights which we are bound by international covenants to guarantee, including the right to adequate health care and education. (32: 12)

**The Honourable Jean Chrétien (Minister of Justice):** The fact that the Charter does not entrench every provision of the [International Covenant on Civil and Political Rights] does not mean that Canada is violating it. The Covenant merely requires states to protect or not violate certain rights. It does not require these rights to be entrenched in the constitution. (36: 13)

**Mr. Gordon Fairweather (Chief Commissioner, Canadian Human Rights Commission):** Legal rights as defined in this Charter are seriously deficient. They contain unnecessary qualifications. It is as if somebody is frightened of something. The rights that ought to be protected, for instance, by Sections 8 and 9 may be seriously circumscribed by the qualification except on grounds and in accordance with procedures established by law. What you should ask witnesses is what this phrase means. If you ask me, I will tell you I have not the faintest idea what it means, and that is why I worry about it. Why is it thought necessary to add it to the clauses protecting legal rights? If it is to restrict the rights set out, surely you are entitled to know the nature and scope of the restrictions contemplated. (5: 9–10)

**Chief John Ackroyd (Chief Metro Toronto Police, Canadian Association of Chiefs of Police):** I will now turn to the Legal Rights section, Sections 7, 8, and 9. The Canadian Chiefs Association fully agrees with these sections as they are now drafted, but we would be strongly opposed to any changes thereto. (14: 7)

## Legal Rights – "Everyone"

**Professor Max Cohen (Canadian Jewish Congress):** What is troubling there for some people, is the word "everyone." Does that embrace people who are in Canada illegally? We think it should include everyone, so that we do not have people here who may be here [il] legally and deprived and are deprivable of these basic rights. (7: 88)

**Professor David Cruickshank (Vice President, Canadian Council on Children and Youth):** Generally speaking we believe that the rights contained in Section 7 through 15 apply to everyone and everyone ought to clearly be taken to mean children, that is persons from birth to the age of majority, whatever that age may be, 18 to 19, it varies from province to province. (21: 30)

## Principles of Fundamental Justice

**Professor Walter Tarnopolsky (President, Canadian Civil Liberties Association):** We have given some consideration to Section 7, and the real difficulty that we see is that the term "principles of fundamental justice" is used interchangeably with the term "principles of natural justice" – a well-known administrative law description referring to fair hearing, and in our Anglo-Canadian jurisprudence has not referred so much to prehearing or to pretrial procedure, which is one of the matters of concern in any provision with respect to life, liberty and security particularly, and which is dealt with particularly in the following Section 8. Now, it is for this reason that when we considered this, the alternative would have been the "due process" clause.

In the last decade – in fact, in the last two decades – since the enactment of the Canadian Bill of Rights, there is no doubt that the due process clause has come in academic circles to mean more and more the over-all *penumbra* of fairness in the administration of justice. However, our courts have not yet adopted that interpretation, and there remains a fear in many circles that any reference to a due process clause, even without reference to property in this clause, could reintroduce the substantive "due process" interpretation in the United States.

Now, one could argue that that is not a very likely reintroduction. Nevertheless, there is a certain fear that a reference to a due process clause might bring that kind of reintroduction. This is why, after consideration of the other articles, we came to the conclusion that a tightening up of the other legal rights would make a general clause not necessary, considering all the difficulties with the rewriting; and this is the reason why we came up with the recommendations we made today. (7: 21)

**Professor Max Cohen (Canadian Jewish Congress):** Why was the phrase "fundamental justice" used, instead of the classical phrase "due process of law"? Well, there is a long story attached to it and I would not go into that except to note procedurally what happened to due process of law in the American system, and you will find that in the Diefenbaker Bill of Rights. (7: 88)

**Ms. Rose Charlie (Western Vice-President, Indian Rights for Indian Women):** Section 7 refers to "the principles of fundamental justice." It would be ridiculous to suggest that a constitution should or could define these principles. But it is surely not too much to ask that these principles be specified, at least broadly. Specifically, could the decision in the *Lavell* case be confirmed under this provision? If so, we are unalterably opposed to it. (17: 85)

**Mr. Chris Speyer, MP (PC, Ontario):** ... Would you not agree with me that there could be a wide interpretation as to what principles of fundamental justice are?

**Mr. Webking (Canadian Federation of Civil Liberties and Human Rights Associations):** I agree, and I think that is not out of step or out of keeping with the concept of the constitution, especially an entrenched one, and entrenched bill of rights. (21: 21)

**Mr. Wilson Head (President, National Black Coalition of Canada):** I have to admit, Mr. Joint Chairman, that these kind of terms, are extremely imprecise, and I do not really know what they mean. What, for example, is "fundamental justice"? Are we talking about due process? Are we talking about some concept of British Common Law, or the Napoleonic Code? Are we talking about the principles of natural justice propounded by Rousseau, or the principles of justice propounded by Plato? I am not sure. So that is what I am saying. It ought to be spelled out. (22: 21)

**Mr. Svend Robinson, MP (NDP, Burnaby):** You have relied very heavily on the concept of fundamental justice in your brief ... and ... you refer to it ... revealing bold initiative. Again this is something of a new course which has not been embarked upon by any of the previous witnesses. In fact there has been some criticism of the inclusion of the words "fundamental justice," because we are embarking upon new waters, as it were, to the best of my knowledge and that of some of the previous witnesses, in that there has not been any significant judicial determination as to what we mean by the concept of fundamental justice. ... Now, what does that mean, and why do you believe this concept is one which will adequately protect the important rights which we are dealing with in these particular sections?

**Mr. Norman Whalen (Vice-Chairman, Canadian Federation of Civil Liberties and Human Rights Associations):** First of all, we agree with you that the concept of fundamental justice does not have a basis in judicial interpretation. However, we believe it will attain an interpretation similar to the concept of natural justice. We have indicated in our brief that, to this extent, we are going to have to rely upon the courts to determine what that will mean. However, we are satisfied that whatever ultimately it is natural justice. That is an awful lot better than the phraseology used in Sections 8 and 9 which is "as established by law," which will permit Parliament to change the law by a simple majority of the House of Commons whenever they felt like it. We have every confidence in the Supreme Court of Canada when we say that.

**Mr. Robinson:** I appreciate that. I am not sure it is entirely well placed in view of their record in interpreting some words.

**Mr. Whalen:** There will be new judges. (21: 14–15)

**Mr. Svend Robinson, MP (NDP, BC):** What is there, Mr. Minister, in Clause 7 contained within the rubric of principles of fundamental justice that is not contained in the remaining legal rights section? What does that section mean, what specifically does it mean, and for example what is the meaning of the right to be deprived of your right to life as long as that is done in compliance with the principles of fundamental justice?

**The Hon. Robert P. Kaplan (Acting Minister of Justice):** Well, that type of statement in a constitution has its meaning developed over years of use, and over years of reference.

**Mr. Robinson:** What does it mean now, Mr. Minister? What is it intended to mean now?

**Mr. Kaplan:** Well, I think generally, the generally recognized rights affecting life, liberty and security are specifically referred to in the provisions that follow, and the reason for a general introductory statement like that is to permit the evolution and expansion of rights of life, liberty and security over time. For example, rights of security at the moment may be just at the dawn of their evolution. What is a right of security? The following provisions, search and seizure, give some reference to rights of security but an evolving democratic society could well develop new ideas of rights of security, and the purpose of that provision is not a kind of flimflam, as you might suggest; the purpose is to open the door.

**Mr. Robinson:** Those are your words, Mr. Minister.

**Mr. Kaplan:** Yes, but that is what you were getting at. It is to open the door for the possibility of rights of security that are not conceived of now, generally recognized now. (41: 15–16)

[The PC Party moved an amendment at committee to add protection for the right to enjoyment of property in section 7 and to change "principles of fundamental justice" to "principles of natural justice." The amendment was defeated.]

**The Hon. Perrin Beatty, MP (PC, Ontario):** ... You will note that we have changed the words "fundamental justice" to "natural justice." We do that because we believe there is a greater body of law defining what constitutes "natural justice" and we are more comfortable with a word included in the charter which is more clearly defined, and we should be very careful, as Mr. Robinson stressed, to be cautious when we are including wording in the constitution to ensure that we know what we are doing.

We believe that "natural justice" properly represents what the vast majority of Canadians want to see take place when it comes to property rights or the right to life or to the security of the person or the right to liberty.

Mr. Chairman, we are opposed to the concept. We could, of course, have included the proposal for due process of law instead of natural justice, but that simply implies that governments have the right as long as it is lawful. As long as they pass legislation to authorize what they are doing, they have the right to go ahead and do whatever they want, and we believe their fundamental principles here regarding process, and whether or not people have a right to be heard and whether or not they have been fairly heard, that this should be included in the constitution when we are dealing with such fundamental areas of individual rights.

**Mr. Jean Lapierre, MP (LIB, Quebec):** ... It is entirely realistic to ask that the notion of fundamental justice be changed and a number of associations, including the Canadian Civil Liberties Association, the National Association of Japanese Canadians, Indian Rights for Indian Women, the National Black League and others, have asked that the notion of fundamental justice be more clearly defined, since it is not a well-known legal expression. For this reason, the members of this Committee are willing to recognize this principle. (44: 12–16)

**Mr. Svend Robinson, MP (NDP, BC):** It was the [Canadian] Bar Association who pointed out that the concept of fundamental justice, as is contained in Clause 7, is one which is virtually unknown in Canadian jurisprudence and that the Canadian Bill of Rights in Section 1(a) contains the concept of due process of law. Now, we recognize that the principles of fundamental justice are subject to some interpretation and expansion as was pointed out by the Minister of Justice the week before last when he was explaining what was meant by fundamental justice.

... I would first of all again like to obtain some clarification from the Minister as to whether or not the words "principles of fundamental justice" and the concept of fundamental justice contained in Clause 7 is intended to incorporate the concept of due process of law from Section 1 of the Canadian Bill of Rights?

**The Hon. Jean Chrétien (Minister of Justice):** Yes, fundamentally, but in terms of procedure there are some nuances and perhaps I can ask Mr. Strayer to ...

**Mr. Robinson:** Certainly.

**Mr. Barry L. Strayer, Q.C. (Assistant Deputy Minister, Public Law, Department of Justice):** Mr. Chairman, it was our belief that the words "fundamental justice" would cover the same thing as what is called procedural due process, that is the meaning of due process in relation to requiring fair procedure. However, it in our view does not cover the concept of what is called substantive due process, which would impose substantive requirements as to the policy of the law in question. This has been most clearly demonstrated in the United States in the area of property, but also in other areas such as the right to life. The term due process has been given the broader concept of meaning both the procedure and substance. Natural justice or fundamental justice in our view does not go beyond the procedural requirements of fairness.

**Mr. Robinson:** ... May I ask, then, what the basis for Mr. Strayer's statement that the concept of fundamental justice has no substantive component? Where is the jurisprudence on that particular section, what evidence does he have to support his interpretation that this might not have a substantive component?

**Mr. Strayer:** We have not been able to find any evidence of that term ever having been given a substantive content.

**Mr. Robinson:** Well, can you point to any interpretation of that term whatsoever within the context of the Canadian legal system that might assist us?

**Mr. Strayer:** Which term do you want?

**Mr. Robinson:** Fundamental justice.

**Mr. Fred Jordan (Senior Counsel, Public Law, Department of Justice):** Yes, Mr. Chairman. This expression appears in Section 2(e) of the Canadian Bill of Rights now in terms of the right to a fair hearing in termination of one's rights and obligations. The Chief Justice in the *Duke* case in 1972 in the Supreme Court spoke about the meaning of Section 2(e) and said a fair hearing in accordance with the principles of fundamental justice, without attempting to formulate any final definition of those words, I would take it to mean generally the tribunal which adjudicates upon his rights must act fairly, in good faith, without bias and in a judicial temper and must be given an opportunity adequate to state his case, and I think that is the classic definition of the rules of natural justice or the principles of fundamental justice.

**Mr. Robinson:** Do you make any distinction, then, between the principles of fundamental justice and the rules of natural justice?

**Mr. Jordan:** Not in light of the interpretation which the Chief Justice gave it in this case here. There is a possibility that in a particular context one could see it as having a somewhat expanded meaning but there is no jurisprudence which would indicate that it is clearly broader than the principles of fundamental justice that have been articulated in all of the various common law decisions. ...

**Mr. Robinson:** Well, Mr. Chairman, I am sorry to belabour this point but it is an important point because this is an important clause and it is a new principle of law. Mr. Jordan, you have pointed out that the concept of fundamental justice has been interpreted with respect to the requirement of a fair hearing. With respect, that is not what we are talking about in Clause 7, we are going well beyond that and we are applying the principles of fundamental justice, whatever they may be, to the right to life, liberty and security of the person. Now, can either you or Mr. Strayer, or perhaps the Minister with his legal knowledge, point to any interpretation of these words in that sweeping context?

**Mr. Strayer:** Obviously not in this specific context because these words have not appeared in a constitution or in any type of statute before, but I am bound to add, Mr. Chairman, that there is a good deal of jurisprudence on the term "due process," both in Canada and the United States, and some of the jurisprudence in the United States gave rise to the problem that we were trying to avoid with the term, "fundamental justice."

**Mr. Robinson:** Perhaps, then, now that you have admitted that this concept of fundamental justice is not found in any statute or any constitution anywhere else in the world to the best of your knowledge in connection with these principles, what is the particular concern with respect to the application of the principles of due process of law which continue to apply, certainly within the federal context by virtue of the Bill of Rights, what specifically is your concern with respect to their application? How could these be applied in a substantive sense to any of the provisions of Clause 7?

**Mr. Strayer:** Well, there are various possibilities. The term "security of the person," for example, could be interpreted in a very broad sense so the term "security" could cover matters of a, say, contractual or property nature. More particularly the question of right to life, gives rise to, if it is interpreted in a substantive way, gives rise to questions about matters such as capital punishment, abortion and so forth, and if one used the term "due process," and by that language imported some of the American jurisprudence under due process, then the result would be what 1 believe the Committee indicated last week they wanted to avoid, and that was prejudging the law or the question on both those issues. In other words, it might somehow have the effect of limiting the options of Parliament in the future on those subjects. (46: 30–4)

...

**Hon. John A. Fraser, MP (PC, BC):** But this is what is worrying me. The indication that we have from the law officers of the Crown – and the point Mr. Robinson is making – that the words "fundamental justice" have not yet been defined by the courts and, as a consequence, Mr. Robinson's concern is that when they are defined there may be a definition which is more restrictive, more confining than we would like or we would be intending at the moment. As a consequence of the well-known rule that you cannot look to the intent of the legislation and that the matter has to be perceived from the words which are present on the page, what we intend to do here is of very little help to the court later when the matter is being dealt with or interpreted. So, what I am saying is this. The first question is, if the words of the Diefenbaker Bill of Rights, relating to principles of due process of law were included, as Mr. Robinson proposes, is it in the opinion of the law officers of the Crown that the inclusion of those words would in any way derogate from what we are trying to do by using the words "principles of fundamental justice"? ...

**Mr. Strayer:** ... Due process would certainly include the concept of procedural fairness that we think is covered by fundamental justice, but we think that "due process" would have the danger of going well beyond procedural fairness and to deal with substantive fairness which raises the possibility of the courts second guessing Parliament or legislatures on the policy of the law as opposed to the procedure by which rights are to be dealt with. That has been the experience at times in the United States in the interpretation of the term "due process."

**Mr. Fraser:** Do I take it that what you are telling us is that, in your opinion at least, by adding the words "due process" we could get a narrower interpretation of justice than we might be by just leaving the words "principles of justice"? These are not easy concepts. They are terribly important right now, because if this Committee, not understanding what is at stake here, let it go on the original wording or accepts the change without understanding the implications, then some day somebody is going to wonder why we were asleep at the switch, and I am worried about it.

**Mr. Strayer:** Well, as I say, in our view, the use of the term "due process" would certainly also protect or require procedural fairness. But it would have the other possibility of narrowing, as it were, the range of discretion of Parliament in matters of policy by possibly opening the door to the courts second guessing laws of Parliament on the basis of the policy involved rather than the question of procedural fairness. In the United States "due process" was used from time to time in combination, for example, with a guarantee over property to provide a basis for courts to determine whether expropriation was justified in the circumstances as a matter of policy, whether the compensation was adequate and so forth. It has been used to second guess public social measures. (46: 35–6)

**Mr. Chrétien:** I would just like to make a suggestion arising out of the discussion, because there might be a compromise here. Mr. Robinson is preoccupied because we used a new term "fundamental justice." Earlier, there was an amendment proposed which was rejected a component of it; the word was "natural justice."

If members of the Committee were more comfortable with the words "natural justice" rather than "fundamental justice," we could accept "natural justice" rather than "fundamental justice," because one has been used before – "natural justice" has been a term used before the courts, and "fundamental justice" is a new phrase. So if members of the Committee are more comfortable with the words "natural justice" we are willing to accept it. But the advice I have received is that "fundamental justice" is perhaps more appropriate, but perhaps marginally so, and I am willing to accept "natural justice." It could cope with some of the preoccupation of the Committee, and it was dropped because the motion in the previous amendment was including the two parts, and the phrase "natural justice" would have been acceptable to us. We can accept that as part of the earlier rejected amendment and take "natural justice"; and for "due process of law," my legal advisers have said that the scope of it, what it might create, if we were to inscribe it and limit even more the powers of the legislatures and give the power to the court to look at, not the form but the substance of the legislation that would be passed in Parliament, would limit very much the legislative power of the different parliaments in Canada. (46: 37–8)

**Hon. David Crombie, MP (PC, Ontario):** Could either the Minister or any one of the gentlemen present tell me what is the difference between natural justice and fundamental justice? ...

**Mr. Barry L. Strayer, Q.C. (Assistant Deputy Minister Public Law, Department of Justice):** The term "fundamental justice" appears to us to be essentially the same thing as natural justice.

It is interesting that this question was debated in 1960 when the Canadian Bill of Rights was before Parliament, as to whether to include the term "fundamental justice" or "natural justice." They finally settled on "fundamental justice." But one of the leading commentators on the Bill of Rights, Professor Tarnopolsky, reviewing that debate at that time and the jurisprudence since has said that it appears to him that the two terms are essentially the same.

**Mr. Crombie:** What are they?

**Mr. Strayer:** Well, fundamental justice or natural justice both involve procedural fairness and that is the content of them. The requirements of natural justice certainly have been pretty well defined over the years by the courts. The term "fundamental justice" has not been used very much in legislation, although it does appear in the Canadian Bill of Rights. But we have assumed it meant about the same thing. Those two terms can be contrasted to due process. (46: 38–9)

...

**Mr. Crombie:** Natural justice and fundamental justice do not deal with substantive matters, only procedural fairness, that is the difference between those two and due process?

**Mr. Strayer:** Yes. (46: 42)

...

**Mr. Crombie:** ... What effect will the inclusion of the due process clause have on the question of marriage, procreation, or the parental care of children?

**Mr. Strayer:** Mr. Chairman, I am sure that anything I could say would be purely in the realm of speculation, but it could be seen to open the door to the courts dealing with the question of abortion, that sort of thing, contraception, which has been dealt with by the American courts. In other words, the courts would be making these policy decisions instead of Parliament.

**Mr. Chrétien:** The point, Mr. Crombie, that it is important to understand the difference is that we pass legislation here on abortion, criminal code, and we pass legislation on capital punishment; Parliament has the authority to do that, and the court at this moment, because we do not have the due process of law written there, cannot go and see whether we made the right decision or the wrong decision in Parliament. If you write down the words, "due process of law" here, the advice I am receiving is the court could go behind our decision and say that their decision on abortion was not the right one, their decision on capital punishment was not the right one, and it is a danger, according to legal advice I am receiving, that it will very much limit the scope of the power of legislation by the Parliament and we do not want that; and it is why we do not want the words "due process of law." These are the two main examples that we should keep in mind. You can keep speculating on all the things that have never been touched, but these are two very sensitive areas that we have to cope with as legislators and my view is that Parliament has decided a certain law on abortion and a certain law on capital punishment, and it should prevail and we do not want the courts to say that the judgment of Parliament was wrong in using the constitution. (46: 42–3)

### The Right to Privacy

**Mr. Fred Pennington (Board Member, Canadian Council on Social Development):** In our opinion, the right to privacy appears to have been addressed in a tangential way by Section 7, by the inclusion of the phrase "security of person." Because of its importance to the democratic process, we suggest the principle of the right of privacy be strengthened by forming a separate section with wording which clearly articulates both the scope and the importance of the concept. (19: 28)

### The Right to Property

[The PC Party moved an amendment at committee to add protection for the right to enjoyment of property in section 7. The NDP opposed the amendment. As described in chapter 3, at first the government committed to support the amendment but then changed its mind several days later, leading to the defeat of the amendment.]

**The Hon. Perrin Beatty, MP (PC, Ontario):** The family farm, family business and family home are some of the most fundamental elements of Canadian society; yet, anyone who has ever dreamed of his own home or a family farm or business, would be disturbed by the fact that while the Diefenbaker Bill of Rights included the right to the enjoyment of property, the Charter of Rights proposed by the government in the constitution is mute on the subject.

Mr. Chairman, it is not uncommon at all for federal constitutions or national constitutions to include recognition of party rights. Indeed, a cursory check of various constitutions we have been able to locate more than 30 countries around the world which include India Constitution the right to own property as one of the fundamental constitutional rights. I will name just a few of them, which I think would be instructive, covering a broad spectrum: Belgium, Portugal, France, Germany, Ireland, Italy, Luxembourg, Japan, and of course, the United States. So what we are proposing, Mr. Chairman, is not novel in any way. It is not an experiment which has not been tried in other areas. It is a recognition of the hopes and dreams of millions of Canadians who believe that the right to own property is a fundamental right which should be enjoyed by all Canadians. Mr. Chairman, this right was included in the Diefenbaker Bill of Rights and it was proposed to us that it should be included in the Charter of Rights in the constitution by the Canadian Organization of Small Business and by the Canadian Bar Association.

Mr. Chairman, concern has been raised as to whether or not this involves an intrusion into areas of provincial responsibility, and it has been suggested from time to time that property rights are exclusively reserved to the provinces. First of all, I would like to point out that there is some property which belongs under federal jurisdiction, for example copyright and patent rights, clearly areas falling under federal jurisdiction.

But in addition to that, we do recognize the fact that the bulk of property rights, for example, control over real property by and large resides under provincial jurisdiction. But I would point out to members of the Committee who are concerned in this area that the position of the Progressive Conservative Party from the outset has been that no provision of the Charter of Rights should apply to any province against its will; that obviously the proposal we have made is that provinces should have the right to determine what provisions within the charter would apply in their jurisdictions and would not be imposed on them by Ottawa. We are establishing a principle here, as we propose to establish a principle in the case of freedom of information, which we believe should extend across the board, but as we felt in the case of freedom of information,

we feel here that because these are areas falling under provincial jurisdiction, the extent to which they fall under such jurisdiction, the provinces should have the right not to have Ottawa simply imposing those
rights and responsibilities on them and they have a right to be heard
and to make that decision, and we are confident, Mr. Chairman, that
sooner or later and eventually all provinces will agree that the right to
the enjoyment of property should be included in the constitution and
that they would move in this direction.

A second concern has been expressed as to whether or not this provision will prevent provinces from legislating in areas of property rights. For
example, concern was expressed at the First Ministers conference about
Prince Edward Island and whether or not they would have the right to
ensure that their land in that province was not held by people from out of
the province who were not there to take advantage of it, and local people
were not deprived of their rights to use property within their province.

Mr. Chairman, it is our contention in the Progressive Conservative
Party that the amendment we are proposing would not prevent provincial governments from making or passing legislation which they
feel was essential and justified. We are asking two things; one, that the
principle of the right to ownership of property should be recognized
in the constitution; secondly, that that right should not be taken away
from anyone unless he has had a fair hearing and this is done by lawful means. We believe that such provisions would not prevent provincial governments from expropriating property if the public interest
demanded it, as long as there were fair hearings and was done legally;
it would not prevent legislation from being passed by provincial governments which would reserve land to local people, if it were done
fairly and by lawful methods. So we do not feel we would therefore
be imposing in the constitution an obligation of the provinces which
would greatly circumscribe the rights of the provinces to operate in
a field under their jurisdiction, but rather that we would, first of all,
recognize a central principle in the Charter of Rights and, secondly, we
would say that all governments have the responsibility in dealing with
their citizens to do so in a way which recognizes basic principles of law,
that it is lawful and done after a fair hearing. ...

Finally, Mr. Chairman, Mr. Robinson indicated that the NDP was not
attempting to take away family farms or to threaten the position of family farms or family businesses, and I accept their word on that, but he
said that a different case could be made in the case of corporations,
and I think, Mr. Chairman, that we should ask ourselves if we have

concerns about whether or not corporations should be entitled to the same rights as we are giving to all Canadians and to small businesses and to family farms.

I think we have a right to ask our friends in the NDP, to ask anyone who is opposed to this provision, what would they propose to do in the case of large corporations, be it even foreign owned multinationals, would they deny them the right to a fair hearing; would they deny them the right to expect that before property was taken away that that should be done by lawful means; and how is the national interest damaged? How is the national interest damaged by conferring these rights to corporations as well as to individuals? Do we not feel that anyone operating lawfully in our society is entitled before property is taken away from them to a fair hearing and to have that property taken away only by legal means. Mr. Chairman, I think that property rights should extend both to corporations and to individuals, and this is why we have moved the amendment in the way that we did. I think it is an amendment which deserves the support of all members of the Committee; and that it be welcomed by literally millions of Canadians.

**Mr. Jean Lapierre, MP (LIB, Quebec):** As you know, the Canadian Bill of Rights grants property rights. Over the summer, in July, consideration was given to including this right in the federal proposal, but a number of provinces were concerned about the inclusion of a provision of this type because of zoning, environmental and industrial development legislation. We are convinced that this new provision will not prevent the provinces from passing legislation and I assure my colleague opposite that their proposal would certainly raise the ire of our colleagues like Mr. Garon, Mr. Leonard and others, particularly in Quebec, except that what they are proposing is quite different. I think that Mr. Beatty has clearly demonstrated that property rights should be included in the new Constitution. Since I am the same man I was yesterday, the same man who made a commitment to his colleagues opposite, I am still willing to go along with their suggestion. ...

For this reason, the members of this Committee are willing to recognize this principle. Also, property rights have intrinsic value in Canada and we are prepared to go ahead with this. (44: 13–16)

### Sections 8 to 11 Generally

**Mr. Alan Borovoy (General Counsel, Canadian Civil Liberties Association):** It would appear that this section [section 8] may be a verbal illusion in the sense that it may pretend to give us something, but in fact, gives us nothing more than we already have. At the moment, there can be no searches and seizures unless they are done in accordance with procedures established by law. We would think that the real problem is, what do some of our laws themselves provide in the way of the power to search and seize.

Let me cite to you a case that received considerable controversy a few years ago, the famous or infamous Fort Erie search and strip drug raid. Just to refresh your memory, the police conducted a drug raid in a small Fort Erie hotel. By the time they were finished their business, they had searched more than 100 patrons they had found in the lounge. In the case of the women, some more than 30 women they found, they had them herded into washrooms, stripped and subjected to vaginal and rectal examinations. In the result, the police found only a few grains of marijuana and they were found not in any of the body orifices but rather on the floor of the lounge. Indeed, what also emerged is that at no time did the police believe that everyone they searched was in unlawful possession of an illicit drug. But apparently under the Narcotic Control Act, there is a power with respect to places other than dwelling houses without any kind of a warrant, even a Writ of Assistance, even that is not required, forcibly to enter, search the premises and, according to the views of the Royal Commissioner who ultimately sat in that matter, search all of the persons found on the premises whether or not each of the persons searched is himself or herself the object of reasonable suspicion. If Section 8 existed at the time of the Fort Erie search, it would appear that we would have no basis to challenge this provision under the Narcotic Control Act.

We would suggest, therefore, that it be amended so as to create an opportunity to challenge the reasonableness of the law itself. The suggestion might be something like, everyone has the right not to be subjected to unreasonable search or seizure. That may be one way of accomplishing this goal.

The same considerations would apply with respect to Section 9. That does, in the case of detention and imprisonment, what Section 8 does with respect to search and seizure. Also with Section 11(d), the provision dealing with bail is the same thing. It would seem to us that we ought to be talking about in the case of arrest and detention something like arbitrary arrest and detention. If we are talking about reasonable bail, we might also talk about reasonable grounds and in accordance with fair procedures. So that not only would the administrative practice be subject to challenge, but also in the event of an overly arbitrary law or a law which creates arbitrary powers, the law itself. (7: 12)

**Ms. Tamra Thomson (Ottawa Caucus of National Association of Women and the Law):** Furthermore, just relating to evidence, we note that going back to Sections 8 and 9, the legal rights concerning search and seizure and detention and imprisonment, such rights are guaranteed in the Charter but they are permitted to be subverted by any procedure established by law. This would allow any legislature or Parliament to subvert either of these legal rights, not to be subjected to search and seizure or not to be detained or imprisoned. We see this as another very important failure to guarantee rights within this Charter and therefore they should be amended to take out the provision which says "in accordance with procedures established by law." (22: 61)

...

**Mr. William Black (Member of Executive Committee, British Columbia Civil Liberties Association):** In many cases it seems that the rights that are given in the first half of the [Legal Rights sections] are snatched away by the second half of the Section. I am sure there have been other submissions to the Committee concerning Sections 8, 9 and 11(d), all of which are qualified by the provision that it is "except on grounds and accordance with procedures established by law." ...

We think in effect this is what those sections then mean. Section 8 means that everyone is protected against unreasonable search, unless Parliament or any provincial legislature decides otherwise. Section 9 means a Parliament or provincial legislature can authorize detention or imprisonment for any reason whatsoever, or indeed for no reason at all. Section 11(d) means reasonable bail could be denied without reason. We hope in your consideration of the proposed Charter that you will strengthen and change these sections. As they now stand we think that they give no rights whatsoever and we would prefer that they be omitted from the Charter rather than stand as they are. (22: 108–9)

**Senator Jack Austin (LIB, BC):** May I take us quickly to Sections 8, 9 and 11, on which you made comments, particularly your criticism of the phrase "except on grounds in accordance with procedures established by law." I agree with your concerns about the wide-open nature of that language and its lack of protection of rights. Do you have a suggestion as to how we could approach a redraft which would take into account the more legitimate concerns of the draftsman in that particular section under legal rights?

**Mr. William Black (Member of Executive Committee, British Columbia Civil Liberties Association):** The draft submitted to the provinces in August by the federal government said everyone has the right to be secure against unreasonable search and seizure. Section 8 of that draft said everyone has the right not to be arbitrarily detained or imprisoned, perhaps unreasonably and arbitrarily would be even more advantageous. Section 11(d) said everyone has the right not to be denied reasonable bail without just cause. I think that the draft of August fulfils many of the objectives that we hoped would be fulfilled. (22: 121)

**Professor Fred Sussman (Chairman of the Committee on Legislation, Canadian Association for the Prevention of Crime):** ... We are of the opinion that the following phrase which appears in all of these Sections, that is Section 8, Section 9 and Section 11(d) should be deleted because it would make these Sections meaningless. The language I refer to is "except on grounds, and in accordance with procedures, established by law." ... We suggest that the following language be inserted: in Section 8, the language "arbitrary or unreasonable" so that the Section would be amended to read "everyone has the right not to be subjected to arbitrary or unreasonable search or seizure." In Section 9 the words "arbitrarily or unreasonably," so that the Section as amended would read "everyone has the right not to be arbitrarily or unreasonably detained or imprisoned." Section 11(d), the words again "arbitrarily or unreasonably" so that in the relevant portions the Section would read "anyone charged with an offence has the right *(d)* not to be arbitrarily or unreasonably denied bail." (24: 43)

**Mrs. Diana Davidson (President, Vancouver People's Law School Society):** We join with the numerous other briefs that have severely criticized the legal rights Sections 8, 9, 11(d) and 12. We are in agreement with the proposals that have been made time and again before you that Section 8 be modified to "everyone has the right not to be subjected to unreasonable search or seizure"; Section 9 be modified to "everyone has the right not to be arbitrarily detained or imprisoned"; and Section 11(d) be modified to read "not to be denied reasonable bail without just cause." (32: 12)

**Mr. Norman Whalen (Vice-Chairman, Canadian Federation of Civil Liberties and Human Rights Associations):** Sections 8, 9, 10(c) and 11(d) are drafted in such a way as to render them seriously inadequate. Each is subject to parliamentary change. ... Parliament, acting alone, can establish the procedure for search and seizure. The protection which entrenchment in a constitution should offer would thereby be denied. We have recommended, Mr. Chairman that in each of these sections the limiting words "and in accordance with procedures established by law" should be replaced by the wording used in Section 7 of the Charter: "except in accordance with the principles of fundamental justice." This would mean that, while Parliament could make the changes in each of these areas from time to time, these changes would always have to be in conformity with the principles of fundamental justice. The Supreme Court would set this standard, and each legislature and the Parliament of Canada would have to meet them. Thus, only by amending the constitution would Parliament or a legislature be able to change the standard of protection which is provided in the Charter. This, Mr. Chairman, is the type of entrenchment which, in our view, is essential, if the Charter of Rights is to have any meaning whatever. (21: 7)

## Section 8 – Search and Seizure

**Professor Max Cohen (Canadian Jewish Congress):** Now, you must have heard the criticism in the last several days about that. It means, really, that all you have to do is pass a law, no matter how severe, and, therefore, it meets the requirement. Clearly, that is not what was intended by the draftsmen. What they really meant was what we think you meant by our amendment on page five of our brief, and it should read something like this: Everyone has the right not to be subjected to arbitrary or unreasonable search or seizure. That is what you meant. Therefore courts thereafter can be guided by and legislatures would have to be guided by, not to be unreasonable in what they state, otherwise, you have no standard. Simply established by law is no standard whatever. It can be the most arbitrary law, the most vicious law and it still will be binding in this particular context. (7: 88)

**Mr. J. P. Nelligan (Chairman, Special Committee on the Constitution of Canada, Canadian Bar Association):** Section 8 which deals with protection against searches and seizures made contrary to law, of course does not protect against unreasonable seizures made under the law. Our proposals and those of most other bodies have always suggested that the prohibition should be of unreasonable searches and seizures. (15: 8)

## Section 9 – Detention or Imprisonment

**Mr. J. P. Nelligan (Chairman, Special Committee on the Constitution of Canada, Canadian Bar Association):** Again, with Section 9, as it is now worded it adds nothing to the law. It should provide that no one should be subjected to arbitrary arrest or detention. (15: 8)

**Professor Max Cohen (Canadian Jewish Congress):** Again, it simply is not good enough. It can be very arbitrary and so we suggest everyone has a right not to be arbitrarily or unreasonably detained or imprisoned; a much more flexible, a much more realistic approach the way in which legislature ought to behave and the way in which the judges will make them behave by having this kind of standard. (7: 89)

**Professor David Cruickshank (Vice President, Canadian Council on Children and Youth):** With respect to the right not to be detained, we hope that one of the things you will consider is that any procedures established by law which allow detention ought to consider separate detention for young persons. This is the existing law but it is not often carried out in practice. I know certainly in rural areas of Alberta it is quite common to use adult jails for children; so that should be made clear. (21: 30–1)

### Government Response to Criticism of Sections 8 and 9 and Opposition Response

**The Honourable Jean Chrétien (Minister of Justice):** … There have been numerous representations made with respect to the legal rights in Section 8 and Section 9. The government is prepared to accept the recommendation of premier Hatfield of New Brunswick and of organizations such as the Canadian Civil Liberties Union, the Canadian Jewish Congress, the United Church, the Canadian Bar Association and others that these clauses be changed to read:

Everyone has the right to be secure against unreasonable search and seizure.

Everyone has the right not to be arbitrarily detained or imprisoned.

In other words, the fact that procedures are established by law will not be conclusive proof that search and seizure or detention is legal. Such procedures and the laws on which they are based will have to meet the tests of being reasonable and not being arbitrary. (36: 11)

…

**Mr. Svend Robinson, MP (NDP, BC):** The final question, Mr. Chairman, on the proposed amendment deals with the matter of mail openings and there was some discussion earlier today about the question of mail opening, the opening of first class mail by members of the Royal Canadian Mounted Police. Is it your view that this particular protection of the right to be secure against unreasonable search or seizure could have any effect whatsoever on the existing opening of first class mail, or possibilities of legislation which the present Solicitor General has indicated he personally supports to permit the opening of first class mail.

**The Hon. Jean Chrétien (Minister of Justice):** We will pass legislation on that and the court will apply its test to it. I cannot decide for the court. The problem of mail opening and the activities of the police to track down people who are criminals or are involved in espionage and whatnot is a different problem and that will have to meet that test.

**Mr. Robinson:** Have you had any interpretations or any advice from law officers of the Crown as to the likely success of a challenge to mail openings of first class mail by the RCMP if this provision is enacted.

**Mr. Chrétien:** I do not know if the law will be changed in terms of mail openings. If the law is changed, it will have to meet that test. (46: 108–9)

## Section 10 – Right to Counsel

**Mr. Alan Borovoy (General Counsel, Canadian Civil Liberties Association):** I then turn to Section 10 and in order to give more practical significance to the various rights that accused people or arrested people would have, we would suggest that this be augmented, that people under arrest be informed of the rights that they are entitled to exercise as soon as practicable after the arrest and that a very key component of this is that they, as you can appreciate, many of the problems that arise with arrested people arise during the course of custodial interrogations. The person is under arrest, he is nervous, frightened, bewildered and he is then subjected to an interrogation.

One of the problems is that in those circumstances, these people may very well make themselves look guilty when they are not or guiltier than they are. The idea of having the right to retain and instruct counsel without delay is of course our answer to that, but in order to give that more practical significance, the suggestion we would make is that in the absence of some imminent peril to life or limb, that people in these circumstances not be subjected to custodial interrogation until they have been advised of their right to counsel and having been so advised, either exercise it or waive their right to exercise it.

I might add in this connection, that on the basis of the research that has been done into this, there is no reason for us to anticipate that law enforcement would suffer unduly from granting these additional protections to accused people. As you know, some such protections were introduced into American law by virtue of the *Miranda* case in the U.S. Supreme Court. Some surveys conducted shortly thereafter indicated that although the rate of confessions dropped after the Miranda rule went into effect, the rate of convictions and crime clearances, which are another way of saying crime solutions, did not drop. So, in other words, it appeared that custodial confessions were not the indispensable element in law enforcement that many people had until then thought. (7: 13)

**Professor Max Cohen (Canadian Jewish Congress):** The next problem of course is to retain and instruct counsel without delay. Now, very important questions arise here. What if you do not have it? You all know of course the famous U.S./Supreme Court judgement in the Moranda Case. In Moranda the Supreme Court and a whole series of cases thereafter made it clear that the failure to inform accused of his rights will poison the proceedings thereafter. The question is, what do we say about that kind of problem in a Canadian charter. We do not go that far. We do not say that the failure to inform will amount to an absolute exclusionary rule that you cannot have evidence therefore which can be adduced because you have not given the man a fair warning as you should have done. We think this should be left to the judge in a case by case process. (7: 90)

**Hon. James A McGrath, MP (PC, Newfoundland):** My concern is that by inserting the words "as soon as practicable" in place of "promptly" you are defeating the very purpose of the section, because "promptly" means promptly; whereas "practicable" means different things to different people. Would you please explain what you mean by that. I do not understand, quite frankly, how you feel, if there is to be the protection afforded in Section 10, and if we are to have an entrenched bill of rights, obviously we must have the kind of protection that Section 10 addresses. It seems to me to be a contradiction in terms there if you change the word "promptly" to "as soon as practicable."

**Mr. Roderick McLeod, Q.C. (Assistant Deputy Attorney General of Ontario, Canadian Association of Crown Counsels):** Sir, we are not wed to the words "as soon as practicable." Our concern with this issue is exactly the same as the concern of the Chiefs of Police. We are suggesting that some courts might interpret the word "promptly" as meaning virtually immediately and that just simply is not practicable in many arrest situations. That is why in our view the Criminal Code for many years has spoken in terms of giving notice, where it is feasible to do so, to allow for the fact situation where, for one reason or another, depending on what kind of a fact situation you are dealing with, how many people there are; where they are; what kind of pressure the police officer is under and he may require some few moments it might be 10 minutes, it might be 20 minutes before he can get to that person and comply with this provision in the constitution, and we are concerned that the word "promptly" just connotes too much immediacy. I really cannot be too much help here, but my understanding is that the French version of this constitution as now drafted does not really translate too easily back into English with the word "promptly." So perhaps it is a draftsmen's problem rather than anything. (14: 15)

**The Honourable Jean Chrétien (Minister of Justice):** Some witnesses have made the point that while Section 10 guarantees the right on arrest or detention to retain and instruct counsel without delay, there is no explicit requirement for an individual to be informed of that right. I am prepared to accept an amendment so that the section will state that: "Everyone has the right on arrest or detention to retain and instruct counsel without delay and to be informed of that right." (36: 12)

## Section 10 – Right to Legal Aid

**Professor Max Cohen (Canadian Jewish Congress):** … We think that in accordance with the international convention there should be a right to legal aid because, as matters now stand, that language will very easily succumb to the theory – well, of course, you are entitled to counsel, but if you cannot afford counsel, then so what, what is your recourse to it. It ought to be clear that now that Canadian society has almost established a rule from coast to coast in the assistance of legal aid in which no one is deprived of their due defence through the absence of counsel, somewhere that is worth stating in a charter of rights so fundamental as this. So, a legal aid system of some kind or the right to legal assistance of some kind is worthy of charter mention. (7: 90)

**Professor Fred Sussman (Chairman of the Committee on Legislation, Canadian Association for the Prevention of Crime):** With specific reference to Section 10(b), where we approved this Section, we suggest that the right to free legal aid be available to the accused with insufficient financial means in criminal proceedings. We are aware that present legislative provisions and arrangements with federal government support by agreement with the various provinces in support of the legal aid schemes in the various provinces have the effect of making legal aid presently generally available and we would like to see that availability entrenched so that it could not in the future be removed. (24: 43–4)

**The Hon. James A. McGrath, MP (PC, Newfoundland):** ... It does seem to me that the danger in entrenching legal rights is that you are affording a great deal of protection for the advantaged people who can afford counsel, whereas not addressing the problem of the disadvantaged who cannot afford counsel. As somebody once said, beggars hang so that jurymen may dine. They only hang poor people.

**Mr. Nick Schultz (Associate General Counsel, Public Interest Advocacy Centre):** On the question of legal aid, as you have indicated, we do have in I think virtually every province fairly comprehensive legal aid plans which remove the pernicious aspect of the penal system where people who could not afford lawyers were simply going to jail because the only people they had advising them were the police officers who were arresting them. However, there is no provision in this Charter which would ensure that those legal aid plans, or something like them, remain in place. What we would propose is that there be some provision inserted in the Charter to ensure that those without means be provided, not necessarily specifying the means but simply that consideration be given to providing the means so that these rights can be enjoyed. That would not necessarily tie the hands of the legislature into saying: you have to have this specific legal aid plan; but a province would have to give thought to establishing a legal aid plan which would redress that problem. (29: 26)

**Mrs. Diana Davidson (President, Vancouver People's Law School Society):** We also support incorporating in Section 10(b) a provision such that those without funds will have independent counsel provided for them. (32: 12)

**Mr. Algis Juzukonis (Council of National Ethnocultural Organizations of Canada):** ... We would also further suggest the inclusion of a provision in the new Charter guaranteeing legal counsel to those Canadians who are not able to pay for it. (22: 78)

**Mr. Jean Lapierre, MP (LIB, Quebec):** ... If we return to your presentation on Clause 10 concerning legal rights where you hope that will be added in the right to receive legal aid freely everywhere in Canada for people who do not necessarily have the means, did your group try to find out who would be paying for that legal aid? (22: 89)

**Mr. Juzukonis:** Yes, Mr. Joint Chairman legal aid exists at the present time under the jurisdiction of the provinces. It comes to a question of principle for us. It is not a question of some sort of program which is necessary. We endorse the Charter of Rights and Freedoms because we believe that is the best way to protect human rights in our Canadian society. But how can we guarantee that protection, when the poorest elements of our society – who are usually the most discriminated against – do not have the same access to legal [counsel] that the more well to do elements of our society have. It is imperative that they be guaranteed that same access to legal counsel that others have available to them. The only way we can guarantee that is to include a provision for legal aid. In our case it is a question of principle and not of program. (22: 89)

**Mr. Svend Robinson, MP (NDP, BC):** ... If there is to be a right to retain counsel, as there should be, if there is to be a right to be informed of this right to retain counsel, what good is either of those rights if the person who is accused of a criminal offence has no money and cannot afford to retain counsel? Should not that be included in the constitution and not left to a statute, a simple statute which can be amended or taken away, to ensure that that right has some substance.

**The Hon. Jean Chrétien (Minister of Justice):** My reply to you is that it is a different thing to pay or not to pay. I do think that to cope with that problem, some time ago in Canada we passed a bill that established a program for helping the individuals who cannot afford to have a lawyer to get them. It is a program that is working very well ...

**Mr. Robinson:** That bill can be repealed tomorrow, Mr. Minister.

**Mr. Chrétien:** I will be in the House and you will be in the House, too and I do not think that it will be repealed.

You have to keep in mind that you cannot put everything in a bill of rights. It is a fundamental law of government – you cannot inscribe all aspects of the Criminal Code in a Bill of Rights and we have legal aid established as part of the Canadian society for a long time. It is not going to disappear. Of course, you know, you say that if it is in a bill of rights it is better but at the same time the minute that you try to make out of a bill of rights the Criminal Code, it is no more a bill of rights. It is basic rights of the citizens, and I do not think that having this tradition in Canada of legal aid for years, that it is appropriate to inscribe it in the constitution. (37: 24–5)

**Mr. Svend Robinson, MP (NDP, BC):** ... Group after group appeared before this Committee asking us to recognize the principle that it is a hollow right to tell someone who has been charged with a serious criminal offence that they have the right to retain and instruct counsel, and they have the right to he informed of that right, but if they do not have any money then it is too bad, that is the end of the matter, because that is the effect of the Charter as it stands now.

The Minister might say: well, there are legal aid provisions in effect in the provinces and the territories, but I would point again to the Minister's own words and the explanatory notes to this proposed Charter and what the Minister has said is this: "However, with few and limited exceptions the rights and freedoms are not constitutionally guaranteed." These are the vital words: What protection has been legislated yesterday can be removed or limited by another enactment tomorrow. Now, Mr. Minister, it is not good enough to say that this legislation which guarantees to those persons charged with serious offences the right to legal aid is the only protection they should have, for as a number of groups have said to us if this right is to mean anything at all it must include the right of the poor to have the assistance of counsel. ...

In view of the representations from group after group after group before this Committee, why has it been decided not to include this fundamental right in the Charter of Rights, and particularly why has it been felt that you are prepared to rely upon an ordinary statute of Parliament and provincial legislatures which can be swept away at any time? (46: 128)

**Mr. Jean Lapierre (LIB, Quebec):** If I may, Mr. Chairman, the position which has been discussed is that legal aid, as you know, is basically a provincial responsibility; all Canadian provinces and territories now have legal aid, with a federal financial contribution. The problem with entrenching your proposed amendment would be in determining the eligibility criteria which differ from province to province. Senator Asselin is no doubt aware of the criteria in Quebec, which are no doubt different from Ontario's and those of the other provinces. We feel that at the present time the system is well enough provided for by ordinary provincial legislation, and we do not see the need to include legal aid in the constitution. I would even go further. Earlier, Mr. Robinson, you spoke of our international obligations. I feel that the provincial measures in existence allow us to fulfil our international obligations quite well, since we do in fact provide legal aid to disadvantaged citizens. ...

**Hon. James A. McGrath, MP (PC, Newfoundland):** I just wanted to ask the Minister if a person is advised of his rights under this section and if he cannot afford counsel, well then, at that point in time surely he is entitled to be advised that there is legal aid which will provide him with counsel and that seems to me to be the thrust of what Mr. Robinson's amendment addresses.

**The Hon. Jean Chrétien (Minister of Justice):** In this system the guy has some rights and in terms of the administration they will say you are entitled to a lawyer.

**Mr. McGrath:** He says: I cannot afford it.

**Mr. Chrétien:** I do not know, we could perhaps give, an Attorney General can perhaps give direction to his police force to advise the person that there is a system of legal aid but we cannot put it into the Charter of Rights how administratively it should be done. We say you have the right to have a counsel, that is the main purpose of this amendment. How after that it is being implemented in the field, of course that is why we have Attorneys General in the provinces and it is not even my responsibility unless we decide to inscribe something in the Criminal Code in terms of a new procedure. What we are giving is the right, the right to counsel, it is as a basic right. How to pay for counsel, it is either the individual or legal aid and it is not a matter of the Charter, it is a matter of operation after the person accused has been informed of his rights. (46: 131)

**Hon. David Crombie, MP (PC, Ontario):** The [US] Supreme Court has held, however, that the amendment imposes an affirmative obligation on the part of the federal and state governments to provide at public expense legal counsel for those who cannot afford it in order that their cases might be adequately represented to the court. The Supreme Court has held that this right extends even to cases involving petty offences if there is a chance that a jail sentence might result. The indigent have been held to have such a right at any critical stage of the judicatory process which the court has confined to post-indictment stages and trial-like situations. In addition, indigents have been given the right to a free copy of their trial transcript for purposes of appeal for their conviction. Congress enacted the Criminal Justice Acts of 1964 and 1970 to implement this right to counsel by establishing a federal defender system to represent those defendants who could not afford legal counsel. I just thought it might be worth pointing out to the Minister that, at least in the Republic to the South which has had the Bill of Rights now for something like 160-odd years, they have at least seen the point that the right to counsel without the ability to afford one indeed is a hollow promise and if you mean something by it, then I think we ought to be able to put our support in giving those who are charged before the courts the ability to pay for a lawyer. (46: 132–3)

...

**Mr. Robinson:** Mr. Chairman, I am concerned that if this right which is proposed in the charter is to have any substance for the poor of this country who are charged with a serious criminal offence, if this is to be a charter for all people in Canada and not just for those who can afford to retain a lawyer, that we should live up to our commitments, the commitments we have under the International Covenant on Civil and Political Rights, and that we should entrench this right in the constitution. It has been suggested that, well the judge can always appoint a lawyer; but, of course, that is purely discretionary and it is not good enough to rely on that. It has also been suggested that the provinces have enacted certain legal aid schemes. Well, as the Minister himself has said, what protection has been legislated yesterday can be removed or eliminated by another enactment tomorrow. We are writing a charter for the future, for decades possibly, Mr. Chairman. This right, if it is to mean anything to the poor, if there is to be any justice for the poor, it must be supplemented by the right to retain counsel and that is the purpose of this amendment, and it is for that reason that I would hope that all members of this Committee would support the proposal. (46: 134–5)

[Both the Tories and the NDP supported the proposed amendment to add a right to legal aid to section 10, but it was voted down by the Liberal majority on the committee, 13–9.]

### Section 10 – The Right to Counsel

**Professor David Cruickshank (Vice President, Canadian Council on Children and Youth):** With respect to rights upon arrest we suggest two additions that would affect young offenders in conflict with the law; one, the right to be informed of your right to remain silent; secondly, the right to have an independent adult, and by this we mostly mean a parent, present during police questioning. These are two rights we think important, as attached to the rights on arrest. The right to counsel we think ought to be expressed in a broader, more definite way, to read that indigent persons including accused young persons have the right to have counsel provided, not just the right to retain and instruct, but the right to have counsel provided at the time of plea and trial. (21: 30–1)

**Mr. William Black (Member of Executive Committee, British Columbia Civil Liberties Association):** Right to counsel is mentioned in Section 10(b) but we are concerned that the right to counsel should be a practical right as well as a right in theory. Therefore, we would urge that first you include in the Charter a provision that people should be informed of their right to counsel and that they should also be informed of the other rights stated in Section 10 and Section 11. Secondly, we propose that the Charter be amended to include the right to be provided with counsel in serious cases if an accused person cannot afford counsel. We do not think that justice is something that can be denied for lack of funds and we believe that in many serious criminal cases, it is absolutely essential that the accused have the assistance of counsel if the accused is to have a fair trial. (22: 109)

## Section 11 – Trial within a Reasonable Time

**Hon. James A. McGrath (PC, St John's East):** I would like to go on to your next suggested recommendation on Section 11(b). This concerns me, because you expressed concern about the use of the phrase "reasonable time" with regard to the laying of a charge. What would you consider to be appropriate? Would you specify a length of time?

**Chief Ackroyd:** I do not think it should be entrenched in the constitution.

**Mr. McGrath:** Where is it to be entrenched? What would be your preference?

**Chief Ackroyd:** I think it would have to be as laid out in the Criminal Code, what the times are for a preliminary hearing, for example, or for a trial. But you are putting the courts in a position of trying to interpret what is a reasonable time. There are cases in the metropolitan Toronto today that are two and a half years and have not come to trial; so, is that a reasonable time? "Reasonable" is a very vague word. So that it can only work if you have a specific time frame laid down that a man should be brought before a preliminary hearing within so many months, and following that, brought to trial within so many months. But to be as vague as to use the word "reasonable" leaves a very broad interpretation for the courts. (14: 14)

**Mr. Svend Robinson, MP (NDP, BC):** Do you have any suggestions on what specific time might be laid down if there are to be specific times laid down, have you given any thought to that?

**Chief Ackroyd:** No, I do not think it is the position of the police to lay down specific times. I would feel that if it is to be entrenched in this Charter it would have to be done by amendments to the Criminal Code.

**Mr. Robinson:** Of course, you appreciate the Criminal Code is not in any way an entrenched document and what could be put into the Criminal Code can also be taken out of the Criminal Code at any time.

**Chief Ackroyd:** Yes, my concern would be with a word as vague as "reasonable," could people then be allowed to go free that are before the court because someone ruled that they were not tried within a reasonable time. I do not know what "reasonable" is. (14: 17)

## Section 11 – The Right upon Being Charged with an Offence to Be Informed of the Specific Offence

**Chief John Ackroyd (Chief Metro Toronto Police, Canadian Association of Chiefs of Police):** Our greatest concern in Section 11 is the word "specific." The Association suggests that that word be taken out and recommends that it read "to be informed as soon as practicable of the offence with which he is charged." The reason we say that is that in the word "specific" many police officers investigating a crime, at the scene of the crime may not know when they are arresting a person and telling him what he is charged with, they may not know whether it is murder or manslaughter: he may not know whether it is false pretences or forgery, those two are very close in the Criminal Code. We may not know whether it is gross indecency, or indecent assault, and the word "specific" ties it down very tightly and we feel it should be removed. (14: 7)

...

**The Hon. James A. McGrath, MP (PC, Newfoundland):** I would like to have an explanation from the government as to why they would use the phrase "without unreasonable delay" as opposed to "promptly," because the whole word "reasonable" causes some concern as to what you mean by "reasonable" and hence what is meant by "unreasonable"? "Promptly" would be a much better word in terms of protecting rights.

**Mr. E.G. Ewaschuk (Department of Justice):** Mr. McGrath, that is obviously so in the classic case where somebody is charged with murder or rape or robbery, but that is not what this section deals with. This section deals with an offence, it deals with federal offences, it deals with provincial offences, and [in] well over 90 per cent of those offences there is no arrest involved so the person is not there and he cannot be told promptly, meaning you have him there, and obviously that is the way it should be done if the person is there.

However, on the other hand, [in] many of these cases there has to be an assessment so maybe documents are taken, its weights and measure, they go back, a decision is made and then they charge the person by laying an information. What they do in those cases then, is they summons the person. They often use the mails. Now, I think some of us know how slow the mails are and is that "promptly" in bringing that notice or informing the person of the specific offence, or where in fact they may have to serve that person, find that person?

So the question was to give more flexibility to deal with the more minor offences, the regulatory offences, summary conviction offences, rather [than] the other; it was decided it would be preferable to use the words "without unreasonable delay" which gives more flexibility than the word "promptly." If we were dealing only with murders, rapes and such, where there was a detention for bail hearing, then the word "promptly" would have been the better word. But we are not dealing with that, but with all of the range of offences. So that is the reason for moving to "without unreasonable delay."

**Mr. Chrétien:** And, Mr. Chairman, if I may, I would add that the Chiefs of Police would be happy with that. ...

**Mr. Svend Robinson, MP (NDP, BC):** ... I share the concern expressed by my Conservative colleagues with respect to the change from "promptly" to "without unreasonable delay." I might also note that the honeymoon between the Conservative members and the Canadian Association of Chiefs of Police seems to have been rather short lived. The Chiefs of Police would be throwing their hands up in horror that their newly acquired allies have deserted them so quickly on what is so obviously a matter which is going to result in rampant crime in the streets. Mr. Chairman, I think we should maintain the word "promptly." That word is the word which is used in Clause 10(a). I would like to remind honourable members of this Committee – and I am sure that Mr. Ewaschuk and the Minister would agree – that this qualification of "promptly" is subject to the overriding test in Clause 1, as are all clauses in the Charter – of demonstrable justifiability. If it can be shown to be demonstrably justifiable that there is a problem in complying with this position of "promptly" then there is no difficulty: that Clause 1 limitation applies to this, and secondly, that the remedies clause in Clause 24 leaves a very wide discretion in the courts and one of the factors they can consider in coming up with the appropriate remedy would indeed be the kind of practical difficulty Mr. Ewaschuk has pointed to. I would oppose the amendment and join with my Conservative colleagues in doing so. (47: 32)

**The Hon. John Fraser, MP (PC, BC):** Again, referring to Black's Law Dictionary, the word "prompt" is defined as "to act immediately;

responding on the instant." I do not have the advantage of seeing other definitions in Canadian cases as to how the word "prompt" has been defined. But I ask honourable members just to look at those words – "to act immediately, responding on the instant." Now, interestingly enough, in the same law dictionary, "reasonable notice," which is what the government amendment is, is defined as "such notice or information of a fact as may fairly and properly be expected or required in the particular circumstances." Now, that is open to different views, as to how much time ought to be required in each case.

I am a little concerned – and I am only speaking for myself here, unlike some of my colleagues on the Liberal side who do not introduce their comments with that caveat, so, I am looking at my very good friend, Mr. Lapierre – that if the general and accepted definition in law of "prompt" is consistent with the one in Black's Law Dictionary "to act immediately, responding on the instant," that could create some problems. On the other hand, "reasonable notice" – and again, I am only referring to the English and not discussing how it may appear in French – "such notice or information of a fact as may fairly or properly be expected or required in the particular circumstances." Having said that, and having pointed out that when we are dealing with words, we had better know what they mean, which makes the work of this Committee under the time constraints we are operating extremely difficult, and I do not think we are doing justice to the amendment. In any event, what I would like to ask is this. The amendment is to Clause 11, and to Clause 11 (a). It says that

Any person charged with an offence has the right
(a) to be informed without unreasonable delay of the specific offence

Now, I want to know what "specific offence" means. That certainly cannot be the charge; because it says "any person charged with an offence," which would imply they had already been charged. If a person is charged with breaking and entering, that is what they are charged with. Then it goes on to say that they have the right to be informed promptly of the specific offence. Does that mean they have the right promptly to be informed that they have been charged with breaking and entering, or does this mean that they have the right promptly, or without unreasonable delay to be given the particulars of the offence?

In trying to help anyone who may be watching this, a charge is one thing. A charge of breaking and entering is the specific charge. It usually is accompanied by the statement that so and so did unlawfully on such and such a day and at such and such a place, break and enter. But there are many other aspects which are called "particulars of the offence" which, of course, can be sought by defence counsel on application, which go far farther than that. I want to know whether Clause 11(a) is talking about the particulars of the offence, or just about the charge itself! If what this means is that you cannot be charged without being told that you are charged, then I follow you; but if it means that you can be charged and told of what you are charged and Clause 11(a) then means you must be promptly or without unreasonable delay given the particulars of the charge, then I want to know what this means. I am not saying this to delay the proceedings of this Committee, I am just asking these questions because we are now dealing with very difficult concepts and we have to know what we are talking about, then this Committee is not doing its job. Somebody else will come along later, as I have said before, and say, "Why did not the Members of Parliament ask a few questions and find out what they were talking about?"

**Mr. Ewaschuk:** If we take the example of somebody shooting somebody – to go back to Clause 10(a) that everyone has the right ... on arrest or detention to be informed promptly of the reasons therefor. So, the policeman puts the arm on the person and says, "I am arresting you for shooting so and so, for killing somebody." He has told him the reason, but he has not told him of the specific charge. Now that is step number one: "Promptly" – he has him there, and he can tell him promptly, assuming that he is not fighting back or there is no flight. Then we go to the next clause – "Anyone charged," the way I interpret that is not that you are being told you are charged with murder, but it is in fact the laying of the information – Section 455.3 of the Criminal Code. You go in front of JP and you lay that information; that is charging somebody with an offence. So we assume, then, that the police have in fact sworn to the murder information, and he is still there.

Well, in Mr. McGrath's earlier example, he is still in the cells, so it is not very difficult to walk down there. That is what Clause 11(a) assumes. You are going to tell him now not that he is being held on a homicide for killing somebody, but that you are charged with second degree murder or manslaughter or first degree murder – you have to go on and tell him that. In the normal course of events, however, what will happen is that you will serve him with an appearance notice.

There may be a summary conviction ticket or, in a great many of these situations, it is actually a summons. You will inform the person that he would be charged on the laying of the information; in fact, if we are assuming in a summons situation he would not be informed until the summons were served on him through the mail or by personal service. Then he would be informed of the specific charge – careless driving, weights and measures, whatever type of offence it may be; but the process, the document that he would be served with would tell him of the specific charge. (47: 34–7)

...

**Senator Martial Asselin (PC, Quebec):** Does the right to be informed promptly mean. ... There is already a time limit in the Criminal Code; as you said earlier, the accused must be summoned to appear before the judge. Does "promptly" refer to his appearance before the court or to his arrest? Does this mean that he has the right to be informed immediately of the reasons for his arrest?

**Mr. E. Ewaschuk (Department of Justice):** I think that is a very good question because we had a lot of argumentation. It seemed to me that what the international charters were really saying was that it is the right to be informed on first appearance in court that you had the right to be arraigned, you had the right to be told of the information. On the other hand, what this is designed to do is to tell you even before you get to court so that you may prepare for court. Some people assume that maybe when you go to court for the first time that you have to go on with your trial. I think that you and I know that that is not so. You are there many times before you are forced on for your trial. The short answer is no, it is not intended merely to in fact put the duty on the court to inform you on your first appearance, your arraignment, to be arraigned, it is in fact to be told before you go to court what the specific offence is either by serving you with a summons, an appearance notice or however the process may be, or warrant, but you are to be told of the specific offence. (47: 39)

**Mr. Svend Robinson, MP (NDP, BC):** I think that if we now go to "within a reasonable time" in the English version that we are probably weakening it even more. Note that the words, for example, "within a reasonable time" are the precise words that are used with respect to the right to a trial "within a reasonable time" and to have the next clause using those same words. Without unreasonable delay strike me as being some sort of compromise. I would have preferred the word "promptly" to remain but I recognize the Minister is attempting to accommodate the Canadian Association of Chiefs of Police and is also not prepared to use the wording which the International Covenant on Civil and Political Rights used in Article 14(3)(a) which refers to the words "to be informed promptly and detail in a language which he understands of the nature and cause of the charge against him." Those are the words which presently bind us, Mr. Minister, but if you wish to yield to the suggestions of the Chiefs of Police in this matter, certainly I will understand.

**The Hon. Jean Chrétien (Minister of Justice):** Mr. Chairman, I have said that we will accept the words proposed by Mr. Tassé, and "promptly" is not acceptable. (47: 41–2)

### Section 11 – The Presumption of Innocence

**Professor Max Cohen (Canadian Jewish Congress):** Now, with respect to [the presumption of innocence] there is a development in Canada in which in certain types of offences the onus shifts once the Crown makes a prima facie case. That was developed very much in Regina versus Sault Ste. Marie. Do you want to speak to that, Mr. Magnet.

**Professor Joseph Magnet (Canadian Jewish Congress):** The point here simply is that a defence of due diligence is not recognized by the Supreme Court of Canada with respect to public regulatory offences which are not true crimes. These would occur mostly at the provincial level and the Supreme Court of Canada now recognizes in Regina and Sault Ste. Marie and Regina and Chapin and in various cases in the provincial courts of appeal, that the onus of proving the defence of due diligence is on the accused, after the Crown has made a prima facie case. Well, we have considered whether the presumption of innocence might disturb the developments, the quite laudable developments of the Supreme Court of Canada in this area and we think on balance that there is no danger that the presumption of innocence will disturb them. (7: 91)

### Section 11 – The Right to Bail

**Professor Max Cohen (Canadian Jewish Congress):** We now come to this question of bail. The language you have here we think could be improved ... by reading not to be arbitrarily or unreasonably denied bail. It seems to me that is the real issue, that bail should not be unreasonably or arbitrarily denied. (7: 92)

**Mr. J. P. Nelligan (Chairman, Special Committee on the Constitution of Canada, Canadian Bar Association):** ... When we come to Section 11 ... on the denial of bail, it should be that there should be no denial without just cause. (15: 8)

**The Honourable Jean Chrétien (Minister of Justice):** There have been many representations made regarding Section 11(d). It has been suggested that the right not to be denied reasonable bail should be subject only to just cause rather than procedures established by law. I am prepared to accept an amendment to read that: "Anyone charged with an offence has the right not to be denied reasonable bail without just cause." This reflects the wording now found in the Canadian Bill of Rights. (36: 13)

...

**Mr. Chrétien:** Mr. Chairman. On several occasions in the course of your proceedings before the clause by clause consideration, several groups have argued that the draft that we had before us and that only stated "except on grounds, and in accordance with procedures, established by law" was much more too restrictive and that we should ensure in a more explicit way this citizens' right. This is why we have changed the wording to "without just cause." (47: 52–3)

### Section 11 – The Right to Trial by Jury

**Mr. Norman Whalen (Vice-Chairman, Canadian Federation of Civil Liberties and Human Rights Associations):** Section 11(c) provides for trial by an impartial tribunal, omitting reference to the jury system which is at the foundation of the criminal justice system in Canada. (21: 8)

**Mr. Svend Robinson, MP (NDP, BC):** I would suggest to you, Mr. Minister, that there is a very serious omission in this particular section, namely, the omission of a guarantee that when Canadians are or a Canadian citizen is charged with a serious offence, that they would have the right to be tried by a jury of their peers. This is a fundamental right in the Canadian criminal justice system, and, indeed, was contained in the 1688 Charter of Rights and is an important element in the United States Bill of Rights; and I would hope that you would be prepared very seriously to look into the possibility of an amendment to include the right to trial by jury in the case of serious offences.

**The Hon. Jean Chrétien (Minister of Justice):** You are right in referring to the existence of the Bill of Rights in the United States. But the application of that has been somewhat restricted by interpretation in the courts and over the years the courts have limited the application of these rights and have declared them to be somewhat limited. Of course, I would like to point out to you that the United Nations Covenant on Civil and Political Rights does not mention a right to trial by jury. Personally, I think it is a well-established Canadian institution laid down in the Criminal Code. But the question arises: Is it necessary to add to it by including it in the Charter of Rights? As far as I am concerned, I have no personal objection. However, I think the problem would be to find the proper test to decide what is a serious offence, and so on and so forth. Perhaps it would be easier and much more satisfactory to leave it as it is in the Criminal Code. If it is a major concern to the Committee, personally if we can find the appropriate words and try to convince the Cabinet of the wisdom of doing it, then, as I have said already, if there is some suggestion on the part of the Committee I am perfectly willing to look into the matter. I would like to clarify the matter that it is covered by the Criminal Code today and it is not judged by my officials as being necessary for inclusion in the Bill of Rights. But I will listen to the views of the Committee. (4: 57–8)

**Mr. Robinson:** A fundamental concept of criminal justice in this country, the concept of trial by jury in the case of serious offences is not even found in the document and when that was raised with the representatives of the Department of Justice they shrugged their shoulders and said, well, we assumed it was in there. We assumed it was in there. Well, Mr. Chairman, why this great rush? (9: 45)

...

**The Honourable Jean Chrétien (Minister of Justice):** A number of suggestions have been made with respect to Section 11 which deals with the rights of anyone charged with an offence. Mr. Robinson, member for Burnaby, British Columbia, has made strong representation to guarantee the right in serious criminal matters to trial by jury. I welcome his representations as being very constructive and would be prepared to accept the following amendment:

> Except in the case of an offence under military law tried before a military tribunal, anyone charged with an offence has the right to the benefit of trial by jury where the maximum punishment for the offence of which the person has been charged is imprisonment for five years or a more severe punishment.

I want to stress that this, like many rights, represents a minimum standard. The Criminal Code will continue to provide for jury trials in many cases where the maximum punishment may be less than five years imprisonment. Jury trials in cases under military law before a military tribunal have never existed either under Canadian or American law. (36: 12)

**Mr. Svend Robinson, MP (NDP, BC):** Certainly, I welcome the proposal of the government to include in the proposed Charter of Rights the right to trial by jury. This is a fundamental right which Canadians have taken for granted for many years, and I appreciate the fact that the Minister has listened to the representations of a number of groups and individuals on this very important question. It was, I think, recognized as early as Blackstone, in Blackstone's Commentaries that the fundamental importance of the right to trial by jury – and I would quote very briefly from Blackstone's Commentaries: "The trial by jury, or the country, per patriam, is also that trial by the peers of every Englishman, which, as the grand bulwark of his liberties, is secured to him by the great charter." That is the Magna Carta. (47: 53)

**Hon. Jake Epp (PC, Manitoba):** I would like to ask the Minister two questions: one, the amendment that the Minister has put forward – would that amendment in fact increase the number of cases which would go to the jury instead of the present practice?

**Mr. Chrétien:** No, I do not think so.

**Mr. E. G. Ewaschuk (Director of Criminal Law Amendments Section, Department of Justice):** We do not have the numbers. But it could affect an increase in the volume in jury trials. If you start viewing the indictable offences in the Criminal Code as a Jacob's ladder and go from the top of the ladder, then you have life imprisonment, then 14 years, 10 years, 5 years – and the most minimal type of indictable trial is the two year trial. So, obviously, having practised in the courts, you know people do not go to jail automatically for two years for a two year offence. Breaking and entering a dwelling house is a life offence, and most young offenders almost invariably get probation for that. It is the rare case where you go to jail for this type of minimal offence. We have identified as far as the five year offence is concerned, the problems which would be created with that; for example, under the Combines Act, if you have a corporation that is involved in a combines; in 1976 the penalty was increased to five years; but the Combines Investigation Act itself says a corporate accused is not entitled to a jury trial. This, in fact, would call for the amendment of that act. In Section 483 of the Criminal

Code we have a bunch of offences some of which are theft, possession, false pretences, fraud under $200 where the Crown goes by indictment and there is no jury trial and the top end is two years.

There are other offences – and I have a list here; keeping a common gaming house, betting house, various types of bookmaking, lotteries, games of chance, betting for a consideration, driving while suspended, where the Crown goes by indictment, fraud in relation to fares – those offences, then, traditionally there has been no right of jury trial, and the right to jury trial would be allowed for all those two year offences. Our concern was not to overly inconvenience the courts. Jury trials are much slower, and civilians have to be brought in and they have to sit, and panels have to be selected. A decision was made that it was reasonable for five years, that, given the fact that people, as we have said, do not go to jail that often for two year offences, that there you have more discharges than fines, that it really was not required in that type of case.

**Mr. Epp:** I appreciate, Mr. Chairman, that very complete answer. Do I take it from you sir, then that the five years you feel even in that case there would be an increase in jury trials? Obviously, you do not have a reading as to how many; that there could or likely would be an added cost factor on the provincial treasury even with the five years. Is that correct?

**Mr. Ewaschuk:** It would be very marginal in the five year offences situation; there as a general rule – there is the odd exception – jury trials are provided for.

**Mr. Epp:** And the two years would obviously increase it substantially as well and plug up the system and you would have not only to spend more money on the system, but also to enlarge the system. Is that correct?

Mr. Ewaschuk: Yes. (47: 53–7)

### Section 11 – Double Jeopardy

**Professor Max Cohen (Canadian Jewish Congress):** We now come to how far the double jeopardy rule, no one can be tried twice for the same offence, will protect war criminals in Canada. Here we have a very serious Canadian, as well as international problem. There are allegations, as you know, that are anywhere from 35 to 200 war criminals, if they could be tried properly, running around this country. The debate has been going on for a number of years. I am not competent to judge the accuracy of those figures, but clearly, there are enough people of competence in this country who believe it is a serious problem to make us wonder how we should handle it.

We feel that it is worthwhile looking at how the United Nations Covenant on civil and political rights handled the matter. If you see the language we borrowed from the Covenant on page 8, you will see we took Article 15(2) from the UN Civil and Political Rights Covenant. I think we should incorporate that somewhere into a Canadian charter, so that even though time will eventually destroy the immediacy of the problem of Nazi war criminals, it at least it is there as a symbolic gesture to a very dark past and that no one should be allowed to run free so long as there is a possibility that we have a war criminal who can be identified as such. So that the doctrine of double jeopardy will not become a defence to anyone who otherwise can be identified in due course as a war criminal.

There is another aspect to this on the top of page 9 which is the extent to which the word offense itself raises difficulties. We think that the double jeopardy rule in the word offense gives rise to some problems and we think the Committee recommends the word offense in 11(f) be replaced by the words acts giving rise to the offense. Because what you can have is, you can have a man tried two or three times for different offenses, even though they are the same set of facts. What we are saying there is, therefore, once you identify a set of facts, no matter how ingenious you may be able to formulate different offenses against him, you ought not to try that man twice on the same set of facts. (7: 92–3)

**Mr. Svend Robinson, MP (NDP, BC):** Mr. Chairman, the purpose of this particular amendment is to reflect in the Charter the representations which have been made to us by a number of groups who are concerned that the development of the law in Canada be accurately reflected in dealing with this particular clause on the subject of what amounts to double jeopardy. (47: 60)

### Section 11 – Compelled Testimony

**The Honourable Jean Chrétien (Minister of Justice):** The Canadian Bar Association and the British Columbia Civil Liberties Association have argued that the proposed resolution should clearly constitutionalize the right of an accused not to be required to testify against himself in criminal proceedings. This longstanding right in our system of justice against self-crimination should be explicit in the Charter. An amendment to Section 11 which would make this clear is included in the material I am tabling. (36: 12)

**Senator Martial Asselin (PC, Quebec):** No one can be forced under the Criminal Code to testify against himself, but does this cover the case of an accomplice who testifies against an accomplice and is subsequently charged with the same offence? Is this provided for, or does the witness have to ask for the court's protection?

**Mr. E.G. Ewaschuk (Department of Justice):** No, that will be in another clause. What this means is only when he is being tried does he have the right not to testify against himself. So that is only when his liberty is at stake during that trial. (47: 43–4)

### Section 11 – Ex Post Facto Laws

**The Honourable Jean Chrétien (Minister of Justice):** Representations have been made by the Canadian Jewish Congress and the North American Jewish Students Association and by members of the Committee to ensure that Section 11(e) and (f) do not preclude the possibility of prosecuting those who are alleged to have committed crimes recognized under international law. The International Covenant on Civil and Political Rights recognizes the right of a country to try to punish a person for an offence that was, at the time of its commission, recognized as such under international law even if not so recognized at the time under domestic law. The Covenant also permits the trial and punishment of a person for an offence for which he has not been tried and punished in another country.

To reflect these principles in the Charter the government is prepared to accept an amendment so as to provide that:

> Anyone charged with an offence has the right not to be guilty on account of any act or omission that at the time of the act or omission did not constitute an offence under Canadian or international law; and has the right if finally convicted or acquitted of the offence in Canada, not to be tried for it again and, if so convicted, not to be punished for it more than once. (36: 12–13)

**The Hon. Jake Epp, MP (PC, Manitoba):** All of us have been concerned that our Bill of Rights would reflect not only Canadian practice and Canadian heritage, but as well our obligations to the international community and specifically as it relates to war criminals. I know the Jewish Students Association and the Canadian Jewish Congress have put forward amendments along these lines. I think it is a better reflection, not only on our Canadian traditions, but also on our obligations internationally and I commend, obviously, the amendment to all members. (47: 58)

**Mr. Ron Irwin, MP (LIB, Ontario):** So there is no misconception on this, Mr. Chairman, the clause does not prevent the prosecution of war criminals. By itself it does not do that. It does not stand in the way of the prosecution, but by itself it does not allow the prosecution. What it does is allow enabling legislation if the Parliament sees fit, so I think that should be clear. (47: 59)

## Section 12 – Cruel and Unusual Treatment or Punishment

**Senator Duff Roblin (PC, Manitoba):** … Have the Chiefs of Police any opinion as to how their stand on capital punishment would be affected by either one of these two sections of the proposed bill?

**Chief John Ackroyd, Chief, Metro Toronto Police Canadian Association of Chiefs of Police:** Well, Mr. Chairman, we did not do any research into this with any depth. We did not do so because we did not feel there was anything in this Charter which would prevent the bringing back of capital punishment if the government of the country so decided. As I understand it, capital punishment in the United States has not been regarded as cruel or unusual treatment because it has been conducted in other places in the world, and therefore, those words may not prohibit capital punishment from being brought back. So we have not really addressed ourselves to it. But these would be my views off the top of my head. (14: 29)

**Mr. William Black (Member of Executive Committee, British Columbia Civil Liberties Association):** We would also recommend with regard to Section 12 which concerns cruel and unusual punishment, that you consider the wording of Article 7 of the International Covenant. As presently worded, it would seem that no matter how cruel punishment would be allowed as long as it were not unusual. And that is also the interpretation that has been given to those words by the Supreme Court of Canada. The International Covenant language would avoid that problem. (22: 110)

**Mr. Svend Robinson, MP (NDP, BC):** I would like to draw to the attention of members of this Committee, Mr. Chairman, that as it now stands the Clause is worded "cruel and unusual punishment." What that means, according to the Supreme Court of Canada, is that any punishment is acceptable within the Canadian context, as long as it is not unusual. It does not matter how cruel it may be, or how inhuman or degrading, if it is not unusual, if it presently exists in Canadian jurisprudence, then it must be accepted and cannot be struck down.

... I believe we should bring this Clause into line with the provisions of the International Covenant on Civil and Political Rights; that we should broaden the possible scope of this protection from cruel, inhuman or degrading treatment or punishment in order that some of the more odious forms of punishment and treatment which presently exist in Canada and which are by no means unusual might possibly be dealt with by the courts. I need only point, for example, to the abuse of the lieutenant governors' warrants. That is not unusual. Unfortunately and sadly, that is not unusual, and that could not be covered because of the fact that though it might be cruel, inhuman or degrading, it is not unusual.

Mr. Chairman, there is the treatment of prisoners held in solitary confinement. While there was a decision of the federal court at first instance that that constituted cruel and unusual treatment or punishment, it is very likely that, had that case been appealed – the government decided not to appeal it – it might very well have been overturned, because solitary confinement under what many regard as cruel and unusual circumstances, cruel and degrading circumstances, is sadly not unusual in Canadian society. (47: 73–4)

**The Hon. Jake Epp, MP (PC, Manitoba):** I would like to ask the Minister whether he has had anyone study Clause 12 and whether any determination has been made as to whether Clause 12 could be interpreted by the courts either as saying that capital punishment is not cruel or unusual, or in fact that it is. Is the clause neutral on the question of capital punishment?

**The Hon. Jean Chrétien (Minister of Justice):** The advice I am receiving is that this clause is neutral – the power to decide on capital punishment will remain the prerogative of Parliament.

**Mr. Epp:** If it is neutral – and I accept your word as being the best knowledge the Crown now has – does that not leave open the possibility that the courts could decide on either side of the case as I have presented it?

**Mr. Chrétien:** The Supreme Court has already decided. They would have to reverse themselves.

**Mr. Epp:** Would it not be possible for them to reverse themselves in view of the Charter now coming into effect?

**Mr. Chrétien:** No, we do not think that would cause them to change their minds and reverse themselves. If we were to use the words proposed or change them, it could cause them to reverse themselves. But if you use those words as exist in the Bill of Rights, the legal situation will remain the same.

**Mr. Epp:** On a philosophical basis, Mr. Minister, do you agree that the question of capital punishment should be left to parliamentarians?

**Mr. Chrétien:** Yes. ...

**Mr. Epp:** I take it from you that you feel, one, that the matter is neutral and that the Supreme Court has judged on it and declared that it is not unusual or cruel punishment, and that your position is that it should be Parliament judging on these questions, rather than the courts. (47: 76)

## Section 14 – Right to an Interpreter

**Professor David Cruickshank (Vice President, Canadian Council on Children and Youth):** With respect to an interpreter we would point out that languages in the ordinary sense are not the only barrier to understanding what goes on in court. In my work as a lawyer in the juvenile courts I have seen frequently a situation where a young person comes out of court having pleaded, having listened to the charges, undergone a trial, and not known a single thing that happened in the court room. It all has to be explained over again to him. So we would like to see you take the concept of an interpreter as far as including the right to an interpreter where age or disability is a barrier to understanding the language and process of the courts. ... (21: 31)

...

**Mr. Yves L. Fortier (National Treasurer, Canadian Bar Association):** At Chapter five of its report towards a new Canada, the Canadian Bar Association had recommended that provisions for using one official language or the other in a criminal case be enshrined in the constitution. We had also recommended enshrining the right to testify in French or in English before any Canadian court. We think that the proposed resolution does not go far enough. We agree with you, Mr. Irwin, to say that asking this question helps pointing out the danger there is in not enshrining such a right. Today's Ontario government is encouraging the use of French. But will tomorrow's government do the same? This is the main reason why, in this field as in others which have been commented upon, we recommend the enshrining of certain fundamental rights. (15: 23)

**Mrs. Diana Davidson (President, Vancouver People's Law School Society):** ... We are taking no position with respect to the official languages or the minority language educational rights, other than to say that in this province it is to the disadvantage of Indian people that they are not able to use their own language in court. We support their right to be able to be tried in their own language and as far as possible within their own culture. (32: 14)

**Senator Guy Williams (LIB, BC):** Your reference to Indians not being able to use their own language in courts, I think that is one of the contributing factors. I was a member of the Parole Committee of the Senate and I found that from Manitoba to British Columbia there were times when 56 per cent of the inmates were our Indian people. But I do see difficulties. In British Columbia alone there are nearly 40 dialects. I originally come from Kitimat. I left there in 1944. There are parents there today who do not speak their own dialect, many of them, and this is repeated in many other reserves. Personally, I cannot see where there will be enough people to supply the need. (32: 28)

**The Hon. James McGrath, MP (PC, Newfoundland):** Well, Mr. Chairman, now that that fact has been so dramatically verified I expect any minute to ask the Minister to give consent to have the amendment withdrawn to be moved on a subsequent amendment. It would be more in keeping with the experience we have had here. However, Mr. Chairman, this is a serious amendment and I am very, very encouraged by the fact that the government has seen fit to accept it because there are a number of people in this country who have a serious hearing handicap. Indeed, I stand to be corrected on this, but there are over 200,000 Canadians who are deaf or have a hearing disability to the point where they are clinically or legally deaf, and it is a serious problem because their handicap is not apparent and it becomes compounded when they are party to legal proceedings. That is why this amendment is so important. It is not without interest to note that we are moving in the direction of recognizing the rights of these people, for example in broadcasting they have mechanical devices now in the public broadcasting system in the United States for the hard of hearing or the deaf. I understand that we are moving in that direction in Canada as well. (47: 87)

## Additional Legal Rights

**Mr. Norman Whalen (Vice-Chairman, Canadian Federation of Civil Liberties and Human Rights Associations):** We would have liked to see included under the heading legal rights, the right to remain silent, the right to retain and instruct counsel in private, the right to have counsel present during questioning and the right to legal aid, as well as the right to be informed immediately upon arrest of each of the rights listed above. (21: 7)

## Chapter Ten

# Equality Rights

**Section 15**

*Non-discrimination Rights* Equality Rights

Equality before and under law and equal protection and benefit of law

15 (1) ~~Everyone~~ Every individual ~~has the right to equality before~~ is equal before and under the law and has the right to equal protection and equal benefit of the law without discrimination ~~because of~~ and, in particular, without discrimination based on race, national or ethnic origin, colour, religion, ~~age or~~ sex, age or mental or physical disability.

Affirmative action programs

(2) ~~This section~~ Subsection (1) does not preclude any law, program or activity that has as its object the amelioration of conditions of disadvantaged ~~persons~~ individuals or groups including those that are disadvantaged because of race, national or ethnic origin, colour, religion, sex, age or mental or physical disability.

### Section 28

*Rights guaranteed equally to both sexes*

**28.** Notwithstanding anything in this Charter, the rights and free-doms referred to in it are guaranteed equally to male and female persons

### Section ~~29~~ 32

### Application of the Charter

(2) Notwithstanding subsection (1), section 15 shall not have effect until three years after this section ~~Act, except Part V,~~ comes into force

## Commentary

No other section was overhauled as completely as section 15 as a result of the submissions of witnesses before the Joint Committee. As originally presented to the committee, section 15 would have protected only "equality before the law" and "equal protection of the law." This language was taken directly from the Canadian Bill of Rights. As discussed in chapter 1, judicial interpretation of the bill led to widespread dissatisfaction with it in academic and human rights circles and helped fuel the drive for a constitutionally entrenched Charter of Rights and Freedoms. In particular, as described in chapter 2, the Supreme Court's decisions in several cases – *Lavell*, *Bedard*, and *Bliss* – provided a very narrow and, many would say, narrow-minded approach to equality. Thus, it is not surprising that, at the Joint Committee, section 15 became a magnet for criticism of the Supreme Court and for argument over the role of the courts generally.

Many witnesses were wary of giving the courts too much power to interpret equality rights given their past record of upholding differential treatment. As David Lepofsky of the Canadian National Institute for the Blind noted, "The courts have a tradition of taking a very restrictive view of civil liberties."[1] Witnesses expressed scepticism as to whether the judges would be up to the task of interpreting a constitutional bill of rights, especially respecting an equality guarantee. This drove the witnesses' desire to be as specific as possible regarding the language in section 15.

No less than seven specific subjects or proposed amendments were proffered: (1) changing the title of the section, (2) changing "everyone" to "every individual," (3) the contents of the equality guarantee generally, (4) the role of the enumerated grounds and the list of those included, (5) the affirmative action clause, (6) the need for an additional clause to explicitly protect the rights of women, and (7) the three-year delay in section 32(2), which provided that section 15 would not come into force for three years.

Some groups feared that the Charter would do too much to prevent differing treatment where such treatment should be permitted. The Church of Jesus Christ of Latter-day Saints thought the Charter might take away "traditional protections" enjoyed by women.[2] The Catholic bishops were worried that a religious school board would be prevented from hiring solely people of a certain religion.[3] Likewise, the insurance industry was concerned that the age and sex provisions would impact their ability to sell insurance products.[4]

Another major concern was the judicial interpretation of section 15 specifically in regard to women's rights. Section 28 was not part of the 6 October 1980 draft of the Charter. At the Joint Committee, several groups called for an additional, explicit statement recognizing the equality of the sexes. Such a clause was proposed as an amendment during the Joint Committee hearings but was resisted by the government and voted down during clause-by-clause. It was thus not part of the amended resolution reported back to Parliament in February 1981. As discussed in chapter 4, in April 1981 the government agreed to an amendment to the joint resolution to add section 28. The amendment passed in the House of Commons 222–0.

One of the primary concerns of the invited witnesses was whether the equality/non-discrimination provision should include a list of protected grounds. The original wording did not include the phrase "and, in particular," implying that the listed grounds were exhaustive. Many witness groups were against this and favoured not having a list at all;[5] others wanted to add more enumerated grounds. Of the proposed additional grounds, physical or mental disability was by far the most widely supported. Other suggested grounds included sexual orientation, parental status, prior criminal convictions, language, marital status, political belief, and an explicit inclusion of Aboriginal rights. As we can see from our current Charter, with the exception of disability none of these grounds was included in the final text. Indeed, there was a failed NDP amendment to add marital status, sexual orientation, political belief, and lack of means to the text.[6] Instead, the government changed the wording to create an illustrative rather than exhaustive list of prohibited grounds.[7] The NDP and the Conservatives proposed amendments to add physical or mental disability, and the Liberal government agreed, adding this ground to the text of section 15.

Equality rights were seen as having the most wide-ranging impact on governments, and that is why section 32 (then section 29) provided for a three-year delay before section 15 came into force. Section 15 was the only provision of the Charter that was not to go into effect upon proclamation. The delay was necessitated, according to the government, to allow federal, provincial, and territorial governments time to review their legislation for compliance with the new equality provision. Numerous witnesses spoke out against this delay; some wanted immediate application, while others proposed more limited delays of a year or several months. However, this delay was not the focus of the witnesses' energy and attacks. That was levelled squarely at the specific language of section 15.

### Section 15 Generally

**Mr. Alan Borovoy (General Counsel, Canadian Civil Liberties Association):** The problem with this, of course, one is always concerned about is how well a section of this kind ultimately be construed by the courts. There is a risk and one never knows exactly how these things are going to be interpreted, but there is a risk that on the one hand it may be too narrow and on the other hand it may be too broad. It may be too narrow because if we state the grounds of unacceptable discrimination in the charter, then we may implicitly be saying that any other ground of unreasonable distinction or discrimination thereby becomes constitutionally acceptable. ...

Is there a risk that if one says, for example, no race discrimination, there can be no discrimination because of race, might that imperil Indian Reserves? To what extent might that be discrimination because of race? To what extent might old age pensions or the Juvenile Delinquents Act be arguably considered discrimination on the basis of age? I am not suggesting necessarily that the courts would give that interpretation, I am only suggesting that the words may be such as to create some problems with respect to it, and what one always worries about is that if the courts, as many of us would think likely, seek to sustain the Indian Reserve system, old age pensions and the like, in doing so they may develop doctrines that might create mischievous precedents for some other situations where we would not want it to apply. (7: 13–14)

...

**Mr. Svend Robinson, MP (NDP, BC):** I do wonder though whether you have considered two points: the first is the wording "equality before the law," followed by equal protection of the law and the desirability of changing that to a different formulation, perhaps equality in the law or equality in and under the law so it is very clear that we are not just talking about the administration of the law but we are talking about the substance of the law. ...

**Professor Walter Tarnopolsky (President Canadian Civil Liberties Association):** ... One just does not know whether the change of the word equality before the law to something such as equality under the law will make a difference. ...

One is guessing as to what is going to be most effective. I think one can say this, that when particularly Mr. Justice Ritchie in the *Lavell* case introduced the conception that the term "equality before the law" really means no more than Dicey, suggested for it, which is, if everyone is equal before the courts of the land. At that point, he also suggested that he was rejecting the American egalitarian conception of the clause. Now, what is being proposed here is with the addition of the words "equal protection," one is specifically indicating the incorporation of American jurisprudence. Whether that is going to be sufficient, one does not know. However, it seems that when there is a combination of the nondiscrimination clause with the equality and equal protection clause that the egalitarian concept is supposed to infuse the equality or equal protection clause. Certainly, this is the approach taken in Article 26 of the International Covenant and Civil and Political Rights in combining the prohibited grounds. 

So, from that point of view, the suggestion where we have placed our emphasis is more on the decision, the hard decision that has to be made either to extend the grounds or not to mention any for the fear that those not mentioned might be excluded. (7: 22–3, 29)

...

**Professor Irwin Cotler (Canadian Jewish Congress):** With regard to Section 15(1) ... our Committee recommends that Section 15 express a general proscription of discrimination and protection of equality before the law with no grounds listed. In the alternative, if prohibitive grounds are to be included, we believe that the prohibited grounds of discrimination in Section 15(1) are incomplete. In particular, we believe that the rights of the disabled require entrenchment in the constitution. ...

As well, we believe that the list of prohibited categories, if they are to be identified, should be expressed by way of the *ejus generis* principle so as not to unduly freeze the proscriptions only to those that are listed herein.

Finally, we believe that the charter should contain an express reference to the rights of women. We suggest adding here an unequivocal principle that this charter guarantees the equal right of men and women to the enjoyment and protection of the rights and freedoms set forth in this Charter. (7: 93–4)

**Ms. Lynn McDonald (President, National Action Committee on the Status of Women):** Equality before the law, the wording proposed in the government's Charter of Rights, and used in the present Canadian Bill of Rights, has been interpreted to mean only that laws, once passed, will be equally applied to all individuals in the category concerned. The law as written could discriminate against women, which is neither just nor acceptable. The courts have been concerned with maintaining the just administration of the law, but not with discrimination built into the law itself. Thus the Supreme Court of Canada decided against Lavell and Bedard, two Indian women who lost their status on marriage to non-status men. If the present wording prevails there is no guarantee that Indian women will not continue to be denied equal rights with Indian men. ...

In view of the Stella Bliss case especially, it is clear that more specific directions need to be given to the courts for the interpretation of equality. Notably it is necessary to specify that discrimination on the basis of sex is proscribed whether the law discriminates against all women or only some of them. NAC recommends the addition of a new clause to Section 15 specifying that discrimination on the basis of specified category is proscribed whether all members of that category are affected or only some. (9: 58–60)

...

**Ms. Lynn McDonald (National Action Committee on the Status of Women):** We would prefer a positive statement, where exactly it goes could be debated. But we would prefer a positive statement, not just the nondiscrimination, partly because of the problems in Section 15(2) in that affirmative action programs could be ruled to be illegal, whereas if there were a positive statement about equality as a good thing to be aimed at, affirmative action programs would be seen as a natural follow-up to that.

**Miss Flora MacDonald, MP (PC, Ontario):** Yes. I realize that; that is Section 15(2) which we are talking about as far as disadvantaged person and putting in the positive statement there, but I would think in Section 15(1) it would be necessary to spell out very clearly that every man and woman has the right to equality before the law, that it has to be put in in much clearer terms in Section 15(1) than it is now.

**Ms. Lynn McDonald:** Yes. Our complaint with Section 15(1) is not that the sex discrimination is not so clear but that the equality before the law is an inadequate wording, because it has been interpreted only to mean equality in the application of the law and has not been interpreted to mean that the laws themselves must not discriminate against women.

**Miss Flora MacDonald, MP (PC, Ontario):** Indeed this is the very wording that had been used in the *Lavell* case to deny the rights of women.

**Ms. Lynn McDonald:** Yes. ... The decisions of the Supreme Court and other courts, the courts generally, have been very bad. When women are the victims of discrimination, judges have been very bad on this. They have been much better on native peoples, much better on ethnic minorities than they have been on women's issues. That is why we think we just have to spell out these things. We just cannot leave that one to chance. (9: 65)

...

**Miss Pauline Jewett, MP (NDP, BC):** Thank you, Mr. Chairman. I wanted to emphasize then and emphasize again now how important it is that the equality of women, women's human right to equality is a positive objective that must in the document be stated as a positive objective. I wanted also to emphasize, and I think you have but perhaps you might want to comment a little further, on the very great importance of changing the wording that is now "before the law," the very great importance of changing that to "in the law" or "in law," because of the fact that the "before the law" clause has been, of course, a part of our common law and it is also a part of the statutory bill of rights and as has been said, has been interpreted in a way not to provide for equality in the law itself.

I am assuming that you would want in Section 15(1) a definite change in the wording that now exists and remove "before the law." What is so very important, it is not the minor fact that we change a word, it is of vital importance to give a clear message to the courts and to the legislatures that their interpretation must be changed. If you use the same words naturally a court will continue to interpret those words the way the court has hitherto interpreted them. Nor is it any good to say, as I think the Minister responsible for the status of women says, that by entrenching the bill you will somehow be giving a message to the courts that they should interpret those words differently. I do not myself believe that is a valid argument to make. In fact I think it is a very flimsy argument to make because the courts in many instances have interpreted the Diefenbaker bill of rights, the Canadian Bill of Rights as if it were entrenched. And the famous *Drybones* decision has never been overturned on that score and therefore, simply now to say that the words will be treated differently, is to me a very weak argument.

In my speech in the House, and I think I was the only one that did speak specifically on the need for change as far as women are concerned, I did make an appeal to all my fellow members of the House and particularly to the 14 women in the House, that we should do as we had done once before this year, get together as we did on the question, Flora MacDonald will recall, of equality for Indian women. I hope that all the women will once again get together to ensure that the changes that you have suggested and other changes might be made.

**Ms. Lynn McDonald (National Action Committee on the Status of Women):** We want to stress that the *Lavell* and *Bedard* cases were lost to women not because of the lack of entrenchment of a Canadian bill of rights but because the judges did not see the issue as a matter of equality because they interpreted "equality before the law" in an extremely narrow fashion. Miss Jewett is quite right in pointing out that the judges did not come up with this narrow interpretation when it was a matter of *Drybones* where the victim of discrimination was a native male, but they were unable to see equality when it was a case of women being the victims. So it was not the lack of entrenchment that has done women in on these very important women's rights cases. ...

**Miss Jewett:** Of course one of the reasons why this is so badly drafted and why women's groups, and we will be hearing later from the Canadian Advisory Council on the Status of Women, have been protesting the present wording is because unfortunately most of the academic lawyers and government lawyers who have been looking at questions relating to equality over the past ten years have not been looking at the problem of women's equality and, indeed, have not been women lawyers and academics. I think your brief shows the benefit to be derived by the fact that young women nowadays are becoming prominent as constitutional lawyers and prominent in the legal profession as well as in the law schools. (9: 68–9)

...

**Mrs. Doris Anderson (President, Canadian Advisory Council on the Status of Women):** Women in Canada know from bitter experience that the discrimination we encounter often originates and is perpetuated by the laws themselves. In other cases, women have not received justice because of the unfortunate interpretation of laws that we believed were there to defend our rights. The wording in Clause 15 is almost exactly the same wording as in the Canadian Bill of Rights and this wording we have found through ten years of testing before the Supreme Court of Canada has not alleviated discrimination for women at all. Equality before the law has meant equality of treatment in the courts and in the administration of the law, not in the law itself.

We would like to see the wording changed in each of the two parts of present Clause 15 and, in addition, we wish to add a further clause. We believe that we need these changes because the guarantee of rights for women, as it now stands, is simply not strong enough. The wording we have suggested we believe would establish as a positive principle that women are entitled to equality. The equality that we envision would exist in the law, not merely in the administration of the law. Clarity in the drafting of Clause 15 is essential so that there can be no misinterpretation of the directive to the court. It must be clearly understood by the public, by the courts and the legislatures that Canadians intend to enshrine in the Constitution a genuine principle of equal rights. (9: 124)

...

**Dr. Noel A. Kinsella (Chairman New Brunswick Human Rights Commission):** We make comments on Section 15 with reference to equality before the law. That is terribly important for us, Mr. Chairman. It is important because that wording, as others have mentioned before this Committee, has to be such that people, like Sandra Lovelace, would not have to seek remedy outside of her own country, but would be able to find justice and equality within Canadian law. She has, as all Canadians have, the right to a domestic remedy against the worst form of discrimination, namely legislative discrimination. (11: 32)

**Mr. Norman Whalen (Vice-Chairman, Canadian Federation of Civil Liberties and Human Rights Associations):** We find in particular, Mr. Chairman, that the rights against discrimination as set out in

Section 15(1) are seriously lacking in two respects. First, the list enumerated is not exclusive. For this reason we recommend that no list be attached, thereby prohibiting discrimination on any basis. Secondly, apart from the right to equality before the law, we would submit that everyone should have the right to equality of service as well as to equality before the law. We would suggest that the provision of equality of service would go a long way towards establishing the rights of the handicapped, minority groups and other disadvantaged groups or persons. (21: 8)

...

**Ms. Pamela Medjuck (National Steering Committee, National Association of Women and the Law, Nova Scotia):** We are therefore not at all confident that the Supreme Court will begin to interpret this clause in a broader way simply because it is entrenched. I think the point is important to be made that entrenchment itself is not a protection. The protection for equality comes from guidelines clearly articulated in a charter. We believe that Section 15 does not set out these kinds of guidelines. Quite the contrary, in our view, these words are likely to receive exactly the same interpretation after entrenchment as before. ...

We do not believe that this subtle change in the wording of the equality clause will be sufficient to overcome the past restrictive interpretation given to the words "equality before the law and the protection of the law." The principle should be generously and broadly stated so that there is no doubt whatsoever that the purpose of the Section is to guarantee to every person their human right to equality in the fullest sense. We are concerned that the word "protection" is too restrictive because this ordinary meaning would not include "benefits" or "privileges." When the phrase "equal protection" was included in the American constitution in 1868, in the 14th Amendment, there were no social welfare benefit programs around at the time. Now we have these programs. We think we should avoid the problem of the litigation the Americans are facing in trying to broaden the word "protection" to include in the constitutional guarantees, benefits. We should learn, from their experience that the courts have had a hard time in stretching that concept. If Canada is taking the opportunity now to offer protection and benefit, it is not too demanding to ask that those words be included.

Also, because the courts have tended to take a strict and very literal interpretation of human rights in Canada, we think that every possible mechanism for guiding them and directing them how to interpret the Charter should be made available. Including the word "benefits" does this, and it is not difficult to put in a few words. We therefore recommend that the words "and equal benefit" be added after "equal protection" in Section 15(1). (22: 56)

**Mr. William Black (Member of Executive Committee, British Columbia Civil Liberties Association):** I would like to run through what we think are the minimum objectives of any right to equality and then compare the language of Section 15 with those objectives. First, we think it is essential that the right to equality protect against all unreasonable forms of discrimination. The right to equality of all things should not be given to some and denied to others. Unfortunately it seems that Section 15, as it is presently worded, may do just that because it provides that everyone has the right to equality "without discrimination because of race, national or ethnic origin, colour, religion, age or sex."

It would seem then that the Charter would not protect against unreasonable discrimination on the ground of political beliefs, or unreasonable discrimination on the ground of physical disabilities or unreasonable discrimination on the ground of sexual orientation. We wish to re-emphasize here that the right to equality does not mean that all groups have to be treated absolutely equally in all circumstances. It prohibits unreasonable and discriminatory distinctions. With that qualification in mind, there seems to us no reason not to extend it generally to all people in society and to prohibit all unreasonable discrimination. In this regard we have had the advantage of submissions of the Canadian Human Rights Commission to this Committee and we believe that either of the alternative proposals that were made in the submission of the Commission would be a big step in the right direction.

A second objective of the right to equality is that it should apply both to equality in the application of the law and in the substance or content of the law. I understand other groups have raised the *Lavell* case before you where the Supreme Court seemed to hold that it did not apply to equality in the content of the law. (22: 110–11)

**Mr. Bruce Smith (President of Toronto Ontario East Stake, Church of Jesus Christ of Latter Day Saints):** Section 15 of the proposed resolution is an attempt to ensure equality before the law and equal protection of the law. We fear, however, that in its present vague form it may have the very opposite effect. Of fundamental concern to us is its potential effect on the family. As a church we have deep and fundamental commitments to the family, upon which all other institutions of society depend. It is in the family that we best learn to work, to love, to forgive, to be committed to justice. It is the family which is the natural and fundamental group unit of society; to change it is to change society itself. Within the family, motherhood and children are entitled, we believe, to special care and assistance. Our concerns may be illustrated as follows:

First, in attempting to remove discrimination because of sex and age, Section 15(1) of the proposed resolution could end up, perhaps inadvertently, taking away from women and children traditional freedoms and practices they now enjoy. Husbands now are primarily liable for the support of their wives and minor children. If this liability is removed, in the name of equal treatment for both sexes, the protection afforded by this responsibility to mothers and children could seriously be weakened, with tragic consequences for both individuals and society. Women who prefer to remain at home and maintain a traditional family could be unable to legally count on child support from their husbands. Great pressures could be brought to bear on a woman not to marry or have children, and to join or remain in the labour force. The potential deleterious effects on family life seem obvious, and must be prevented.

Second, if the law must be undiscriminating towards sex, it could follow the laws outlawing wedlock between members of the same sex would be invalid. The argument of a homosexual male, for example, could be, "If a woman can legally marry a man, then equal treatment demands that I be allowed to do the same." As a church we are totally opposed to the extending of constitutional protection to homosexual marriages. While it cannot be stated with certainty whether this or any other consequence will result from the vague wording of Section 15(1), the possibility cannot be precluded.

Section 15(1) would not provide traditional protection of women against military service. Although Canada does not at present have compulsory military service, the possibility of such being required in the future cannot be overlooked. If women were found physically qualified, they would, unless exemption is provided, be required to be treated exactly the same as men, including service in combat zones in time of war. ...

The impact of Section 15(1) on sexual offences against children cannot readily be ascertained, but could be extremely damaging. If children are not provided special protection by reason of their age, but are treated the same as adults with respect to sexual acts, what will be the impact on their wellbeing? As a Church, we deplore, in the strongest terms, sexual relationships outside of marriage. But perhaps our strongest condemnation falls upon those who abuse children sexually. These innocents require special protection by society against both hetero and homosexual offences. (29: 8–10)

**Senator Renaude Lapointe (LIB, Quebec):** What do you consider as a reasonable and natural distinction between the sexes, and do you not think that women are able to make the distinctions for themselves?

**Mr. Bruce Smith:** If I heard the question correctly, Mr. Chairman, what do we think is a reasonable and natural distinction between the sexes, and then the second part of the question. ...

**Senator Lapointe:** Do you think that women are able to make these distinctions for themselves?

**Mr. Regan Walker (Executive Secretary, Toronto Stake, Church of Jesus Christ of Latter Day Saints):** Mr. Chairman, certainly women are ready and able to make any sort of natural distinction. That is not the problem that we are addressing in this brief. The problem is that perhaps the openness of the language of Section 15 could be subject to judicial interpretation such as would leave women and girls and children et cetera in certain instances in an unfavourable position under the law, and we are thinking in terms of such things as co-ed washrooms, housing institutions, the military, et cetera. In other words, there are no exceptions admitted in the language of Section 15 such as would comprehend a situation like that, if interpreted strictly by a court. (29: 16)

## Enumerated Grounds: General

**Mr. J. P. Nelligan (Chairman, Special Committee on the Constitution of Canada, Canadian Bar Association):** Dealing with some rights which we feel are not broadly expressed or not sufficiently broad. We feel, for instance, in Section 15, that the right to equality before the law should not be limited to specific kinds of discrimination. We feel that the individual should be protected against all forms of unreasonable discrimination by a general recognition of the right of the individual to equality before the law. On that point, and again I think some of the other groups have discussed it, because of recent decisions in our courts it would appear necessary to make it clear that that equality is not merely before the law but equality in the law. I would not myself have thought a few years ago that was necessary but now, on the basis of experience, we feel that refinement of the language should be provided. (15: 8–9)

...

**Mr. R. G. L. Fairweather (Chief Commissioner of Canadian Human Rights Commission):** We ask you to change Section 15 of the Charter to a general proscription of discrimination with no grounds listed, as suggested by the Minister of Justice for Canada in his July document, a much better formula for protecting against discrimination than what has come before your Committee in September. (5: 8–9)

...

Failing that, I believe the list should be expanded to include physical and mentally handicapped, marital status, situation de la famille, sexual orientation and political belief. And may I remind the Committee that this is the non-discrimination section that I am dealing with, that having an inclusive list does not thereby say that the Canadian Human Rights Commission or Parliament is making any statement about sexual preferences or political beliefs, or so on, it is saying that people should not be denied employment opportunities because of these beliefs. Sometimes this is mixed up and I get letters from people saying we are advocating a certain lifestyle or a certain preference. It is not my business to advocate, or my colleagues. You would rightly be outraged if we were in the business of advocating lifestyle. (5: 8–9)

...

**Mr. Noel Kinsella (Chairman, New Brunswick Human Rights Commission):** ... Rather than have the exclusive list of grounds which is presently within the wording of Section 15 of the resolution before you, that you would use terminology like "grounds of discrimination such as" and list whichever ones you wish to list, and try to come close to the list of prescribed grounds of discrimination that you would find in the provincial and federal human rights acts of Canada, because they have already been accepted, and then put at the end "or other status"; and the courts, then, would be focusing very clearly on discrimination, these kinds of things and the so-called *ejusdem generis* principle of statutory interpretation which will be applied. (11: 40)

...

**Mr. Ron Irwin, MP (LIB, Ontario):** Under the Charter of Rights age is included as an item along with race, national or ethnic origin, colour, religion and sex. Under the Bill of Rights it is excluded, it is not in that column. Do you see this as diluting the interpretation of that particular section? Do you see the inclusion of age in the Charter of Rights as a good thing or should it be separated off into another category?

**Mr. Alan Borovoy (General Counsel, Canadian Civil Liberties Association):** The suggestion that I made earlier was that while we would like to see age discrimination prohibited in many contexts, there was some nervousness about establishing a blanket constitutional provision because of the possibilities of some situations arising where age would be an altogether reasonable category of distinction.

That being the case, the suggestion was that it ought not to appear in this form but rather what ought to appear is a general prohibition against unreasonable distinctions or discrimination followed by a selection of some categories that are almost always inappropriate, and there we would say they would be regarded as presumptively unacceptable. (7: 29)

**Ms. Pamela Medjuck (National Steering Committee, National Association of Women and the Law, Nova Scotia):** ... New grounds may be recognized in the future which we cannot now anticipate. To achieve this, either no list should be included in Section 15(1), or words such as "on any ground including" should be added before the list to clarify that it is not all inclusive.

Our first preference would be to include no list at all to provide for the more expansive possible application of the section. However, we do recognize the concerns of groups such as the mentally handicapped who may prefer the protection of a list of grounds which includes them. ...

A number of grounds which should receive judicial scrutiny have been left out of the Charter. The more obvious ones are: marital status, physical or mental handicaps, political belief, sexual orientation and previous conviction. It is important to include marital status because often discrimination against women is disguised in this form. The language of Section 15 should permit the court to scrutinize legislation on these grounds. The present wording of Section 15(1), because it provides a finite list of prohibited grounds, will not permit the necessary expansion. (22: 58–9)

...

**Senator Duff Roblin (PC, Manitoba):** Coming to that point about guidelines, I would like to express my real interest in your proposals to change Section 15. That has to be one of the most important sections of this bill and I am much attracted by your first preference that you read out to us a little while ago because your preference for Section 15(1) I think clearly sets out the overriding goals that we are seeking here, in a much more satisfactory way than the rather negative way in which it is phrased in the bill itself. I also like the way you have divided the two principles of equal rights and then reinforced it with Section 15(1), which comes under the heading of compelling reasons that must be advanced.

My problem with the way it is written now is that it is limited to certain subjects such as race, sex, colour, national or ethnic origins, religion and so on, but I suppose it is conceivable that there may be other rights which might be included under a rule of compelling reason. Would it be possible to add a phrase like "or the like" or some phrase like that, that would indicate that we are not necessarily limited to those specific categories that you show there? Is it possible to get a more flexible approach?

**Ms. Deborah Acheson (Member of the Steering Committee, National Association of Women and the Law):** Yes it would be possible to draft so it said that a compelling reason must be shown for any distinction including the following categories, some words to that effect. I have not quite addressed myself to it.

All we are doing in Section 15(1) is setting a standard through those cases where discrimination can almost never be justified and we are leaving it open to the courts discretion to decide whether it will use a compelling reason test or a reasonableness test with respect to the other cases. (22: 64)

...

**Ms. Lynn McDonald (President, National Action Committee on the Status of Women):** NAC recommends that the specified categories in Section 15(1) be amended to include marital status, sexual orientation and political belief. We do not elaborate here but these are included in other codes and we would recommend they be included here. (9: 58–9)

...

## On Age and Mandatory Retirement

**The Hon. Jake Epp, MP (PC, Manitoba):** From your experience as a Commissioner of the Human Rights Commission, could you give us examples of if this proposed resolution had in fact been in effect with the prohibitions in Section 1, can you give us some specific examples of the restrictions it would have given or caused both to rights and freedoms and also to the Commission?

**Mr. R. G. L. Fairweather (Chief Commissioner of Canadian Human Rights Commission):** Yes. One was given last night, if I know correctly, by the Minister of Justice for Canada. It might be that generally accepted standards in this country for mandatory retirement, the anti-discrimination part having to do with age, could be challenged and rendered meaningless as a reform mechanism, because the generally accepted standards now are quite illiberal, if I may use that word in this place. The generally accepted standards for Canada are to push people out at certain ages. I greeted this charter with excitement when I saw that the Government of Canada had included age, but when I see the language of Section 1, I wonder. ... (5: 11–12)

...

**The Hon. Jean Chrétien (Minister of Justice)** [in response to Mr. Hawkes, MP]: So you are asking me to answer a question about the effect of the charter on compulsory retirement at age 65. I think we have to ask ourselves whether it is discrimination to force people to retire at 65? I do not know how compulsory retirement at age 65 will be interpreted in light of the provision in the charter for no discrimination because of age.

The courts could interpret that this is discrimination. I think the important thing right now is to make sure that there is no blatant discrimination. Of course, we would have to take into account conventional practices regarding retirement in Canada. Now, as to whether this is in direct conflict with the charter, I do not know what sort of effect the charter would have. In my own mind, I think that the courts could examine whether or not compulsory retirement is justifiable by looking at both the charter as a whole and section 1 in particular which states that the charter "guarantees the rights and freedoms set out in it subject only to such reasonable limits as are generally accepted in a free and democratic society with a parliamentary system of government." So the test will be to determine whether this is truly discriminatory in the light of section 1. The courts will decide.

**Mr. Jim Hawkes, MP (PC, Alberta):** Mr. Minister, just to check the translation, I think the basic message was: I don't know. In social policy terms, sir, the definition of bad legislation as it affects people are those three words: I don't know. (4: 199–20)

...

**Senator Duff Roblin (PC, Manitoba):** There is another clause in this act which has to do with fundamental freedoms, and it forbids any discrimination among Canadians on the basis of age. As a municipal man, perhaps you see some problems here in that so many social policies, indeed educational policies, do have age clauses in them. I wonder whether you think this is a matter which should be clarified before we go too far into the question of fundamental freedoms and discrimination, or whether you think it can be dealt with in the ordinary course of business if this age clause should come into effect?

**Mr. Dennis Flynn (Federation of Canadian Municipalities):** I think, Senator, it probably should be clarified. There are some real problems now in my own municipalities with various pension plans and the aging of people and the forced retirement of those persons. There is a bill before the legislature of the province requesting that that be lifted, be changed, and that the age question be entirely readdressed. As a federation, we have not given consideration to that matter.

**Senator Roblin:** I guess if the age qualification comes into effect some of us will be faced with it, and I just thought I would bring it to your attention. (9: 14–15)

...

**Mr. Svend Robinson, MP (NDP, BC):** You make some proposals for changes to the proposed Section 15 of the Charter, and of course as it stands now that section includes prohibition on the grounds of age, and you would make certain additions to that and change it to read "without discrimination." I wonder if you would comment, please, on the effect that this might have. Some witnesses and others have expressed concern about the effect this might have on various provincial and federal statutes, and if you would specifically direct your mind to Section 43, I believe it is, of the Criminal Code? [Section 43 of the Criminal Code of Canada – the so-called "Spanking Law" – provides, "Every schoolteacher, parent or person standing in the place of a parent is justified in using force by way of correction toward a pupil or child, as the case may be, who is under his care, if the force does not exceed what is reasonable under the circumstances." In 2004, the Supreme Court of Canada upheld the constitutionality of the law but severely restricted its application.[8]]

**Professor Cruickshank (Vice President, Canadian Council on Children and Youth):** Well, I think that would be something the Committee should realize that you are assigning to the courts. In effect, by keeping Section 43 in force and passing the equality before the law section you are assigning to the courts the job of deciding whether or not that will be struck out of the Criminal Code, and I as a lawyer would certainly try to make a persuasive argument that the phrase "age" ought to be used to strike that section out of the Criminal Code. (22: 44–5)

...

**Mr. Ron Irwin, MP (LIB, ON):** I feel comfortable with five or six things in Section 15. I feel comfortable with them. I will ask you about them. You mention age. How do you feel about the others—non-discrimination because of race; non-discrimination because of national or ethnic origin; because of colour; non-discrimination because of religion, non-discrimination because of sex. Now those are as old as the bills of rights of the forties and the Diefenbaker Bill of Rights. Do you have problems with those?

**Professor Russell (University of Toronto):** Some of them are not. Some of them are rather novel. I cannot speak for the whole world. But I think I know the Canadian record. Age is rather latter-day as an addition to the list; national origin has not been in all drafts. They all would present some difficult questions for the courts.

To take age, personally I treat it differently as a basis for discrimination than the other categories, because we all age and we all go through the ages of life and our social institutions and our laws make all kinds of discrimination based upon age: children cannot do certain things that adults can do. Adults have responsibilities and opportunities up to a certain age which they do not have after a certain age and so and so forth. Age is something we all experience together as long as we live. I have great difficulty in seeing why our legislatures should be barred from discriminating on the basis of age just like that. I do not think that is wise. (34: 153)

## Enumerated Grounds – Others

**Miss Nicole Dumouchel (Board Member, Canadian Council on Social Development):** As the Committee has been told, neither physically nor mentally handicapped persons would be protected by this section. We would also point out that discrimination on the basis of sexual orientation, marital or family status, political belief or socio-economic status would not be provided by Section 15 as drafted. Clearly, a statement which will guide through judicial decisions for decades should be both flexible and inclusive in order to accommodate changing social conditions, as well as to safeguard the rights of the present populace. We believe handicapping conditions, sexual orientation and socio-economic status, marital situation and political belief should be added to the list and that the clause should be rendered more flexible by adding "such as" preceding any description of status. This section should include as well prohibition of discrimination in both the substance and application of the law. (19: 30)

...

**Mr. Les Benjamin, MP (NDP, SK):** What is your view as to incorporating or including the matter of political belief? There may be the right
to belong but this is a nondiscrimination because of political beliefs, is
that an area again that should be left up to Parliament and legislatures
through general law?

**Mr. Norman:** Well, again, I take the latter point. I think it ought not
to be specified in a great list which strikes this Committee and then
both Houses of Parliament as being right for today. I am sure it will not
strike you as being right two or three, let alone five or ten years from
now. (20: 20)

...

**Mr. Svend Robinson, MP (NDP, BC):** I think there may be some
misunderstanding here, Mr. Chairman, perhaps the witness could clear
it up. You indicate that one of the three areas that you do not believe
should be included is political beliefs, which I find somewhat surprising for people who have in some cases fled from oppression on the
basis of political belief. Are you aware of the fact that political belief is
included in the International Covenant on Civil and Political Rights,
and presumably, now that you are aware of that, you would agree that
at least should be included?

**Mr. Nicolas Zsolnay (President, Canadian Citizenship Federation):**
I remember that was in. We had briefs that this should be accepted by
Canada but I would still be very careful on that. Do you wish to include
Nazis, for instance, as a protected political belief or not? That is a very
dangerous thing. I would like to have a law but not to have it in the
constitution. What are the political beliefs of Paul Rose? I mean, thank
you, I had enough of that. Should we protect him and to what extent. So
we must be careful. We are not against dealing with these things but we
think a special law would be enough on human rights, ordinary human
rights bill or law, but not in the constitution where this can be twisted
by a sympathetic judge or so. This is how we would like to interpret it.
(29: 62-3)

**Mrs. Diana Davidson (President, Vancouver People's Law School
Society):** With respect to the list of proscribed discriminations, we ask
that that list be greatly expanded to proscribe discrimination on the
basis of political affiliation, physical or mental handicap, sexual orientation, belief, opinion, expression and from discrimination on the basis
of lack of means.

It has been suggested to me that there is a hesitation about including
sex as one of the proscribed classes because it is desired to avoid the

result that women are conscripted to war. Now, that is one of the few rights that women have ever managed to get hold of, and I suggest that women are very willing to work so that men have that right, and did work during the Viet Nam crisis in the United States, to try and assist their fellow human beings, to wit the men, to acquire that right; but if the desire is to avoid the conscription of women, then rather than limiting the express proscription of discrimination on the basis of sex, include a section that women are to be exempted from compulsory military service. (32: 13)

**Mr. Svend Robinson, MP (NDP, BC):** Now turning to your comments on Section 15, the proposed antidiscrimination section, as you have particular comments on some of the concerns which have been expressed with respect to those additional grounds which might be added? ...

**Mrs. Diana Davidson (President, Vancouver People's Law School Society):** With regard to the addition of these grounds, first of all, with regard to political affiliation, it makes little sense to have a protection in Section 2, and no protection in Section 15. With regard to the physically or mentally handicapped, it is not possible to represent ourselves as civilized people when we have that large group of persons who are excluded. (32: 13, 20–2)

### Enumerated Grounds: Concerns about Age or Sex

**Mr. P. D. Burns, Director (Canadian Life and Health Insurance Association):** Our concern basically centres on Section 15(1) of the proposed Charter of Rights and Freedoms. ... In particular, our concern rests with the words "without discrimination because of age or sex." ... We strongly believe that legislation of this type should be applied only to prohibit unfair or unreasonable differentiation between individuals and, unfortunately, wording such as you have before you now could be interpreted to prohibit any and all differentiation between individuals based upon stated grounds and could have an unintended impact on many aspects of Canadian society. ...

The function of the private health insurance industry or insurance process, really, is to reduce each individual's exposure or risk to financial loss by pooling it with the risk of other individuals. For this risk sharing process to operate on a private voluntary basis – and those words are the very key, "private and voluntary" – it is, we think, essential that a charge assessed against each individual be reasonable in relation to the risk which is being shared and also in relation to that risk that that individual brings. In other words, that the cost of insurance be reasonable in relation to the benefit likely to be received.

Efforts to meet this requirement have led insurers to consider many individual characteristics in the structure of premiums and benefits. Variations on such bases as age and sex are common to reflect the obvious variations in mortality and morbidity related to or arising out of these factors; for example, the appropriateness of varying life insurance premiums by age is almost self-evident. The appropriateness of varying premiums by sex is probably more contentious, but we think equally well founded. Variations in life and health insurance premiums on these bases is not prohibited in any jurisdiction in Canada or elsewhere of which we are aware, and we believe it is not your intent that such would be prohibited under the proposed Charter. (33: 87–92)

**Mr. P. D. Burns, Director (Canadian Life and Health Insurance Association):** If the word "discrimination" is meant to distinguish between certain groups of people and the nature of the risk they bring in joining that pool as Mr. Galloway has described it, it is certainly true that the life insurance, or any form of insurance works on the basis of what I prefer to call "risk classification," rather than "discrimination." I am concerned in Section 15 that some people might interpret it literally to say that if two individuals, one of whom is 19 years old and the other being 91 years old, and each one buys life insurance, for example, that they would get it for the same price. I think that most of us would concede that such an example is absurd. But you then go on further down the line and say "can you demonstrate that a certain group of people bring a higher risk because of certain characteristics, and is it valid to distinguish the additional risk that they bring as they become members of that group?" Is it valid to charge them the same price, or should they pay more or less according to the character and nature of the risk they bring? (33: 95)

**Mrs. Lise Bacon (Canadian Life Insurance Association):** The fact that women live longer than men is reflected in life insurance premiums. In this case, there is discrimination against men. If we think of the risk assumed in the case of annuity insurance, since women have a much greater life expectancy than men, there is discrimination against women in this case. Simplistic generalizations should not be made. Actuarial procedures and life expectancy must be taken into account. It is assumed that even as infants, females are better equipped to deal with life than males. I think such assumptions are made at a rather early age. However, they are not about to change, despite the different lifestyles women now have and the different work they now perform. It is very fashionable to talk about stress these days, but women experience the same pressures in a constantly changing society. Nevertheless, we still do not have a standard premium for men and women. (33: 96)

### Enumerated Grounds – Disability

**Mr. Noel Kinsella (Chairman, New Brunswick Human Rights Commission):** I think it would be very appropriate for this Committee to look very carefully at including as a prescribed ground physical disability, in addition to the reason that we would be drafting a constitution during the international year of the physically disabled. It seems to me that we ought to be talking about drafting a constitution in terms of the social values of the closing years of the second millennium and not to go back to 1215 and the Magna Carta principles and philosophy, so there is the type of ground which, to my way of thinking, is an obvious thing which you put in. But at the same time if you are going to have grounds, I do not think you can put everything in. (11: 42)

...

**Mr. R. G. L. Fairweather (Chief Commissioner of Canadian Human Rights Commission):** The list of grounds presented in that section is incomplete. In particular, no promise of equality under the law is made to the disabled. We must give this undertaking to the disabled that they are entitled to equal rights, not to do so is to perpetuate stereotypes and attitudes that are more crippling to the disabled than any handicap. Not to do so because of arguments about the financial costs involved in opening up our society to the handicapped would also be wrong. Costs are not relevant to the guaranteeing of the right to equal protection of the law. (5: 8)

**Mr. Paul Mercure (President of the Canadian Association for the Mentally Retarded):** We are asking that the rights of handicapped persons be protected in the new constitution. ...

**Mr. David Vickers (Vice-President, Canadian Association for the Mentally Retarded):** The year 1981 will be International Year of the Disabled. It would be an appalling commentary on our Canadian values if we failed to entrench in that year, in our new constitution, protection for all Canadians who live with a handicap whether real or perceived. The usual objection raised to inclusion of handicapped as a prohibited ground of discrimination is that such a measure might obstruct programs designed to remedy the effects of the long history of negative discrimination. We believe that the usual exceptions to affirmative action programs can relieve this concern. And you have dealt with that in the subsection to Section 15.

There is a second objection from those who say that in order to benefit from antidiscrimination clauses a person would first have to identify himself or herself as handicapped. This objection can be overcome if the terminology used is defined broadly, such as we find in a definition of "handicapped person" which can be found in the U.S. Rehabilitation Act of 1973. There "handicapped person" is defined as any person who has (a) a physical or mental impairment which substantially limits one or more of such person's major life activities; (b) has a record of such impairment, or (c) is regarded as having such an impairment. It is noteworthy that particularly under subsection (c) of this definition the focus is clearly on the act of discrimination rather than on whether the person discriminated against can be fitted into the protected category. That is the essential purpose of the statutory definition. (10: 7, 10: 12–13)

...

**Mr. Ron Kanary (Vice-Chairman, Coalition of Provincial Organizations for the Handicapped):** Of most importance to disabled people in Canada is that disability or handicap should be included as grounds protected from discrimination under Section 15(1) and we recommend this amendment to you. ... The all-party House of Commons Special Committee on the Disabled and the Handicapped in its first report to Parliament in October of this year stated: "Should it be the will of Parliament to entrench Human Rights in a patriated constitution, your Committee believes that full and equal protection should be provided for persons with physical and mental handicaps." ...

Hence, if disability is not among the listing in Section 15(1), complaints of discrimination on grounds of disability will be dealt with using whatever resources the commissions have left over after dealing with complaints on grounds which are listed in Section 15(1). Inadvertently, the Canadian Charter of Rights and Freedoms will create a first and second class of rights to protection from discrimination. We believe we have a compelling case for the inclusion of disability or handicap as a prohibited ground of discrimination in the proposed Canadian Charter of Rights and Freedoms. ...

A constitution is most basic and fundamental legislation. As such it deals with basic and fundamental issues. The issue as to whether Section 15(1) of the charter of rights and freedoms in the constitutional bill

should be amended to include "disability" is also a basic and fundamental matter. (12: 26–31)

**Mr. Peter Lang, MP (LIB, Ontario):** The argument of cost has been
used against the inclusion of the disabled in Section 15(1). Mr. Derksen,
I wonder if you have any comments on this?

**Mr. Jim Derksen (Coalition of Provincial Organizations for the
Handicapped):** This seems to be based on the idea that simply to place
disability or handicap in Section 15(1) without any limiting clauses
might result in the courts imposing disruptive change on our society:
for example, that all buildings without elevators be equipped with
elevators. Now, we see that religion, sex and age are also included
in that section without any limiting clauses. We see that Section 1 or
Section 15(3) as proposed by the Human Rights Commission, would
allow the courts to interpret the reasonableness or the justifiable
necessity of limiting that protection from discrimination for age, sex
and religion.

Sections 1 and 15(3) would make possible an interpretation, in regard
to protection from discrimination on the basis of age, by the courts
that would uphold 18 as the minimum age for, say, the purchase of
liquor, firearms, voting in federal elections. There seems to be a misunderstanding that there is no comparable limiting clauses in existing
statutes, and no comparable precedents in existing case law to limit
reasonably, where justifiably necessary, that right to protection from
discrimination. ...

We believe, in fact – and this has been shown by the strong economies of Northern Europe – that enabling disabled people to participate
in society would be an extremely cost effective course of action for this
country to take. ... We believe the cost argument which underlies much
of the resistance or objections to the inclusion of disability in the constitution is not a real one. (12: 37–9)

**Mr. Lang:** Are there any other governments which have provided
protection from discrimination for the disabled, and as a second caveat
to that, can you give us any information on the economic factors
involved with these governments, and in particular whether they have
presented any impediment?

**Mr. Derksen:** Well, I can say that Nova Scotia, New Brunswick,
Prince Edward Island, Quebec, Manitoba, Saskatchewan and Alberta,
all give comprehensive protection from discrimination to the disabled
through the ordinary legislation of human rights acts. Some of these
have been in place since 1974; others are more recent. There is no

indication that these provinces are at the brink of bankruptcy because of that protection. (12: 39)

**Hon. Richard Hatfield (Premier of New Brunswick):** I would like to add to the list that restricts Parliament for restricting rights that I have proposed. I would like to add to that list the physically handicapped as well because I do think that they have a special problem and that the constitution should see to it that they are not discriminated against because of a handicap. (19: 49)

**Mr. Ron Irwin, MP (LIB, ON):** You say that physically handicapped, mentally handicapped should be on, I think you called it a tier system. Many people have come before us and said unequivocally the physically handicapped should be in the Charter, but I think your experience is important. You are suggesting there are different types of rights that the physically handicapped have and we have to look at each one and what is reasonable. I put to you that maybe it is a good idea to put the right to employment of the physically and mentally handicapped in the federal charter and leave the right to services and so on to the human rights charters?

**Mr. Ken Norman (Chief Commissioner, Saskatchewan Human Rights Commission):** Well, sir, I think that, as in my response to Mr. Benjamin on the question of the Charter, it is a constitutional document getting down to the detail of talking about a work place as distinguished from services or accommodation. I think that is a step in the wrong direction because even the work place alone, every human rights law in this country that deals with physical disability, and certainly those laws when they deal with mental disability, we have heard so from the Association of Mentally Retarded in their briefs to us as recently as last Friday, necessarily needs to have a reasonableness distinction standard because we have in this country all sorts of special employment provisions for people with multiple handicaps and disabilities, and they need to be addressed in a sensitive way by an agency or agencies, departments of labour included with human rights agencies, and I think to simply have a clear proscription is to invite the court to wonder what in the world to do with that, because it seems to be an invitation to upset a number of apple carts that have been put together by every government. (20: 24)

**Mr. David Lepofsky (Member, Ontario Division Board of Management, Canadian National Institute for the Blind):** Handicapped people in the struggle for equality and equality of opportunity find that not only do people discriminate in the access to jobs, buildings, facilities, services and housing, but that, in fact, legislators, persons passing laws have also experienced the same negative attitudes towards the handicapped and have passed laws which are in fact discriminatory. Accordingly, the major thrust of our presentation is that it is necessary that they should be included in Section 15 of the Charter of Rights, the so called equality or nondiscrimination clause, and be referred to as a protected class, mentally or physically handicapped persons.

We are not looking at this as a means of getting jobs or housing, because that is something which is done at the federal or provincial Human Rights Code level, and we are actually lobbying for that. Here, we are concerned with not just human conduct which is discriminatory, but legislation which discriminates.

Why should we be included in Section 15? Why are handicapped people entitled to equality before the law and to the equal protection of the law? To begin with, I am sure you have all come to the conclusion yourselves and you have heard from other groups, as the clause is presently drafted it is unarguable, unquestionable that handicapped persons are not entitled to equality before the law. By this exclusion, it perpetuates in our constitution an attitude which, as I have mentioned, is prevalent in society, some notion of handicapped people as second class citizens, people who need to be taken care of, not given independence, protected, not given the opportunity of equality. ...

The final reason that I would like to articulate for including handicapped in Section 15 concerns an argument that some have raised against it: namely, that the costs occasioned by including the handicapped would be excessive. I have several responses to that argument. Number one, I would ask what those costs would be. I am not altogether clear and I would submit that there probably are not that many. Intuitively nothing really comes to mind as being excessively costly. Secondly, I would submit that unless this Committee is going to go through the process of looking at every liberty enumerated in the Charter of Rights and say how much will this one cost, should we include it, is it too expensive? Unless we are to do that with every single liberty then there is a certain inequality to simply looking at one group, namely the handicapped, and say that they will be excluded on the basis of a cost argument. And so, if that argument is presented before this Committee, I would ask that you bear that in mind. And finally, if that argument is presented before this Committee, that is that including handicapped would be too costly, I would ask you to bear the following argument in mind, or the following point in mind. To say that the cost is too excessive is to assume that handicap inclusion is the absolute lowest priority of every government in Canada, that we have spent every last dollar of revenue we have taxed and collected and that there is no money left. If you were to look at the priorities of the various governments, provincial and federal, of spending, you might find that there are others that are lower priority than handicapped equality and you might find that it might be worth including the handicapped in the constitution and perhaps let some more inconsequential programs go by the board. I do not think it is fair to simply say it costs too much, therefore we cannot do it. ...

More importantly, it is our view that the courts have a tradition of taking a very restrictive view of civil liberties. Now, that is not by way of criticism or by way of anything less than respect for the members of the judiciary, but it is something which is, nonetheless, true. I think that it will be necessary and it is our submission that it will be necessary for strong direction to be given to the courts through very specific wording directing them to invalidate discriminatory legislation.

Our concern is that there is a danger of misleading people if the Charter does not include the handicapped. There is the danger that people will believe that in Canada under such a provision, egalitarian liberties are truly safeguarded, there is equality for all. Without handicapped inclusion such is not the case. And it is not only unfair to handicapped persons to deny them equality, but it is a risky venture for the public to be misled into believing that all minorities are protected when they are in fact not. Our concern, as I said at the outset, is dealing with public attitudes. Public attitudes are something which we must battle at various levels. At the constitutional level we are battling public attitudes as they are manifested through legislation and this is a battle which is both serious and crucial.

Finally I would close by saying that there is an oft stated adage that justice is blind; in fact it is a cliché. Our concern – and the underlying concern of this presentation – is that while justice may have had the opportunity to experience blindness, we are asking for blind persons, as well as for other handicapped persons, to be given at last an opportunity to experience justice. (25: 6–14)

**Senator Richard Donahoe (PC, Nova Scotia):** Do you feel that the position of the handicapped is going to be very much improved and very much enhanced if this procedure is followed with or without your suggested amendments?

**Mr. Lepofsky:** ... This would provide a means or mechanism for handicapped persons and other interested groups, to challenge legislation which is discriminatory. If these provisions are not put in, then it would signal to the disabled that it is the prevailing view in Canada that handicapped people are not entitled to equality before the law and that the kinds of discrimination that are experienced by any handicapped person in their everyday life are in fact representing a pervasive view which in fact has been articulated through the actions of the framers of the new constitution. ... It would be a signal to the Canadian people that as regards handicapped persons, who in the past have either been a forgotten minority or a lesser class of citizen – and I say this was not intentional or out of malevolence; but it has happened nonetheless – that a new era has dawned and that as deeply felt a concern is being presented to Canada as can be expressed through a Charter of fundamental rights as acknowledging this liberty. (25: 15–16)

**The Honourable Jean Chrétien (Minister of Justice):** I know that many witnesses have recommended either that the grounds for non-discrimination be widened to include handicapped persons or others or that there be no specific enumeration and that more discretion be left in the hands of the courts. The government has studied these representations with great care. The position of the government is that certain grounds of discrimination have long been recognized as prohibited. Race, national or ethnic origin, colour, religion and sex are all found in the Canadian Bill of Rights and are capable of more ready definition than others.

I want to make clear that the listing of specific grounds where discrimination is most prohibited does not mean that there are not other grounds where discrimination is prohibited. Indeed as society evolves, values change and new grounds of discrimination become apparent. These should be left to be protected by ordinary human rights legislation where they can be defined, the qualifications spelled out and the measures for protective action specified by legislatures. For example, it was only four years ago that federal human rights legislation specifically provided protection for the handicapped in the area of employment. Recently the Special Parliamentary Task Force on the Handicapped chaired by David Smith has recommended changes and improvements in the Human Rights Act with respect to the handicapped. The government will be acting on some of the recommendations of the Task Force. The government is also proposing to act on some of the recommendations made by the Canadian Human Rights Commission in this area and will propose amendments to the Human Rights Act. But if legislatures do not act, there should be room for the courts to move in. Therefore, the amendment which I mentioned does not list certain grounds of discrimination to the exclusion of all others. Rather, it is open-ended and meets the recommendations made by many witnesses before your Committee. Because of the difficulty of identifying legitimate new grounds of discrimination in a rapidly evolving area of the law, I prefer to be open-ended rather [than] adding some new categories with the risk of excluding others. (32: 13–15)

...

**The Hon. David Crombie, MP (PC, Ontario):** While one could understand and indeed applaud excluding age because of its impact on social programs, I also note that you did not include in your list of case by case protective areas, you use sex, race, colour, national or ethnic origin or religion and you did not include either sexual orientation or the handicapped, mental or physical, in your preferred list and I wondered why you did not.

**Ms. Mary Eberts (Legal Counsel, Advisory Council on the Status of Women):** I think that the rationale would be the same as that for age and it has been pointed out by, for example, the Lamontagne-McGuigan Committee that to include marital status in a list of distinctions that are always regarded as unreasonable would create practical problems with the administration of a number of social programs, for example, and our formulation remains the same: we have two tiers; where the ground is specifically mentioned in Subsection 2 of our proposal we intend that to be a signal to the courts that distinctions based on those grounds are categorically wrong, we should never have them.

**Mr. Crombie:** Which problems?

**Ms. Eberts:** Race, sex, colour and so on. Whereas distinctions based on other grounds can be judged by a court to be reasonable in certain circumstances and unreasonable in other circumstances, so that once again, as I mentioned in my initial presentation, a statute which denied a driver's licence to someone on the basis of marital status could well be challenged and found to be unreasonable, even though marital status is not explicitly mentioned. So that we hope that our formulation would be flexible enough to cover both sort of hard core types of distinction and also those that required more flexibility. Also, there is nothing in our formulation to prevent either the province or the federal government from passing detailed and articulate legislation to prevent specific kinds of discrimination on the basis of any category.

**Mr. Crombie:** So it is clear in my own head, Mr. Chairman, you have in your two orders of protected rights, as it were, age, sexual orientation and handicapped, mental and physical, are clearly in the second order which need to be dealt with in a case by case manner as opposed to categorical; is that what you are saying?

**Ms. Eberts:** Yes, that is right.

**Mr. Crombie:** Were you surprised to find yourself in a different category than the Human Rights Commission on the matter?

**Ms. Eberts:** Well, I think the Human Rights Commissioner, although he proposed first of all the alternative of having no explicit categories and secondly, the alternative of having vast numbers of them, recognized in his written presentation to you that within those numerous, numerous categories that he suggested might be there, there would be the need for different interpretation and he suggested in his written submission that he would say that the courts should be told that race and sex could never be reasonably justifiable and our proposal is in accord with that submission of his but we think that our proposal provides that direction to the courts, that his proposal unfortunately where you have a long list of categories makes it very difficult for the court to extract guidance as to which are to be regarded as the categorical ones and which are to be regarded as the sort of first tier of reasonableness ones, whereas ours makes it fairly clear how the distinction is to be drawn.

**Mr. Crombie:** I might say, Mr. Chairman, and indeed with kindness, that you may want to familiarize yourself with the brief of the Canadian Association of Mentally Retarded who take a somewhat different view. (9: 146–7)

[An amendment sponsored by the Tories and supported by the NDP to add "physical and mental disability" was adopted by the Joint Committee.]

## Enumerated Grounds – Sexual Orientation

**The Hon. David Crombie, MP (PC, Ontario):** There is another change contained in your recommendations, and that deals with the question of discrimination with respect to sexual orientation and I wonder if you could advise the Committee of the experience of your Commission with respect to reported and dealt with discriminatory acts in relation to sexual orientation in this country?

**Mr. Gordon Fairweather (Chief Commissioner, Canadian Human Rights Commission):** Messrs. Chairmen, I think the Committee will be very surprised when I say that the public is ahead of the legislation in provinces and in our nation on this issue. We wrote to many major employers that fall in our jurisdiction and they said sexual preference is not relevant to the ability to do a job. I myself would want to tell you, and my bias is coming out, I thought that many employment policies of companies would not be as liberal as they turned out to be.

**Mr. Crombie:** We like to use the word "fair-minded" if you do not mind.

**Mr. Fairweather:** Fair-minded? Whatever word you like. It has no relevance. This is an anti-discrimination rights section, it is not an espousal of a style. And we also piggybacked the survey, you will be glad to know that we piggybacked it as it saved us some money, a couple of thousand people, and the majority said that sexual preference should not be a bar to holding a job, and I have always felt, I fought as a Member of Parliament and tried to have it changed at that time. Quebec has it and the social policies of Quebec have not come [tumbling] down.

**Mr. Crombie:** Is it the only province?

**Mr. Fairweather:** The only province. It went through in 1977. It was added to the proscribed ground.

**Mr. Crombie:** Thank you very much, sir. Thank you Mr. Chairman. (5: 24–5)

...

**Mr. Peter Maloney (Member of the Executive Committee, Canadian Association of Lesbians and Gay Men):** Members of the Committee, you have heard from four people that come before you today who are very concerned that there be some guarantee of the rights and liberties, the equality before the law, the equal protection of the law, for the gay and lesbian members of our community.

... You have heard them before from the Chief Commissioner of the Canadian Human Rights Commission who, in his presentation to you before this Committee and in the brief from the Canadian Human Rights Commission, indicated to you that he felt that the Charter ought to be amended in one of three ways: additional grounds, additional proscriptions against discrimination ought to include, among other things, sexual orientation if it was felt necessary in the Charter to list specific grounds. We take the position and we adopt the position in the brief that, the preferred position of Mr. Fairweather and the Canadian Human Rights Commission, that there be sort of a general global anti-discrimination clause, ought not to prevail.

That his second preference is our first preference, namely that there ought to be a general statement against discrimination followed by a listing of specific groups who are traditionally discriminated against. (24: 28)

**Mr. Jean Lapierre, MP (LIB, PQ):** You are asking us to include sexual orientation in Section 15. You are aware that many other groups have made the same demand. In one paragraph, you say: "It seems unlikely that the Courts would interpret the right to equality as failing to protect against racial or religious discrimination, but there is a real chance that they would not interpret Section 15 as protection [of] gay men and lesbians. ..." On what basis do you make this statement ...? Section 15 states that everyone has the right to equality before the law, particularly with respect to sex, but you do not find that adequate. Is there a legal basis for this?

**Mr. Maloney:** The case that goes to that point in the Supreme Court of Canada is the *Vancouver Sun* case in which a local gay newspaper in Vancouver attempted to place a simple advertisement saying gay newspaper, so many dollars subscription, write to box so and so; and you may be aware that the British Columbia Human Rights Act provides one of those general clauses that purports to catch all kinds of groups. The Supreme Court very narrowly decided on that case in a way that leads us to believe that the courts of this land are likely to interpret a broad general catch-all position that does not specify particular groups in a way that would be prejudicial to gay people. One of our concerns is of course that no matter what way you phrase such a general provision that there is always a judicial out if there is not a specific list that follows and takes over from the general. (24: 35–6)

**Mrs. Diana Davidson (President, Vancouver People's Law School Society):** It seemed, other than that, the statistics are all different with regard to the number of people that the inclusion of the discrimination on that basis would be of interest to us as a country but it would be of interest, of course, to those persons whose sexual orientation is not heterosexual and the statistics with regard to that is that that involves a group of anywhere from 8 per cent to 35 per cent of people; but even if you take the 8 per cent they also have parents and brothers and sisters and husbands and wives and children and so on and it is desirable not to have some sort of discussion going on in schools advocating a certain sexual behaviour; but it is desirable to avoid the situation where you have a person who is making a wonderful contribution and all of a sudden an irrelevant detail about their personal, private life is used to discredit them and deprive the community henceforth of their contribution. In any event, this is a Charter of Rights and I cannot say that it is covering the minorities when it leaves out such a large minority. (32: 20–2)

...

**Mr. Svend Robinson, MP (NDP, BC):** There are two other areas that I would also ask exactly the same question on. Immediately following the passage of the Charter would it also be your intention that the courts could interpret this Charter to exclude discrimination on the grounds of sexual orientation?

**The Hon. Jean Chrétien (Minister of Justice):** It might. That will be for the court to decide, it is open ended,

**Mr. Robinson:** But at the time of the passage of this Charter you would not preclude that as a possibility?

**Mr. Chrétien:** We say other types of discrimination and we do not define them. It will be for the court to define them. (39: 17)

[An NDP amendment to add sexual orientation to the list of enumerated grounds was defeated.]

## Reasonable Distinctions

**Ms. Mary Eberts (Legal Counsel, Advisory Council on the Status of Women):** The problem is that courts and others are only too prone to find that distinctions made on the basis of sex are reasonable distinctions. The argument goes something like this, and it is an argument that was made by a former Justice Minister, Mr. David Fulton when the Canadian Bill of Rights was considered by this House in 1960. Men and women are different, they reason. The difference is apparent and the difference is natural and, therefore, it is natural to have male-female differences entrenched in the law. However, we know that not all the differences between men and women are natural. Vast numbers of them are culturally imposed. There is, for example, nothing in the structure of a woman's arm that necessitates that doors be opened by men for women rather than the other way around. This is a cultural pattern.

Others of these differences are in the eye of the beholder only, and the fact that there may be some biological differences between men and women should not make reasonable all distinctions imposed in the law or even most of them. We certainly need a stronger indication for the courts about what is and is not reasonable as a basis for distinctions in law. The Chairman of the Canadian Human Rights Commission gave his view when he appeared before you that limitations will almost never be reasonably justifiable [or] demonstrably necessary on the grounds of race, sex or colour. Chief Justice Laskin suggested in Bedard and Lavell that sex, race and the other categories in the Bill of Rights at present should be regarded as prohibited grounds of distinction. Our Prime Minister has also said in 1971 that race and sex discrimination in particular are doubly unfair and it is our submission that these particular kinds of discrimination, which people cannot avoid no matter what they do should be subjected to stronger measures.

What route is open to us to make it clear to legislatures and to courts that a simple reasonableness test is inadequate to bring to bear against the stubborn evil of sex discrimination? Well, I suppose we can trust to fate. We could hope that Canadian courts will employ not just the simple reasonableness test described by Justice Minister Lang, but also the idea that some [bases] for distinction are invidious and should be subject to strict scrutiny by the courts, upheld only when the government can show a compelling state interest for requiring the distinction. This latter test has been developed in American jurisprudence as a companion to the reasonableness test. Together they form a two tier approach with the tougher strict scrutiny tier being applied to types of distinctions regarded as the most serious.

We are not too hopeful that trusting to luck will bring about this result. To begin with, there is just no guarantee that Canadian courts will adopt the strict scrutiny approach if left to their own devices. Moreover experience in the United States has shown that simply adopting a strict scrutiny approach may not achieve the result either. American courts are in a complete muddle about whether sex should be subjected to strict scrutiny or not. Sometimes they say yes, sometimes they say no, let us just subject it to a middle category test.

There is in our view no need to adopt uncertainty when we are forming a new constitution for Canada. We have, thanks to the chance to contribute at the outset to the nature of our charter, a chance to get it right the first time around. We can include language, meant as a clear signal to the courts that whatever they may think about other bases of distinction, certain bases of distinction should never be regarded as reasonable.

Our proposal for a change in Section 15 can be found at page 13 of the English version of our brief, page 14 of the French and it is also included in the summary of recommendations. We propose that the Section read:

every person shall have equal rights in law, including the right to equality before the law and to the equal protection and benefit of the law.

> Such equal rights may be abridged or denied only on the basis of a reasonable distinction. Sex, race, colour, national or ethnic origin or religion will never constitute a reasonable distinction except as provided in Subsection (3).

Our proposal does two things: it accepts the idea that some distinctions may possibly be reasonable or practical. That is the idea behind Subsection 1 and the first sentence of Subsection 2. This is, if you like, our first tier of analysis. Under this section, for example, a law denying drivers' licences to married women might well be struck down even though there is no guarantee of equality before the law on the basis of marital status.

We also feel it necessary to tell the courts what basis of distinction just will not be reasonable and that is the second sentence in Subsection (2). The matters enumerated there correspond closely to those highlighted by Mr. Fairweather before you and by the Prime Minister.

We think that if we keep the list of "never reasonable categories" which are explicitly expressed rather short, the courts and the legislatures cannot help but get the idea that in these cases they should and can respond to a signal to regard them as most grave. We should point out, however, that our proposal does not prevent the provincial and federal legislatures from broadening the legislative protections given to those with particular handicaps, given on the basis of age or whatever. The legislators are not hampered by the proposal we have put forward if they desire to expand protection for human rights. What we propose is that everyone in the country will be guaranteed a basic and very secure minimum protection which can expand as judicial awareness of trends in Canadian society gets a chance to operate on cases that come before it. (9: 126–8)

**Mr. Lorne Nystrom (NDP, SK):** I want to ask you why you are calling for a test of reasonableness in the case of race, national or ethnic origin or colour? Because it seems to me, sir, that even in times of emergency, war, great emergency in this country, that there should not be any discrimination whatsoever on the basis of a person's colour, or his national or ethnic background. I do not believe that anything should justify discrimination on the basis of those factors, regardless of how dire the emergency may be.

**Mr. Wilson Head (President, National Black Coalition of Canada):** Yes, I agree with you on that ... that there should not be any discrimination at any point, whether in times of war, insurrection, or apprehended insurrection or whatever the situation may be, on the basis of race, creed, colour or any other criterion. So, that should be an absolute. (22: 18–19)

**Ms. Pamela Medjuck (National Steering Committee, National Association of Women and the Law, Nova Scotia):** No guarantee of equality is ever absolute. The court does have an inherent power to define the boundaries of any rights in the Charter. For example, we are all willing to include protection for freedom of speech, and yet we do not ever intend this to include freedom to defame others or to slander others. Rights do exist and are propounded in an absolute sense, but aspects could never be existing in it, so we have to give our court direction as to how to restrict them and when. Thus, the court will have a duty when interpreting Section 15 to determine which distinctions amount to discrimination and which are reasonable and should be allowed.

The American courts have developed a "suspect classification" test in relation to discrimination on certain invidious grounds. For example, race can rarely form a proper basis for differential treatment in law. In such cases the onus is on government to prove a compelling state interest for the distinction in order for the law to be upheld. The court must not only evaluate the purpose of the legislation, but must also determine if the purpose could be achieved in another nondiscriminatory way. However, a majority of the American court has not yet applied this "suspect classification," sometimes called "strict scrutiny," test to distinctions made on the basis of sex. It has, rather, adopted a middle test somewhere between "strict scrutiny" and "reasonable distinctions" to apply to sex inequality cases.

Professor Beverley Baines has identified five different tests which the Canadian courts have developed to aid interpretation of the equality clause in our present Bill of Rights. The best of these appear to resemble the "reasonable classification" test which the American court applies to cases of discrimination on grounds other than race or sex. The Canadian court has never applied the "strict scrutiny" test in any discrimination case. Because immutable characteristics, such as sex and race, are unrelated to the ability or capacity of a person, we believe that a strict standard must apply to them. In the words of the paper presented by the Canadian Human Rights Commission, distinction should almost never be made on these grounds. We would like to point out, while we do support Mr. Gordon Fairweather's comments that these distinctions should never be made, we cannot agree with his recommendation which includes that age should be included with race and sex. We do not believe that. Otherwise we are supporting his principles; not the wording of his recommendations. To ensure that our courts will take this approach, we believe it will be necessary to clearly state the standard in Section 15. We therefore recommend that Section 15 specifically provide that a compelling reason must be given for any distinction on the basis of sex, race, national or ethnic origin, or religion.

Regarding other prohibited grounds, age, physical or mental handicap, marital status, political belief, sexual orientation and previous conviction, we would emphasize that not all "inherent" classifications are necessarily invidious, to use the American term. The example of age comes immediately to mind. While some legal distinctions on the basis of age are improper and therefore ought to be prohibited by Section 15, many distinctions based on age are perfectly appropriate because they fairly relate to different levels of capacity. It is appropriate, for example, for children who have been convicted of committing criminal offences not to be given as severe a penalty as adults. Equally, we do not want to have the vote in Canada extended to children four years of age. These types of reasonable distinctions are acceptable in law. This is not to say that unfair, unreasonable distinctions on the basis of age should be tolerated.

Certainly Section 15 should forbid discrimination on this ground. Our point is that the judiciary should apply a different, a more stringent, test to laws which distinguish on the basis of the invidious or the suspect categories, such as sex or race, than to laws distinguishing on other bases, age, handicap, et cetera. To achieve this, Section 15 of the Charter must make it clear that a suspect classification test, that is, a strict scrutiny test, should apply to certain types of discrimination. To fail to do so will result in this standard for all differential treatment being reduced to the lowest common denominator, i.e. the reasonable classification test. (22: 56–7)

**Miss Pauline Jewett, MP (NDP, BC):** I wondered if you had given any consideration to this ticklish matter of what is a reasonable distinction and what rights might be abridged or limited on the basis of a reasonable distinction. Some people would argue for example that in the case of age you do not have complete rights for everybody of every age, children and older people alike, and in what areas there should never be allowed a "reasonable distinction" or "equality on the basis of a reasonable distinction."

**Ms. Lynn McDonald (President, National Action Committee on the Status of Women):** The matter of "reasonable distinction" is a very tricky one, and one that we would be very worried about. I think the important point is that some characteristics are immutable, sex is and race is, and we do go through different ages. Questions of income and social class, these are changeable things, people's occupations, their abilities and so forth. Of course, there are reasonable distinctions that have to be made. The Unemployment Insurance Act has to distinguish between people who are unemployed and people who are employed. That is a reasonable distinction. But we have to be very careful when it is a matter of an immutable characteristic such as sex and race. "Reasonable distinction," there have been court cases in which this has been argued or a "valid objective" and of course this has been traditionally very detrimental to women because one could always think of some good objective. Protective legislation, so-called protective legislation has been of this sort. It has made a reasonable distinction, it has been for the benefit of women and it has not been in practice. So we would be leery of anything along those lines. (9: 69)

## On the Relationship between Section 15 and Aboriginal Rights

**Mr. Wilson Head (President, National Black Coalition of Canada):** We are very much concerned that where the rights of the native people are abrogated, then none of our rights are safe. Our view is that the native people have been treated very badly in this country, and we have never given them the rights they deserve, in spite of treaties which have been signed, and in this sense Canada has had a shameful history, a history which is still being repeated today; and we feel very strongly that the rights of all people, in this connection, native people, Chinese, browns, South Asians, Pakistanis, wherever they come from, as well as blacks, should be protected. We are very pleased that this act looks at some of the other questions which have not been covered before, but not all. It does not yet address itself to marital status, it does not address itself to the handicapped, and it seems to us that these are the kind of things that ought to be included. (22: 10)

**Miss Mary Simon (Member, Inuit Committee on National Issues):** The Canadian constitution, therefore, must make it clear that the right to equal protection under section 15 cannot be invoked to challenge legally our unique status and rights. (16: 12)

**Ms. Rose Charlie (Western Vice-President, Indian Rights for Indian Women):** Section 15 deals with "equality before the law." We find this provision thoroughly unsatisfactory and we believe that all thoughtful

Canadians should agree with us in demanding something more substantial. As it has been interpreted by Canadian courts, the requirement of equality before the law has been understood as entirely formal in character, as the notorious *Bliss* and *Lavell* decisions indicate. As this provision is now interpreted, equality before the law would be satisfied if there were a law specifying that all Canadian citizens with the surname Trudeau shall be decapitated and if all and only Trudeaus were decapitated. This is simply not good enough. Equality before the law requires clearer and more specific definition. We realize that this is not [an] easy task. Some differences in treatment are certainly warranted. Cabinet ministers, judges, medical doctors, and policemen, among others must have rights and duties which are not possessed by other Canadians. At the very least, the types of justified inequalities should be stated with some clarity. And, to speak to our own main concern, these types certainly should not allow continued inequality between Indian men and Indian women. (17: 85–6)

**Mr. Harry Daniels (President, Native Council of Canada):** It would be inconceivable that our collective rights could be entrenched without explicitly protecting them from legal actions which argue that aboriginal rights are discriminatory. We are not just another disadvantaged group but a historic national minority with rights corresponding to that status. (17: 112–13)

**The Hon. Jean Chrétien (Minister of Justice):** There is only one aspect that I have some problems with, which is the non-discrimination aspect of the charter, how that will affect the Indian Act in relation to the status of the women who marry white men. This problem will not be resolved and it might be that in the delay of three years as proposed in this charter of rights, in relation to the non-discrimination clause, that we might be forced to legislate in the Indian Act in relation to the rights of the Indian women, despite the fact that in 1969 I promised the Indians that we were not to change it without their advice and consultation. (3: 85)

...

**Miss Flora MacDonald, MP (PC, Ontario):** I want to touch briefly on the whole question of the lack of rights for Indian women in this country and I hope that the Indian Rights for Indian Women's groups will be able to appear before this Committee. But the charter as it is now written would, in fact, entrench, in my opinion, the abhorrent clause, Section 12(1)(b) of the Indian Act, into the constitution of Canada and make it even more difficult for Indian women to gain their rights. If you follow through from Section 15 to Section 24 and Section 25, you will find that it would lock in the wording of the very clause that denied Jeanette Lavell the right to be regarded as an Indian, even though she is a full blood Indian woman. If something is not done about this, if some change is not made to take that particular situation into consideration, you will find that the Sandra Lovelaces of this world who have to go to the United Nations now to seek redress against discrimination are going to have to continue to go to the United Nations rather than to the Government of Canada or the courts of Canada.

I wonder if you would comment on how you see the Sections 15, 24 and 25 locking in the discrimination that now exists against Indian women.

**Ms. Betsy Carr (National Action Committee on the Status of Women):** Thank you. The situation here is really desperate for Indian women. Unless we can spell out the understanding of the present situation where there is a built in discrimination and there has been, as Miss MacDonald has just explained to us, the rather invidious situation where Indian women in Canada have to go abroad to look for redress in this, to my mind it is like pouring concrete over a very unjust situation. It will be set for all time to come if the wording here is not changed to accommodate it. I am not really prepared to explain any definite wording and how to handle this. We are not constitutional experts. We think we see some of the soft spots. We think we see what needs to be done. We return it to you people with your expertise to get our ideas into this Charter of Rights. (9: 66–7)

...

**Ms. Lynn McDonald (President, National Action Committee on the Status of Women):** Well, there are several points here. On Sections 24 and 25, we do not feel that Section 25 is an adequate adjunct to Section 15. Section 25 says that laws which are contrary will be inoperative. Contrary to the charter, but what provision of the charter? You see, the Indian Act is contrary to Section 15(1) of the charter, but it is not contrary to Section 24 of the charter. So there is an ambiguity there, it would have to be interpreted by the courts and the courts have been terribly bad on these issues. We would have to trust the Supreme Court of Canada really to understand and to come out, given that there is an ambiguity and to treat the equality as being the more important consideration there, and we do not have confidence that that would be the decision that would be made. We do not think it should be left to chance, we do not think there should have to be litigation for years in order to find out what would happen. (9: 75)

## Affirmative Action

**Professor Walter Tarnopolsky (President Canadian Civil Liberties Association):** On the matter of the affirmative action or, in Canada as they are called special programmes provisions, Section 15(2), 1 think that the point made by the Canadian Human Rights Commission is certainly one we do not disagree with, namely, that we do not want to have to refer to it so broadly that there is no possibility of the review in the sense of the programme being designed specifically for a bona fide amelioration of a person or group of persons; in other words, taking past history, there seems to be no doubt that it is possible with the clause quite as broadly as it is to include affirmative action programmes that we in the Canadian Human Rights Commission would not have considered to be such. So that on that particular point, I do not think that our position on the affirmative action programme is really any different than that submitted to you by the Canadian Human Rights Commission. (7: 23)

**Professor Irwin Cotler (Canadian Jewish Congress):** ... the Committee supports the principle of affirmative action as set forth here in the charter and as earlier set forth in Section 15 of the Canadian Human Rights Act. These components of affirmative action can be discerned in fact from the affirmative action programme with respect to francophones and the public service which itself was a consequence of the [Bilingualism and Biculturalism] report.

Our only reservation therefore is with respect to the question of the incorporation or application of quotas in that regard. If I may, I would just like to excerpt from a brief that I had occasion to participate in on behalf of the Canadian Civil Liberties Association in the consideration of Section 15 of the Canadian Human Rights Act at the time, wherein, we stated that in view of the controversies elsewhere ... we were referring then to the situation in the United States ... it would be prudent to note that our recommendations here need not entail any suggestion of reverse discrimination or benign quotas ... and here is the key phrase, we are not necessarily asking that qualified whites be rejected, for example, in favour of unqualified non-whites. What we are asking is that more non-whites be encouraged and assisted to qualify and compete. ...

Many Canadian universities have themselves developed special admission programmes for native students with resulting increases in the rates of native enrolments. In certain ways then, Section 15 of the Human Rights Act simply legalized practice and philosophy that was already well entrenched in Canada before it and I suggest that Section 15, Subsection 2 of the charter affirms that principle and we associate ourselves with that principle with the caveat as expressed therein with regard to the matter of quotas. (7: 94)

**Ms. Lynn McDonald (Member of the Executive, National Action Committee on the Status of Women):** We believe that this clause on affirmative action programmes is intended to include women, but nowhere is this expressly stated. Given the sorry record of the courts on women's rights cases, this is not a matter to be left to judicial discretion. Should affirmative action programmes be established we do not want to have to spend years in court proving their legality. The National Action Committee recommends adding to Section 15(2) the words "including women." (9: 58–60)

**Miss Flora MacDonald, MP (PC, Ontario):** Section 15(2), that is the one which I think could kill any affirmative action program that is now in effect in Canada if the courts so decided of if they moved in much the same way they have in the past as far as women's rights are concerned, because it talks about this, it says: "(2) This section does not preclude any law, program or activity that has as its object the amelioration of conditions of disadvantaged persons or groups." But by and large women are not seen as a disadvantaged group and yet any affirmative action program that is in effect for women could be killed by an interpretation of that section.

**Ms. Lynn McDonald (President, National Action Committee on the Status of Women):** This is a very dangerous one. Incidentally, I would like to make the point that I am not aware of any real affirmative action programs in the country at the present time in the sense of a program intended to enable women to catch up. The ones which exist simply are to prevent further discrimination, to keep women from falling below where they ought to be. For example, if women constitute 40 per cent of the people who have a certain skill, they should get 40 per cent of the jobs in that area. It is not suggested they ought to [have] 60 per cent to compensate for the fact they only had 20 per cent before. There are not any programs which would actually disadvantage a man to my knowledge in Canada, but should that happen, should there be genuine catch-up programs, there is a very real danger that they would be ruled to be illegal by the Supreme Court. If we sound to be in contempt of court, it is for very good reasons.

**Miss Flora MacDonald (PC, Ontario):** Hear, hear. (9: 65–6)

...

**Ms. Lynn McDonald (President, National Action Committee on the Status of Women):** We do not agree with that. Women, today, on average earn 60 per cent of what men do for fulltime work. It is very difficult to imagine the tables being turned so much that men average only about 60 per cent of what women earn. It cannot be within our imagination that the tables would be so badly turned that men, as a group, would be disadvantaged so as to require affirmative action programmes.

What we worry about is the fact that women are about half the population of the country. Would the courts decide, women being half the population of the country, that they constituted a group in that sense, a disadvantaged group? I can hear a judge saying, "Women are not a disadvantaged group. My wife has never ever been disadvantaged."

If you read the cases, you will see remarks of this sort. There has been a terrific inability among judges to understand inequality against women, and I do not think we can leave this one to chance.

**Senator Joan Neiman (LIB, Ontario):** I understand your concern, but I still feel if the other sections were strengthened and women had recourse to the law under the equality sections, eventually those inequities which are now in existence would gradually be eliminated.

**Ms. Betsy Carr (National Action Committee on the Status of Women):** I wish I could share your optimism that all the other things we are asking for would be granted. I hope that would be so. But we want to be sure that this is quite clear in this particular case, in case the wording is not quite to our liking somewhere else. (9: 72–3)

**Ms. Mary Eberts (Legal Counsel, Advisory Council on the Status of Women):** Subsection 15(2) as proposed is designed to permit legislative programs for the benefit of disadvantaged groups. That is not in our view, even as it stands in its present version, designed to require such programs and that is a distinction that we feel important. It is designed to permit programs that would otherwise be struck down by the courts because they violate Subsection 1, and our comments on this section are predicated on our understanding that that is what the purpose of the section is.

We think that the present draft, however, has some deficiencies. First of all, it extends protection to affirmative action programs, if you will, that need not be authorized by a legislature. We think that this protection is too sweeping. A private employer, for example, may dream up a sort of crazy affirmative action program in order to justify its discrimination against women or against Indian people or against people who belong to a particular racial minority and we do not feel that this kind of private initiative which is carried on without the benefit of the legislative framework should be rewarded by protection in the charter of rights. Affirmative action is rather a special and heavy-duty remedy against discrimination and we do not feel that it should be available on a random basis to anyone who cares to dream up a program.

We also feel that the section is deficient because it does not tie itself in with the groups mentioned in the proposed Section 15(1). Anyone who proves that they are disadvantaged, so-called, could under the present proposal try to justify a program which discriminates against Indian people, against women, against those who may well be really disadvantaged in our society. For example, a program brought forward for the benefit of those poor souls who did not attend Upper Canada college might be justified under Section 15(2) as it now stands, even though that program discriminated against Indian persons who are trying to live on $1500 a year.

We recommend that Section 15(2) be cued in to groups that are mentioned explicitly in Section 15(1), because after all Section 15(2) exists only to prevent Section 15(1) from cutting down a beneficial program and there is no need to have its scope go any wider, and indeed there may be harms brought about because its scope does go wider. (9: 126–7)

**Senator Florence Bird (LIB, Ontario):** Under part 2 of Section 15. Now, I am not trying to be difficult but I simply do not understand two things: first of all, you are worried about a private company or employer using affirmative action for the wrong group. Well, surely the courts would bring that out very quickly, I would think; but are you suggesting in order to have an affirmative action program, for instance, in the public service, as I hope we have that you would have to have an act of parliament, that is you would have to get permission from Parliament or from the legislature every time you brought in an affirmative action program. You would have an awful lot of acts, it would seem to me to be rather awkward and I do not understand.

**Professor Nicole Duple (Advisory Committee on the Status of Women):** We feel that any program, whether it is positive or negative, will have some incidence on other groups of the population which are not beneficiaries, or who are not affected by such a program. That is why we feel that it is extremely difficult to let the legislatures, or the Government of Canada, or the provincial governments establish programs without any legislative framework. We prefer to encourage those programs which are supported by law. And indeed that is why we are asking that the programs be established under the law.

**Ms. Mary Eberts (Legal Counsel, Advisory Council on the Status of Women):** There was a further point that we chose the language of our proposed Section 15(3) rather carefully to say that it limits the authority of Parliament or the legislature to authorize any program or activity envisaging that there may well be general legislation on the subject of the public service which would enable the passage of regulations or the passage of guidelines or directives to implement a particular program and thereby achieve flexibility, but that the basic policy decision as to whether, for example, the legislation would allow the Public Service Commission to promote programs designed to achieve equality should be a legislative one. It is not each particular program that would have to be authorized but there would have to be an initial grant of discretion to the body setting the program up so the legislature would have passed on the principle. (9: 142–3)

**Mr. Francis Young (Legal Advisor, New Brunswick Human Rights Commission):** First, I would like to deal with paragraph 15(2). The New Brunswick Human Rights Commission supports this paragraph in principle but proposes that it be amended in order to avoid a possible problem.

It is recognized today that affirmative action programs are essential to the reintegration into Canadian society of disadvantaged minorities who, for many years, have suffered the cumulative effects of discrimination. Programs like this would be precluded under paragraph 15(1) so it is essential that it be maintained in paragraph 15(2).

However, the Commission feels that the scope of paragraph 15(2) is too wide since it authorizes not only affirmative action programs provided for by law but also those which are not.

Therefore, our Commission recommends that only programs undertaken in accordance with the law fall under paragraph 15(2). ... This would avoid removing the affirmative action programs from the scope of paragraph 15(2) which is essentially a continuation of paragraph 15(1) or the exaggerated affirmative action programs like those which include "quota" for example. On the other hand, programs which have been entrenched in the law would not lead to abuse as frequently. (11: 32–3)

...

**Mr. Wilson Head (President, National Black Coalition of Canada):** We believe, for example, that the reference in this constitution to "affirmative action" is very well taken. We believe that, in order to overcome the long, 300-year history of discrimination against blacks in Canada, that affirmative action is a necessity.

We feel that if one simply opens up equality of opportunity – and we do not believe that is true now, but let us say that it is true – it would take another 100 years before we are able to make up for the past discrimination or the past history of discrimination over the last 200 or 300 years in Canada. (22: 9)

**The Honourable Jean Chrétien (Minister of Justice):** Section 15(2) of the draft Resolution permits affirmative action programs to improve the conditions of disadvantaged persons or groups. I am proposing an amendment to read: "Subsection (1) does not preclude any law, program or activity that has as its object the amelioration of conditions of disadvantaged individuals or groups including those that are disadvantaged because of race, national or ethnic origin, colour, religion, sex or age."

This section permits programs designed to achieve equality which might otherwise be precluded by the rules against discrimination in subsection 15(1). The amendment will not preclude other programs to assist the disadvantaged – be it on grounds such as handicap, marital status or other bases of discrimination identified by the courts. It is simply an assurance that an affirmative action program based on a recognized ground of non-discrimination will not be struck down only because it authorizes reverse discrimination for the purpose of achieving equality. (32: 15)

## Amendments to Section 15

**The Honourable Jean Chrétien (Minister of Justice):** I want to take this opportunity to congratulate all of the witnesses who testified on this section. I want specifically to compliment the Advisory Council on the Status of Women for a particularly fine brief as well as for an impressive presentation before you. The work of the Council has greatly influenced the government as have the presentations of the many witnesses who have spoken on this subject on behalf of women's groups, the handicapped, and others. A provision on "equality rights" must demonstrate that there is a positive principle of equality in the general sense and, in addition, a right to laws which assure equal protection and equal benefits without discrimination. To ensure the foregoing and that equality relates to the substance as well as the administration of the law, I would be prepared to accept an amendment to Section 15(1) so that it would read:

> Every individual is equal before and under the law and has the right to the equal protection and equal benefit of the law without discrimination and in particular without discrimination based on race, national or ethnic origin, colour, religion, sex or age. (32: 13–14)

...

**Senator John Connolly (LIB, Ontario):** The magic word seems to be "in particular" and I wondered whether the old hackneyed phrase, "without limiting the generality of the foregoing," which is very familiar to the lawyers and to the bench, at least my generation of lawyers and judges, whether you may have the effect of that phrase and the use of the words "in particular." I wonder whether there is something about the words "in particular" that create the open ended list that is contemplated.

**The Honourable Robert P. Kaplan (Acting Minister of Justice):** ... The advice we are given from the lawyers, and I will ask them to enlarge upon it, is exactly that, that using this expression "in particular" means that other forms of discrimination and discrimination based on other characteristics of the individual would be covered by the general introductory words. ...

**Mr. Roger Tassé (Deputy Minister of Justice):** We are confident in the department that what the clause says here would entail, in effect as we have being saying, an open ended clause or open-ended list of possible grounds for discrimination but underlying, in effect, to the courts that they would have to accept that there are some grounds on the basis of which discrimination is not acceptable. It would have to be open to them to decide whether there are additional grounds. ... (41: 18)

**Mr. Svend Robinson, MP (NDP, BC):** Mr. Chairman, I will attempt to ask a question rather than make a speech. ... Is it your intention or that of the drafters of the Charter that it would be open to a court to proscribe discrimination on the grounds of marital status, political belief, sexual orientation and disability. ...

**Mr. Kaplan:** ... It would be open indeed to a court to do that. I do not see any particular advantage of the expression that you have proposed over the one which is proposed in the bill. (41: 21–2)

## Title of Section

**Ms. Pamela Medjuck (National Steering Committee, National Association of Women and the Law, Nova Scotia):** First of all, a point we would like to bring up, though not of great significance to the public but is of significant legal interpretation concerns the title of Section 15. In the Charter the government proposes, the title is Non-discrimination Rights. We believe it would be helpful to subsequent legal interpretation if the title were equal rights. We would like to avoid the use of a negative term which does not set out the affirmative standard that Section 15 is aspiring to. Therefore, we recommend to the Committee that the title of Section 15 be changed to equal rights. (22: 55)

**The Honourable Jean Chrétien (Minister of Justice):** There has been much discussion of the non-discrimination provisions of the Charter as found in Section 15. I want to deal with this in some detail. First, I want to state that I agree with the proposal made by the Advisory Council on the Status of Women and the National Association of Women and the Law that the section be entitled equality rights so as to stress the positive nature of this important part of the Charter of Rights. (32: 13)

## Explicit Recognition of Equal Rights of Men and Women

**Mr. R. G. L. Fairweather (Chief Commissioner of Canadian Human Rights Commission):** The charter of rights should contain an explicit reference to the rights of women. We suggest adding the following unequivocal principle: "this charter guarantees the equal right of men and women to the enjoyment of the rights and freedoms set out in it." Scholars will know, and deputies and senators will know this is not special language, it comes from international treaties now ratified by Canada. (5: 9)

**Mr. Svend Robinson, MP (NDP, BC):** Now, turning to Section 15 of the proposed charter, the section which you have emphasized in your brief, as it is presently worded would you agree that this section fails significantly to ensure equality of status for women in this country?

**Mr. Gordon Fairweather (Chief Commissioner, Canadian Human Rights Commission):** I think there are very good reasons to do as we and some others have suggested, to make a specific statement about the rights of women. If I were pressed on this, strictly lawyer to lawyer, I would like to think this is enough.

But a constitution is not only a document of lawyers, but also a document of people, poets and others, at least I hope it [is]. I think the clear enunciation we have suggested that comes from tested international jurisprudence would protect women better than this.

**Mr. Robinson:** That is a political ...

**Mr. Fairweather:** We are in politics, too. We are in attitudinal change, and not in partisan politics.

**Mr. Robinson:** Speaking on behalf of the Commission, Mr. Fairweather, in your recommendations you have certainly said the section, as now worded, is not adequate to protect equality of status for women and you have proposed some specific amendments to that section.

**Mr. Fairweather:** Yes; I have done that, because I am appalled by some of the judicial interpretations which have flown in the face of what most of us believe should be the rights of women in society, and have also flown in the face of Bills of Rights that I know are only federal charters, but I can reel them off and you know them just as well as I do – Canadian decisions like Laval and Bliss and others which are saddening to those who had hoped that the Supreme Court of Canada could do better.

**Mr. Robinson:** And, presumably, it is because of those decisions on the wording as it now exists that you are making your recommendations?

**Mr. Fairweather:** It is because of these decisions that we must have an entrenched Bill of Rights in this country to remind the judiciary that there have been changes in Canadian society. There is no mystery about the origin of entrenchment. It will be the statement of the Parliament of Canada about how serious they are about enshrining these rights, and the *Bliss* and *Laval* cases as well as the *Indian Act* cases and so on would be overturned, as they should be.

**Mr. Robinson:** Presumably, though, you would want to make absolutely sure that, in formulating the wording of the anti-discrimination section, or equality section, that those kinds of decisions could never again be made in interpreting Section 15?

**Mr. Fairweather:** Exactly; that is why we are here today, Mr. Robinson. Exactly.

**Mr. Robinson:** Thank you. (5: 15–16, 24–5)

**Mrs. Diana Davidson (President, Vancouver People's Law School Society):** Also, this section requires strengthening by making clear that the Charter applies equally to men and women. (32: 13)

**Miss Pauline Jewett, MP (NDP, BC):** I wonder what you would think of adding one clause to that section and the clause would be, after the Canadian Charter guarantees to every person the rights and freedoms set out in it and the equal rights of women and men to the enjoyment of these rights and freedoms, so that you have it right out in front at the beginning.

**Mrs. Doris Anderson (President, Canadian Advisory Council on the Status of Women):** Well, my reply to that is very positive.

**Miss Jewett:** Is there any legal problem with that, Mrs. Eberts?

**The Joint Chairman (Mr. Joyal):** Mrs. Eberts?

**Ms. Mary Eberts (Legal Counsel, Canadian Advisory Council on the Status of Women):** Well, I do not think there is a legal problem. I think that from the discussions that we have had among our group concerning possible changes to the Charter, our main difficulty with the language such as you have proposed would be that if that were the only language guaranteeing women's rights to equality in the Charter, we would find it not strong enough, but if that were part of the general hortatory introduction, then we can see it only as a beneficial addition, as long as it did not have to carry the full freight, as it were.

**Miss Jewett:** Carry the full freight, no indeed, I was thinking only of having a fairly positive thrust at the very beginning as far as equality of men and women are concerned, before you move on to other distinctions. (9: 137)

### Three-Year Delay for Section 15

**Professor Maxwell Cohen (Canadian Jewish Congress):** ... We cannot understand why there should be the three year delay with respect to Section 15, bringing into effect. It appears to be from the notes to the document distributed by the government that the problems of age create difficulty. We think that on a closer look into this matter it will be discovered that the phasing out problems wherever they take place, really do not require a delay in the whole process which this particular provision provides for, and we think, therefore, the Committee recommends the delay be restricted to the age provision alone and not to Section 15 as a whole, and even the age provision we think, probably, actuarially, it may not be as severe as it is believed to be. (7: 99)

**Senator Joan Neiman (LIB, ON):** ... I think members of the legal profession from Ontario who are present will certainly remember the chaos which was created in our province a few years ago when the Family Law Reform Act was implemented almost immediately after its proclamation. The legal profession, the officers who had to administer or observe the law, men and women who were directly affected by that law, all had many, many problems, because it just was proclaimed one day and suddenly put into effect the next day. It was almost impossible to deal with it, because that law cut across so many other laws. I think there needs to be a transitional period. I am not arguing for three years. I think it is going to take three years to amend all of the laws which might be affected by the provision of this charter.

I quite understand your concern, and the concern of the many women that you are representing, that three years is a long way down the line as it appears to be. But I think, in very practical terms, a transition period of some kind is necessary, and probably the periods could be allowed to vary depending upon the laws involved. Would you feel that kind of amendment would be acceptable? (9: 74–5)

**Ms. Lynn McDonald (President, National Action Committee on the Status of Women):** On the moratorium, let me emphasize that on the question of the native women's rights, the discrimination has been known about for years and it has been complained about for years, it was a recommendation of the Royal Commission on the Status of Women in Canada, that report was tabled in Parliament almost ten years ago. In a couple of weeks it will be ten years ago. This has been known about for a long time, that there are wordings – it would not take a long time and it has been a lack of political will, it has not been the necessity of working out detailed legislation or administrative procedures. We certainly have been lobbying on issues of housing, for example, which would be relevant to this for a long time. We just do not think there is any excuse for this ten year moratorium – pardon me, a three year moratorium. A Freudian slip there. (9: 75)

**Senator Florence Bird (LIB, ON):** ... You discussed the idea that three years before the legislation is applied is much too long and you think all of the provinces could change all their statutes in six months and you quote the Royal Commission on the Status of Women, which after ten years has only two-thirds of the recommendations that have been implemented. Now, there is a difference here. The Royal Commission was instructed to enquire, report and make recommendations about what steps the federal government should take to give women equal opportunities in every aspect of Canadian Society, but the Government was under no obligation and neither were the provinces nor the private sector to whom we made our recommendation, there was no obligation, while in this case, there is a definite obligation that in three years time it is law and no nonsense and the laws have to be changed.

Now, I know how impatient women are and heaven knows I am impatient myself having been Chairman of that Commission, but I do think there is a difference between the recommendations of a Royal Commission and a Charter of Rights which lays down a certain rule and a certain cut-off day. I am just saying this, I suppose, to lay at rest the worries and doubts of all the thousands of women who are going to sleep better at night when they have an entrenched Bill of Rights.

**Ms. Mary Eberts (Legal Counsel, Advisory Council on the Status of Women):** The point that the governments are legally obliged to enact the reforms necessary to bring legislation into line with the charter is one that we do not quarrel with but we wish that if that is the effect, if that is intended to be the effect of Section 29, it can be made explicit. Right now it seems as if the intention to bind governments to change their law in three years is implicit in Section 29 and not explicit. Moreover, the problem remains of what happens to women who are denied the recourse to the courts during that three-year period. It may well be, as a neophyte trial lawyer I think I can say that if you have to wait three years, your witnesses have gone, your facts are not there and those women are going to be in the bitter situation of having their rights guaranteed on paper and they are not going to be able to secure their achievement.

So if it is desired to have a moratorium for three years, then we would regard it as most desirable to make two things explicit: first of all, that governments are bound to embark upon a program of reform; and secondly, that no one is going to lose the right of recourse to the courts in the interim and in that kind of situation where your understanding of the bill is made explicit, then the moratorium would be easier to live with. (9: 144–5)

**Ms. Deborah Acheson (Member of the Steering Committee, National Association of Women and the Law):** Speaking as a lawyer who has been involved in two appeals to the Supreme Court of Canada, I can tell you from my personal experience, the first one took three years and the second one took five years to wend its way from the Supreme Court of British Columbia to the Supreme Court of Canada. The proposal contained in Section 29(2) means that even if this were brought into force next year, we are then talking about a six-year delay until we have a legal pronouncement from our highest court, and that is simply not acceptable. I have an alternative proposal. It seems to me that it would be quite simple to use the sort of procedure that one uses in the Crown liability acts, that is where a prospective litigant wishes to sue with respect to a declaration under Section 15(1), the litigant gives the government three months notice of the intention to issue a writ. The government then has three months to consider its position and decide whether or not it is going to make the necessary amendment. It is simple and it is effective and it would bring immediately to the attention of the government those areas of urgency which were of great concern for those people suing, and would result in having legal decisions within a much earlier period of time, and if we are going to enact the Bill of Rights, for heaven's sake, let us get on with finding out what it means. (22: 68–9)

**Mr. David Lepofsky (Member, Ontario Division Board of Management, Canadian National Institute for the Blind):** ... Finally it is our submission that Section 29 (2), which provides that the equality clause will go into effect later than all other parts of the bill should be repealed, simply because there is no good reason in our view why egalitarian liberties should be delayed. If anything, they should be accelerated. (25: 13–14)

## Chapter Eleven

# Language Rights

*Official Languages of Canada*

16. (1) English and French are the official languages of Canada and have equality of status and equal rights and privileges as to their use in all institutions of the Parliament and government of Canada.

(2) English and French are the official languages of New Brunswick and have equality of status and equal rights and privileges as to their use in all institutions of the legislature and government of New Brunswick.

~~(2)~~ (3) Nothing in this Charter limits the authority of Parliament or a legislature to advance the equality of status or use of English and French.

*English and French linguistic communities in New Brunswick*

16.1 (1) The English linguistic community and the French linguistic community in New Brunswick have equality of status and equal rights and privileges, including the right to distinct educational institutions and such distinct cultural institutions as are necessary for the preservation and promotion of those communities.

*Role of the legislature and government of New Brunswick*

(2) The role of the legislature and government of New Brunswick to preserve and promote the status, rights and privileges referred to in subsection (1) is affirmed.

17. (1) Everyone has the right to use English or French in any debates and other proceedings of Parliament.

(2) Everyone has the right to use English or French in any debates and other proceedings of the legislature of New Brunswick.

18. (1) The statutes, records and journals of Parliament shall be printed and published in English and French and both language versions are equally authoritative.

(2) The statutes, records and journals of the legislature of New Brunswick shall be printed and published in English and French and both language versions are equally authoritative.

19. (1) Either English or French may be used by any person in, or in any pleading in or process issuing from, any court established by Parliament.

(2) Either English or French may be used by any person in, or in any pleading in or process issuing from, any court of New Brunswick.

20. (1) Any member of the public in Canada has the right to communicate with, and to receive available services from, any head or central office of an institution of the Parliament or government of Canada in English or French, as he or she may choose, and has the same right with respect to any other office of any such institution where ~~that office is located within an area of Canada in which it is determined, in such manner as may be prescribed or authorized by Parliament, that substantial number of persons within the population use that language.~~

(a) there is a significant demand for communications with and services from that office in such language; or
(b) due to the nature of the office, it is reasonable that communications with and service from that office be available in both English and French.

(2) Any member of the public in New Brunswick has the right to communicate with, and to receive available services from, any office of an institution of the legislature or government of New Brunswick in English or French.

21. Nothing in sections 16 to 20 abrogates or derogates from any right, privilege or obligation with respect to English and French languages, or either of them, that exists or is continued by virtue of any other provision of the Constitution of Canada.

22. Nothing in sections 16 to 20 abrogates or derogates from any legal or customary right or privilege acquired or enjoyed either before or after the coming into force of this Charter with respect to any language that is not English or French.

**Minority Language Educational Rights**

*Language of instruction*

23. (1) Citizens of Canada ~~whose first language learned and understood is that of the English or French linguistic minority population of the province in which they reside have the right to to have their children receive their primary and secondary school instruction in that minority language if they reside in an area of the province in which the number of children of such citizens is sufficient to warrant the provision out of public funds of minority language educational facilities in that area.~~

(*a*) whose first language learned and still understood is that of the English or French linguistic minority population of the province in which they reside, or (*b*) who have received their primary school instruction in Canada in English or French and reside in a province where the language in which they received that instruction is the language of the English or French linguistic minority population of the province,

have the right to have their children receive primary and secondary school instruction in that language in that province.

*Continuity of language instruction*

(2) ~~Where a citizen of Canada changes residence from one province to another and, prior to the change, any child of that citizen has been receiving his or her primary or secondary school instruction in either English or French, that citizen has the right to have any or all of his or her children receive their primary and secondary school instruction in that same language if the number of children or citizens resident in the area of the province to which the citizen has moved, who have a right recognized by this section, is sufficient to warrant the provision out of public funds of minority language educational facilities in that area.~~

Citizens of Canada of whom any child has received or is receiving primary or secondary school instruction in English or French in Canada, have the right to have all their children receive primary and secondary school instruction in the same language.

*Application where numbers warrant*

(3) The right of citizens of Canada under subsections (1) and (2) to have their children receive primary and secondary school instruction in the language of the English or French linguistic minority population of a province

(*a*) applies wherever in the province the number of children of citizens who have such a right is sufficient to warrant the provision to them out of public funds of minority language instruction; and
(*b*) includes, where the number of those children so warrants, the right to have them receive that instruction in minority language educational facilities provided out of public funds.

## Commentary

Language rights were the subject of much impassioned debate at the Joint Committee. Most speakers spoke about language rights in the abstract, with very little discussion about the text of sections 16 to 23. Discussion about language rights (sections 16 to 22) was often lumped together with minority-language-education rights (section 23).

The majority of the debate centred on whether to force the provinces to provide bilingual services and, if so, which provinces. Although several provinces had previously expressed their willingness to be bound to provide services in both languages, at the time of the Charter debates only New Brunswick was willing to entrench its bilingualism in the Constitution. The refusal of other provinces – especially Ontario – to similarly bind themselves received much criticism from advocates of minority-language rights. Likewise, the federal government's unwillingness to impose provincial bilingualism on the provinces – especially Ontario – sparked accusations of betrayal and political dealings. This was a divisive issue within the Liberal caucus as many caucus members strongly supported extending official bilingualism to Ontario; but ultimately, Trudeau and his Cabinet were unwilling to alienate Ontario Premier Bill Davis by doing so.

Many witnesses and some committee members thought that the majority-anglophone provinces should be bound to respect the rights of the French minorities because Quebec was already bound to respect the anglophone minority in that province. Manitoba was also similarly bound by section 23 of the Manitoba Act, 1870. There was much discussion of section 133 of the BNA Act, which enshrined "institutional bilingualism" for the federal government and Quebec, and whether it should be expanded.[1] For reference, section 133 provides the following:

Use of English and French Languages

133. Either the English or the French Language may be used by any Person in the Debates of the Houses of the Parliament of Canada and of the Houses of the Legislature of Quebec; and both those Languages shall be used in the respective Records and Journals of those Houses; and either of those Languages may be used by any Person or in any Pleading or Process in or issuing from any Court of Canada established under this Act, and in or from all or any of the Courts of Quebec.

The Acts of the Parliament of Canada and of the Legislature of Quebec shall be printed and published in both those Languages.

Discussion of Section 133 often overlapped with discussion of minority-language-education rights as well, although, as Minister Chrétien admonished, "Clause 133 is institutional bilingualism. It has nothing to do with education. ... So do not start getting them both mixed up."[2]

Most of the debate centred on the four provinces with the highest levels of other-language minorities: Quebec, Ontario, New Brunswick, and Manitoba. Several witnesses thought institutional bilingualism should be imposed on New Brunswick and Ontario; others called for (certain levels) of bilingualism everywhere. However, throughout the debates, Minister Chrétien steadfastly maintained that the federal government would not impose anything on the provinces.

Premier Richard Hatfield of New Brunswick appeared in front of the Committee and supported the extension of institutional bilingualism to his province, and amendments were made. Section 16.1 was added in 1983 after patriation.[3] The premiers of PEI and Nova Scotia appeared and promised to enact provincial legislation to protect the rights of their French-speaking minorities.[4] The premier of Saskatchewan also appeared and did not make any legislative promises, but pledged to promote French-language rights in the province.[5] In contrast, the Social Credit Party of Alberta was strongly against any minority rights based on language, but the Alberta NDP was in favour.[6] The premier of Ontario was conspicuously absent.

There was a mild amount of concern about the threshold for providing services in the minority language. The expression "where numbers warrant" or "a substantial number of persons" was criticized as vague.[7] The CBA called for the threshold to be determined either by a constitutional formula or by the courts.[8] A few witnesses spoke in favour of protecting other language rights – for instance, through section 15(1). However, the text of section 22, which specifies that sections 16 to 21 are without prejudice to the protection of other languages, seemed to make this a low-priority subject.

The minority-language education-rights provision (section 23) also attracted spirited debate, focusing on the issues of who qualified for the right, the content of the right, and the restriction on that right in being eligible for public funding.

## Language Rights Generally

**The Honourable Jean Chrétien (Minister of Justice):** Language rights have been a topic for much discussion and debate before this Committee and indeed in many other forums across the country. Let me state clearly the position of the government.

First, our objective is to enshrine in the Constitution the provisions of the Official Languages Act. This means that there will be a constitutional guarantee that English and French are the official languages of Canada and have equal status in all institutions of the Parliament of Canada and the Government of Canada. In addition, it means that there will be equality of status of English and French in the courts established by the Parliament of Canada. Finally, it means that Canadians will have a constitutional guarantee of their rights to receive services from and communicate with their federal government in the official language of their choice.

Second, the policy of the government is to give a constitutional guarantee to all Canadian citizens of the French or English speaking minority in each province to have their children educated in that minority language wherever there are sufficient numbers to warrant the provision of such minority language education. By so doing, the government is giving effect to the principle agreed to by the Premiers in St. Andrews in 1977 and in Montreal in 1978. The Premiers agreed, and, I quote, that: "Each child of the French-speaking or English-speaking minority is entitled to an education in his or her language in the primary or the secondary schools in each province wherever numbers warrant." It is this principle which the government is enshrining. Our position is that in the area of language rights we will not impose anything on which the premiers have not agreed.

Third, the policy of the government is to encourage and expand the protection of both official languages in every province, with the support of provincial governments. It has never been the policy of the government to impose institutional bilingualism on any province. Much as I would like to see Ontario become officially bilingual, with French-language rights within the context of its legislature, translation of legislation, and services to citizens before the provincial courts, all of this with constitutional guarantees, I have to agree with the view Claude Ryan expressed in Toronto last Thursday. He said, and I quote: "I would never impose it on the province of Ontario. It must come from the province of Ontario. This must be crystal clear."

Fourth, it is the policy of the government to protect the acquired rights of Canadians to have their children educated in English or French if that is the language in which they received their own instruction in Canada and if that is the minority language of the province in which they live. (36: 15–16)

**Hon. Richard B. Hatfield (Premier of New Brunswick):** Those of us who believe in the citizenship of Canada, must believe that, if the constitution says, as does the law of Parliament, that there are two official languages in our country, which I believe is a political necessity and reality as well as a political advantage to a country, then I think we must see to it that that status is in effect particularly as it affects a large number of Canadians. (19: 56)

**Mr. M. F. Yalden (Commissioner of Official Languages):** In other words, why entrench constitutional language rights and why cut off the legislative powers to change the situation for the better? I think all members of this Committee are well aware of the answer. It is because the legislative record has simply not been good enough. Who is there around this table who can really say that in the soon to be 115 years since Confederation, either the federal parliament or the provincial legislatures have acted consistently to protect the official language minorities? ...

Beyond these very practical considerations in favour of entrenchment, there are, I believe, symbolic reasons which go to the heart of our situation as a Canadian nation. For better or for worse, language has always been a matter of concern in this country; for worse, because it has too often been the cause of deep and painful division; for better, because at times it has shown itself a source of richness and diversity that is the envy of other nations. It is precisely because of this symbolic dimension which will profoundly affect our national cohesiveness in the future, as it has in the past, that we need to keep what Premier Blakeney has called the Confederation bargain by seeing to it that language rights are clearly and unequivocally recognized in our fundamental constitutional law. These are the reasons, or the main ones, why I favour entrenchment – why I very much favour it. If, therefore, I am here today to discuss the merits of the proposed resolution, it is not because I disagree with the basic principles underlying the government's proposals. It is, rather, to ask you to look at the wording as carefully as you can and to see whether the text is acceptable as it stands. (6: 10–11)

...

**Mr. M. F. Yalden (Commissioner of Official Languages):** In conclusion, Mr. Chairman, I should like to observe very simply that language rights are similar to other fundamental rights in that they limit, or should limit, the power of the state to encroach on the liberty of the individual. Indeed, other such rights often do not mean much unless one is allowed to live in one's own language. In this sense, of course, language rights have another dimension as well, for they also create the conditions in which languages and the cultures they express can flourish in dignity and without fear of assimilation.

Are the language provisions in the resolution before us likely to bring about such conditions while at the same time protecting English and French speakers from possible encroachments by the state? The answer, I believe, is yes and no. I am glad they are there but I wish they were better. I wish they were more generous and open and less mindful of political considerations and social apprehensions. It is in this sense that I believe that significant improvements can be made to the present text without risking any undue trauma to the body politic and I urge you in your work over the next few weeks, and in your report to Parliament, to try and bring those changes about. (6: 14–15)

**Mr. Dennis Flynn (Mayor of Etobicoke, National Executive, Federation of Canadian Municipalities):** In the Federation's approach to constitutional change, we perceive these as guiding principles: ... First among our objectives must be the creation of a constitution which will allow French-speaking and English-speaking societies to achieve their full and varied cultural aspirations, while recognizing the special rights of our native peoples to their particular traditions. ...

In our opinion, constitutional reform, in order to enshrine these principles should include the following provisions:

> Equality of status for the two official linguistic communities. The free and equal character of the partners in the federation must be emphasized to achieve a feeling of security and belonging.

> A bill of human rights must be enshrined in the new constitution to ensure justice and equality for all Canadians. Among others, linguistic rights must be assured. Canada will not be able to endure and flower as a political entity without such a bill of rights, which would bind, at the same time, the lawmakers and the executive branch of the different governments. These rights cannot be left to the generosity or intolerance of a parliamentary group.

We suggest that equality of opportunity, for the members of our two official linguistic communities should be an important part of the linguistic rights of this bill. More precisely, it is necessary to assure for all our citizens across the whole country, accessibility in the two official languages to the following services:

(I)     Education;
(II)    Courts (particularly criminal courts);
(III)   Governmental services (federal and provincial);
(IV)   Radio and television;
(V)    Bilingual laws (federal and provincial).

Accessibility should not be based on the number of citizens involved, except in the field of government services. ...

In conclusion, may I summarize the Federation's recommendations and stress our commitment:

V.     We recognize that cultural or linguistic freedom essential to the success of a Canadian federation can only be assured by a comprehensive reform of many laws, provincial as well as federal;
VI.    We express strong support for the fundamental principles of equality of status and equal rights as to the use of the English and French languages. (9: 8–10)

**The Hon. David Crombie, MP (PC, Ontario):** I do not think there has been a brief which has gone so far as that one with respect to municipalities that the Federation has undertaken. I may stand to be corrected that they have gone that far, but I do not recall it, but at any rate I am very impressed that you have it before us. (9: 21)

**Mr. Florent Bilodeau (Director General, Association culturelle franco-canadienne de la Saskatchewan):** The language provisions, sections 16 to 23 inclusively, do little more than recognize federal bilingualism to a certain extent and confer education rights that will not have much real effect. We know that the survival and development of Francophone communities implies far more than this.

The proposed resolution, as now worded, also ignores a number of sectors which affect people daily, such as services that fall under provincial jurisdiction. The proposed resolution says nothing about this, as if the Canadian constitution were a federal document and not a national one that defines the relationship between all of the governments that make up Canada and provides complete protection for citizens. This is a serious shortcoming and we know what effect it will have, since the government of English-speaking provinces have never been very inclined to respect the rights and needs of the French-speaking population. (12: 8–10)

We recognize that the inclusion in the Canadian constitution of the principle of equal status for French and English in Parliament, in legislation and before the courts confers a real right on the individual. Affirming the status of French in the constitution would certainly have a symbolic value, but it is a great concern to us that the proposed resolution falls well short of providing the strict and vital minimum for the French-speaking population of Saskatchewan. We are painfully aware of the fact that these few provisions of the proposed resolution will be a decisive and irreversible step in the history of French-speaking minorities in Canada. With certain exceptions, we consider that the premiers of English-speaking provinces are responsible for the watering down of our rights in the proposed constitution. This is particularly true of our premier, who, although he is aware of our position, has remained silent on the issue. In its official position on constitutional reform, our government completely ignores its responsibility to its French-speaking population and gives the impression that the issue does not interest it in the least.

We have the following recommendations to make on the aspects of the constitution which are of particular interest to us. First, a clear and unequivocal recognition of the Canadian duality and of the two founding nations. Secondly, the recognition of the responsibility of provincial and federal governments of ensuring the equality of status of the Francophone population and of encouraging the development of Francophone communities through appropriate legislation and policies. Thirdly, the recognition of the right of the minority to education in the language of the official minority, without regard to the number of students, and the recognition of the principle of control over and management of Francophone schools by Francophones. Fourthly, a more generous and precise definition of access to federal services in the language of the minority Finally, the recognition of the legal status of the French language in Saskatchewan, before the courts and in the legislative assemblies, as provided for in certain provisions of the Northwest Territories Act. (12: 10–12)

**Miss Jeanine Seguin (President, La Federation des Francophones hors Quebec):** Mr. Chairman, evidently a translation is welcome but there is quite a difference between having a translation and living. We need institutions in the field of social services, community services and education; we need homogeneous education boards; we need to be able to manage our own institutions. (37: 47)

**Senator Martial Asselin (PC, Quebec):** When you say that Canada should be a bilingual country, I do not believe you mean that all anglophones should speak French, and that all francophones should speak English everywhere in Canada. That is not what you are asking?

**Mr. Antonio Sciascia (Legal Adviser, National Italian-Canadian Congress):** I do believe however that we should institute bilingualism in those areas where there is a concentration of francophones and anglophones. I think that we should start in those provinces where there is already a fairly large language minority. It would be a start at least. But the ideal objective would be that some day every Canadian shall speak both languages. Yes, that should be the objective, the ideal. (23: 13, 16–17)

**Mr. Grant Notley (Leader, Alberta New Democratic Party):** On the issue of language rights, it is our view, members of the Committee, and here we agree with the Premier of Saskatchewan who has suggested that language rights are not essentially human rights, as they are Canadian rights. They are rights that exist because of Canada's history, because of its background, because of its development. But we feel that in fact there should be a recognition right across the country of language rights, not just in some provinces but we feel right across the country. In this respect we go perhaps somewhat further than any of the submissions that I think you have heard to date from at least provincial governments or political parties. ... (33: 104)

...

**The Hon. David Crombie, MP (PC, Ontario):** I would like ... to offer some general thoughts which I have found important and I think perhaps others have as well, when it comes to the question of language policy. I think one of the tendencies we have, Mr. Chairman, in this country is to assume that when we deal with language policy of Canadians that somehow we are all alone and isolated and the world does not either have anything to say to us or pay any attention to what we say about language policy. But I think we start off with a single fact, that in this space ship earth, in this world, there are approximately 2,500 languages, and there are only about 150 countries to go around to serve them all; any country's attempt to try to deal with more than one language within one geographical space is certainly paid attention to by other countries who have the same problem.

Many countries in the Western World have had to deal over the past 450 years [with] two, three or four languages. Newly emerging countries in Asia and Africa have many tribal languages and dialects which have to be dealt with. So the first point I would like to make is that we are dealing with something which is of world-wide significance, and how we deal with it is very, very important.

Over the years, Mr. Chairman, countries have sought to deal with more than one language in one country in a number of ways – territorially, where they have said in certain parts of the country there will be one kind of language and in another part of the country, another language. The best example of that would be Belgium, where territorial bilingualism is rigidly adhered to. We also have personal opportunities with respect to more than one language in other countries. That is true in Switzerland as it is in Finland.

We have, as well, Mr. Chairman, institutional bilingualism in relation to certain services from government. Most countries, Belgium, Switzerland, Finland, to use three examples, also have that kind of bilingualism. One lesson which comes out of the world experience, Mr. Chairman, is that most countries attempt to solve it in relation to their own conditions. Indeed, that is what Canada has done. Canada, by and large, has organized its language rights and liberties in respect of Canadian traditions. ...

I think it is important to recognize that throughout the whole history of this country, we can pick language policy as the one trail you could pick through the three and a half centuries. I guess, that either English-speaking or French-speaking people have been here. You can pick one or two which are very significant, Mr. Chairman: in 1774 there was the Quebec Act. It is important to remember that that act established, or if you like, re-established the rights of the French-speaking Canadians with respect to their religion and systems of laws. That was confirmed in 1791 and drowned [sic!] in 1840. In 1867 and subsequent years, we attempted to arrive at policies which would allow the survival of both languages so that both may coexist. That long history netted out one other, in my view, at any rate, fundamental principle in this country and that is that we rejected two extremes: the extreme which says that all of Canada should be English-speaking; and we rejected the tradition which said that there should be an independent French-speaking state, north of the 49th parallel. I reject those two. There are some Canadians who do not, but I do and I think members of this Committee do as well.

I could go through the record and show, Mr. Chairman, how provinces in this country have done with respect to the use of both English and French. Again, I do not have the time for that. It is unfortunate that I do not have the time, because looking at the province of Ontario – a province I know very well – people would be surprised to learn of the number of government services which are offered in both languages. Indeed, I shall not speak any further of institutional bilingualism of that nature as noted in Clause 16, nor with educational matters, because that is dealt with in Clause 23. We have by and large, adopted a Canadian pragmatic, practical way of offering services and educational facilities in both languages differently over a time in provinces. What I would like to deal with, Mr. Chairman, is something which I consider to be not a major step forward, but can become so.

I want to deal very specifically with the question of what languages we use in the courts, and legislatures. Mr. Chairman, the situation as it now stands today is that in the province of Manitoba both official languages have the right to be used in the courts and in the legislatures by virtue of Section 23 of the 1870 act. In the province of Quebec, as a consequence of Section 133 of the British North America Act, both official languages have the right to be used. In the province of New Brunswick, as a consequence of their own volition, both official languages have the right to be used. In the province of Ontario, only one official language has the right to be used – English.

Had I been able to have more time, Mr. Chairman, I would go into an extremely long list explaining how the Province of Ontario, my home province, has done more in the past 10 years with respect to bilingual services than at any time in the history of the province. Indeed, Mr. Chairman, when it comes to the question of the courts and the legislatures the province of Ontario has seen the need. It should come as no surprise to people, though often it does, that one may speak French in the legislature of Ontario. Indeed, Mr. Chairman, in 1979 Ontario adopted the policy of having a bilingual situation with respect to the criminal courts anywhere in the province. Also, in 1978 there was the adoption by provincial law of ten designated areas so that there would be bilingual services in French and English for those areas where there was a sufficient concentration of the language and now encompasses some 77 per cent of Franco-Ontarians. I mentioned that because the problem that I see is that even though both French and English can be used in the courts and the legislature, the only right given is to the English language.

If I can put my problem succinctly, it is this in short: I can find no principle which allows me to accept the proposition that an English speaking Canadian should have the right to speak in the legislature of the Province of Quebec or plead in the courts of the Province of Quebec and a French speaking Ontarian should not have the same right. That is the nub of the problem. I am one of those therefore, Mr. Chairman, who believes that the Province of Ontario should preach what it practises. The Province of Ontario does offer that facility. It simply holds back the right. I think that is an inappropriate – indeed, an unjust – way for us to continue. There may well have been historical views which were acceptable to some in the past, but I do not think there is going to be any foundation for them in the future.

I wish to conclude – because I know I have strained my five minutes – by looking at some of the reasons, for one moment, why there has been some difficulty in accepting that proposition. First of all, there has been some suggestion that we ought to impose that right of French speaking Ontarians on the Province of Ontario. As you know, Mr. Chairman, I am utterly opposed to that process – indeed to any kind of imposition, of any unilateral action, in fact. I think the history of the Province of Quebec and of Ontario – indeed of all the provinces of this country – is such that at any time rights or lack of rights are imposed, then this country has suffered. So that, firstly, I think it is important that I do not suggest – and I have never suggested, and I would oppose as I have every item in this constitutional proposal where there is unilateral action by the federal government to impose anything on a province.

Secondly, Mr. Chairman, there are some people who have suggested that, although it is only a small step, it is only symbolic, and it is not very important, that it is only a symbolic act; that symbols are not very important; that if you can already do it in the province of Ontario, why make a big issue out of it only for the sake of a symbol. Well, Mr. Chairman, symbols are extremely important. I do not need to lecture or offer modest thoughts to members of this Committee to establish that symbols have been important to humankind since they have been around. Millions upon millions and billions of people have been organized on the basis of the symbol of the Cross. People in this country have organized and gone to war and have died on the symbol of the Maple Leaf. Symbols are extremely important. We can no longer afford in this country a symbol which says that if you are French in Ontario you have a lower collar than English in Quebec. This is unacceptable in terms of any symbol I know of for unity in the future.

Certainly, Mr. Chairman, if there was one principle that the future must use, when it comes to the final step, after 350 years, of two peoples warring in the bosom of a single state – Lord Durham's phrase – the one principle is that of equality. There is no other principle which is acceptable. And I speak to that. Finally – and I hope not drawing too grand a sweep to it, although it is a small step, simply confirming what Ontario already does, and making it a right rather than a sufferance, I think it would have a bit of a breakthrough for us. If you read the history of this country, as many of us have, we are struck by the imagination and the courage of early Canadians. I think we have suffered considerably in the past number of decades with an acute case of timidity, Mr. Chairman; we have tended not to want to deal with things and have attempted to solve our problems by avoiding them.

It seems to me that, if we intend to take the future, then the only way in which I know how we can do that is to make sure that we, first of all, deal with ourselves and find out who Canadians [are]; we are Canadians and we come from many countries, speaking many languages and from many cultures, and we have organized ourselves as a political entity, as the rump of two empires, the French Empire and the British Empire. Maybe, finally, if we admit and clearly understand that we may be able to tap the resources of this country.

Let me say, finally, that there are some people – and I have received a lot of advice this morning – who wish that I would let sleeping dogs lie and not raise the matter. I am not one of those who believes you ought to rush in where angels fear to tread; I have lived a public life where I understand the importance of the middle ground and compromise. I used to make my living doing that. But I also know from personal experience that change does not come by itself. Although everyone I have talked to so far has said "David, I agree with you in substance, but ..." It is the "but" that bothers me. It is the "but" that holds the country back. So, Mr. Chairman, when the motion comes forward, if it is a motion which deals with those sentiments, then it will be a motion which I will support if it is worded in relation to the sentiments I have offered. Thank you. (48: 62–6)

**Mr. Nystrom, MP (NDP, SK):** I think the question of languages is, perhaps, one of the most, if not the most, sensitive of issues in many countries around the world, certainly in Canada. We, as Canadians, have spent more time on language debates, on misunderstandings and misconceptions of what the Official Languages Act means and of what bilingualism means, than on any issue in the last 20 or 30 years. I was elected back in 1968 and shortly thereafter, we introduced in Parliament the Official Languages Act by the Prime Minister, and I am proud to say I was one of the members of Parliament who supported that act, and supported, again, a few years later the reaffirmation of that act in Parliament. ...

Now, I do not really know as much as I should know about the province of Quebec; but what I do know about that province is that many Quebecois believe that their language is not really equal to the English language in Canada and many parts of this country. I think if we want to make sure that French-Canadians, Quebecois are really at home in Canada, we must have the equality of the two languages, even if in some cases it is more, symbolism. Now, David [Crombie] has referred to the fact that in Ontario one can speak French in the Legislature and there are now, of course, provisions where the French language can be used in the courts of Ontario. These are very important steps. There is another very important step, which may be more symbolic than anything else, and that is to enshrine some of these rights in the constitution.

He has referred to the possibility that we may be having before this Committee a motion to that effect, and I only want to make one appeal to you. I do this because of a sensitivity of issue, because of the fact that it is so easy to misunderstand, so easy to distort, and because of some of my frustrations in the last few days over the way it has been misunderstood by some people and distorted by others – and I can only think of some open-line hosts who totally distort the issue and do not do this country a service in telling people what we mean by equality of language in Ontario and Quebec.

Because of that sensitivity, because of the potential explosiveness, and because of the fact we want to do something that is positive for francophones in this country outside of Quebec, particularly in Ontario because there are so many francophones in Ontario, that we should seek in this Committee, as Mr. Crombie has said, to come up with a motion which would be unanimous, if that is possible. I know when you have 25 people on a Committee and dealing with an issue as sensitive as language with people from so many different regions of the country as we have here, that may be difficult.

But I, Mr. Chairman, do not think it is impossible. I think we can do it. I am hoping that we can do that, and that sometime before the end of these proceedings we could have an all party agreement and all member agreement, which is unanimous, and which will provide the wish and the hope that we can have the same services in the province of

Ontario for the francophones as exists in the province of Quebec for the anglophones. We said a long time ago that we intend to move a motion regarding this area but before we do that we hope that we can come to some kind of consensus, all of us, unanimously. (48: 66–7)

**The Hon. Bryce Mackasey, MP (LIB, ON):** Mr. Chairman, I think the tone set by Mr. Crombie and my very close friend Lorne Nystrom is one that should prevail on all the sections because the fact remains that the French language and the French culture is one of the greatest protections we have in the country against assimilation from the United States. Its very existence as an official language which our government brought in, which Parliament supported, that by itself has developed into one of the great forces against assimilation.

... There are two things I would like to see before I leave Parliament: that right to French speaking Canadians enshrined in the constitution, not only in Ontario but everywhere; and I would like to see freedom of choice brought back to the Province of Quebec so that new Canadians coming to that province have a choice to be educated in either language. They are both fundamental to me. (48: 67–9)

### Section 20 – Communications by the Public with Federal Institutions

**Mr. Lorne Nystrom, MP (NDP, SK):** I just wanted to ask the Minister's officials a question or two on Clause 20. The wording here refers to "any head or central office of an institution of the Parliament or Government of Canada," in terms of bilingual services. Can you explain a bit more what that means, "any head or central office"? Of course, "head office" is a head office, but does "central office" mean a regional office, or head office? Do the words mean the same thing?

**Mr. Roger Tassé, Q.C. (Deputy Minister of Justice):** Well, we wanted to make sure that we covered all possible arrangements which may be made for the distribution of government services. It could be a department like the Department of Veterans Affairs, which would be a head office of an institution of government. But it could also cover the head office or central office of government agencies; it could be a board, a corporation. In effect, I suppose we wanted to make sure here that we were not missing any central agency of government in a broad and general sense. That is why we have used these two words.

**Mr. Nystrom:** And in proposed Clause 21(a) as well, there are the words "significant demand." The reason I ask these questions is that we have always had controversy of what "where numbers warrant" means, and so on. I was wondering whether there is anything you would like to put on the record about that which may be helpful? Would "significant demand" be ultimately decided by the courts?

**Mr. Tassé:** That is correct, Mr. Nystrom. If in the original Clause 20 as tabled in Parliament, that determination in the final analysis was to be made by Parliament. But under this revised text, the court will ultimately decide these questions, whether there is in effect, a significant demand or not. (8: 83–4)

**The Honourable Jean Chrétien (Minister of Justice):** These policies [excerpted earlier in this chapter] have not changed. It is in this context that I would like to explain the amendments which the government is prepared to accept to the language provisions of the Charter of Rights.

First, Premier Hatfield had, in his appearance before this committee, requested on behalf of the government of New Brunswick that the Charter confirm that English and French are the official languages of New Brunswick, that the use of both languages in the courts and legislatures and statutes of New Brunswick be guaranteed, and that the right of the people of New Brunswick to communicate with and receive services from their government in either official language be guaranteed.

I am very pleased to be able to table amendments to Sections 16–20 giving effect to the proposals of the Premier of New Brunswick. I want to take this opportunity to congratulate Premier Hatfield on his statesmanlike approach to Canada. When other provinces are prepared to emulate Premier Hatfield, the amending formula as presently drafted will allow them upon resolution of their legislature and of the Parliament of Canada to give constitutional protection respecting the use of the English and French languages in their provinces. Mr. Hatfield has assured us that the amendments being tabled before the committee today will be approved by the New Brunswick legislature as soon as it resumes its sittings.

The second amendment with respect to language rights deals with the rights of Canadians to communicate with and obtain services from the federal government in either English or French. The amendment meets the concerns expressed by the Commissioner of Official Languages that Section 20 should ensure that the right to communicate with and receive services from any federal office in either official language is based, not on the number of persons in an area using the languages, but on their being a significant demand for communications with and services from any office in the language. In addition, as suggested by the Canadian Bar Association, the amendment would leave to the courts rather than to Parliament the ultimate determination of where other federal offices should provide bilingual services. (36: 16–17)

## Institutional Bilingualism: The Extension of Section 133 to Other Provinces

**Mr. M. F. Yalden (Commissioner of Official Languages):** So far as official bilingualism at the provincial level is concerned, it [i.e., the draft resolution] simply perpetuates the status quo. The rights pertaining to language use in the courts and legislatures in Quebec and Manitoba provided by Section 133 of the BNA Act and by Section 23 of the Manitoba Act are maintained. But what of Ontario and New Brunswick? The Resolution as drafted extends no such constitutional protection to them. Yet more than 90 per cent of the Francophones outside Quebec live in these provinces and there is little difference between their combined minority populations and the official language minority population of Quebec.

Why then perpetuate this obvious imbalance? If the Resolution as a whole attempts to avoid a checkerboard Canada, why carry forward this particular inequity? New Brunswick, we know, is ready to accept constitutional provisions relating to the courts and the legislature, in accordance with the basic principles of its own Official Languages Act. This leaves Ontario as odd man out. Can we really accept, especially when we know that such arrangements would not impose an intolerable burden on anyone, that the province with the largest Francophone minority of all should simply be omitted from a constitutional requirement to respect the French language in the legislature and the courts? What kind of constitutional rights are we talking about that apply to one official-language minority but not to another, to one province but not to its neighbour?

A further and major omission in the matter of the courts is the right to a criminal trial in the official language of one's choice. (6: 11)

...

**Mr. Lorne Nystrom, MP (NDP, SK):** I would like to ask the Minister why, in view of the deep-rooted principles of the Liberal Party on linguistic equality, did he not apply the same principles that are in Section 133 of the BNA Act to the provinces of New Brunswick and Ontario where are situated the two largest Francophone minorities anywhere in this country outside of the Province of Quebec?

**The Hon. Jean Chrétien (Minister of Justice):** At no point during the long debate on the constitution in Canada has the federal government proposed to impose Section 133 on any provinces. Any provinces that wanted to bind themselves are welcome to do so. I have to tell you that I am personally disappointed that there are not many provinces today that want to do that. In 1971 there were seven provinces that were willing to bind themselves by Section 133, and now we are down to the two, Quebec and Manitoba, who are obligated by the constitutional text, and the province of New Brunswick is still willing to bind itself.

... In the course of the summer the Ontario government said that they were not interested. Of course, we know that the rest of the governments who were interested in 1971 are no longer interested, or are, I do not know, but they have not given us an indication during the summer.

**Mr. Nystrom:** ... Supposing Quebec wants to be taken out of Section 133, and they make that request to the federal government, will he accede to that request? Or if Manitoba wants to be removed from the strictures of the Manitoba Act, will he accede to that request? ...

**Mr. Chrétien:** There is a difference between what I call acquired rights and new rights. These rights were established in the constitution long ago. They have, by historical reasons, kind of disappeared in Manitoba along the road, but they were in the constitution long before today. I think that it is a principle in law that before you take away acquired rights you have to be very careful, and they are rights that have been acquired in Quebec and in Manitoba. I do not want to go back on that. Now we have one more province that wants to bind itself by Section 133, it is New Brunswick, and I applaud them and I hope that there will be many more provinces. It is not the view of the government that we should force the provinces. If it is the view of this committee, I would like to know.

**Mr. Nystrom:** In other words, the answer to Manitoba and Quebec would be no.

**Mr. Chrétien:** No, I do not want to take those acquired rights from the people who have them. (2: 26–30)

...

**The Hon. Bryce Mackasey, MP (LIB, Ontario):** Prejudice is not something that is limited to language or anything else. I have to make that point because somehow in my concern for this issue over the last few years too many academics, too many intellectuals – and I am excluding politicians for the moment – have found a very facile, easy solution to our problem, that Quebec become totally unilingually French and the rest of Canada become totally unilingually English, and somehow all the problems will disappear, according to the academics of the greater Toronto area. I can assure you that when this happens you will have separation, when you have two sizable groups in this country ceasing to communicate spontaneously, as we do. It is important and imperative that the French language be given total opportunity of expanding and being recognized as an official language, not only in Quebec but across this country. This is why I welcome the unselfish attitude of Premier Hatfield in New Brunswick who understands that New Brunswick, despite its obvious limitations geographically and economically, is vibrant because it has somehow been able to meld these two great cultures. And that has been the experience in Quebec for as long as I lived there, which was a long time. One of the tragedies in recent years is that somehow in order to redress what were legitimate complaints in that province, complaints which I suggest did not flow from the educational system but from the business community, the insensitivity of multinationals and insensitivity of Canadian corporations, insensitivity that was reflected for instance in actual forbidding of the French language to be spoken in the workplace. These things have been rectified, thank goodness, and it makes Quebec a better place.

I must remind Mr. Nystrom and others that if it were not for Section 133 the right of English-speaking Canadians who reside in Quebec to be heard in the court of Quebec in their own language would be something waived and disappeared as a result of certain provisions of Bill 101.

I happened to say, and continue to repeat, that the relationship between the English and French in Quebec should be an example to all of Canada, and the constitutional changes that we propose should make it possible for that joie de vivre, that relationship, that intercommunication between the English and French in Quebec to have an opportunity to flourish across Canada. You are not going to get a sizeable French minority, Mr. Nystrom, in Saskatchewan, if you are unwilling to extend to that province the type of provisions and protection that the minorities should have resulting from section 133. (2: 34–5)

...

**Mr. Jean Lapierre, MP (LIB, PQ):** Like my colleagues, I wish to welcome you, Mr. Minister. I really appreciated Mr. Nystrom's magnanimity with respect to Section 133 of the BNA of 1867. I can only regret that his magnanimity does not encompass all provinces. What is good for others should be good for oneself. I would be very pleased to second a motion which would have Section 133 apply to all provinces. (2: 40)

...

**Mr. Eymard Corbin, MP (LIB, NB):** Mr. Minister, Mr. Chairman, I am happy to hear the minister say that he believes the courts will interpret "in which the number is sufficient" or the word "reasonable" based on the treatment which English speaking minorities are given in Quebec. That is what the minister has said, is it not?

**Mr. Chrétien:** Yes. If I was defending the francophones outside Quebec, I would call that province as my first witness so that the bench could hear how English speaking minorities in Quebec are being treated.

**The Joint Chairman (Mr. Joyal):** Mr. Corbin.

**Mr. Corbin:** The text of the resolution will remain unchanged.

**Senator Martial Asselin (PC, PQ):** Yes, but people have to wait before the courts can interpret the provision.

**Mr. Chrétien:** We must have confidence in the courts. Having confidence in the provinces has not proved very satisfactory over time.

**Mr. Corbin:** Obviously, we have to trust the courts, Mr. Chairman. Otherwise this exercise would be fruitless since all hopes founded in law are eventually left to interpretation before the courts. In any case, I am a little more encouraged by the minister's remarks than I was when we began consideration of the resolution. However, it appears to me that there is no backbone in this country. There does not seem to be enough determination on the part of the provincial premiers to recognize that we must recognize and grant, in the text of this charter, the same rights which anglophones have in Quebec at the present time. Frankly, I must admit that this obviously political game escapes me totally. I know that politics is the art of the possible, I know that as far as possible there was a desire to respect the texts which were adopted in 1971 and that the federal government did not want to give itself more rights than it has at the moment or take any away from the provinces. However, in my opinion it is an opportunity missed. The amendment of the constitutional provisions has not requested the provinces to take a more affirmative, a more positive stance. The minister may tell me that this is beyond his jurisdiction, but I have, nonetheless, to express my regret.

**Mr. Chrétien:** Obviously, Mr. Corbin, it is refreshing to hear that we have not been bold enough. Many have told us that we have gone too far. (3: 17–18)

**Senator Martial Asselin (PC, PQ):** And during this summer's conference, how many times have I heard Quebec representatives say that they hoped the English provinces would do for francophones what they were doing for anglophones in Quebec and that is exactly what we are putting into the Constitution at this point. ... What are the rights of the French minorities you are protecting? Is there anything being said for French minorities, say in Ontario, where there are 600,000 French Canadians and where your law does not apply, where you do not even apply or try to have applied Clause 133. I do not know why the representative from New Brunswick, Mr. Corbin, has let it be understood that there was negotiation of certain rights, I do not know. Anyway, the Acadians in New Brunswick as well as the French Canadians in Ontario are not at all affected by that law. (3: 55–6)

...

**Senator Duff Roblin (PC, Manitoba):** I notice that the Province of Manitoba is expected to provide French in the Courts and French in the legislature and it certainly does provide French in the schools right now. And in that Province 5.4 per cent of the population are francophones. Well, in looking over the statistics I find there are four other provinces in Canada who have more francophones among their population than Manitoba. There is Quebec, there is New Brunswick, there is Ontario and there is Prince Edward Island. Now, I would like to ask the Minister by what exercise of logic he decides that these rights should be accorded to Manitoba francophones but not accorded to francophones in other provinces which have more of that element in their population?

**The Hon. Jean Chrétien (Minister of Justice):** Those rights have not been given to the Manitoba francophones by this Parliament, it was given by the Fathers of Confederation in the same way that the rights of the anglophones in Quebec were given. It was inscribed in the constitution. What you are asking me is why is it there. It was decided by the Fathers of Confederation. The point I make is I do not want to turn back the clock, I want more provinces to bind themselves. That is a good argument that you are using, that in New Brunswick there are many more francophones than in Manitoba in relation to the population and already Mr. Hatfield has said that he will use the mechanism provided in this constitution to bind the Province of New Brunswick in 133. (4: 137–8)

**Mr. Alex Paterson (Co-president, Positive Action Committee):** As English speaking Quebecers we have borne witness to the use of both languages not only in the Legislature but also before the courts in our province. Whether it is Montreal where there are nearly one million

English speaking people or in the Beauce where only a handful reside, whether it be a civil or criminal trial, any witness or litigant can testify or plead in both languages. Even under Bill 101, this right, while limited for corporations in civil trials, never attempted to prevent witnesses or litigants from speaking English in the courts. The bilingual courts of Quebec are a source of pride to our bar and bench and an example to our country.

To give a personal example, when I was a third year student, I went to the Beauce during summer and I was often in the courthouse and even in the Beauce where I was almost the only English speaking person there, it was always possible and I was always welcome to speak as a witness or as a lawyer in English. In my fourth year, I went to Rimouski for a whole summer and even though I was almost the only English speaking person in Rimouski, once again, I was always welcomed when I spoke English before the bench in Rimouski.

Now, when people from Ontario tell me it is impossible, it is not practical because we do not have enough French speaking people in certain areas of Ontario I wonder, since it is possible in Rimouski, since it is possible in St-Georges-de-Beauce, since it is possible everywhere in Quebec for an English speaking person to speak English before the courts, how is it that in Ontario it is impossible to address a court in French? (7: 53–5)

...

**Professor Irwin Cotler (Canadian Jewish Congress):** Recommendation number two: we believe that Section 133 of the BNA Act and its equivalent section, 23 of the Manitoba Act should be extended to New Brunswick and Ontario. Section 133, which the courts in ... both the Quebec decision [in *Blaikie* and] in the Manitoba decision in *Foret*, rightly called a fundamental rule of law principle enshrines French and English as the official languages of the courts and legislatures of Quebec and Manitoba. We believe that this should be extended to Ontario and New Brunswick as was initially recommended in Bill C-60, again in the Canadian Bar Association Report, and earlier today in the Positive Action Committee Report and the federal proposals of August 22.

It does not appear to us to be sufficient, though we are encouraged by the fact that New Brunswick has rights of this kind in its own Provincial Human Rights Charter and has been responsive to the suggestion that it be included in this charter as well, or that Ontario is moving and we are encouraged by those developments in that regard. (7: 95)

...

**Mr. Eric Maldoff (President, Council of Quebec Minorities):** The next point we would like to bring to your attention is the question of Section 133 of the BNA Act. We see this issue as vital, we believe that Section 133, which guarantees the right to use English and French before the legislatures and courts, as it stands right now, of Canada, the Province of Quebec and the Province of Manitoba, should be extended at least to apply to New Brunswick and the Province of Ontario.

Our Quebec experience indicates that this is possible and people can live with this, it is a workable recommendation. Indeed, we have pleaded as the Council of Quebec Minorities on many occasions with Mr. Bill Davis, the Premier of Ontario, that he should move to see Section 133 expanded to apply to the Province of Ontario. As recently as November 11 we cabled the Premier of Ontario and urged that he take this step.

In light of the recent experiences we have lived, certainly in Canada and in Quebec, we know that it is vital that a gesture of this nature be made. It is an important step forward, it is an important affirmation of the fact that English and French are Canadian languages. We note with great pleasure that Senator Roblin and Messrs. Crombie and Nystrom have in fact indicated their support for this proposal. (8: 31–2)

...

**Mr. Simon de Jong, MP (NDP, BC):** Yes, my last question, Mr. Chairman. How important is it to Quebec that Section 133 be extended to Ontario for the people of Quebec, for the majority, for the French people of Quebec, the symbolism and the importance that they would attach to this.

**Mr. Maldoff:** I cannot emphasize this strongly enough how important the inclusion of Section 133, granting rights in the legislature and courts of Ontario is to the French speaking people of Quebec. We have recently lived through an experience, and I should say, we are trying here today to speak in a positive light, but we have recently lived through a very divisive experience in Quebec, a very difficult experience. It seems that many Canadians are forgetting about the experience that we have recently lived through. One of the questions that was most difficult to answer was when a French speaking Quebecker would say, why should I be part of this country if I do not feel at home in this country. It is essential that English and French speaking Canadians feel at home in Canada, and a major step in that direction would be the guarantee that in areas which are most crucial to the survival of the two linguistic groups and that is access to courts, access to justice and the legislatures, that both these groups feel secure and confident. (8: 43)

**Mr. Bryce Mackasey, MP (LIB, Ontario):** Thank you, Mr. Chairman. I welcome our witnesses. As there is not much time left, I would simply like to hear your opinion on the alternative proposed by Mr. Nystrom and by others two weeks ago of extending Section 133 and Section 23 of the Manitoba Act to include the provinces of Ontario and Manitoba. Do you agree or do you feel that this amendment should also include the Province of Saskatchewan?

**Mme Irène Chabot (présidente, Association culturelle franco-canadienne de la Saskatchewan):** In our opinion, these rights should not be extended to include Ontario and New Brunswick in particular, but all the provinces, without exception. There is no reason why they could not fall under those provisions. Neither Ontario nor New Brunswick would suffer from every other province being included in the resolution and it would be up to the provincial governments to do their share to make sure it was respected. (12: 25)

**Miss Jeanine Seguin (President, La Federation des Francophones hors Quebec):** Despite the richness of the French language, there is no word that could properly describe how grateful Francophones outside of Quebec would be to those around this table if everyone were to decide to become fully involved in this project, which will change the future of our country. I do not think that there would be a word in French to express our appreciation if everyone wanted to extend section 133 to all of the provinces. (13: 40)

**Mr. Jean Lapierre, MP (LIB, PQ):** Mr. Premier, you say in your brief that: "I agree that a new Constitution should preserve the existing constitutional rights, privileges and obligations respecting the French and English languages."

**Hon. J. Angus MacLean (Premier of Prince Edward Island):** Mr. Chairman, it is with regard to language rights you speak now? Language rights are a very difficult and emotional problem with varying difficulties and problems from place to place throughout the country. We have great sympathy for the percentage of Acadians in Prince Edward Island whose mother tongue is French. In absolute numbers they are rather small because our total population is rather small. We have taken action, in the last year we have, as I mentioned in my brief, passed legislation to assure certain rights to people whose first language is French. (14: 99–100)

I might add, however, that that is nothing new, it just puts it in legislation, the practice has long been in use even before Confederation, admittedly with varying degrees of extent, perhaps, in some situations their position is better than others. For example, in fairly recent years our school system in Prince Edward Island has been consolidated and this resulted in less opportunity for people to be educated in their language as compared to the situation when schools were small, very small, and there were pockets of people whose mother tongue is French. They were a smaller system, they were more easily accommodated.

However, I also wanted to say that both languages are used in our legislature but there would be practical problems for us with regard to some things. We as a government are trying to take some action to provide services in both languages where this is appropriate, and so on. But there is a danger in situations of this sort, of imposing a very heavy load on taxpayers for a very small benefit. When I say that, I do not want to leave the impression that rights should be measured in terms of economics. They should not be, any more than our judicial system should be. However, I feel that prominent in the realms where language rights are strictly at the present time in provincial jurisdiction, that the provinces should be trusted to do what they should do under those circumstances. I think we have to have faith in ourselves as Canadians. I see the honourable member shaking his head. Maybe his faith is shattered. I do not know with regard to that, but mine is not. (44: 99–101)

**Hon. John Buchanan (Premier, Government of Nova Scotia):** We have no objection to the entrenchment in our constitution of matters which are totally federal in nature, and which do not infringe upon the rights and privileges and powers of provinces: none whatsoever. As far as linguistic rights in Nova Scotia are concerned, I think you were present at College Ste. Anne when I said that we were prepared to, and will, at the earliest opportunity, enact legislation in Nova Scotia to protect the linguistic rights of the Acadian people in the Acadian areas of Nova Scotia. You supported that at the time, and I believe you still do.

**Miss Coline Campbell, MP (LIB, NS):** That was not entrenchment.

**Mr. Buchanan:** Well, it certainly is going to be entrenched in our provincial legislation. (17: 43)

## Institutional Bilingualism: Manitoba

**Mr. Joseph E. Magnet (Counsel, Societe franco-manitobaine):** On Sections 17, 18, and 19, these deal with the right to use the English and French language before Parliament, federal courts and in the printing of federal statutes. In our view, this is not enough. It perpetuates the status quo which, with respect to Franco-Manitobans, means decline and dismemberment, not the regeneration which in our view the constitution should encourage. We suggest that to protect Franco-Canadian minorities these protections should be explicitly extended to other Franco-Canadian communities.

We refrain from speaking specifically for our sister francophone associations but we wish to emphasize that with respect to Manitoba, healthy development of the Franco-Manitoban community requires these protections to be extended by constitutional text to the Manitoban minority. It is true that Section 23 of the Manitoba Act now contains most of these guarantees, not all of them. We think that the educational impact of including reference to the courts and legislature of Manitoba in these sections would be considerable. It would reaffirm Canada's commitment to the principle of duality and it would impact this fundamental precept on the Canadian consciousness. Furthermore, if these protections are extended to Manitoba, they become part of the charter and therefore difficult to amend. (10: 25–6)

### New Brunswick's Adoption of Official Bilingualism

**Hon. Richard Hatfield (Premier of New Brunswick):** I trust that in view of the fact that the government of New Brunswick, and without any doubt I am sure the legislature of New Brunswick, that you will acknowledge and accept our request that the elements of the Official Languages Act of New Brunswick be entrenched now, before the resolution goes to Great Britain, so that they will be there when the constitution comes back to Canada.

I hope that you will, however, recognize that the resolution is inadequate when it comes to providing for equity as far as the French speaking people are concerned outside the Provinces of Quebec and New Brunswick. I hope that you will find the way to either protect the rights of the largest number of French speaking people outside of Quebec and New Brunswick, that is to say the Canadians living in the Province of Ontario, that you will find a way to protect their language rights and that they will be operative and applicable within that province, because if you do not then you are perpetuating an inequity and I can tell you a nation cannot sustain very long an inequity of this kind, and I would hope that you would not want to be party to the perpetuation or the enshrinement of such an inequity.

I believe that if you cannot find a way and if you cannot get an assurance that the French speaking people will be protected in the Province of Ontario, then I think you have to consider very seriously removing the imposition on the Province of Quebec with regard to English language instruction for Canadians in the Province of Quebec and go back to the original, again the original convention which is that the province has the right to determine how language is to be given or provided as far as education is concerned, which is a provincial responsibility.

I hope that this can be done in order that we can continue to see happen in this country what I believe has happened in the Province of New Brunswick whereby we have come to terms with this phenomena of our country, come to terms with this resolution, I think, of the founders of this country but certainly the resolution of the people of New Brunswick, which is that it is possible and it is to the betterment and the advancement of the people to acknowledge and to enjoy the benefits of two languages and all that comes from that. That has been our experience in New Brunswick, we do not have the ideal and we are still making improvements and we will continue to make improvements, and if you grant our wish here today or in the resolution we will be forced by the constitution to make improvements.

I hope that you will see the wisdom of what has been happening in New Brunswick and accept the fact that that is in the best interests of Canada and that we must move that forward in that province which has the largest numbers, as I said, of French speaking Canadians outside the Provinces of Quebec and New Brunswick. (19: 48–9)

...

**Hon Richard B. Hatfield (Premier of New Brunswick):** I do not think the people of Quebec wanted that or supported that or voted for that in the referendum, that their language, rather than be treated as a Canadian language it would be treated as a language of a minority. The people who speak French in this country are not minorities. That is what the Official Languages Act says and that is what I want the constitution to say. They are not minorities, they are Canadians. They are Canadians who exercise a right to speak one of the Canadian languages. (19: 59)

**Mr. David Berger, MP (LIB, PQ):** But yet we have a province such as Ontario which has the largest French speaking population outside of Quebec, I think perhaps over 400,000 or maybe half a million French Canadians, and they are reluctant to take that step still, 12 years later, and you correctly pointed out that this is not something that Mr. Trudeau has brought up as he is accused of doing very frequently, but it goes back to Mr. Pearson's time and before that time. So the question I ask you is: when and how?

**Professor Maxwell Cohen (McGill University):** I have no difficulty with my answer, Mr. Berger. I think the time is ripe to put to rest the ghost of Lord Durham's report and that goes back an awful long way and I think it is time to face up to that aspect of the Canadian reality, and if we do not do it we make for the profound discomforts which in part explain our present crisis. (34: 93)

...

**The Hon. Bryce Mackasey, MP (LIB, Ontario):** I have got to come back to Premier Hatfield when he was here, ... when he was here he was discussing with Mr. McGrath and others, he said this, if 1 may reread it, he talked about 1971, being one of the few that was around at that time, and he said in that year we had a substantial number of problems and were prepared and said so, to go to their legislatures and ask that the official languages of French and English be recognized at the provincial level, or that Section 133 should apply to them. I wish I had the constitution of Canada in Canada, which is what you are saying, so that that agreement could have been put in that constitution at that time. I want to tell you that I think we could have avoided [the election of the PQ in] 1976, I think it could have been avoided if we had had our own constitution. (34: 143)

...

**Professor Peter Russell (University of Toronto):** I am particularly concerned about the right to use either of our official languages in the parliaments and legislatures of Canada and in the courts of Canada, and I am dissatisfied with this proposal that, for one thing, it does not extend the right to use both official languages to Ontario where there is a very, very large, as you know, francophone minority and it seems to me as a matter of principle absolutely essential that the rights that our constitution already affords the English minority in this respect in Quebec should be extended to the French minority in Ontario, and I cannot think of any reason or principle for not having the right in both places. That is the prime example and that offends my sense of justice and I think it makes this charter, we are talking about trying to do something for Quebec, I think it makes this charter very unsatisfactory to many people in Quebec for that simple reason.

**Mr. Eymard Corbin, MP (LIB, NB):** Now, I come from a linguistic community which comprises close to a million French speaking Canadians who do not live in Quebec. New Brunswick has shown some sense of justice in that respect inasmuch as in 1969 under Louis Robichaud, the Liberal Premier, and in more recent years under Richard Hatfield, a Progressive Conservative premier, we have come a long way fast and I feel very strongly that we have a heck of a lot of catching up to do in other parts of the country, and in that connection I think there is enough goodwill, there is more than sufficient goodwill in Ontario to go the way New Brunswick has, not in a condescending way, not in a paternalistic way, but in the way that you yourself have suggested to us, Professor Russell, and so again I commend you for your comments and I feel more reassured as a Canadian, not one coming from Ontario, but one currently living in Ontario with his family for the last ten years, and I hope you will do what you can to foster this continued development of good will and better understanding amongst Canadians of all linguistic and cultural backgrounds. (34: 157–8)

**The Hon. John Fraser, MP (PC, BC):** What I am asking you is this. How do you morally justify letting down about 400,000 French speaking people in Ontario by arguing that you do not impose it on Ontario unless you impose it in British Columbia where we do not have a large speaking French population, or Alberta, or Saskatchewan where it is small, or Newfoundland. Now, there is something that is not very nice about the reasoning that the Minister and the government is trying to put up to justify their position, and I say, Mr. Minister, that what you leave us with is the impression that when you came right down to it you did not have the guts to do what you wanted to do. You admitted that you have wanted to do it and what you have done is you have sold out the next largest francophone population outside of Quebec in Canada. You may be able to justify it by politics but I do not understand how you can justify it morally.

**The Hon. Jean Chrétien (Minister of Justice):** We have selected, to begin with, the area, as I explained earlier in my testimony, that the most vital area for the francophone outside of Quebec is the area of education, and we have solved that problem. I am very pleased to see that outside of Quebec that is very little controversy about the proposition on education in French all across Canada, and I am very pleased with it. There are some controversies in Quebec, but that is the most important thing. We feel that it is very much within the confines of the province of Ontario about how the speeches are made in Ontario in the legislative assembly, or how the law is translated or not translated and other types of problems of that nature very much in the area of the provincial authority of Ontario, that it was not for us to do it for them, that they should do it themselves; and this has been the policy of the government since 1970. When Mr. Nystrom quoted what Mr. Trudeau said, and I agree, why I am pleading with Ontario and why I am not pleading with Saskatchewan is because there is a bigger group of francophones there.

But the policy remains the same, and I do not mean to imply that we were ready to impose that in 1978. That was not true, Mr. Nystrom, it was an opting-in provision, and it is still there, it is still there. When there is a constitutional matter that affects only one province it can be implemented by a resolution of that province and approved by Parliament of Canada. So if Ontario, if there is election, and I do not think that Mr. Davis is taking some chances because in Ontario the majority of the Francophones for years have voted Conservative in their elections, generally speaking. You know, there was the area of Cornwall. For example, now they have an NDP but before it was a Conservative for years. In Northern Ontario, the same thing; in Hawkesbury, the same thing; and if he does not care about those people who have voted for him and led them down the path, that is his own risk. (37: 35–6)

**Miss Desantis (National Italian-Canadian Congress):** We are told that Canada is presently bilingual, but if we go across the country we realize that this is not the truth. If we really want to say that Canada is bilingual we have to set up a program that effectively makes Canada bilingual. Then in Ontario and in New Brunswick we already have conditions which would allow for the extension of Section 133 to those provinces and it seems but petty politics to refuse to allow Section 133 to be also applied to those provinces, otherwise the whole notion of bilingualism is just a lovely notion and not something that we really want to achieve for Canada. (23: 13)

**The Hon. Bryce Mackasey, MP (LIB, Ontario):** That is why I was pleased with the paragraph on page 15, I think it is, where you say that you do not object to the constitutional entrenchment of French and English language rights. That is important, coming from a man of your stature, because we have had briefs which acknowledge that historical fact. The right to use French or English or the right to receive some government services in either of those languages is also very important. It is not, after all, a right which we claim as humans; it is an essential fact of Canada, and if the French community of Saskatchewan is going to survive it needs to be serviced in its own language. If it cannot survive, then there is no reason that French speaking Quebec should encourage the existence within its community of a strong English presence.

Would you go so far as to extend under certain circumstances, and Mr. Nystrom, for instance, has made the point that he intends to bring in an amendment extending Section 133 to Ontario and New Brunswick, would you be prepared to have him include in this amendment the same provisions for the Franco-Saskatchewanians which were demanded here by your community, and I do not ask that to embarrass you, I ask you as another concerned Canadian who I think has the same view of this country?

**Honourable Allan E. Blakeney, Q.C. (Premier of Saskatchewan):** Now, back on the language issue. I basically share your view of Canada that we will not survive as a bilingual country, we will not survive as a country if we have unilingual blocks. Accordingly, there must be some ability of Anglophones to exist as Anglophones in Quebec and Francophones to exist in Ontario and New Brunswick, and, yes, in Saskatchewan. This is not only directed to those Francophones or Anglophones who may be in a minority position now in parts of Canada, but also, as I say, to the Francophone majority in Quebec who ought to have some right to move across Canada, including to Saskatoon; or the Anglophone majority in Saskatchewan who should have some right to move to Quebec City and expect some services. ...

I am not now asking you to sympathize with me, but it is not a popular cause in Saskatchewan because the Francophone group in Saskatchewan alone is a very small linguistic group, well below Cree. And as for Ukrainians or Germans or others, they are much more numerous than the Francophone community. About 2.9 per cent. ... Well, I think the answer is, if you want Section 133 in its current terms, the answer is no. If you are asking if the entire contents of Section 133 is being rejected, the answer is no. (30: 42)

### Bilingualism in the Legislature

**Mr. S. McCall (Positive Action Committee):** We recommend that the right to speak both French and English in the Legislature be extended throughout Canada, that this is not just a bit of empty symbolism but an important right if you are a Canadian to be able to speak either of the two official languages in any Legislature in Canada. (7: 79)

**Professor Irwin Cotler (Canadian Jewish Congress):** Number one, that every person has the right to use English and French in any of the debates or proceedings of the legislatures of any province. This indeed was a recommendation made to you earlier today by the Positive Action Committee. It has been made by the Canadian Bar Association Committee in the study to the new constitution and it was contained in the initial federal constitution proposals to the provinces of August 22, 1980. The absence of such a right, Mr. Chairman, would effectively, we believe, prejudice the rights of official language minorities in one of the most important public fora in this country, the Parliaments of the various legislatures. (7: 95–6)

**Mr. Eric Maldoff (President, Council of Quebec Minorities):** If English and French are indeed Canadian languages, Canadians must be able to use either language in the Parliament of Canada and in the Legislative Assemblies of all of the provinces. Our experience in Quebec certainly indicates that this is relatively easy to achieve and at very little cost. (8: 31)

**The Hon. Bryce Mackasey, MP (LIB, ON):** What about the use of French in the legislature?

**Mr. Robert Andrew, MPP (Progressive Conservative Party of Saskatchewan):** Well, I am not sure that we would really approach the question any differently than the existing government of Saskatchewan does now and I think from the resolution which calls for "where numbers warrant" in the schools. I think obviously the call has not come into the legislature, there is I think one French speaking member who happens to sit on our side, he does not use the language very much and I really cannot see until such time as the need arises there and I cannot really see it as sort of a burning question in Saskatchewan provincial politics as to whether or not.

**Mr. Mackasey:** But this particular group did, speaking as representatives for minority groups.

**Mr. Andrew:** Well, I fully grant that they are and that they are advancing the question of without regard to numbers, and I think primarily that is in the City of Saskatoon. I think the bulk of it, the gravel burgs and these places where they are properly provided with French education, French language. (32: 140–1)

### Bilingualism in the Courts

**Mr. M. F. Yalden (Commissioner of Official Languages):** Section 19 entrenches the right to use either language in courts established by Parliament, and Section 21 confirms the existing constitutional right to use them in the courts of Quebec and Manitoba. But beyond this, it ought to be a basic principle of justice in Canada that an accused person in a criminal case has the right to a trial in his own official language. I am of course aware that Parliament amended the Criminal Code in this direction some two years ago and that the new provisions have been implemented by provinces like Ontario and New Brunswick. Is this not all the more reason, however, for them to be clearly enshrined in the constitution, at least with respect to those provinces in which by far the largest proportion of the minority resides? (6: 12)

**Mr. Fraser:** I do not know whether it was Mr. McCall or Mr. Paterson [who] said, when speaking of bilingualism in the courts, and I think you said it is inconceivable that an accused cannot be tried in their own language. Now, I think it is inconceivable where you have a significant minority and where you can provide the services, but it is much more difficult in some other parts of the country. Presently, under the Criminal Code, amendments went through several years ago which established the federal authority with the power to declare this in different provinces and we have not been able to do it yet in British Columbia because of a real problem in having sufficient people who can speak French competently, and I am not talking about those who like myself who have struggled away to learn it on a functional basis, but to speak competently enough to serve a litigant within the courts, so I would be interested in your views? ...

**Mr. Alex Paterson (Co-president, Positive Action Committee):** I appreciate that, but it seems to me, and I have to bow to your much more familiar knowledge of British Columbia, but it seems to me that if you have in the order of 40,000 [French-speaking] people, albeit scattered to a degree, you can not have a court outside the house of the man that is faced with a criminal trial, but it is hard to believe that you can not bring a man to a court in British Columbia, be it Vancouver, Victoria or elsewhere, and provide for a criminal trial in that centre. (7: 77–8)

**Mr. Eric Maldoff (President, Council of Quebec Minorities):** Next we would feel that the right to use English and French in legal proceedings instituted by the Crown where the liberty of the individual is at stake must be guaranteed. Nothing is more fundamental than a person's right to his liberty and this protection must be ensured to Canadian citizens. Our next point would be that the government, at this time, all levels of government play an increasingly greater role in the lives of the citizens of this country. In view of the role government is playing and the ever expanding role it is playing, Canadians of either language must be able to communicate with their government, whether it be federal or provincial, in either of the official languages. ... (8: 32–3)

**Mr. Joseph E. Magnet (Counsel, Societe franco-manitobaine):** Sections 17 to 19 of the proposed resolution are, in our view, seriously deficient in making no reference to the quasi-judicial and administrative sides of government. The truth is that this is where the significant contact between citizens and governments occur. Our view is that language guarantees should filter down into the administrative sector. We suggest that statutory adjudicative agencies like the CRTC or the discipline committee of the Manitoba Law Society, should strain towards bilingualism. We think further that where necessary to promote the French language in Manitoba, administrative tribunals should strive towards the bilingualism goal. (10: 26)

**Mr. Ron Irwin, MP (LIB, Ontario):** ... It is my understanding in Ontario right now that judges, lawyers and reporters are made available in criminal cases and you either change the venue and go where they are available or they will provide them at the place of the original offence. And it is also my understanding that in certain selected areas, in Small Claims Courts, they are now having civil trials in French. I was talking to a judge recently, Judge Stortini, who indicated he had just finished one where a third of the people spoke only French, a third spoke only English and a third spoke both or understood both, and the pleadings came in partly in French and partly in English; this was Small Claims, and it took a little longer but it worked. Now, is that your understanding of the situation in Ontario as far as what they are doing?

**Miss Jeanine Seguin (President, La Federation des Francophones hors Quebec):** Mr. Chairman, I must recognize that there has been some progress done in Ontario. It is true to say that we Francophones now have the right to be criminals in French. That is good and I am happy about it. Secondly, we have to be logical with ourselves and honest, and we must recognize that it is in French also for the small claims. But there is still the civil court, there are still some steps to be taken, but honestly I must say there has been some progress in Ontario during the last 10 years. In this day and age people move very fast and we find it is too slow. We would like that it be done faster and we hope that this committee can help us to accelerate things. (37: 48)

**Mr. J. P. Nelligan (Chairman, Special Committee on the Constitution of Canada, Canadian Bar Association):** Our report would have guaranteed that a person should have the right, if accused of a criminal offence, to be tried in his language. (15: 10)

**Mr. David Copp (Vice-President, British Columbia Civil Liberties Association):** We ignore large sections of the Charter with the general outlines of which we agree, though we do find drafting problems. For instance, with respect to language rights in the courts, Section 19 is unacceptably narrow. The right to use either official language should extend from the Supreme Court of Canada at least to the courts mentioned in Section 96 of the BNA Act, that is to superior, district and county courts, and should apply at least in serious criminal cases. However, let me turn to the main issues, beginning with general principles. (22: 103)

**Senator Jack Austin (LIB, BC):** The points you have made, yes, of course. Could I take you, and I am hurrying along because the clock is running on me, could I take you to page 12 of your brief. I found it most interesting that you were suggesting extending the use of the two official languages to provincial courts, having the same jurisdiction as the B.C. Supreme Court and B.C. Court of Appeal, and you know that your suggestion requires us to impose ourselves on the legislature of the province of British Columbia but your recommendation is we should do so.

**Mr. William Black (Member of Executive Committee, British Columbia Civil Liberties Association):** It seems to us, at least with respect to serious criminal matters, for an accused who is a citizen of Canada not to be able to have the case argued in the language that that citizen understands is a very severe intrusion on that citizen's rights, especially since there is a similar protection for the English minority in Quebec. We think it is reasonable to have comparable protections in other parts of the country where French is a minority. It would cost something but we think the cost is well worthwhile.

**Senator Austin:** I want to say that I agree it is reasonable and I hope it will prove to be practical. (22: 121–2)

### Section 22 – Other Linguistic Groups

**Mr. J. P. Nelligan (Chairman, Special Committee on the Constitution of Canada, Canadian Bar Association):** ... We would have preferred a more positive statement of the rights of Canadians belonging to linguistic groups other than English or French. (15: 10)

**Mr. Andriy Bandera (Council of National Ethnocultural Organizations of Canada):** ... Mr. Chairman, our Council advocates linguistic and cultural tolerance and understanding. We reject the fossilized and xenophobic perception of Canadian society based on a static and retrospective view of past privileges or the fallacious concept of two founding peoples who have somehow become more equal than others. We therefore ask, Mr. Chairman, that this committee give the strongest possible consideration to the suggestions contained in our brief which includes the following points:

One, an inclusion of general language rights or, in our phraseology mother tongue, as a nondiscrimination right in Section 15(1). Two, an additional clause in Section 15 which would not preclude any programs, laws or activities designed to protect and develop any linguistic and cultural rights in Canada. Three, a provision that would extend or enable provincial legislatures to extend the status and use of other languages other than English and French. Thank you, Mr. Chairman. (22: 79)

**Senator Arthur Tremblay (PC, Quebec):** Would you go so far as to say, Mr. Yalden, that the right to trial in one's own language, particularly in criminal cases, should be extended not only to francophones and anglophones, but also to natives and other language groups?

**Mr. Max Yalden (Commissioner of Official Languages):** Mr. Chairman, I find the question of native languages and languages other than French and English somewhat difficult, but I think we should try to be as generous as possible. A person who speaks a language which the court does not understand or who does not understand English or French should certainly have access to an interpreter. Should we go further than that? Should entire trials be conducted in another language? I do not think so. Native languages are another matter. Members of the Committee have perhaps noticed that I have not referred this evening to languages other than the official languages, English and French. (6: 30)

**Professor Manoly Lupul (Director, The Institute of [Ukrainian] Studies):** We do not wish to see our language rights trampled upon again as they were during World War 1, when legislation was passed by provincial legislatures in the western provinces which prescribed the teaching of the Ukrainian language – together with all other languages other than English – in the schools of the prairie provinces. We do not wish to see the continuation of discriminatory clauses in our constitution, clauses which have relegated Canadians of origins other than Anglo-Celtic or French to a lesser status in a country in which they are allegedly to be "equal" citizens, too. (14: 54)

## Minority Language Education Rights

**Mr. M. F. Yalden (Commissioner of Official Languages):** Turning now, Mr. Chairman, to the vital area of education, we can I think take heart that Canadians are increasingly accepting in every province of this country the principle that minority language children have the right to be educated in their own official language. Even some opponents of entrenchment, as I understand it, are apparently prepared to make an exception for minority language education rights. It is therefore natural that any constitutional document should reflect this widespread consensus. ...

I have serious reservations about Section 23 as it is now drafted. The problems that I see with the present formulation are essentially the qualification of citizenship, number one; and the criterion of sufficient number, number two. To these I should add the further observation that Section 23 offers no guarantee to the minorities regarding the administrative control of their own educational institutions.

On the subject of sufficient number, I have been struck not only by the inclusion of this provision as by the way it has been formulated. Citizens, and I quote: "have the right to have their children receive their primary and secondary school instruction in that minority language if they reside in an area of the province in which the number of children of such citizens is sufficient to warrant the provision out of public funds of minority language educational facilities in that area."

As I have suggested, the purpose of a constitution is to enshrine in broad but unambiguous terms those fundamental and generally applicable principles we hold to be important. The provision I have just read seems to me to miss this mark on several counts, and I quote:

1. it clearly sets out to distinguish between those who can and those who cannot enjoy this right;
2. the more words are added for greater precision (e.g. "warrant the provision out of public funds of minority language educational facilities in that area"), the more they suggest new problems of interpretation;
3. it suggests that minority-language education may sometimes cost more than our society can or wishes to pay. (6: 12, 14)

**Mr. Joseph E. Magnet (Counsel, Societé franco-manitobaine):** Let me come on to minority educational rights. Minority educational rights are critical to the development of the Franco-Manitoban community. This is the key. We must tell you frankly that we are unconvinced our needs are the same as the needs of the anglophone minority in Quebec. We want to impress upon you the needs of the Franco-Manitoban community which are distinct. Our need is for schools, for freedom of choice in schools. That is the long and short of it. That has been our primary need since 1870 and it is still the crucial ... essential foundation upon which a healthy Franco-Manitoban community must be built. So we have suggested that with respect to Manitoba, freedom of choice prevail; that public funds support minority language education; that the administration of the schools wherein the French language be confined to the minority community. In regions which have small populations we understand that a separate school may not be practical. So in such cases which would be exceptional cases, we would think that a French classroom would suffice in an otherwise English school with an English school administration.

We would extend this right to immigrants to Manitoba. We do not think that the Government of Manitoba should be entitled, against the will of such immigrants, to force immigrants to assimilate to the Anglophone stream. There is enough cultural pressure on immigrants to do so. ... Finally, ladies and gentlemen, on the question of educational rights, we think official language immersion education is the way of the future. It has already had significant beneficial regenerative effects in Manitoba and elsewhere. So we propose that the constitution recognize the right to official language immersion education. (10: 26)

**Mr. Florent Bilodeau (Director General, Association culturelle franco-canadienne de la Saskatchewan):** What hurts the most is the way in which educational rights are dealt with. The intention of Section 23(1) is clearly positive, as it gives us the right to educate our children in French. But we are very concerned about the wording of this section, not only because of the ambiguity of certain terms that are used, but because we fail to see how we in Saskatchewan will be able to avail ourselves of this right, given the restriction placed on it in the section.

It must be realized that in Saskatchewan, there are no French schools and even fewer French school boards. There would have to be enough people to warrant providing the necessary facilities. The number will in all probability be very high and we will have trouble reaching it, since we are dispersed throughout the province and have to deal with a hostile and uncomprehending majority. We will be the ones who will have to bear the psychological and financial burden of legal action.

Even if we did take legal action, nothing guarantees that we would win. If the courts were eventually called upon to decide, without any more direction than is given in section 23, whether the number of children justifies the providing of services in a [certain region, it is more than likely that the courts would reference the opinions of] the legislators and school officials. This means, more or less, that the decision would be made by the majority.

The principle of access to French schools may go nowhere and it would be doubly humiliating for Franco-Saskatchewaners to know that other groups, like Anglo-Quebeckers and certain categories of immigrants, can exercise the right to go to a minority school, as provided for in their constitution, while they, the Franco-Saskatchewaners, cannot, under the same constitution and in the same country. ...

We would like to dissociate ourselves from the strategy of blackmail, by which Quebec's position on the patriation proposal makes it responsible for the misfortunes of Francophones outside Quebec. As the only state in North America where Francophones are in the majority, Quebec has to protect its French-speaking population and it is important for us that Quebec Francophones be strong and dynamic. Despite the intention of Section 23, the legal right to education in the language of the minority is meaningless for Franco-Saskatchewaners. If we cannot achieve this without depriving Quebec of the means of ensuring the survival of its French-speaking population, we will consider ourselves losers.

We have the following recommendations to make on the aspects of the constitution which are of particular interest to us ... the recognition of the right of the minority to education in the language of the official minority, without regard to the number of students, and the recognition of the principle of control over and management of Francophone schools by Francophones. (12: 10–11)

**Miss Jeanine Seguin (President, La Federation des Francophones hors Quebec):** Our fifth recommendation, that section 23 of the Constitution Act, 1980, be reworded so as to ensure the recognition of the rights of Francophones outside Quebec to education in their language from the pre-school to the post-graduate levels inclusively and of the right to schools and homogeneous school boards as well as to the administration of their educational facilities. (13: 30)

**Mr. J. P. Nelligan (Chairman, Special Committee on the Constitution of Canada, Canadian Bar Association):** The minority language educational rights provision seems to us the most important of the linguistic rights affecting the provinces in our report, we say: "The constitution should guarantee the right of a parent to have English or French as the language of instruction of his children in publicly supported schools in areas where the number of people speaking that language warrants this course." (15: 10)

**Mr. Juzukonis (Council of National Ethnocultural Organizations of Canada):** What we would suggest is something to the same effect as was presented before this Committee by the Ukrainian Canadian Committee where a modification of Section 23 should read, we would suggest, and by no means am I suggesting the language is rigorous, that every citizen of Canada and every resident of Canada should have the right to choose his or her language of instruction. Obviously we are talking about the official languages. (22: 99)

**Mr. Eymard Corbin, MP (LIB, NB):** I fully appreciate the points which you have brought to our attention but I would like to urge you to do more and to proceed with greater haste. I believe that my colleague, the Honourable Bryce Mackasey, put things very well when he said that you had a unique opportunity in Canadian history – I am sure that your name will go down for other reasons as well – but it is very important at this time for all men of good will to settle once and for all this question of our two official languages with equal status throughout our country. It is not a matter of shoving French down our throats, as has often been so wrongly claimed in the west. I think that you have understood this quite well, Mr. Premier, but there persists a serious injustice towards one of the founding peoples of this country in several Canadian provinces and I am urging you to do more and to proceed with greater haste. Once our constitution has been patriated, whatever the parliaments should decide, I hope that you and the other provincial premiers will be able to come to a satisfactory agreement as quickly as possible on this point with the federal government.

I do not know if the problem is basically one of money. The Premier of Ontario, who was recently involved in a by-election in the National Capital area, told us here that the basic reason for his refusal to extend Section 133 of the British North America Act to the Province of Ontario was a matter of money. I cannot accept this. As a representative of one of the less rich provinces, as you pointed out in your opening remarks, would you be willing to accept that the federal government provide you with financial assistance for minority language education, provided there was no infringement of your provincial jurisdiction in this field? Would you accept financial support from the federal government to encourage the efforts which you are already undertaking?

**The Hon. Allan Blakeney, Q.C. (Premier of Saskatchewan):** The short answer to Mr. Corbin's last question is yes. We would certainly have no great difficulty in working with the federal government, particularly in accepting their money, encouraging French language education. The problems are not only money. There are problems of the perception that people in a small rural area see as to what is happening to their community. (30: 51–2)

**Professor Joseph Magnet (Legal Counsel, Ontario Conference of Catholic Bishops):** Now, on the separate question of minority language education rights, the proposed resolution, as drafted, fastens on a numbers test. We are not impressed with a numbers test. We are impressed with the principle, with the freedom of choice in minority language education rights. I think Mr. Mackasey would agree with me here, and, indeed many other groups which have appeared before this Committee have taken that position – the positive action group, for example, is one. That is our position.

I think the point that Bishop Carter was trying to make, and made very well, and which I would like to re-emphasize is this. If you take a numbers test and make the right fasten on the numbers test, the difficulty is you would then have to answer at the legislative level precisely the kinds of questions you are asking. But we do not think these should be asked at the legislative level. We think the right is there. The implementation of that right is at present unforeseeable. Supposing, for example, that we gave freedom of choice in minority language education rights across the board, and we have a French speaking family in Northern Manitoba in a predominantly English area that demands a French school, it may be that the implementation of that right would not warrant a school, and it may be that the implementation of the right may not warrant a classroom; it might be that that right could be satisfied at the parents' option, sending their child to St. Boniface, if the parent so desires; in any case the onus would be on the legislature to make provisions to satisfy that right, and if the legislature takes steps which, in the opinion of the person entitled to that school, were not sufficient, then the courts can be called in. (33: 70–1)

**Mr. Louis Duclos, MP (LIB, Quebec):** No, 23. Quebec does not agree with Section 23, Mr. Minister, as you know quite well.

**The Hon. Jean Chrétien (Minister of Justice):** No, but …

**Mr. Duclos:** It will have to change Bill 101 because of Section 23 and in spite of its disagreement it will no longer have any choice.

**Mr. Chrétien:** We are ensuring certain rights in the field of education. Using the same logic, why do you not ask Mr. Nystrom why he does not want it to be applied in Saskatchewan?

**Mr. Duclos:** It is not Mr. Nystrom's problem nor is it mine.

**Mr. Chrétien:** Let me explain the problem. Why should we impose Section 133 on Ontario and not on the other provinces? Because of the size of the French-speaking population? It is not a matter of numbers. If we proceed in this way for education as far as the other provinces are concerned, we should have to do likewise in other matters. We have concluded. Mr. Ryan expressed the same opinion last week in Toronto, that such an initiative would have to come from the population of Ontario.

Mr. Corbin, a Francophone from outside of Quebec, stated yesterday to the Committee that such a step would have to come from the population. The provincial government is responsible for this and this has always been the government's position; 133 applies to Quebec, the equivalent applies to Manitoba because of rights flowing from the 1867 constitution and the Manitoba Act. [end 38: 80] New Brunswick is being brought in through the resolution and we shall continue to pressure the other provinces to do likewise.

**Mr. Duclos:** In that case, let us impose Section 23 on Quebec when the population of Quebec so decides in the same way as Section 133 of the constitution will be applied to Ontario at their request.

**Mr. Chrétien:** There is a great difference, because Section 23 enshrines in the constitution the agreement reached in Montreal in 1978.

**Mr. Duclos:** It is not correct to say that. It is not right! The province did not ask for this provision to be enshrined in the constitution, Mr. Minister. The provinces agreed on reciprocal agreements that might or might not have been revoked at any time if conditions in each province that was party to the agreement were to change. The situation is completely different. I do not want to hear that argument anymore.

**Mr. Chrétien:** Well, you have attended three of the sixty-four sessions ...

**Mr. Duclos:** I am not a member of the Committee, so ...

**Mr. Chrétien:** Nor are you obliged to. If you do not want to hear the arguments anymore, well you need not come. I will tell you what I said, I find your double standard quite shocking. For the first time in the history of Canada, we are going to give francophones the constitutional right to have French schools in Canada and we are telling Quebec that English speaking Canadians in Quebec will be entitled to the same type of education as francophones outside Quebec. If you do not want us to do that for French speakers, I am not very impressed with your nationalistic feelings.

**Mr. Duclos:** Oh for heavens sake! (38: 80)

**Mr. Rod Sykes (Leader, Social Credit Party of Alberta):** My point is that they are not ignored, they are recognized. They are an important part of our population, but if you are saying that they must have special guarantees in Alberta I would say that all of the other 20 or 30 racial groups would not accept that because special guarantees have no place in Alberta. They are not part of our history. Anybody can come to Alberta and settle on equal terms including the French Canadians, who are most welcome.

**Mr. David Berger, MP (LIB, Quebec):** I would ask you again, sir, to perhaps answer the question that I put to you earlier directly and that is when will French speaking Canadians or Europeans or French speaking human beings for that matter have the constitutional guarantee in Alberta to educate their children in French?

**Mr. Sykes:** I hope that no racial group will ever have any special rights over any other racial group in Alberta and that I think is the attitude of most Western Canadians. (33: 179)

**The Hon. Jean Chrétien (Minister of Justice):** In looking for the root of the problem, we felt very strongly that the most acute problem is always education. When you cannot send your kids to your mother language schools, official language schools, it is very difficult, especially today with TV and so on, for French-speaking families outside of Quebec to keep the language in the family. So personally I felt education was extremely important, and a lot of the problems we have today exist because it was not guaranteed in the constitution for all of Canada in the past. Of course, when there is no French there is no problem; it is only for the francophone, so if there is none there is no problem, or virtually no problem. (2: 43–4)

## The Government Amends Section 23

**The Honourable Jean Chrétien (Minister of Justice):** I have said that the provision for minority language education rights in Section 23 is based on the agreement of the provincial Premiers at St. Andrews and at Montreal. You have heard many representations on this section. All representatives of official language minorities agree with the principle of guaranteeing minority language rights in the constitution although many suggestions for improvements have been made.

Senator Rizzuto in particular has pressed for a guarantee for acquired rights. The amendment I am prepared to accept provides for such a guarantee. Basically, the amendment provides the following:

There will be two alternative qualifications for minority language education rights. Under the first alternative, if a citizen has received his primary instruction in Canada in one of the official languages, he may send his child to school in that language if it is the minority language of the province in which he lives. Under the second alternative, a citizen whose mother tongue is English or French may educate his child in the language of his mother tongue if it is the minority language in the province where he lives.

All children of a Canadian citizen will be able to receive their primary and secondary education in the minority language in which any one of the children has commenced his education in Canada.

The present Section 23(2) deals with the provision out of public funds of minority language educational facilities in an area of the province where there are sufficient numbers to warrant it. This section has been criticized as being too restrictive.

Therefore, I am proposing an amendment which will not refer to the provision of "educational facilities" but rather to "the provision out of public funds of minority language instruction." This avoids the implication that the obligation is limited to physical facilities, but rather it extends to that obligation to provide instruction by whatever method is appropriate and can therefore take into account technological advances as talked about by the Commissioner of Official Languages. (36: 16)

## The Extension of Language Rights to Other Services

**Mr. Alex Paterson (Co-president, Positive Action Committee):** The other aspect to our brief, the concept is found in the Beige Paper. It was not mentioned I think by the Canadian Bar [Association] and perhaps in some other briefs, is the right to have access to health and social services wherever the numbers warrant in English and French.

We raise this point urgently in Quebec because although we have had, unlike the other provinces in most cases, we have had our hospitals that are recognized as English speaking hospitals. We have had our social service institutions that are recognized in the same way. We have seen in the last five to ten years an erosion of the possibility of these services off the Island of Montreal. We give as examples in our brief the Jeffrey Hale Hospital in Quebec that was certainly started and existed for many years as an English speaking hospital, now for demographic reasons is not. We have seen the Brome-Missisquoi Hospital in Cowansville slowly now unable to deliver, in its entirety, services to the

English speaking population. We have seen the same thing at the Barrie Memorial Hospital in Ormstown, we have seen problems arise in Ville Marie Social Service Centre which is the main institution that delivers health services to the English speaking population on the Island of Montreal and now, due to sectorization which I will not go into details to this Committee, but its ability to deliver services to people outside the particular geographical area that the government has given to it in which to supply the services is now somewhat threatened.

Entrenchment of the right to health and social services would be a big step towards guaranteeing that in the future if the demography of the City of Montreal changes and if the demography off Island continues to change because there is no statistical argument, the fact is that the English speaking population off Island is diminishing, the entrenchment of these rights would ensure that the delivery of social services which is, in our estimation, a cultural event when you are treating a person for a problem of old age, when you are treating a teenager for pregnancy, counselling, when you are doing marriage counselling, it is a cultural problem. In this country, surely we should be able to assure people that they have those problems dealt with in English and French and even in other languages where possible, but when it comes to enshrinement, at least that the right to have these services in the English or French language should be entrenched.

We have been told by our friends in the other provinces that services in themselves are not a must, the right to administer the institutions that deliver those services is key. So, they have pleaded and we will plead in education that [it] is not sufficient to have the services, the entrenchment of the right to administer should also be there.

With that, I simply conclude and turn the microphone to my friend, Mr. McCall, on the note that we sing a tune of entrenchment for all the minority French and English people across this country in the hope that it will unite and not divide because we are convinced, having lived through the experience [end 7: 54] in the legislatures and in the courts of Quebec, that it is a unifying factor, bilingualism, in these institutions and it is a unifying feature for Canada that we believe could be held up to an example to the world in the next constitution of Canada. (7: 53–5)

**Mr. Yves St-Denis (President, Association canadienne-francaise de l'Ontario):** As far as radio and television are concerned, French and English networks should cover all regions of the country. Full and equal participation in Canadian life depends on access to Canadian institutions on which culture, information and mass communication depend.

All Canadians should therefore be entitled to essential services in the field of communication in their official language. With modern technology, this should be no problem.

The same can be said about medical and social services. Anglophones and Francophones should be entitled to medical and social services in their own language. Furthermore, Anglophone and Francophone minorities should be able to administer their own social and health care institutions in those communities where they make up an important minority. (8: 33)

**Mr. Florent Bilodeau (Director General, Association culturelle franco-canadienne de la Saskatchewan):** Section 21 states that the official languages provisions will not abrogate or derogate from any right, privilege or obligation that exists or is continued by any other virtue of any other provision in the constitution of Canada, but no mention is made in Schedule 1, which lists the legal provisions of the constitution of Canada, of the Northwest Territories Act of 1877, on which the official status of French in Saskatchewan is largely based.

## Chapter Twelve

# Judicial Review, Enforcement, and Remedies

**~~Primacy of Charter~~**

~~25. Any law that is inconsistent with the provision of this Charter is, to the extent of such inconsistency, inoperative and of no force or effect.~~

**~~Laws respecting evidence~~**

~~26. No provision of this Charter, other than section 13, affects the laws respecting the admissibility of evidence in any proceedings or the authority of Parliament or a legislature to make laws in relation thereto.~~

*Enforcement*

*Enforcement of guaranteed rights and freedoms*

**24.** (1) Anyone whose rights or freedoms, as guaranteed by this Charter, have been infringed or denied may apply to a court of competent jurisdiction to obtain such remedy as the court considers appropriate and just in the circumstances.

*Exclusion of evidence bringing administration of justice into disrepute*

(2) Where, in proceedings under subsection (1), a court concludes that evidence was obtained in a manner that infringed or denied

any rights or freedoms guaranteed by this Charter, the evidence shall be excluded if it is established that, having regard to all the circumstances, the admission of it in the proceedings would bring the administration of justice into disrepute.

*Primacy of Constitution of Canada*

**52.** (1) The Constitution of Canada is the supreme law of Canada, and any law that is inconsistent with the provisions of the Constitution is, to the extent of the inconsistency, of no force or effect.

## Commentary

*Judicial review* refers to the power of the courts to determine whether legislation is compatible with the Constitution and, if necessary, strike it down as unconstitutional. Before 1982, the courts exercised the power of judicial review under the Constitution in division-of-powers cases; they not infrequently declared laws *ultra vires* federal or provincial powers under section 91 or 92 of the BNA Act (as it then was). The Canadian Bill of Rights gave the courts a limited power of judicial review over federal laws, but the courts only once exercised this to declare a law inconsistent with the bill in the *Drybones* case[1] referenced frequently in the debates. The entrenchment of a charter of rights would fundamentally change the equation between Parliament and the courts, and as seen throughout the debates, most of the participants knew this. Thus, discussion about judicial review frequently took place in the context of the debate over entrenchment itself.

The debates about judicial review were principled and vigorous and often prescient. Many comments centred on the balance between the legislature and the judiciary, and of these, most were wary of giving more power to the judiciary. Witnesses and committee members who opposed entrenchment were quite clear that they feared giving too much power to the judiciary (see Canada West Foundation; Public Interest Advocacy Centre; The Hon. Allan E. Blakeney, Q.C., Premier of Saskatchewan; Mrs. Gwen Landolt, Campaign Life Canada; The Hon. Angus MacLean, Premier, Prince Edward Island; the Hon. David Crombie, MP; Mr. Jim Hawkes). They voiced concerns that empowering the courts meant that important decisions of social policy and individual rights would be determined by the Supreme Court of Canada; of course, this is precisely what has happened. Most groups and committee members, however, favoured entrenchment. Some were quite explicit in stating that they trusted the courts over Parliament (e.g., National Black Coalition of Canada; British Columbia Civil Liberties Association; Mr. Brian Tobin, MP).

There was relatively little discussion about the issue of the availability of remedies when rights were infringed under the Charter. This is perhaps surprising given the controversial American experience both with the exclusionary rule and with court supervision in areas such as desegregation and prison management. For whatever reasons, witnesses generally did not turn their attention to the issue of remedies. Several groups called for an explicit remedies clause; only the Canadian Association of Chiefs of Police thought this was unnecessary, asserting that as the current law provided sufficient recourse, section 26 of the 6 October 1980 draft Charter would have preserved the existing law regarding the admissibility of evidence. Several groups called for the adoption of the American exclusionary rule. The government responded to these concerns about remedies by tabling the amendment to the Charter deleting section 26 and adding an explicit enforcement clause in section 24. Section 24(1) deals with general enforcement and remedies and section 24(2) with the exclusion of evidence.

## Opposition to Entrenchment: Transfer of Power to the Courts

**The Hon. J. Angus MacLean (Premier, Prince Edward Island):** One argument against entrenchment is that in the course of deciding what is meant by a broad phrase such as freedom of religion, judges will be asked to make decisions which shape the character of our community. I maintain these decisions should be made by the elected representatives of the people. I recognize that this is an arguable point, there are good arguments on both sides of the issue, and that neither one is perfect; but inflexibility or rigidity is not the problem of my government, I perceive it as a problem on a different level. (14: 82)

**The Honourable Allan E. Blakeney, Q.C. (Premier of Saskatchewan):** I know that some people believe it is a good idea to state our aspirations in a constitution and to allow the judges to make all the qualifications. I think the essence of government is making a fair number of these qualifications and I say that the judges are not well qualified to do this. They do not have the expertise or the staff. They cannot set up task forces and they cannot find out what the problems are. They may not be terribly sensitive to what the public wants. Therefore, I tend not to be in favour of a ringing declaration of what we say we are going to do when we know we are not going to do it and to allow the judges to put in the qualifications. (30: 38)

**Mr. Grant Devine (Leader, Progressive Conservative Party of Saskatchewan):** We support human rights but reject the suggestion that those rights be enshrined in the constitution. Entrenchment will mean courts legislate human rights but courts are not the proper vehicle – the legislatures and Parliament are. Human rights are not negotiable and should not be traded for rights over resources. (32: 116)

...

**Mr. Devine:** The problem as I see it is that the courts are not as sensitive to the change in social modification and economic change as you are, as someone in Parliament or a legislator to deal with that – the problems which have resulted in the United States because it is enshrined; maybe we can have a better system than that.

**Mr. Brian Tobin, MP (LIB, Newfoundland):** You talk about the courts. But ... you said that entrenchment would mean irregular and many calls upon the court to legislate human rights. The courts are not the vehicle, you say, but the legislatures and Parliaments are. You are saying that I am better qualified than the courts to protect human rights. I say to you that it was Parliament and the legislatures, not the courts, that interned the Japanese during World War II. I think that is a striking, shocking and a shameful example and we should not allow that type of thing to happen again. So how do you square that with your position on human rights?

**Mr. Devine:** Let me say one thing and then I would like to turn it over to my colleague. I believe in the United States the rights are enshrined in the constitution and there were similar problems with the Japanese.

**Mr. Tobin:** With one big difference: the Japanese in the United States were released much quicker, four years quicker; their property, their houses – and this is an essential difference, and if you were listening to the delegation who were here representing the Japanese and Asian peoples of this country you would have heard that they pointed that out during their representations, that in the United States – and it does not excuse what happened – but in the United States the Japanese people were released much quicker and their property, lands and wealth were returned to them very quickly, based on the rights enshrined in the

United States constitution. Now, in Canada there was no provision, and it took years, and in many cases people's property was never returned to them. I think that is an example we cannot ignore. History tells us that Parliament is not perfect and may not be in the future.

**Mr. Devine:** That may be true. ....

**Mr Tobin:** ...What are the particular problems that you envisage? You talk about the courts and the package as a whole being divisive. What can be so wrong with entrenching human rights?

**Mr. Devine:** I can refer to a couple of examples of the kinds of situations you can get into when you are having it dealt with by the courts as opposed to the legislature. ... That is the inflexibility of interpreting the law by the courts as opposed to the flexibility and sensitivity that you have as an elected member in dealing with social change. (32: 133–5)

...

**Miss Maureen Mahoney (Public Affairs Manager, Alberta Chamber of Commerce):** I think when you entrench a charter of rights, you are giving in effect, more powers to the court. You are giving the Supreme Court positive legislative functions which will, in effect, detract from the role of the elected representatives. There is the possibility for legislating in those areas.

**Senator Carl Goldenberg (LIB, PQ):** Well, are you suggesting that by asking the courts to interpret the law that you are taking powers away from the legislature? Who else [should] interpret the law?

**Miss Mahoney:** No, not taking away powers; but the responsibility that the people give to their elected representatives to make laws for them, reflecting the rights that they want and to have included, and at whatever point in time.

**Senator Goldenberg:** But all this point about the courts making laws: the courts do not make laws. The case has come to the courts because it is alleged that laws are violated. That is when they come to the courts. The courts are intended to correct the situation. (27: 63–4)

...

**Mrs. Gwen Landolt (Legal Counsel, Campaign Life-Canada):** ... The most important effect of an entrenched Charter of rights would be that it would give rise to a shift in power from Parliament, which is subject to public opinion, to the Supreme Court of Canada, which is not. This shift in power would then open the door to a wide list of areas in which, for the first time, the judiciary, rather than the legislature, will have the final say. We have only to look to the United States where the United States Supreme Court has the final word on any legislation passed by the United States Congress, to determine the tremendous consequences that would result from a transfer of this power.

It is appropriate, also, to look to the decisions of the U.S. Supreme Court on constitutional issues, as the United States constitution contains many of the phrases that are contained in the proposed Charter of Rights and Freedoms. Examples of these are: the right to life, which has been interpreted by the U.S. Supreme Court to exclude the unborn child; freedom of religion has been interpreted by the United States Supreme Court so as to prohibit the Lord's Prayer in public schools; freedom of expression has been used by the U.S. Supreme Court to strike down some state obscenity laws.

There are inherent difficulties involved in transferring final power to the Supreme Court of Canada. For example, the Supreme Court's decision may well not reflect public opinion. Parliament is sensitive to public pressure, whereas the Supreme Court of Canada is not. Accordingly, the decisions of the Court may well reflect the views of the nine individuals in the Court rather than that of the general public, which will be permanently and deeply affected by the court's decisions. But the argument that it is beneficial that a decision on individual or minority rights should be made by a court rather than being left to the good will of the majority or the government of the day, may have been valid in the last century, when illiteracy was high and the communications system was poor. Public opinion, under those conditions, may well not have been an informed one.

However, in the latter half of the 20th century, with the very high literacy rate and almost instantaneous communications system, coupled with a majority of people with a genuine awareness of the need for civil rights, it would appear essentially undemocratic and an apparent anachronism that judges, who are appointed by the executive, who are not responsible to the people, and who are protected from removal by tenure, be given this tremendous power to impose their will on the elected members of Parliament. It is a concern to all of us that just five individuals, bare majority, could rule on the great social and political issues of the day contrary to and regardless of the wishes of the general population. (34: 117–23)

...

**The Hon. David Crombie, MP (PC, ON):** You are one of the few persons who has come before this Committee who has indicated that their personal preference is not to entrench rights in the Constitution. ... [You said] that there would be a political burden imposed on the judiciary. Some people have felt that what that means is that by the adoption of a Charter of Rights, and entrenching it in the Constitution, we would move speedily to a more Americanized system for our judiciary. I wondered if you felt that way and indeed if you have any elaboration you would like to make as to what you think the consequences will be for our judiciary if we entrench rights in the Constitution.

**Professor Peter Russell (University of Toronto):** I believe that a Charter of Rights only guarantees a change in the way in which certain decisions are made. It does not guarantee rights or freedoms, it guarantees a change in the way in which decisions are made about rights and freedoms. Rights and freedoms raise, every case, difficult policy decisions. Take any right or freedom in your Charter, just start with the right of free expression, free speech. We can all immediately think of a whole range of policy issues as to what the limit of that freedom should be. Is it an abridgement of the right of freedom of expression to require broadcasters to have a certain amount of Canadian content? Is it a breach of free expression to prosecute people for violating the obscenity provisions of the Criminal Code and so on and so forth. They are difficult decisions and those decisions will be made as the result of a Charter in a different way from the way in which they are made now. The way will be different in this sense: the court will basically, and fundamentally it will be the Supreme Court, will essentially set down the basic guidelines on how far you can go in expressing those rights or enjoying them and how far government can go in limiting them.

Government will be in a sense given direction by the courts. The courts will say how far you can modify free broadcasting by having Canadian content. Both the courts and the legislatures will continue to be active, as they are in the United States, but there will be almost a transfer of functions. The court's function, instead of taking general standards set by the legislature and interpreting them and then the legislature, if it finds the court is going too far or not far enough, correcting the courts, it will be the reverse. It will be the courts, in a sense, correcting the legislature. Now, among other things, that tends to put a lot of political focus on the judges. They will have the kind of focus on them that you ladies and gentlemen are used to having on you. They will be in the limelight, make some fundamental policy decisions and they will be open inevitably, as you ladies and gentlemen always are, to criticism no matter which way they go, whether they interpret the Charter very conservatively or very liberally. That will subject them not only to a burden of political criticism, it will also greatly expand of course their work and give them less time for the other kinds of business that courts normally deal with.

Now, if Parliament and the legislative people want that change, that is the kind of change they will get. It is not all bad, I do not think it is all good, but it is very problematic. (34: 148–50)

**Mr. Jim Hawkes, MP (PC, AB):** I want to thank you this evening, you said with some clarity, some words that I immediately identified with and they were sets of words that I had not had before, but you said clearly that the Charter of Rights will not protect rights, but simply transfer the jurisdiction over rights to another source. And I did not have it phrased in that kind of sense. ...

**Professor Russell:** Just so I can keep the record straight, I did not say they would not protect. I said it would [no]t guarantee ...

**Mr. Hawkes:** Okay.

**Professor Russell:** ... because the results of judicial decisions may well be seen to be more protective of rights than legislative decisions, although I think it is a toss-up. Often legislatures are more protective of rights than courts. That frequently occurs. Just to give one example discussed before, I do not know here, but you take the question of capital punishment and whether it is cruel and unusual and should be unconstitutional.

Our legislature, the Parliament of Canada, is being pretty protective if you like, of the right of the minority of people who are involved in that, and has taken a position that in my view protects rights pretty well. The courts sometimes, take the United States has gone back and forth on capital punishment and is now expanding the acceptability of capital punishment, so you cannot tell in advance whether rights will be better or worse protected. Your process is changing. That is the point. You are not guaranteeing anything but a change in the process. ...

Right now, a lot of Canadian observers of our Supreme Court, sometimes rather characterized as a rather cautious conservative court on issues of civil liberties and a Bill of Rights, but that is very apt to change through criticism, professional criticism, a new generation of lawyers and different appointments to the bench, so there will be some dynamic developments likely if you have this Charter. Thank you very much. (34: 167–70)

**The Hon. David Crombie, MP (PC, Ontario):** Mr. Chairman, the power of that court should also be understood and not mitigated by simply saying that, well, heavens, if we do not like it, we could always pass another law. It is not true. A great quote from Charles Evans

Hughes who was Chief Justice of the Supreme Court in the United States in 1930, and he said, quote: "The constitution is what the judges say it is." So do not misunderstand – I feel a little wary of the law officers of the Crown and the Minister constantly saying, "Gee, folks, do not get excited, we are not increasing anybody's power." You are not just increasing the power and rights of the courts, you are increasing the power of the judges to determine social and political policy in this country, and let us not try and undersell that point. ... (49: 33–6)

**The Hon. Mr. Justice Clyne (Counsel, Canada West Foundation):** My position is that it is a grave mistake to entrench such rights in a constitution rather than incorporating them in an ordinary statute such as the Canadian Bill of Rights, especially when the amending procedure in the proposal which is before you is so rigid and inflexible.

... We certainly should have human rights in the constitution, but that is what the ordinary man in the street feels is a good thing; he does not realize that he is substituting the opinion of a judge on very undetermined issues instead [of] a judgement of his elected members of Parliament. Now, I am in favour of the law being made by elected members of Parliaments under the democratic process; judges should interpret the law; they should not make it. The enactment of a constitutional Bill of Rights puts judges in the position of making political decisions rather than the legislators.

Lord Denning, the Master of the Rules in England, is one of the great legal minds on the bench today. He has not hesitated to give moderate interpretations of the law, but in a recent speech in the House of Lords he said that if judges were given power to overthrow acts of Parliament, they would become politicized. Then appointments would be based on political grounds and their reputations would suffer accordingly.

There is no doubt that in deciding whether an act is constitutional, judges have the right to overrule Parliament and the legislatures. Lord Denning went on to say that

> one has only to see in the great constitutions of the United States of America and of India the conflicts which arise from time to time between the judges and the legislatures.

I hope we shall not have such conflicts in this country and I respectfully agree entirely with what Lord Denning said.

Now, just let me refer you to some of the very vague and general terms of the proposed constitution which would give judges virtually a free hand in interpreting acts of Parliament and the legislatures. Just take for instance this section with which you are all familiar: "The Canadian Charter of Rights and Freedoms guarantees the rights and freedoms set out in it, subject only to such reasonable limits as are generally accepted in a free and democratic society with a parliamentary system of government." Now, ladies and gentlemen, I submit to you that those terms are so completely vague that any judge is going to have great difficulty in deciding what his duty is in respect of an individual statute, altogether too vague and I submit unworkable.

Now another section to which I draw your attention and which I hope might be revised: "Everyone has the right to life, liberty and security of the person and the right not to be deprived thereof except in accordance with the principles of fundamental justice." Now you are leaving it entirely in the discretion of a judge without giving that judge or court any guidance which he should expect to receive in an act of the legislature. (12: 100–2)

...

**The Hon. James McGrath, MP (PC, Newfoundland)** [responding to Guy Lafrance of Canadian Association of Chiefs of Police]: What you [are] saying would still not address the problem you have identified in your opening paragraph on the general philosophy, when you make the statement: "Under the Charter, the individual judge will have the power to overrule Parliament on a number of matters, including such questions as the powers and duties of policemen in the enforcement of the criminal law, and we do not approve of this." In other words, there is really no way that an entrenched Bill of Rights can satisfy you in this particular concern. You either have entrenchment or you do not have entrenchment. You cannot have it both ways. ... (14: 13)

**Mr. McGrath:** I would like now to turn to the Association of Crown Counsel. ... I was intrigued by your suggested changes to Section 1, and your general philosophical approach to the whole business of entrenchment. I found in there a contradiction. You talked about a role for Parliament in clarifying and defining rights. Yes, if we have an entrenched Bill of Rights, Parliament surrenders that role to the courts. It is the courts that clarify and define rights. Can you explain what appears to be a contradiction in your evidence? (14: 14)

**Mr. Roderick McLeod, Q.C. (Association of Crown Counsel):** We are not taking a position because, in our view, you cannot take one. The question simply cannot be answered "yes" or "no." It is a question, rather, of do you give everything to the courts and leave Parliament with nothing? I suppose that is absolute full entrenchment. Or, you give no power to the courts and leave everything to Parliament, which is the other end of the scale.

We are suggesting that it is only when you know the precise wording, especially with Section 1 – and I would respectfully agree with your comment that that is the key to the whole thing – but it is only when you know the wording that you know what amount of power, if you will, has been transferred from Parliament to the courts. It is our suggestion that you can retain, with Parliament the power to clarify or define, yet, at the same time, give to the courts the power to protect the very rights themselves by not permitting Parliament to abrogate or take the rights away. (14: 15)

**Mr. McLeod** [responding to question on whether his association supports entrenchment]: ... Perhaps the best way to look at it is to take an example. If one assumes that there is a charter of rights with a clause in it guaranteeing a freedom of religion and a government official of some kind denies, let us say, a certain organization the status of tax exemption or the right to solemnize marriages or something of that nature, and that citizen feels his rights under the Charter have been infringed, he would take action in the courts and the court would make a ruling. Now, if there is complete and full entrenchment with Parliament having no right to clarify and define, then it would be the court and only the court that would define what freedom of religion means.

If, on the other hand, Parliament shared that role with the courts in the fact situation that I have given, let us assume that the court ruled in the man's favour and overturns the action of the government against this man. After having done that, the legislature of the province in question would be free to legislate so as to define or clarify what was meant by freedom of religion. If that were to take away some of this man's rights, if he thought it did, he could go back to the court and ask the court to overturn what the government had just recently done. The court on that second occasion would then decide whether the provincial legislation was legislation which defined or clarified freedom of religion or whether it was legislation that abrogated the right to freedom of religion. If it was the latter, the court would have the power to strike down the legislation; if it was the former, the court would not because Parliament would have played its role of clarifying or defining that right. That is the type of distinction we seek to make with respect to Section 1. (14: 24–5)

**Mr. Bruce Smith (President of Toronto Ontario East Stake, Church of Jesus Christ of Latter Day Saints):** Finally, we must express concern about the possible effects of the proposed resolution on the relationships between courts and legislatures in making legal policies. The vagueness of the wording of key sections of the proposal, Section 15(1), for example, will necessarily vest the courts with a potential for policy-making unforeseen, and perhaps unforeseeable, when the proposed resolution was drafted. We believe it important to recognize that we do not know what kind of content and interpretation the courts will give to the language of the proposal over the years it will be a constitutional document. No one denies, of course, the good intentions of those who drafted the proposal. But it will take time and extensive litigation before the precise meaning of the vague words and phrases contained therein becomes clear. Most importantly, we cannot foretell what directions those interpretations will take. While fully recognizing the seriousness of that problem, we are concerned also that the extensive litigation and legal interpretations necessary could further shift law-making power from elected legislatures to nonelected judges. It could further accelerate the trend to govern by judicial decisions rather than by passage of law, and upset the division [*sic*! separation] of powers essential to any parliamentary democracy. ... (29: 10)

## Indeterminacy of Judicial Review

**Mr. Jim Hawkes (PC, AB)** [responding to Ms Hill, Canadian Council on Social Development]: Just to perhaps make you feel a little better, when you say that you are saying about exactly the same thing as the Minister of Justice said to us in his 13 hours of testimony: I do not know, was the rather consistent response to detailed questions about the impacts on people, on social rights. He said it would have to be decided by the courts and I made the comment that that is my definition of bad legislation, that as legislators we have a responsibility to be quite sure in our own mind what those impacts are likely to be before we put them into law, and especially preeminent law in the country. (19: 33)

**Mr. Rosenbloom (Legal Counsel, Nishga Tribal Council):** I would like to respond to that, Mr. Oberle [MP, PC – BC], because I think you have raised a very fundamental question that I am sure is on the minds of everyone in the Committee, and that is that if the concept of aboriginal title has not been defined from A to Z, would it be dangerous to enshrine the concept or the doctrine in the constitution? That certainly has been spoken about in this Committee and outside as being a dangerous situation.

Clearly, once you enshrine the doctrine of aboriginal title, there will be judicial interpretation made on the meaning of that term. We concede that once there has been an entrenchment of the principle, that principle will require continuous interpretation by the judicial bodies of this nation, but that is no different, Mr. Oberle, from the requirement to continuously go through a definition process in terms of freedom of speech, freedom of assembly, freedom of religion, issues about whether under freedom of religion Jehovah's Witnesses can refuse to have their children take blood transfusions; issues about freedom of assembly, whether that freedom entitles a group to obstruct traffic through a roadway. Every day in this country the courts are being called upon with the present Bill of Rights to define what is meant by the principle as it is placed in the Bill of Rights. Indeed, if you look at the history of the United States with their Constitution and their rights enshrined in a document, the courts are being called upon to give an interpretation.

It is the essence of this country that the courts go through an interpretation process, a definition process to refine principles that are placed in documents and in legislation in a general way. We do not pretend that the courts will not be called upon to take your move one step further, but we say that it is false to say we cannot enshrine the principle of aboriginal title in the constitution because we are not completely sure of all its elements for definition, but you are willing to enshrine all the other freedoms as listed in your Charter that I suggest are equally vague, that equally will call upon the courts of this nation to interpret, and we say that we just want equal treatment in terms of aboriginal title with all the other freedoms that are in their present day form in the Charter as the Charter is before you. Thank you. (26: 33–4)

**Mr. Wilson Head (President, National Black Coalition of Canada):** ... It seems to us that the way that is done best is through the courts. I for one am not a great believer in the courts in many respects. I realize the slowness. I realize the courts take a lot of time, I have known cases where the case becomes moot while it is being tried because you wait two or three years to get a court case, a hearing or a judgment. However, I am reminded of the very tremendous work that has been done in the United States Supreme Court. I lived in the United States, I went through a segregated school system, I lived in segregated housing, I lived in ghettos, brown or black ghettos. I went to all-black schools, and yet the Supreme Court of the United States, which had ruled in 1918 and in 1896 that segregation was legal and that it did not violate rights, that same Supreme Court in 1954 ruled that segregation was ipso facto illegal. It was basically against the Constitution of the United States, it was a denial of due process, and since that time the Supreme Court has consistently ruled in that favour in the United States and has oftentimes overturned the laws of state government and others who would restrict the right of blacks to vote, to hold office, to live in certain parts of town, to have their children educated, et cetera.

So in that sense, then, I would prefer that the constitution be interpreted not by the Parliament or by the legislatures of the various provinces, but by a court which would presumably operate on the basis of not being pressured by the political climate at that particular time. (22: 11)

...

**Senator Duff Roblin (PC, Manitoba):** I would like to draw you out a little, perhaps, on one of the observations you make concerning entrenchment, because you pose one of the dilemmas of entrenchment when you say that although the expanded role of the courts opens another forum for the adjudication of the human rights issues, there are dangers to be avoided in granting the courts greater powers. You make some very good points about the dangers of an insensitive bench who perhaps find themselves unable to deal as imaginatively as some of us would like with the problems before us. I recall that I think it took the Supreme Court in the United States, where there is an entrenched Bill of Rights, what is it, 40 or 50 years to decide that separate but equal was not equal and that only equal is equal. I think that underlines very clearly one of the dangers we have in placing too much faith that the courts are going to solve all our problems. Maybe there is an advantage in having this entrenched feature but we must be aware that we do not become disillusioned with some of the results that we are going to get. ...

**Ms. Debra Acheson (National Association of Women and the Law):** With respect to the first comments you have made, I should stress that the concern is not only an insensitive bench, and I would not use the word "insensitive" myself to describe the Supreme Court of Canada. The concern is that the Bench have clear guidelines. You cannot expect the court to operate in a vacuum, which is what the present proposal does. You have to indicate to the court what the standard is that you expect the court to supply to you in their decisions. (22: 63)

...

**The Hon. Perrin Beatty, MP (PC, Ontario):** Gentlemen, much of your presentation tonight dealt with the question of the worth of constitutionalizing a Charter of Rights, what the benefit is to Canadians of actually writing it into the constitution to make sure that it is put beyond the reach of Parliament or the legislatures to take away rights unilaterally. I gather that essentially your rationale is, from the point of view of Canadians, the advantage to constitutionalizing rights is that it puts limits on the ability of Parliament or the legislatures to act if political constraints are inadequate in terms of protecting the public interest.

There may be times that political constraints would be enough to stop the government from doing something that was wrong and that would be fine, but there would be other instances where those political constraints would not be strong enough, therefore it is necessary for the citizens to have recourse to the courts to protect their rights; is that correct?

**Mr. William Black (Member of Executive Committee, British Columbia Civil Liberties Association):** I think that is part of it. It seems to me there are two other ways in which entrenchment helps. One is that many times a law may be fair in most applications but a particular application of a law may take away a person's rights. That instance will come to the attention of a court that has to consider the matter but will not necessarily come to the attention of Parliament or the legislature. If it did come to their attention they would probably do something about it, but many times it will not, so a Charter of Rights allows the court to deal with that problem rather than waiting perhaps for decades for Parliament to have time to deal with the problem.

Secondly, courts consider matters somewhat slower, sometimes, than Parliament, and while justice delayed is sometimes justice denied, sometimes it may have the advantage of allowing reconsideration of the matter in calmer times and we think that is still another advantage in addition to the one you mentioned of an entrenched charter.

**Mr. Beatty:** That is a very interesting comment in the present context. (22: 122–3)

...

**Mr. Frank Oberle, MP (PC, BC):** Mr. Grenke, I would take from your comments that you would be against the entrenching of a Charter of Rights. I have very strong feelings about that myself, and particularly I feel strongly about it because I do not believe that an entrenched Charter of Rights is workable in the British judicial process, in the British advisory judicial process as we have adapted it from Great Britain and I draw from the understanding that I have from the system in Germany and to some extent in the United States. You have a constitutional court in Germany that does nothing else but deal with constitutional questions and the individual has free access to these courts. There is no adversarial nature to that process, and half of that particular court is elected by the members of the Lower House and the other half by the members of the Upper House so there is accountability back to the people.

In the American system, of course, the appointment to the Supreme Court is ratified by the Congress and the Lower Courts are elected by the people; again accountability. I cannot believe that you can have one without the other and I feel very, very strongly about that, but as 1 say your brief is somewhat vague in this regard. Do you share with me the same fear that if we entrench the Charter of Rights in the context of the British judicial process that we have here, that you would have a situation where the courts would not only make the laws but they would also interpret them. Do you share that fear with me?

**Dr. Arthur Grenke (Historian, German-Canadian Committee on the Constitution):** To some extent, yes, but I am sure that the people who are drafting this particular bill are aware of this to some extent and all I am trying to say is that they be aware of what they are doing, that they be aware of the limitations and the advantages derived, that this be done intelligently and that they take cognizance in particular of the problems which a bill may involve us in the future.

**Mr. Oberle:** In the way I look at the situation there are two crucial questions that have to be answered by the guardian of the rights that we are about to entrench. The first question is, of course, what is the extent to which each individual in a society, in any organized society, has to surrender a portion of his freedom and his independence and his right to accommodate the community, the common good to the collective will, and having asked that question, then the question arises, what is the common good, the collective will, and if the Supreme Court of Canada were to define both these questions, in my opinion that would be exceedingly dangerous and would be a practice that is not consistent with western democracy but would be a practice, rather, that is consistent with so-called democracies behind the iron curtain.

**Mr. Grenke:** I would not go so far as to say that. (26: 44–5)

...

## Remedies and Enforcement

**Professor Max Cohen (Chairman, Select Committee on the Constitution of Canada of the Canadian Jewish Congress):** Finally, we come to two new ideas in the presentation, one is the question of enforcement and the other is the question of the emergency doctrine. I think I will let Professor Magnet speak to the enforcement issue since he made some enquiries based upon our concern that the only way you can enforce this charter now is to wait for a case to come up in the ordinary civil or criminal way, but what happens if somehow there is harm done or on its way to being done and you do not have an ordinary civil or criminal proceeding en route. Perhaps you would just like to speak to that Professor Magnet.

**Professor Joseph Magnet (Special Advisor, Canadian Jewish Congress):** We have any numerous examples of this, but to take the two most obvious, the *Hogan* case in the Supreme Court of Canada, it recognized the violation of legal rights under the Diefenbaker Bill of Rights, the court said: Well, we see no remedies clause here, we cannot grant a remedy.

Similarly, as you know, under Section 23 of the Manitoba Act there is a proscription there that acts be published in English and French. What is the remedy for failure to comply? Well, we think that to deal with problems like this, as well as the full panoply of rights which will be entrenched in the charter, that an enforcement clause is crucial, that the charter would be hollow without it and we think that this is in conformity with our international obligations under the Covenant on Civil and Political Rights, the text of which is set out for you. There is also a right in the Covenant to damages which is set out for you in the brief.

We are concerned that the courts not run wild with enforcing the charter. We do not think that the charter applies fully to the private sphere. We do not think that the charter constitutionalizes tort law, nor do we think it constitutionalizes contract law or property law. We do not think that if a particular person does not receive an invitation to a Scottish home, for example, that he has a right of action under the constitution. We restrict our submission in the enforcement clause to public authorities.

Similarly, we note that the enforcement clause we have proposed entitles the court to grant mandatory relief, that it can order the public authority to redress the right to grant a remedy as well as injunctive relief in cases of default, and our enforcement clause is, on page 14. Everyone entitled in law to the performance by a public authority of an act or omission shall, in cases of actual or threatened default, be entitled to full and effectual relief by mandatory or restraining order of a superior court to compel the performance of the act or omission. Pecuniary compensation shall be awarded in appropriate cases. (7: 99–100)

**Mr. Francis Young (Legal Advisor, New Brunswick Human Rights Commission):** I would now like to turn to the question of violation of the charter. The proposed text is grievously lacking. In some cases, citizens cannot take advantage of guaranteed rights while under other provisions, they cannot exercise their rights efficiently.

Section 25 should state that any law, regulation or order in council that is inconsistent with the provisions of this charter is, to the extent of such inconsistency, inoperative and of no force or effect. This would mean that what could not be done directly by a law, could not be done indirectly through a regulation. It is also essential that Section 25 outlaw activities which violate the provisions of the charter as most of these sections will probably be infringed upon more often by government activities than by anti-constitutional legislation.

Also, a new section should be added to the charter to provide for efficient recourse, like injunctions, statements, inadmissibility of evidence and damages. This recourse is necessary for the application of sections 8 and 9 and of paragraph 11(d) which, because of their special wording, cannot be implemented at all by section 25. Even if this additional recourse were to be added, there would still be no guarantee that anyone could take advantage of it, at least under the sections of the charter which do not affect particular individuals. For example, an individual would not necessarily always be able to go before the courts if the obligation to publish the House of Commons proceedings in both official languages were not respected. The charter would have to give all individuals the right to take legal action even if the violation did not affect him or her as an individual.

Also, Section 26 should be struck and the court should be given the discretion of admitting evidence based on the specific circumstances. (11: 33)

**Mr. Kiesewalter (Co-ordinating Chairman, German-Canadian Committee on the Constitution):** Mr. Mackasey, how would you deal with the court cases? Which courts? We are not familiar with any provisions being made for dealing with the problems that may arise. Who is going to apply the law of the land?

**The Hon. Bryce Mackasey, MP (LIB, ON):** Well, eventually, people who feel that their constitutional rights which are enshrined are being infringed upon by some authority, can go all the way to the Supreme Court, and the Supreme Court will be dealing not with a Bill of Right[s] which is not enshrined, such as Mr. Diefenbaker's laudable piece of legislation, but with rights which are fundamentally enshrined in the constitution. It will then be for the courts to determine whether the case comes within the definition or intent of the constitution. If you are asking me who would enforce it, then it would be the Supreme Court. (26: 50–1)

...

**Mr. Nick Schultz (Associate General Counsel, Public Interest Advocacy Centre):** ... Moreover, special provisions are necessary to instruct judges in the Charter's interpretation. ... But the Charter must still contend with a legal tradition steeped in the notion of Parliamentary supremacy. There must be clear statement, firstly, that the Charter confers substantive, not merely procedural rights. Secondly, there must be a clear statement that the Charter is to be interpreted as an entrenched constitutional Charter and not as an ordinary statute. Thirdly, there must be a statement that the Charter has primacy over all other statutes. Fourthly, there must be a statement that doubts as to the interpretation of any provision of [the] Charter should be resolved in favour of the individual and not of Parliament. Fifthly, there must be a statement that courts be authorized to examine the background to the constitutional acts in interpreting them; namely, that courts be authorized to examine the debates of Parliament, the reports to Parliament, and so on, so that our courts will understand fully the context in which the acts were drafted. Finally, in this regard, individuals must be assured an inexpensive, quick and authoritative remedy when their rights are infringed. (29: 20)

**Mr. Svend Robinson, MP (NDP, BC):** My final question relates to a matter which is touched upon somewhat peripherally in your brief and that is the question of remedies. Would you agree that ... that the proposed Charter as drafted now simply does not contain adequate provision for recourse by citizens whose rights have been violated, to the courts, and that they may be able to obtain adequate remedies; that there should indeed be some much clearer formulation of the right of access to citizens to the courts to obtain remedies for violation of these rights rather than simply stating that the law is inoperable. ...

**Mr. Victor Paisley (Canadian Bar Association):** ... The constitution should guarantee access to enforce the Bill of Rights ... we should point out that one of the remedies that the court might otherwise have available to it is to exclude evidence unlawfully or improperly obtained, and there is precedent under our existing law for the state to deprive a person of a guaranteed right and for the evidence thereby obtained to be admitted. That is clear law as it now exists. This provision that is going to be entrenched in Section 26, forbids the court from enacting or interpreting the law in a way that would deprive the state of the fruit of the poison tree, as it were. (15: 20–1)

**Mr. Chris Speyer (PC, Ontario):** Gentlemen, I agree with you that if you believe in the value of entrenchment in the Charter of Rights, that this particular document is very badly drafted. I would like to direct a comment to you. Mr. Tarnopolsky in his writing has said that one of the failures of the Diefenbaker Bill of Rights was that we, as legislators, did not give a sense of direction to the courts as to what we wanted the courts to do in the event that there was a violation of those rights. Do you accept the criticism that if we are going to have a Charter of Rights that we should have included some type of remedies when there is a breach of those rights?

**Mr. Norman Whalen (Vice-Chairman of the Canadian Federation of Civil Liberties and Human Rights Associations):** I do not necessarily think that follows. It may give some assistance, but I do not think it is normal in constitutions to find this type of penalty clause, although it is normal in legislation. I think the greatest failing of the Diefenbaker Bill of Rights was the very fact that it was only an act of the Parliament of Canada, and was not part of the constitution. It was not entrenched.

**Mr. Speyer:** Surely, the freedom of speech and the freedom of assembly, which are included in the Diefenbaker Bill of Rights, have the same rational impact as that which is in the Charter of Rights, and the difference is what interpretation the courts are going to place and what remedies the courts are going to give for a violation of those rights.

**Mr. Whalen:** I agree with you up to a point. Are you suggesting that there should be a penalty clause in the constitution so that if you breached clause one you will have a fine of fifty dollars?

**Mr. Speyer:** No, no. I was just wondering whether you had given any thought to the provision of remedies.

**Mr. Whalen:** No, we have not given any thought to that matter.

**Mr. Edwin Webking (President of the Canadian Federation of Civil Liberties and Human Rights Associations):** My only reaction to that would be that the act of entrenchment is itself such a process in constitutional law that it would not be necessary to provide remedies or penalties, for that matter, because the direction that you noted as criticism relative to the Diefenbaker Bill would be eliminated or done away with simply by making that particular piece of legislation the supreme law or part of the supreme law of the country. Then, anybody who felt that they were being denied whatever that piece of legislation guaranteed them, could take action to pursue a remedy through the courts, if that were the way they were advised to go. (21: 20)

**Mr. David Copp (Vice-President, BC Civil Liberties Association):** The third main issue which 1 wish to raise is that the proposed Charter provides inadequate remedies to persons whose rights are infringed by official action. A charter with the remedies of this Charter will turn out to be a hoax for many persons in many circumstances. I refer now to Sections 25 and 26.

First, Section 25 reasonably provides that laws that are inconsistent with the Charter are, to the extent of their inconsistency, inoperative. This does not go far enough, because many official standards which are not laws may be objectionable. For instance, a rule within a penitentiary could authorize a cruel punishment. In this case, a court asked to protect inmates in light of Section 12 of the Charter should have the power to strike down the offending rule without having to interfere with any statutes. Accordingly, we suggest that Section 25 be amended to follow Section 26 of the discussion draft of August 22, which reads "that any law, order, regulation or rule that authorizes, forbids or regulates any activity" in a manner inconsistent with the Charter may be declared inoperative.

The existing Charter provides no remedy for any violation of the Charter other than the striking down of legislation. Section 26 even eliminates the possibility that the courts might rule that evidence obtained in a way that violates the Charter is inadmissible in a legal proceeding. The result is that rights in the Charter are explicitly protected only from legislative infringements. It is obvious, however, that many official actions not explicitly authorized by legislation can be in violation of the Charter. For instance, administrative officials and public agencies could violate the Charter by their actions and there may be no remedy available to aggrieved persons. Consider Section 8, which sets out one of the legal rights. It prohibits unlawful search and seizure. ...

Surely we need not argue that remedies are required and that it would be valuable to list them. Accordingly we recommend the wording in Section 27 of the discussion draft which allows a person to apply to the courts to obtain relief or remedy by way of declaration, injunction, damages or penalty. Now, in many cases the Charter could be violated in the course of obtaining evidence that someone has committed an offence. In many such circumstances the only effective remedy would be for the court to refuse to admit such illegally obtained evidence.

Section 26 would prevent the courts from providing this remedy even in the most extreme circumstances.

Accordingly, in order to give full effect to the legal rights, we believe that at the very least Section 26 should be deleted so that the courts may exclude evidence gained by means of violation of the Charter if they think it is appropriate. Ideally we think Section 26 should be amended to provide that evidence obtained by means which infringe upon or violate the rights listed in the Charter shall not be admissible in judicial and quasi-judicial proceedings. This, the exclusionary rule, is necessary because the use of illegally obtained evidence in obtaining convictions discredits the judicial process and the law enforcement system and would undermine respect for the Charter of Rights. Convictions for illegal acts should not rest on grounds themselves tainted by illegality. (22: 107–8)

...

**Mr. Svend Robinson, MP (NDP, BC):** Now, on that question there [are] some who suggest, including the Canadian Association of Chiefs of Police, that you do not need a remedies section, because there is already provision, for example, for the laying of criminal charges against police officers who violate the law or the provisions of the proposed charter. What would be your comment on the suggestion that we do not need a remedies section, and that it is sufficient to have laws rendered inoperative which violate the proposed Charter?

**Mr. William Black (British Columbia Civil Liberties Association):** Our answer to that, I guess, would be that the whole concept of a charter of rights is based on the assumption that we cannot assume that all the rights which would be available to us at this moment would be available to us forever. The whole principle of entrenchment is that at some future date, for some unforeseen reason, the rights which now exist, or even the common law remedies which now exist, may be restricted by an act of parliament or a provincial legislature or by some other means. And that is why we need an entrenched charter of rights.

So, of course there are other means to protect rights in Canada. Canada has rights now. The danger is that those rights can be taken away so easily. We are in favour of an entrenched bill of rights in many cases, not to create new rights or extend them, although in some cases we have made recommendations along those lines; but to ensure that the rights we now have will also be available in the future.

**Mr. Robinson:** Presumably, though, you would agree that, without a remedies section, many of the rights which Canadians might think they would have, would, in practice, be nonexistent.

**Mr. Black:** As Professor Copp has pointed out, many of the sections refer, not to law, but to the acts of public officials, that a person arrested should be informed of the reason for his arrest and so on. It is public officials, rather than law which would take away those rights. Yet, the only remedy is Section 25 which refers to discriminatory laws, without giving any remedy with regard to discriminatory acts by public officials. (22: 116)

...

**Mr. Jean Lapierre, MP (LIB, PQ):** The only thing that bothers me a bit is that you have recommended that an independent commissioner be appointed. I thought that the legal interpretation and enforcement of the charter was to be left up to the court. I am not convinced that it would be constitutionally appropriate to appoint an independent commissioner. I do not know whether you have really thought about this or whether you are just paying lip service.

**Mr. Peter Maloney (Canadian Association of Lesbians and Gay Men):** Oui. We have some difficulty with leaving it to the courts. Our experience with the courts is that litigation is an extraordinarily expensive and time-consuming thing. Individual cases can surely be brought, but it has been our experience that most of the discrimination in this country is in fact structured and built in, as it were. One needs a more active intervention to seek out instances of discrimination and to seek redress.

**Mr. Lapierre:** Fine. That is why I think we should have a redress clause which would provide for special remedy without creating another judicial or quasijudicial body, since we do have a legal system that must be respected. (24: 36–7)

**Mr. Svend Robinson, MP (NDP, BC):** ... I would refer to Section 26, the comments which have been made on that Section, and the suggestion has been made that that Section should, in fact, be removed from the proposed Charter and that that would leave the courts a discretion, as I understand you to be saying, to exclude evidence which brings the administration of justice into disrepute.

How would you square that suggestion with your suggestion that there should be a remedies section – a suggestion, by the way which I think makes eminent sense – if there is to be a remedy section for breaches of the proposed legal rights section of the Charter, surely that remedies section would confer upon the courts some discretion to exclude evidence which has been obtained in a manner which violates specifically the proposed legal rights contained in the Charter. That is my understanding of the purpose of a remedies Section.

**Professor Fred Sussman (Canadian Association for the Prevention of Crime):** The remedies Section, as I recall the terms in which I phrased it in suggesting it, would be a remedies section which would provide, in effect, for a court proceeding which would seek as a remedy mandatory or an injunctive order of the court, or in particular cases, would make provision for damages. That, I think, you can see is an entirely different matter from the exclusion of evidence, for example, which may be described as the fruit of the poisoned tree.

**Mr. Robinson:** In view of that, I would say that there are those who believe – and I do not believe there has been any suggestion to date that a remedies section should not provide remedies for breaches of the proposed legal rights contained in the Charter.

Would you agree, then, that by merely deleting Section 26, unless the Supreme Court of Canada reversed its position, a course of action which they do not take lightly, that the situation in Canada would remain, to the best of your knowledge, speaking now on behalf of the Association, that evidence obtained would be admissible if relevant, even if that evidence tended to bring the administration of justice into disrepute?

**Professor Sussman:** No: because it is open to the relevant legislatures and in criminal legislation, assuming that the constitutional division of powers remain the same in that respect, it will be the Parliament of Canada – your question was on what assumption? Was it on the assumption that the Section were deleted?

**Mr. Robinson:** The law will remain the same. Assuming that the Section were deleted and there is no indication that Parliament intends to move on this, the state of the law would then be that the evidence would be admissible as long as it is relevant, would it not?

**Professor Sussman:** In the immediate moment, yes. The Charter speaks for a stretch of time reaching into the indefinable future.

The point is that one can anticipate the future. One believes that Parliaments may develop differences of opinion from their present position, and courts may, too.

Personally, I am one who believes that courts particularly tend to rise to the height of the document that they are called upon to interpret. (24: 50–1)

**The Hon. Jean Chrétien (Minister of Justice):** The Canadian Civil Liberties Association, the Canadian Jewish Congress, many members of this Committee and other witnesses expressed the strong view that the Charter requires a remedies section. This would ensure that the Courts could order specific remedies for breach of Charter rights. I would be prepared to see a new section stating that:

> Anyone whose rights or freedoms, as guaranteed by this Charter, have been infringed or denied may apply to a court of competent jurisdiction to obtain such remedy as the court considers just and appropriate in the circumstances.

This would ensure that an appropriate remedy as determined by the courts would be afforded to anyone whose rights have been infringed whether through enactment of a law or by an action of a government official. (36: 19)

...

**The Honourable Jean Chrétien, Minister of Justice and Attorney General of Canada** [talking about parallel French and English school systems]: ... So the court orders you to provide that school.

This was not included in the original charter, and it is extremely important. So it is incorrect to claim that we reduced the scope of our action, when in fact we did the exact opposite, and radically; you will remember the comments, people saying that the courts would make decisions but the government would not act. Clause 25 resolves this problem; it gives the courts the power to decree solutions. ...

**Mr. Eymard Corbin (LIB, NB):** Finally, Mr. Minister, Mr. Chairman, could you specify what you mean by a competent court? In Clause 25 mention is made of a competent tribunal where school questions could be appealed.

**Mr. Chrétien:** Those cases will go before Canadian tribunals depending upon the origin of the problem and there will be an appeal process, according to the normal rules of procedure, up to the Supreme Court.

I could ask Mr. Tassé to be more specific about that. ...

**Mr. Roger Tassé (Deputy Minister, Department of Justice):** Thank you, Mr. Chairman. In fact, that clause which sets up a recourse before the courts could be used in any case where the charter of rights is violated. Those violations could be ... [interrupted]

**Mr. Corbin:** Not only language rights.

**Mr. Tassé:** All legal guarantees or democratic freedom deemed to be granted by the charter can be argued before the various court levels. These could be argued within the framework of civil procedures, criminal procedures or could even be done within the framework of obtaining redress. For example, in a school case, the main thrust of the action undertaken might be to ask for redress. The competent tribunal is therefore mentioned so that those seeking justice might have the possibility to invoke the guarantees granted by this charter in any debate. It might be before a county court, a provincial court or whatever court is competent to hear the case set before the tribunal. (38: 38–40)

...

**Mr. Jim Hawkes (PC, AB):** I have a supplementary to the line of questioning established by Mr. Hnatyshyn. Are the courts a body or authority? The courts themselves, the Supreme Court, is that a body or authority?

**Mr. Roger Tassé (Deputy Minister of Justice):** Mr. Hawkes, the key word here is, are the legislative powers – the court does not have legislative powers.

**Mr. Hawkes:** What about the clause of the constitution that we passed, I believe yesterday, that dealt with the remedy clause and in particular, you brought up the issue of Clause 23 and I thought in our discussion yesterday, the courts could in fact require a school board or a school district to establish a school facility which – you would not consider that as a legislative function, an increase in the powers of the court? The whole remedy clause does not increase the power of the court to, in effect, legislate.

**Mr. Tassé:** I do not think, Mr. Chairman, it would be proper to describe these powers that the courts would have under Clause 24 as being legislative powers. The courts would adjudicate when remedies are sought under the constitution. But they would just be interpreting this under the constitution and they would ensure that its intent and spirit are carried through, but I do not think that we can say that in effect they would be, in so doing, exercising legislative powers.

**Mr. Hawkes:** Do the American Courts legislate?

**Mr. Tassé:** Oh, I think that there are some people that would argue in the loose sense, that perhaps in coming to some decision, in the interpretation, in perhaps a political sense that they may be exercising powers by refining the constitution powers that may look like the exercise of legislative powers, but our Supreme Court in Canada, for example, has been over the year interpreting the constitution. They have been saying, for example, that Parliament has the power to legislate in matters of radio and aeronautics. I do not think anyone would say that in a strict sense, that when they were so doing, they were exercising legislative powers. They were just adjudicating matters that were before them under the constitution.

**Mr. Hawkes:** But surely, when you hand them this charter, you hand them new powers and new responsibilities that will make our system very much like the American in that as you call it, loose sense of legislating powers.

**Mr. Chrétien:** What we are doing Mr. Hawkes, is we are giving rights to the Canadian citizens.

**Mr. Hawkes:** You are giving rights to the courts.

**Mr. Chrétien:** No, the right ...

**Mr. Hawkes:** And powers to the courts ...

**Mr. Chrétien:** The courts interpret the right. The rights belong to the Canadian citizens. When you go in front of the court, you say I have this right. Not only yes or no.

**Mr. Hawkes:** You give them the power to enforce. The courts have the powers, not the people.

**Mr. Chrétien:** Yes, but you know the courts, you know, are there. This is a segment of our society. They are there to interpret the law and, of course, they have to play the role. Otherwise you know, you will have a system where the citizens have no recourse to the court. And the laws, you know, that will be the arbitrary system absolutely, from the legislature.

**Mr. Hawkes:** In other words, you are telling me this is no restriction on that increased power on the courts; that this clause cannot be interpreted even by the courts themselves, as limiting their powers.

**Mr. Tassé:** I think, Mr. Chairman, the powers of the courts under the constitution will be, under that charter, is spelled out in clause 24. In clause 24 it spells out precisely what the role of the court will be under that charter, in adjudicating matters coming before it. So I am not too sure that I see the significance of your question, because even if one were to assume that in effect the courts might be covered by that clause, I do not know whether it would have any significance at all, because the role of the courts under the charter is set out in clause 24.

**Mr. Hawkes:** I think something that is bothering me is the frequency that we have had of "I do not know." I think the most bothersome part of this whole exercise is that we are restricted in time, restricted in witnesses and far too often we get the response "I do not know." ... (49: 28–31)

**Mr. Svend Robinson, MP (NDP, BC):** The B.C. Civil Liberties Association, the Canadian Civil Liberties Association, and the Canadian Federation of Human Rights and Civil Liberties Association all called, Mr. Minister, through you, Mr. Chairman, for specific reference to the right to remain silent and not just from the moment from which a person is charged, but from the moment of arrest. ...

Mr. Minister, perhaps you could clarify, or one of your officials, what remedy you might envisage being applied under Clause 24 of the proposed Charter of Rights if the right to be informed of one's right to retain and instruct counsel without delay were abrogated? What possible remedy might there be applied by the courts if that right were violated?

**Mr. Chrétien:** We say that the court has the discretion to apply the appropriate remedy. (46: 126)

## Chapter Thirteen

# Multiculturalism

---

*Multicultural heritage*

**27.** This Charter shall be interpreted in a manner consistent with the preservation and enhancement of the multicultural heritage of Canadians.

---

## Commentary

Section 27 was not part of the 6 October 1980 draft of the Charter. It was added during clause-by-clause, as proposed by Minister of Justice Jean Chrétien when he appeared before the Joint Committee in January 1980, in response to requests by various groups appearing before the committee for explicit recognition of multiculturalism.

## Multiculturalism Generally

**Mr. Jan Kaszuba (President, Canadian Polish Congress):** This pronounced multicultural policy has been supported by all the major political parties of Canada both in provinces and federally. We must say and I believe that the multiculturalism is a way of life in Canada. I mentioned all these facts because we are coming to the heart of today's problem, the Canadian constitution. In the Polish Canadian Congress we take this position: we are, as a group, for the patriation of the constitution, we are for the entrenchment of the Bill of Rights in the constitution, of course, with suitable changes in the proposed text, but we are also in agreement that we must have an entrenchment of the multiculturalism in the Canadian constitution. We consider this a must. Thank you. (9: 103)

**Mr. Jan Federorowicz (Canadian Polish Congress):** In the brief we say that the constitution should clearly state in its preamble that Canada is a country which has been created out of ethnic culture and linguistic diversity. It should affirm the right of every group, not merely people of French or British origin, to preserve and cultivate their various languages and cultures within the broader Canadian context. We go on to suggest that this is not a process of constitutional reform that we want to undergo very often. It is painful at the moment, it has been going on for 50 years, let us get it done and let us get it done right.

On the other hand, if continuing immigration, particularly from non-French or non-English speaking parts of the world, decisively changes the ethnic composition of this country, as indeed it has been doing since the last World War, then a document which singles out the so-called "founding races" for special mention or special privilege, because of historical accident will become either irrelevant or, what is worse, perhaps racist. ...

So if the constitution is to be equal, then, for all Canadians, not just English or French Canadians. I would like the new constitution to recognize that I, too, am a Canadian, that my language, though unofficial, is a Canadian language; that my culture is a Canadian culture; that I have as much right to pursue and develop my cultural and linguistic interests as any other Canadian, and that my government, which I support with my taxes, will help me in this endeavour.

Either Canada is a multicultural country, and this fact is recognized not only in the constitution of this country but in the practice of the government, or we should stop beating around the bush and admit that there is only room for two chartered ethnic groups in this country and it is official policy, by carrot and stick, to induce all other groups to assimilate into one of these two. If the latter case turns out to be the real intention of all of this, then that is a policy which I totally reject and I suspect it is a policy which you would have trouble convincing a third of this nation to accept. (9: 107–8)

**Mr. Nicholas Zsolnay (President, Canadian Citizenship Federation):** Our movement was a pioneer in the developing interethnic and intercultural relations on a wide scale among Canadians. De facto, the chain of citizenship councils across our country became the cradle of Canadian multiculturalism. The multiethnic fact of contemporary Canada was first recognized by the B and B [Bilingualism and Biculturalism]

Commission and then elevated to legal status by policies of the federal and several provincial governments.

Consequently, and obviously, we wish to add our voice to previous suggestions for the entrenchment of multiculturalism, the right to pursue and to preserve ethnocultural heritages. Our preference would be a new section within the act, eventually combined with Section 15 establishing cultural rights and freedoms in the context of unreversible multiethnic facts of the Canadian social fabric. A minimum requirement seems to be the enshrinement of multiculturalism, either in a preamble to the Charter or to the constitution. (29: 52–3)

**Mr. Rudnyckyj (Canadian Citizenship Federation):** I think that in all our constitutional planning, there is one deficiency, namely the danger of so-called transparent or invisible citizens. These are one-third of the population. I call them itrophones, anglophones, francophones – and "itrophones" is a term introduced in 1974 in linguistics. One of the very important points in our presentation is that concerning multiculturalism which is so far only a policy but not constitutionally secured as a provision. In my opinion, our minimum requirement is to give it recognition in the preamble to the constitution or to constitutionalize the whole policy as it was presented by the Prime Minister in 1971.

So this is a point which, in my opinion, is very important as far as invisible or transparent Canadian citizens are concerned. We spoke about the inborn citizens in relation to the previous delegation. We want to stress also the danger of invisible or transparent citizens who do not exist legally, constitutionally, but who can be made visible and non-transparent if our point, namely, the entrenchment of multiculturalism, or even, as a minimum requirement, that the preamble should mention this in the introduction to the new Canadian Act. (29: 59–60)

**Mr. Laurence Decore (Chairman, Canadian Consultative Council on Multiculturalism):** The Council is completely convinced that all ethnocultural groups recognize the importance and place of the French language in Canada. Multiculturalism respects the linguistic status of English and French as defined in the Official Languages Act and in the resolution. We respect both the historical claims and the present realities on which official bilingualism is based. All ethnocultural communities have a special interest in guarding against the drowning of cultures in what is called the Anglo-American sea. They see continued viability of the French language as one of the cornerstones of cultural pluralism.

In short, Mr. Chairman, the policy of multiculturalism does not challenge the status of Canada's official languages but complements it.

By promoting a climate of cross-cultural sympathy and linguistic opportunity, multiculturalism works to establish the prerequisite for Canadian unity in a bilingual and in a multicultural framework.

When Parliament agreed to support the multicultural policy in 1971, the ethnocultural groups were pleased that there [sic] existence was officially recognized. Since this policy was unanimously supported by all parties, we interpret that, I think all must interpret that as meaning that multiculturalism was therefore a national policy involving all Canadians. As a national policy and an integral part of the Canadian reality, multiculturalism surely must be included in the Canadian constitution, the fundamental national framework for all Canadians, present and future.

Our Council recommends that a preamble be added to the resolution and that in that preamble a recognition of Canada's multicultural society be clearly stated. What we are suggesting is not new or untoward, for in the final report of the Special Joint Committee of the Senate and the House of Commons on the Constitution of Canada, which was co-chaired by Senator Gil Molgat and Mark MacGuigan, the following recommendation was made in Chapter 10 dealing with language rights: "The preamble to the constitution should formally recognize that Canada is a multicultural country." (29: 123–5)

**The Hon. Jake Epp, MP (PC, Manitoba):** I say to you quite frankly that I would like to see the concept of multiculturalism enshrined in the constitution, and I think even that concept would have to be evolved somewhat, even once it was in the constitution in terms of what it really means in our future together. What I am interested in – and I have stated pretty clearly the way I think we should go, and having some responsibilities in that area from this side – what I would like to know from you is this: do you feel we have now reached the point where other people, such as this present government as well – do you have the feeling now that there is enough of an awareness through the work of this Committee and the government itself, that collectively, jointly, we can get that concept put into our constitution as we amend it?

**Mr. Laurence Decore (Chairman, Canadian Consultative Council on Multiculturalism):** Mr. Chairman, we had a unique experience in May of this year. Our Executive Committee travelled to St. John's, Newfoundland. For two days beforehand, I and another gentlemen travelled around Conception Bay and stopped at some of the fish plants and talked to the people.

First of all, I did not know very much about Newfoundland. That was the first time I had ever been there. When somebody told me that there was a unique culture, a Newfoundland culture, I discounted that. But I am convinced that there is. I think it is a tremendous culture and a most interesting kind of lifestyle. I found it was closer to travel to London and to Paris from St. John's, Newfoundland, than it was to go back to Edmonton, my home. That is kind of earth shattering. I suppose I should have known that from my history. But it was then that I came to the reality of that fact.

Many people in Newfoundland did not even know that there was 700,000 Canadians of Italian origin living in Toronto. Most Albertans do not know that there are 500,000 or 600,000 Newfoundlanders living on an island with a distinct culture. Many Newfoundlanders do not know that there are some 600,000 Canadians of Ukrainian origin living mostly in Western Canada. What I am trying to say is that even I have not been able to articulate the concept well enough for Canadians to fully appreciate and realize how immense this country is and how wonderful it is. So, there are a lot of things which have to be done. Our Council was trying to do some of those things and putting it into the constitution is one of the important aspects.

**Mr. Epp:** Do you feel we have arrived at the stage where we can now convince a sufficient number of people, both in government and society that it is important to do that?

**Mr. Decore:** There is just a little step to take. (29: 143–4)

**Mr. Waddell, MP (NDP, BC):** I want to ask you specifically with reference to multiculturalism. It seems to me that we have three choices in dealing with it: the first is there can be no mention at all in the constitution; the second one could be that there is a mention in the preamble of a constitution. Now, I do not see any preamble here but there could be a mention in the preamble. Now, that could be some sort of affirmative guidance to us, a kind of let-us-show-the-nature-of-the-country-we-are, but perhaps of no legal authority; and the third possibility would be that it could be mentioned in the body of the constitution, let us say in Section 15 here, which would give specific legal rights. I wonder whether you would agree with me that those are the choices, there may be other choices, and which choice would you prefer?

**Mr. Dietrich Kiesewalter (Co-ordinating Chairman, German-Canadian Committee on the Constitution):** If I may answer, I think we would prefer to have it in the body of the Charter that you have in front of you rather than in the preamble. The preamble, to me, would be more of a statement of intent. I think our Ukrainian friends recommended an addition to Section 15 and it reads as follows: "Everyone has the right to preserve and develop their cultural and linguistic heritage." I think this would be quite acceptable to us. (26: 47)

**Mr. Nicolas Zsolnay (President, Canadian Citizenship Federation):** ... We wish to add our voice to previous suggestions for the entrenchment of multiculturalism, the right to pursue and to preserve ethnocultural heritages. Our preference would be a new section within the act, eventually combined with Section 15 establishing cultural rights and freedoms in the context of unreversible multiethnic facts of the Canadian social fabric. A minimum requirement seems to be the enshrinement of multiculturalism, either in a preamble to the Charter or to the constitution.

**Mr. Marek Malichi (Canadian Polish Congress):** Well, perhaps I could make one or two brief comments on that. I think Section 15(1), which deals with the right to equality before the law and equal protection of the law without discrimination, that really deals, I suppose, more in the sense of discrimination rather than preservation of cultural rights, but it appears to be the only paragraph here that remotely comes to the idea. Ethnic origin simply means that: Origin; it does not mean the present; it means where we came from but not what we are now. There is no reference to the preservation of language, there is no question of the use of other languages other than say, in the courts or in the Parliament. (9: 113)

**Professor Maxwell Cohen (Faculty of Law, McGill University):** I have had this put before me before, Mr. Chairman, and I am sure you have had it in a much more sophisticated form. We have an official multicultural policy in Canada. Does one transmute that generalized multicultural concept into a constitutional concept? That is a very difficult question.

My initial response is to say: Let us by all means support multiculturalism, but if you ever entrench it, you are opening a series of doors that may be very difficult to manage, both politically, financially and legally. The provinces will have great trouble in handling many otherwise thoroughly integrated Canadian minorities who want their own particular cultural image reflected in the school curriculum, in teaching rights, etc., etc., etc. I suspect, Mr. Chairman, that though all Canadians in this multi-ethnic society strongly support most ethnic cultural policies, it is quite another step to entrench them in a constitution per se. (34: 96–7)

## Chapter Fourteen

# Denominational Rights

---

> *Rights respecting certain schools preserved*
>
> **29.** Nothing in this Charter abrogates or derogates from any rights or privileges guaranteed by or under the Constitution of Canada in respect of denominational, separate or dissentient schools

## Commentary

Section 29 was added at the Joint Committee. It had no precursor in the 6 October 1980 draft of the Charter tabled with the committee. It was necessitated because of concerns expressed by denominational, separate, and dissentient schools that sections 2 and 15 of the Charter would trump the rights that these schools had under section 93 of the Constitution Act, 1867. This apprehension was exacerbated by the inclusion of what was then section 25 in that 6 October draft of the Charter, which provided, "Any law that is inconsistent with the provisions of this Charter is, to the extent of such inconsistency, inoperative and of no force or effect."

Representatives from Newfoundland were particularly concerned about the lack of explicit protection for denominational schools in the Charter because Term 17 of the Terms of Union between Canada and Newfoundland, pursuant to which Newfoundland had joined Confederation in 1949, gave Newfoundland exclusive jurisdiction over education. Historically, all education in Newfoundland had been denominational.

The government responded in two stages. First, in January 1981, when Minister of Justice Jean Chrétien tabled amendments with the Joint Committee, he proposed deleting section 25 from the Charter and creating section 52(1) in its place, which provides, "The Constitution of Canada is the supreme law of Canada, and any law that is inconsistent with the provisions of the Constitution is, to the extent of the inconsistency, of no force or effect." The effect of this clause – as later confirmed by the courts – was to put section 93 of the Constitution Act, 1867 and the provisions of the Charter on the same normative and legal plane. This was what the proponents of denominational schools were seeking at the Joint Committee.

However, this did not suffice to allay the concerns of denominational supporters, who sought explicit recognition that the provisions of the Charter would not alter existing denominational school rights. Thus, during clause-by-clause later in January, the government agreed to the amendment that became section 29 of the Charter.

### General

**Reverend Father Raymond Durocher (Expert Researcher, Conference of Catholic Bishops of Ontario):** The problem we have is that the right which is presently recognized in our constitution not be put in danger by other rights that are being asked for presently in the new constitution; in other words those rights might threaten the existence of our separate schools or Catholic schools. That is our only concern and we would like to ask the committee members to see to it that other rights which might be asked for not threaten the right which is presently recognized by the BNA Act in the matter of our Catholic schools. We believe that those schools, of course, should be financed by taxpayers. We believe that the present situation in Ontario is not equitable because companies' monies cannot go to separate schools and I believe that is a denial of a right and that is a form of discrimination. However, those are perhaps things that should be seen to at the provincial level. What really concerns us, in particular, is that that right be recognized. ...

I would just like to add a point, having been engaged in school battles in both Manitoba and in Ontario where the situation was quite difficult. Reading back parliamentary debates, very much like these that are taking place here, in 1865, I think it is very useful to do that and I hope when they look back at your debates they will say the same thing.

There was no intellectual or principled approach to the question of religious education or denominational education. It was not a question of the churches being established in Britain and therefore there should be some establishment here. It was purely a political decision.

If you were to read the debates, you will see that someone got up and said, "We, English protestants" not distinguishing between protestants and English. He said, "We, English protestants, are very well taken care of now; but we are not sure we are going to be well taken care of in confederation, because the Lord knows who is going to be in the majority." Therefore, he said, "We want guarantees of things now which we thought we would be getting eventually anyhow in Quebec." And he laid down two or three guarantees. But the decision to do that had nothing to do with some position about religion or some position as regards language.

They did not say that churches and state be separate. Nobody thought about that. They said: "What do we have to do in order to get a Confederation?" There is in this country a long tradition of this kind of school, and it is very much adhered to at the present time and these people are not going to go into Confederation unless they have some guarantees that these things are going to be continued. So it was decided that the denominational schools, in that case are meaning protestant English school in Quebec, would be guaranteed and they would have two or three extra things over the market, as they say in French, to sweeten the pie a little bit. It was a purely political decision, a judgment about the things which were very important at that time to Canada.

There was no guarantee for the language at that time because it was not a problem. When Mr. Cartier got up he said that somebody mentioned the dissentient English schools, and he said that there were no such schools in this province, that there were no dissentients; that there was no right of dissent on the ground of languages, because there was no problem. Those who spoke French went to French schools. Those who spoke English went to the Protestant. But that did not mean it was not an integral part of Canada which they were putting together. If I may return to one of Mr. Crosbie's questions, I think he said something about when do we stop looking into this question and exploring it.

**Some hon. Members:** It was Mr. McGrath.

**Rev. Durocher:** I am sorry. But what I would like to say is this. If confederation were being debated today, there can be no doubt in anybody's mind that French would be entrenched. There can be no doubt about that, because there would be no Canada. That is exactly the argument which took place with regard to religion a hundred or so years ago and one which is still valid today. We do not want any religious wars in this country. We have a very good system going and we might as well keep on improving it.

I believe that Archbishop Plourde leans in in that direction, that it is one of the integral parts of Canada. It was not entrenched at the beginning because there was no problem at that time. But now that we have grown and we have more problems, I think it is just as important to have entrenchment of the French as it is to continue entrenchment of the denominational schools.

**Rt. Rev. Plourde:** ... I would [like] members of this honourable Committee to understand well that when we ask for the entrenchment of rights for denominational schools, we are not doing so because we want the schools to uphold the principles of our Church. We are not asking members of this Committee to recommend denominational schools because we want to help the Catholic Church. We are not seeking any favours for the Catholic Church. When we ask for Catholic schools, it is because we think that there are values in that type of teaching which is going to be of use to society as a whole.

Our stand on Catholic schools stems from the type of men and women we want to produce for society tomorrow so that society would be a better place to live in. We are working and asking for that for the benefit of society and not for ourselves. We are still being accused – and I think that is very backward – in certain quarters that we are doing this just to safeguard our Church and to produce vocations of priests. I want to make sure that our position is well understood, that when we claim to have the right to denominational schools, we are simply asking the right to exercise our best contribution to the well being of our society. (33: 65–9)

**Miss Coline Campbell, MP (LIB, NS):** Now on denominational schools, one quick question. What is the percentage of children in Ontario starting school under the separate school system?

**Rev. Durocher:** The separate school system of Ontario educates 35 per cent of the elementary pupils of the province of whom 95 per cent of the francophone children are in the schools too. (33: 71)

**Bishop Alexander Carter (President, Ontario Conference of Catholic Bishops):** We realize that in the history of Canada, dating from the union of the two Canadas up to the time of Confederation and then the BNA Act, that certain rights of Catholic schools, denominational schools, were protected by the BNA Act. We are concerned that under

376  The Charter Debates

the present proposed legislation that these rights might not be protected adequately. Indeed we might lose some of the rights we inherited that are part and parcel of the heritage of our country, if the constitution itself does not enshrine those rights, and even perhaps, in certain places where they have not been understood or fulfilled, they could perhaps be even more clearly delineated. ...

The introduction of individual human rights legislation into the political structure of modern nations necessarily causes some friction where authoritarian regimes have prevailed. So, I am sorry, I am really talking more on human rights, but we are concerned mostly with education and I will come back to that.

Care is usually taken in all instances to avoid direct conflict with national characteristics rooted in historical, geographical, cultural and other experiences of the people. For example, the hereditary nature of the British monarchy is not considered as a case of discrimination against the rights of any Canadian citizen to reach a pinnacle of political power. To avoid confusion, as to denominational school rights, we recommend that a provision be inserted in the Charter of Rights and Freedoms in Section 24, that such rights and freedoms are not to be construed so as to adversely affect the rights and privileges with respect to denominational schools conferred under Section 93 of the BNA Act, 1867.

So on this question of human rights, ladies and gentlemen, although we do not think it is wise to confuse the patriation procedure with introduction of massive changes, we do point out that both denominational rights as enshrined for over a century in Canada's constitution and human rights as proclaimed by the United Nations would justify a greater expansion of educational freedom at this time.

We insist on maintaining our rights partly because this keeps the door of justice and tolerance open for many others who share our belief in the primacy of religious and parental option in education. On this point, you realize that our own teaching, the belief that we hold is that the parents are the first educators and that the church and the state help the parent fulfil that basic right that is theirs and exercise the freedom which is theirs by their very role of parent. (33: 59–60)

**Mr. Phillip Hammel (President, Canadian Catholic School Trustees Association):** Catholic school trustees from across Canada support the concept of a repatriated constitution for Canada. Especially, we believe that the rights of minorities must be constitutionally entrenched, for the majority, in the normal course of events, will have its way. It is with some regret, therefore, that the Canadian Catholic School Trustees

Association, after having reviewed the proposed Canadian Charter of Rights and Freedoms, must express its disappointment and deep concern with respect to the future rights and privileges of publicly funded Roman Catholic Separate Schools rights and privileges which have been ours since the formation of this country in 1867. ...

We must, in the second instance, express our sincere concern that the future of existing, publicly funded Catholic schools is not adequately ensured by the proposed Charter. Although Section 93 of the British North America Act undoubtedly remains in effect as law, our concern, is that attrition of our rights through judicial judgements and interpretations based on the proposed Charter will eventually jeopardize both the religious values and the objectives of Catholic schools. We are particularly concerned that Section 25 of the proposed Charter, which establishes the primacy of the Charter with supremacy over all other laws, provides a basis for encroachment upon our rights, as provided by Section 93 of the BNA Act, whenever there would appear to be some inconsistency between Section 93 and specific terms of the Charter.

Coupled with the primacy of the Charter, we see Section 2, which provides for freedom of conscience and religion, and Section 15, which provides for equality before the law and equal protection before the law without discrimination because of religion, among others, as providing to the individual rights which will take precedence over the denominational group rights. We are particularly fearful because we recognize that the courts will, in the final analysis, determine the specific applications of these sections, and we are not unaware of developments in the United States where a similar dependence on the courts has ultimately reached the point where prayer is banned from an educational system originally founded in a Christian religious context. We are fearful that emphasis upon individual rights by the courts would erode group rights – such as rights in regard to: staffing policies and practices, enrolment criteria, prayer and religious practices in schools, extension of Catholic schools where some are now limited to specific grade levels, and indeed, participation in public funding to such an extent that Catholic denominational schools would remain Catholic in name only. ...

Finally, although Section 24 indicates that the Charter is not intended to affect any rights now existing in Canada, we are fearful that the primacy of the Charter, coupled with interpretations and reinterpretations made by courts in the future, poses a serious threat to the meaningful existence of Catholic Schools.

The Canadian Catholic School Trustees Association requests reconsideration of and amendment to the proposed Charter in order to protect Catholic minority rights to publicly funded Catholic Schools. We have taken the liberty of appending to this submission proposed amendments for consideration. ... We are suggesting that we add a new section after the present Section 24 which concerns itself with undeclared rights and freedoms, and we are suggesting that the guarantee in this Charter of certain rights and freedoms shall not be construed as preventing or limiting:

> any rights or privileges, by any provision of the constitution of Canada, granted or secured with respect to separate, dissentient or other denominational schools;

> the establishment or extension by authority of public statute or otherwise of any separate, dissentient or other denominational school or system of schools, or of any scheme of funding from public revenues or otherwise for the support of such school or system as is deemed appropriate; or

> the operation of any separate, dissentient or other denominational school or system of schools in accordance with its denominational requirements including, but not limited to, the right to follow a selective policy with respect to enrolment on the basis of sex or religion and to employ persons subscribing to the tenets of a particular religion. (19: 6–9)

**Reverend Patrick Fogarty (Executive Secretary, Canadian Catholic School Trustees Association):** I think it is customary to consider historic rights at times as remnants of a past age which have no relevance to the conflicts in modern society with a sort of up to date prestige which would embody individual and, perhaps, communal rights. But the American Bill of Rights, upon which many others are modelled, was not only progressive in its thinking and forward looking, but was also a document which responded to the realities of the situation of the day. The same grass roots pressures were at work when the French Revolution came along, and when the Magna Carta was embodied in the British law.

We are trying today to suggest that we are at a point in our nation's history when it is important to fight for the individual's rights as best we can without neglecting the roots from which we have come. The roots from which we have come in regards to denominational publicly funded school systems is part of the covenant which made this country a nation of the sort that it is. What we are trying to suggest is that the historic evolution of those rights under the British North America Act should be part of the constitution and have equal validity with the thrust to grant individual rights.

In our attempts to do this, I think there is a parallel between the attempts to gain equal status before the law in the new constitution, if you will, as far as group rights are concerned vis-à-vis individual rights, that there is the same historical base for trying to institute in the new constitution the rights of the francophone minorities to their own language education; particularly in view of the fact that when in the early days, for instance, people, such as Louis Riel, referred to "nos ecoles," our schools, that they were protected under the new constitution, it meant for him, French Catholic schools.

The situation, as it has evolved in the province of Manitoba, shows that unless things are spelled out exactly, people's interpretation of them in courts of law or sometimes through remedial legislation, as was the case in the province of Manitoba, just does not solve the problem unless we have specifically mentioned the inherited rights of groups in a way which enshrines them in the constitution giving them equal import and prestige with the new thrust to gain the proper rights for individuals. So that I do feel that we are at a point in our history where we can build upon the tradition of our country in trying to break new ground without neglecting the roots from which we have come. (19: 10–11)

**Senator John Connolly (LIB, Ontario):** I think you would probably agree that when the British North America Act was originally passed there were probably two difficulties, at least the historians refer to. One was the constitution of the Senate, the second one was the denominational school system as provided in Section 93. Now, I do not know whether the idea of the importance of the Senate is too popular an idea today in some quarters, but I think it is not unfair to say that Section 93 was really the Ark of the Covenant so far as the constitution was concerned, and I think without that the union might not have been possible. (19: 16–17)

### Relationship between Individual Rights and Group Rights

**Miss Coline Campbell, MP (LIB, NS):** In Section 15, under the present proposals, we have the right of religion. If you look at Section 1, it talks about "reasonable limits." Now, if you have a women's washroom, it seems to me it is in reasonable limits of the job description that it be a female attendant. Similarly, if you have a separate school board it seems to me to be within the reasonable limits of religion that you hire a teacher of that religious belief. I think there is a fear that you are going to lose these rights. It seems to me one has to be reasonable in looking at a Charter of Rights.

If you look at what the Human Rights Commission proposed about Section 15, which was a straight statement, and Section 1 which allowed the courts the final say on looking at reasonableness, would that interpretation not allay your fears as to the rights to denominational schools, along with Section 93, the rights to denominational schools at the time of union?

**Rev. Father Raymond Durocher (Conference of Catholic Bishops of Ontario):** Well I am glad you brought that example up. The Ontario Human Rights Commission has now proposed a very considerable rewrite of the existing legislation and have agreed with us that the usual protection accorded to religious groups is not sufficient to be adequate for constitutional purposes. So the bill has been brought forth, and they are going to add a clause to the effect that none of the provisions of this act are to be construed in such a way as to be in conflict with the rights and privileges of separate schools which are decreed in this province. So that we would not have to have recourse to the natural or group rights as a denomination which other people might have. It is recognized there that there is a constitutional guarantee and that the Human Rights Code of Ontario is subject to that constitutional guarantee. That is what we want to have put in this Charter. (33: 71–2)

**Miss Coline Campbell, MP (LIB, NS):** I was saying that under Section 15 in the proposal – and there are amendments coming; and I tend to like the Human Rights proposal for Section 15 giving equal rights; but regardless of that, under Section 15 it says that one of the freedoms is the right to religion. If you look at that and relate it to the reasonable limitation, then for a person to say that it is not part of a job description in a separate school system that the provision of the requirement under the separate school system would be covered. I do not know if you understand what I mean.

**Professor Joseph Magnet (Legal Counsel, Ontario Conference of Catholic Bishops):** Well, if I could just add a word or two to that, I do not think so. The reason is that the right of Section 15(1) is a right to equality before the law without discrimination because of, inter alia, religion. That is an individual right. The right which this Conference has been concerned about and made a statement on is the collective right of religious schools which is not found in this Charter, but is found at Section 93 of the British North America Act and at the equivalent provisions for provinces entering after Confederation. So, our concern is that Section 93 might be modified – which is a collective right – might be modified by some of the individual rights in this Charter.

I could see that Section 93, the right to denominational schools, might come into conflict with the very section to which you have drawn our attention – Section 15. Might not a teacher in a denominational school say that if he does not qualify denominationally to teach in that school, he is being denied the right to equality before the law without discrimination on the basis of religion? I think he might well say so. But our concern is that it would be intolerable that we should have a constitutionally protected system of denominational schools without the ability to enforce the denominational character of those schools. Our concern, therefore, is that the individual rights which are in the Charter do not impact to the detriment of the collective right in the existing constitution of Canada, in Section 93 and the successor sections.

**Miss Campbell:** Having said all that, just one quick matter. There is jurisprudence in the United States for my position.

**Professor Magnet:** But the jurisprudence in the United States to which you refer arises under a constitutional guarantee to nondiscrimination and also to a constitutional guarantee which prevents the establishment of religion.

In this proposed resolution there is no antiestablishment clause, and therefore, it simply reflects the Canadian theory which has been true throughout the history of this country that the basic Confederation pact protects certain denominational reasons. Indeed, you might say establishes, but certainly we would not think an antiestablishment clause would be possible in Canada. (33: 71–3)

**The Hon. James A. McGrath, MP (PC, Newfoundland):** Are you aware that representations have been made to the Committee by very influential witnesses which one would certainly expect to have influenced the Committee with regard to providing a clause, for example, in Section 15 which would deal with sexual orientation? The impact of that, of course, means that somebody who would publicly advocate a life style that would be against the mores or the teaching of the Roman Catholic Church, for example, a publicly avowed homosexual, you would be in a position where you would have to hire that person as a teacher.

**Mr. Phillip Hammel (President, Canadian Catholic School Trustees Association):** That is certainly one of the things we fear. As I have indicated in my statement, we are concerned about selective hiring practices. We believe that one of the major purposes, indeed, the major purpose of our schools is of course, the Catholic formation of our young people. Any life style which contravenes the teaching of our church, therefore, would be a disqualification to work in that kind of situation. Therefore, we feel we must have the right to suggest to any individual who does not accept the Catholic faith to seek employment elsewhere. (19: 11–13)

**Mr. Lorne Nystrom, MP (NDP, SK):** I noticed with interest, you said … and I am quoting: "We are fearful that emphasis upon individual rights by the courts would erode group rights." I am very happy to see that in there because last spring or summer I asked the Prime Minister a question in the House about enshrining collective rights in our constitution. He threw back the question at me, well, what are collective rights, how do you define collective rights?

So, I think this morning, you have given us another definition of collective rights. We have had before, as Mr. Chairman knows, a number of groups before our Committee arguing that we have collective rights in terms of language legislation in the Official Languages Act, the French language and the English language. We have also had a number of aboriginal groups before this Committee the last few days talking about the need for their collective rights being enshrined in the constitution. So, now we have at least three different arguments for collective or group rights, including yours and the denominational rights. I am very pleased to hear that. …

I wanted to ask you whether or not you can elaborate as to what some of the specific concerns may be. I expect for example you might be concerned about the right to hire Catholic teachers for Catholic schools because everyone has the right to equality before the law and to the equal protection of the law without discrimination, based on race, national or ethnic origin, colour, religion, age or sex, is that one of the concerns and could you elaborate a bit more on this for us, please.

**Mr. Hammel:** Yes, of course we are concerned about the right to discriminate in our hiring practices. We feel that since the primary purpose of our schools is the Catholic formation of the youngsters of the Catholic faith, that just as you would wish to be able to hire an expert in science to teach a science class so you would hope that in a school where religion was paramount you would have people who were well versed in that particular religion and who also of course support and respect that religion. So, certainly, that is of primary importance and we simply, as I suggested before, when someone who, perhaps very sincerely, has a question of conflict of conscience, when his own conscience conflicts with that or organized religion, then I think he simply disqualifies himself from continuing to be employed in this kind of a situation. It is simply, as Father suggested, one of the privileges of denominational schools, which must be a fact, or they simply cannot exist.

**Mr. Nystrom:** In other words, it might destroy the whole concept of denominational schools?

**Mr. Hammel:** Certainly, yes. If, for example, the individual conscience takes precedence over the religious teachings of the particular group, in this case our Roman Catholic Church, then pretty obviously we no longer have a Catholic school. If 80 percent of our teachers have renounced the faith, then pretty obviously we no longer have a Catholic school.

**Mr. Nystrom:** As I said to you earlier, I am really in favour of enshrining collective rights, I really believe that, but I want to ask you the same question that I posed to the Mennonites of Canada, and that is in Section 15 they use the word "everyone" has the right to equality before the law. Now, I am not a lawyer, I am not sure if you are either, but is there any jurisprudence you have looked at where the word "everyone" could be interpreted as a collective word or group word?

**Mr. Hammel:** I cannot quote specific cases to you but our advice is that that word "everyone" refers to individuals rather than groups. (19: 13–16)

**The Hon. Jake Epp, MP (PC, Manitoba):** The other point I would like you to comment on is this, and we have had one other group before us, a charter of rights tries to entrench or its purpose is to entrench individual rights and freedoms. That is a meritorious concept. The difficulty I have at this point, and with your brief, and I want to say I agree with your approach, is the fact that as we look at a charter we seem to be moving away from what I believe were the moral laws on which this country was founded, and that in an effort to guarantee rights of the individual to move to a state which is based on humanism, that is the total value of the individual, and I know that can be misinterpreted immediately, the minute I say that, and I am not against individual rights, but as we move toward an approach where the rights of the individual become so paramount that the collective rights of a group, or what we call group rights, can in fact if not be removed, can at least be reduced, and as I have been sitting in this Committee I have been wrestling with those two concepts, that what I fear intrinsically is that what we are doing is that, as we protect rights, we are doing two things, apart from the value of protecting individual rights: One, we are changing the basis on which laws have come down to us to the present day, the moral basis; two, the difficulty for groups which have always given society a moral fibre, such as your group, and the Church; that in fact, its ability to strengthen the moral fibre of society is being reduced.

I would like to comment on it, because I say to you quite frankly – and I am wrestling with these two points of view and torn between these two points of view – I do not want to be part of a procedure which reduces the ability either of parents or of the Church to make collective decisions which, I believe, have great value for society.

**Mr. Phillip Hammel (President, Canadian Catholic School Trustees Association):** I can only respond by saying I am in agreement. We believe that the essence of our stand is the maintenance of moral values and standards. The major characteristic of our denominational school system is the inculcation in our young people of those moral values and standards. As a result, we believe, in regard to your dilemma, that we must somehow protect groups which are in the face of a materialistic, humanistic approach in society; we must protect groups which are, in effect, promulgating moral values which, as you say, are traditional and are the basis of our society in its origins. I would simply say in regard to your dilemma that in Saskatchewan, Ontario and also in Alberta, provincial human rights codes do, indeed, provide for the protection against discrimination in certain areas, one of which is religion in the case of denominational schools.

**Senator John Connolly (LIB, ON):** "Discrimination" is a terrible word use.

**Mr. Hammel:** Well, at one time "discriminate" was a complimentary type of term; but in recent years it has acquired a derogatory connotation. The word simply means to be selective in how you approach certain aspects of things, and we prefer the original definition, and we plan to be, and would like to be and intend to continue to be discriminating. So, I would suggest that if we can in provincial human rights codes provide for that form of exemption, surely we could do it at the national level. (19: 18 –21)

**The Hon. Bryce Mackasey, MP (LIB, ON):** You know, Father, I come from a school system where I learned the words "God save Ireland" deep in Quebec before I learned the national anthem. I think our dilemma will not be resolved regardless of how wise we are. That dilemma has been well expressed by Senator Connolly and Mr. Epp, and Mr. Nystrom, weighing collective rights or group rights against individual rights. You have expressed concern about what has happened in the schools of the United States and the fear that it might happen here. But one thing you must bear in mind is that there is a fundamental difference in the two constitutions, in that the United States constitution prohibits the establishment of a religion, whereas ours goes exactly the other way by guaranteeing religious freedom, which makes for a very fundamental, a very big, difference. Inherent in all our legislation and in the proposed constitution is the insistence that our religious values and systems be maintained; whereas the Americans stress individual rights to the point where they prohibit the establishment of religious groups or religion. So I do not believe that your fear that we might find ourselves in the dilemma which applies to the United States is a valid one in that sense.

**Mr. Hammel:** If I may respond, we have to be very concerned in the sense that, although the initial starting points were different and we recognize the whole concept of the separation of Church and State in the United States, yet, when we have such phrases as "equal protection of the law without discrimination," which I think are almost identical in both countries, and when I think you have to admit, perhaps, that once we start dealing with these kinds of things, the results of American cases, will, indeed, be presented in our courts, then we do have some fear.

**Mr. Mackasey:** I am sure you are entitled to have a fear, and it is a legitimate fear. But I am saying there can be no perfect document, a fact which I think you have already recognized. For instance, the freedom of religion is now expressed very commonly in provincial jurisdictions now, and I am not aware that it has presented any particular problem. I know of no case which has gone before provincial rights commissions which has created this clash between individual rights and religious freedoms. Are you aware of any?

**Mr. Hammel:** No, sir.

**Mr. Mackasey:** Hopefully, it would not happen.

**Mr. Hammel:** The Caldwell case in British Columbia although that is still to be heard.

**Mr. Mackasey:** I said hopefully. I presume it will not become a problem. Although it could, theoretically, go to the courts. You have a valid argument. All of us are faced with the dilemma of morality. Nothing has been said with which I can disagree. I, too, am concerned about the breakdown in authority and old values. Perhaps it is a question of old age creeping up, or it might be the result of my upbringing. But I think we all agree that you cannot legislate morality, and that the solution has to be an educative one and not a statute. Maybe I am wrong.

**Mr. Hammel:** Perhaps what that suggests is that we must provide for that kind of education, which is what we are here espousing.

**Mr. Mackasey:** I agree, and perhaps some wording or phraseology in the constitution could eliminate intolerance or create tolerance – but, as I have said, we all agree. (19: 21–3)

**Senator John Connolly (LIB, ON):** Now, I wonder whether there might be some sense in redrafting, if we get to that stage of it, where we have a heading in the document talking about "group rights" or "collective rights" as distinct from the individual rights that are referred to in Sections 2 to 15, because while I have mentioned four different groups [Section 93 BNA Act; Section 16–23 Charter – i.e., language rights; Section 133 BNA Act; and "Native" – i.e., Aboriginal rights], there may be many other groups, undoubtedly there are many other groups that would like to see some reference to their immediate requirements in a constitutional document, and if we are to provide a framework do you think we should have such a framework in a document as it is being redrafted? ...

**Professor Max Cohen (McGill University):** ... If you do not mind, Senator Connolly, I will give you a brief but very inadequate answer to your second question. The classical Anglo-Canadian, Franco-Canadian civil rights tradition has been individual, not collective rights. You and I had rights, the group as such was not known other than very, very special cases, I suppose. We did not have minority treaties as they had in eastern and central Europe. That was very unfamiliar ground to us. However, life changes that and we now have, it seems to me, a political acceptance in Canada that there are [*sic*] a form of group identification that deserves constitutional treatment, native rights is one. We have it in the BNA Act, as you pointed out, in Section 93 and Section 133. And therefore, it does not surprise me that we should have reflection of that, and your Committee will have to look closely at the extent to which you could have it, but the final question you put before me is a more difficult one. (34: 96–7)

### The Impact of Section 15

**Honourable Allan Blakeney (Premier of Saskatchewan):** On Section 15 let me mention one particular concern about the possible impact of that section, and you will recall it as the nondiscrimination section, on the system of separate schools which exists in Saskatchewan and a good number of other provinces. On the face of it, the use of public funds to support denominational schools is a clear violation of Section 15 which prohibits discrimination on the basis of religion, since you are only going to do it for one religion and not all of them. Are separate schools saved by other sections of the Charter or by other constitutional provisions? Perhaps so, perhaps not. What about the discriminatory hiring and staffing practices and enrolment criteria which are part and parcel of a religious school system? Will they be jeopardized by the language of Section 15? Well, our lawyers have looked at this and they say on balance perhaps not but it is far from clear. And while I fully agree that there are other provisions in the U.S. Constitution, and important other provisions, we all know that aid for parochial schools has been struck down, partly on the grounds that it is discriminatory on the basis of religion. (30: 15–16)

**Mr. Jim Hawkes, MP (PC, Alberta):** Missing from your brief – and I would like you to address it – but there is a concept which has floated in and out of our world in these hearings; I think there is a general agreement amongst all members of this Committee, that individuals need protection from government. But a lot of groups have come to us saying that collectivity, whether we talk about a separate school or a native tribe, needs protection from the state. Perhaps the next level of conundrum is the protection from individual rights: that was expressed to us clearly by one group in terms of separate schools, that if they do not have the power to discriminate on the basis of religion, for instance, then how can they hire a Catholic school teacher, for instance, to teach Catholic values to Catholic children. I am wondering if that is just an oversight or whether you have considered it and then decided it was too complex a matter to deal with and left it.

**Mr. Grant Notley (Leader of the Alberta NDP):** I would say that in terms of our discussions as a Committee, to be completely accurate, for your information consideration by the council of the [New] Democratic Party which approved the document did not go into that specific question of the problems of collective groups as compared with the individual. We have, of course, seen some interesting cases in Alberta with respect to our Individual Rights Protection Act and our Human Rights Act. You may recall several years ago a decision which was made with respect to the Alberta School Act on the Mennonite school question, the category four schools, a rather significant decision was made by a provincial court judge, and at that time we felt it should have been referred to the Supreme Court of Alberta for a more definitive ruling.

**Professor Garth Stevenson (NDP, AB):** I think that in many ways there are difficulties certainly in putting down in precise terms any Charter of Human Rights to a degree that we have to rely on the common sense of the courts in dealing with any particular set of words and phrases and an interpretation related in some way to the prevailing values of the time. The point about Catholic School boards being prevented from hiring a Catholic teacher to teach religion may be a good debating point, but I find it extremely difficult to imagine that the Canadian judiciary would [interpret] the Charter of Human Rights in that fashion.

**Mr. Hawkes:** It depends upon the words, because courts are bound to interpret the words that we give them as legislators.

**Professor Stevenson:** There is a great deal of creativity in the judicial process, particularly when you are dealing with human rights, and the American experience shows this. But I am not suggesting for one moment that there should not be great care taken in the drafting, but we did not go into details very much in our brief. (33: 114–15)

**Mr. Mark Rose, MP (NDP, BC):** Under the matter of denominational schools or independent schools as I would prefer to call them, I do not have many problems with that concept of the moment. I did one time; I do not so much anymore. It seems to me there is a group right existing there and the right for parents to have some say rather than simply the state over what kinds of education people have for their own children. However, what concerns me is a recent case here involving a denominational school, a Catholic school, in which a Catholic teacher married a divorced person. Now, you have your group right to hire a Catholic teacher, you want that enshrined or at least you want that clarified. Now, when these group rights come into conflict with individual rights, what gives? Which right is superseded.

**Professor Joseph Magnet (Legal Counsel, Ontario Conference of Catholic Bishops):** I do not think it is possible to give an answer to that in the abstract. What you have posed there, I would like to write it down so that I could give it to my constitutional law students on their exam, that is precisely the kind of conflict for which we have courts. We cannot see precisely how these rights will come into conflict and when such a conflict arises what we need to have is all of the facts of that case and all of the policy materials of that case brought before the courts for a decision on that narrow question.

**Mr. Rose:** Just so that everybody understands the question, in a denominational school a Catholic teacher, a woman, married a divorced man, presumably a Protestant, and as a result lost her job. So it seems to me a direct conflict between individual rights, the right to choose one's mate, and the right of a group to hire someone who apparently or presumably supports the values of that group. That is one point, and you have answered it. (33: 85–6)

## The Need for a Clear Statement on Denominational Rights

**Miss Coline Campbell (LIB, NS):** Thank you. You are talking about a particular province. I am talking about a general statement of the right with the reasonable limitation clause, Section 1 – and that has had a lot of criticism. But it seems to me that overall where you have been given a protection of denominational schools under Section 93 and where it is a provincial matter under Section 93 ultimately the education in the province – does not that Section under a Charter of Rights and Freedoms protect you under that reasonable clause?

**Reverend Father Raymond Durocher (Conference of Catholic Bishops of Ontario):** You are introducing a Charter of Rights and you are giving it priority or primacy over everything else, it changes the situation in regard to guarantees in Section 93, because Section 93 then becomes just one of the provisions of that constitution and which actually could be subject to the Charters. That is why we think the situation is being changed to the detriment of the guarantees we have at the present time. There should be some clear statement that the new Charter which we most heartily approve is not to be construed as to limit the rights which we enjoy at the present time. (33: 72)

## Newfoundland

**Archbishop A. L Penney (Chairman, Denominational Education Committees of Newfoundland and Labrador):** In Newfoundland and Labrador, Mr. Chairman, we have a very unique situation with regard to a system of education. First of all, we have a system of education which is a public system of education, based in a denominational framework, and this public system of education based in a denominational framework is operated through a partnership of the government of Newfoundland and the churches in Newfoundland which are recognized for educational purposes.

This partnership is carried on through the joint services of the Department of Education representing the Government of Newfoundland and the Denominational Education Committees representing the churches. And in Newfoundland and Labrador there are three denominational education committees. There are the Integrated Education Committee, the Pentecostal Education Committee and the Catholic Education Committee. ...

Not only that, Mr. Chairman, but I would also like to submit to you that these rights of classes of people in Newfoundland to education, these rights are a very integral component of the very social fabric of our province. It is one of the distinguishing characteristics of the Province of Newfoundland in having the rights of people, all classes of people to education interwoven so intimately and so widely in the social fabric of the province. These rights guarantee the totality of education, both in regards to the truths communicated as well as to the opportunity of complete growth and development afforded to the student to enable him or her to live in our society, or in the society in which they find themselves.

I would submit to you that it is no exaggeration to state that if our denominational school rights were not protected to the extent that they were protected in the Terms of Union and in particular, in Term 17 of the Terms of Union in 1949, that due to the very narrow percentage points, a per cent and a half difference in the swinging of Confederation, or not having Confederation, Confederation very easily could never have happened at that time, but these rights were guaranteed in such a very minute and in a very thorough way.

I would also like to submit to you Mr. Chairman, and to help you to come to appreciate the very distinctive flavour of the denominational system of education in Newfoundland and I would, in bringing this to your attention, I would like to point out to you – I do believe it is on page 4 in the brief, Section 63 of the Schools Act. It states there:

> No School Board shall refuse admission to any school under its control solely on the ground that that child is of a religious faith which is not the denomination or one of the denominations of the school, if there is no school of his own religious persuasion reasonably available to him.

Section 64 states:

> No person shall, in any college or school aided by money granted under this Act, impart to any child attending it any religious instruction which may be objected to, in writing, by the parent or guardian of that child.

The saving feature of these two sections Mr. Chairman, I would like to underline, is the fact that in the 104 years that these have been on the statutes, that they have never been contested in court. That is an indication of the harmony in the quality of the relationship that exists within our public school system, being denominationally based. (35: 50–3)

**Bishop Martin Mate (Bishop of the Anglican Diocese of Eastern Newfoundland and Labrador):** Honourable Joint Chairmen, in Newfoundland and Labrador, as has been mentioned, we have now, as we have had for many generations, a public school system, denominationally based. When we came into Confederation great care was taken to recognize, protect and safeguard the system.

At present, for us in Newfoundland and Labrador, denominational rights in education are strongly entrenched in legislation. We are all confident that it is not intended that the Constitution Act, 1980 will adversely affect these existing rights and privileges. However, the absence of clear and precise statements aimed at the protection and preservation of these rights in the proposed Charter, a Charter that guarantees rights and freedoms to individuals, raises real concerns over the possibility that rights and privileges with regard to denominational schools could be eroded.

Specifically, the enactment of the proposed Charter, being a constitutional document of great authority, gives to the court of this and future generations the power of interpretation, interpretation in novel, unforeseen and unexpected ways in light of the evolving value system of Canadian society as interpreted and applied by the judges then presiding. The constitutional entrenchment of the Canadian Charter of Rights and Freedoms gives to the judges of this country the authority to declare unconstitutional, therefore illegal, any action of any group or institution that the court considers to have interfered with any of the rights and freedoms enumerated in it.

Our Committee therefore, representing approximately 97 per cent of the population of our province who are affiliated with the denominational groups now recognized in law for educational purposes, asks that the proposed constitution be amended to state specifically that rights and privileges with respect to denominational schools now enshrined in the present constitution of Canada, are rights and freedoms guaranteed under the proposed new Charter of Rights and Freedoms, and that the guarantee in the Charter of certain individual rights shall not abrogate or derogate from existing denominational rights.

... For the consideration of the Special Joint Committee on the Constitution of Canada, we propose the following draft amendments for inclusion in appropriate places in Part I of the constitution act, 1980:

> Any right or privilege with respect to denominational, separate or dissentient schools granted or secured under Section 93 of the Constitution Act, 1867, formerly named the British North America Act, 1867, as amended, or under any provision of the Constitution of Canada in substitution thereof, shall be a right or freedom guaranteed by the Canadian Charter of Rights and Freedoms.

> The guarantee in this Charter of certain rights and freedoms shall not be construed or interpreted as abrogating or derogating from any right or privilege with respect to denominational, separate or dissentient schools granted or secured under Section 93 of the Constitution Act, 1867 formerly named the British North America Act, 1867, as amended, or under any provision of the constitution of Canada in substitution thereof. (35: 53–4)

**Senator William Petten (LIB, Newfoundland):** As you point out in your brief, the Church sponsored the first schools and continued to do so for some 110 years, until 1836 when the government of the day decided to vote a little money, as I understand it, to help the cause of education. So one can see, because of the early involvement of the Church with education, that a partnership evolved between church and state and it has proved, in my opinion and in the opinion of many others, most satisfactory.

Having been born in and spending the first 40 odd years of my life in and around St. John's, and attending the denominational schools, I am well aware of the feelings of my fellow Newfoundlanders concerning our unique system of education. Your Grace will recall at the meetings with the Minister, which you referred to just a few moments ago, the Honourable Jean Chrétien, his assurance that our system of education in Newfoundland would not be changed and it was not the intention of the government to effect any changes whatsoever to our educational system and the conditions upon which Newfoundland and Canada agreed to when they entered Confederation in 1949, they would remain intact. It is not the intention to change the constitution which is not now only an important part of Newfoundland's heritage but that which has also become an important part of the Canadian mosaic.

... Bishop Mate, what would you think if it were somehow made clear that the Charter of Rights and Freedoms did not supersede any other part of the constitution, including Section 93? Do you think that this would alleviate your concerns about the effects of the Charter of Rights and Freedoms on the denominational school system? That is my question, sir.

**Bishop Mate:** I think I will ask our counsel to answer that one.

**Mr. James Greene (Legal Counsel, Denominational Educational Committees of Newfoundland and Labrador):** Senator Petten. Our brief sets out at some length the specific areas of our concern because it seems to us that the Charter of Rights, and I think I should make it clear that none of us here today are against the idea of recognizing and, indeed. enshrining individual rights, but it is a question which I know this Committee has considered on a number of occasions, the relationship between individual rights on the one hand, and group or collective rights on the other; and there is distinct danger, it seemed to us, particularly when it would be left to the courts of future years to determine just what was intended in that regard, and particularly in view, for example, of such sections as Section 25 of the draft act now before you which provides that any law that is inconsistent with the provisions of this Charter is, to the extent of such inconsistency, inoperative and of no force and effect.

That seemed to us to put the Charter of Rights on a special plateau and any law I suppose could be interpreted as meaning any other part of the constitution act, and if that were so, then perhaps simply referring to Section 93 or reconfirming Section 93 perhaps would not give us sufficient comfort in regard to the continued entrenchment of our rights because Archbishop Penney, in making his representation, referred to the fact that Section 91(1) of the BNA Act, which coincidentally came into the constitution of Canada the same year that Newfoundland did, it is the BNA Act number 2 of 1949, that gave the Parliament of Canada certain rights to legislate in the constitutional areas but removed or said that these rights did not extend to certain areas. I am sure all honourable members are aware of the limitations which Section 91(1) imposes now on the Parliament of Canada. One of these is that it may not make laws prejudicially affecting the rights and classes of persons with respect to schools.

... [Noting that the Prime Minister and the Minister of Justice had publicly stated that it was not the intention of the draft resolution to affect existing denominational rights] ...

Judges are not, in my opinion, are not entitled to consider the intention of legislators where they have clear words to follow, and if that is indeed the intention then we would see no objection to making two things very clear: one, that existing rights, and with the sole exception of the fact that we are now, the Pentecostal assemblies of Newfoundland are asking to have an amendment made to the constitution of Canada which was asked for by the legislature of Newfoundland 10 years ago, we would ask that that be acted on; but apart from that we are asking nothing new, we are not asking to have further rights given to us or any deeper entrenchment than we now have. We are simply saying please preserve to us the rights we now have, do not put us in the position of having to argue before some courts in years to come: oh, by necessary inference our rights are protected; or the Prime Minister of that day said it was not intended; or the Minister of Justice said we did not mean to do it.

... We ask two things in that regard, that first of all it be made clear that existing group rights in education be themselves declared to be rights under the Charter of Rights; and secondly, to avoid any doubt or uncertainty in the future we ask a declaration that the cataloguing, the setting forth of individual rights, such rights as freedom of conscience, freedom of religion, commendable though they be, that it be made clear that no individual can assert that right where to do so would be to jeopardize or call into question rights, analogous rights which those enjoy or other citizens enjoy as groups because there is perhaps no greater present demonstration in our law of a right of religion or a right of freedom of conscience than the school system that we enjoy in Newfoundland and which many of our fellow Canadians enjoy in other ways. I am quite satisfied that it is not the intention of the legislators to effect that by their wording but to put it beyond doubt it is our respectful submission, Senator, that express wording be used to that effect. (35: 62–5)

**Mr. Raymond J. Halley, Q.C. (President, Canadian Bar Association, Newfoundland Branch):** During the late forties Newfoundlanders in a national convention considered terms of union that were presented by Canada. These terms were debated for approximately a year and a half and after deliberation in a referendum Newfoundlanders chose to join Canada. Newfoundland became a province of Canada at midnight, March 31, 1949. These terms of union, which have been the centre of debate in our province concerning these constitutional proposals, confirm the Labrador boundary decision of the Privy Council which was given in 1927, and also provided for the organization and funding of our denominational, educational school system. Newfoundlanders have always believed that the terms of union could not be changed without the consent of the people of the province. ...

Regarding the Charter of Rights and Freedoms, there are two issues there, Section 2 concerning freedom of religion and Section 6 concerning the mobility provisions. Section 17 of our Terms of Union, as I mentioned, provide for the preservation of the denominational school system but also provide that these schools be funded publicly. There is concern, and we also expressed it, that the right of freedom of religion which is inherently good could be interpreted by the courts, as has been done in the United States, and could be detrimental to these denominational schools and their funding. Our concern is heightened in that Section 25 of the act provides that any law which is inconsistent with the provisions of this charter is, to the extent of such inconsistency, inoperative and of no force. We recognize that there are two points of view with respect to this matter concerning freedom of religion: one is by virtue of Section 25, term 17 would become inoperative, not binding; and the other view is that in our courts, in the Canadian courts they will view the definition of freedom of religion in light of Section 17 and in light of the history and tradition of the denominational, educational school system in the province. (9: 76–80)

...

## Amendment to Add Section 52

**Mr. Ron Irwin, MP (LIB, Ontario):** I have two questions. I would like to address my first question to Mr. Tassé, with the Minister's permission. I would like to address my first question to the Deputy Minister of Justice, and my second question to the Minister. Mr. Tassé, as you know, we had several religious groups attend here. They were very influential and very concerned religious groups across the country, who have expressed concern that although they favour strongly freedom of religion, nevertheless, they wish positively to discriminate within their own religions; for instance, that in the case of the Catholics, a rule that a teacher must be a Catholic in order to be teaching in that system is a positive discrimination as far as they are concerned. They want to make sure that the Charter of Rights, Section 15 and the right contained in there, dealing with nondiscrimination because of religion, does not affect that right positively to discriminate within a group.

I have noticed that you have added an amendment; the Minister has suggested an amendment, 52(1) as follows:

52(1) The Constitution of Canada is the supreme law of Canada, and any law that is inconsistent with the provisions of the Constitution is to the extent or the inconsistency, of no force or effect.

Can you explain to the Committee the legal process by which you would draw an inference – which I would assume you are drawing – that these positive rights to discriminate within religious groups will be protected?

**Mr. Tassé:** In the resolution before the Committee, that is to say the one without amendment, there is a Section 25 which provides, in effect that the provisions of the Charter would prevail, supersede, any provisions of the constitution. The question has been raised – and you have mentioned it – as to what the effect would be of the inclusion of freedom of conscience and religion on a section like Section 93 of the constitution which provides for denominational schools and protects them. A doubt has been raised to the effect that Section 2 would prevail over all other provisions of the constitution. that we would not unwittingly have imperilled the protection which had been given to denominational schools under Section 93.

That is the reason why we thought it would be preferable to have in Section 52 a reference to the supremacy of all the provisions of the constitution: but the sections of the Charter and the other provisions of the constitution, like Section 93, would have to be interpreted in relation to one another, and there is not one, like Section 2, which would supersede the other one. We are pretty confident that we are not affecting denominational schools here, and that teachers can continue to be hired in the Catholic, Protestant or whatever religious stream, and that it would be a bona fide requirement for the job in these schools that in effect they share the faith of the school system in which they would be hired. (38: 51–2)

**The Hon. James McGrath, MP (PC, Nfld):** Thank you, Mr. Chairman. I have a supplementary question to the Minister, having to do with group rights with regard to the provisions of Section 15(1). We have heard from the Roman Catholic School Trustees, the Bishops of Ontario, the Denominational Education Committees of Newfoundland, expressing concern about group rights. Indeed, one group felt that they should be given their right to discriminate, using the word "discriminate" in the traditional context and not in any racial sense as it has come to be used.

I would like to know if the Minister can tell the Committee what, in his view, would be the impact of Section 15 on, for example, the right of separate schools to hire teachers, particularly in the context of the provisions of Section 52 of the Charter. Could Section 15, for example, be used to prevent separate or private schools from hiring teachers who had to conform to the teachings or moral standards set by that particular school or religious denomination?

**The Hon. Jean Chrétien (Minister of Justice):** Mr. McGrath, you must have been absent from this room yesterday when we had a long exchange on that very issue. I gave that guarantee. Mr. Tassé explained the process under our questioning by Mr. Irwin.

**Mr. McGrath:** If you have already dealt with the matter yesterday, then I will not take up the time of the Committee further.

**Mr. Chrétien:** We said that there was no problem. It would be possible for any Catholic or other school board in Canada to keep hiring people of the same belief.

**Mr. McGrath:** It would be possible but will it be open to challenge?

**Mr. Chrétien:** It will not be open to challenge.

**Mr. McGrath:** Thank you. (39: 18–19)

**Mr. Brian Tobin, MP (LIB, Newfoundland):** I would like to go back to Section 52. Mr. Irwin mentioned the amendment regarding the primacy of the constitution of Canada. The earlier proposal in the Canada Act put forward made the Charter of Rights supreme, and any other law in Canada, or for that matter, in the constitution, inconsistent with the Charter will be over-ruled by the Charter of Rights. The amended version now says that the constitution in total and the Charter are supreme.

Now, what I am asking you in particular and for clarification is about Term 17 of the Terms of Union. May I assume from this, then, that Term 17 of the Terms of Union, the term which guarantees the right to denominational education systems of schooling in Newfoundland, that right is equal to the individual right spelled out in the Charter of Rights? Is that a fair assumption?

**Mr. Chrétien:** That is a view expressed by Mr. Tassé earlier. The [Charter of Rights] will have no supremacy over the [rest of the] constitution. This [Charter] of Rights, for example, the provision for freedom of religion, in the [Charter] of Rights, will not have supremacy over Section 93 of the constitution or resolution 17 of the Act of Union of Newfoundland to Canada.

**Mr. Tobin:** So you are saying, in your opinion, it is not conceivable that, based upon the rights provided for in the Charter of Rights, individual rights, it is not conceivable for one to test the collective rights, let us say, of the churches in operating a denominational school system anywhere in Canada? I am particularly concerned about Newfoundland.

**Mr. Chrétien:** Yes, that is correct.

**Mr. Tassé:** That is correct. In effect, Mr. Chairman, what I said earlier about Section 93 would equally apply to Section 17 of the Terms of Union between Newfoundland and Canada. (38: 55)

*Chapter Fifteen*

# Aboriginal Rights

*Undeclared Rights and Freedoms*

~~24~~ 25. The guarantee in the Charter of certain rights and freedoms shall not be construed as denying the existence of

(a) any aboriginal, treaty or other rights or freedoms that may pertain to the aboriginal peoples of Canada including any right or freedom that may have been recognized by the Royal Proclamation of October 7, 1763; or
(b) any other rights or freedoms that may exist in Canada.

**PART II**

**RIGHTS OF THE ABORIGINAL PEOPLES OF CANADA**

*Recognition of existing aboriginal and treaty rights*

**35.** (1) The existing aboriginal and treaty rights of the aboriginal peoples of Canada are hereby recognized and affirmed.

Definition of *"aboriginal peoples of Canada"*

(2) In this Act, *"aboriginal peoples of Canada"* includes the Indian, Inuit and Métis peoples of Canada.

---

*Land claims agreements*

(3) For greater certainty, in subsection (1) *"treaty rights"* includes rights that now exist by way of land claims agreements or may be so acquired.

*Aboriginal and treaty rights are guaranteed equally to both sexes*

(4) Notwithstanding any other provision of this Act, the aboriginal and treaty rights referred to in subsection (1) are guaranteed equally to male and female persons.

Note: *Section 35(3) and (4) were added in 1983, after the* Constitution Act, 1982 *was proclaimed. See Constitution Amendment Proclamation, 1983 (see* SI/84–102).

---

## Commentary

As discussed in the introduction and in chapter 3, Pierre Trudeau's government did not originally plan to entrench Aboriginal rights. Rather, the plan was to deal with Aboriginal issues in a subsequent round of constitutional negotiations to commence immediately after patriation.[1] It was envisioned that the content of Aboriginal rights would be agreed upon through negotiation at that time. Many witnesses – both Aboriginal and non-Aboriginal – expressed strong dissatisfaction with this plan. Mr. Donald Rosenbloom, legal counsel for the Nishga Tribal Council, stated, "To suggest that we patriate the constitution and then seek the consent of the provinces of Canada defies and ignores the history of the provincial government and its relationship to the native people of Canada. ... There will never be consent from the provinces to enshrine the principle and it is for that reason that we use our words cautiously when we say that the suggestions of the Prime Minister and that of the present Minister of Indian Affairs that Indian people should patiently wait until patriation, is, indeed, a suggestion which has to be a sham. There will be no entrenchment after patriation."[2]

The Trudeau government's rationale for originally not entrenching Aboriginal rights is briefly articulated at the beginning of this chapter

by Minister of Justice Jean Chrétien. Saskatchewan Premier Allan Blakeney testified before the Joint Committee that he opposed entrenching
Aboriginal rights because of his general approach to a charter of rights
and freedoms: "that one does not dare assert that which you are uncertain about, and I think it is fair to say that we are uncertain about the
nature, scope and extent of the historic rights which pertain to Indians,
Inuit, Metis or other native peoples."[3]

The only provision in the draft Charter before the Joint Committee
that touched on Aboriginal rights was section 24 (which became section 25) and did so only by negative implication. More than one-third
(thirty-seven) of the witnesses who appeared before the committee
argued for entrenchment, fewer than half of whom were representatives of Aboriginal peoples.[4] Due to space limitations, this chapter is
unable to reproduce this aspect of the debate before the Committee. It
is no exaggeration to say that it would fill a book in itself. It includes
accounts of the history of Indigenous peoples in this country and their
relationship with the Crown. Many Aboriginal groups emphasized the
promises made by the British Crown to Aboriginal nations and tribes
generally and specifically in the Royal Proclamation of 1763. A few references are included to give the reader a flavour of both the substance
and the fervour of the discussion.

The Royal Proclamation was frequently described as the cornerstone
of Aboriginal rights and Aboriginal title in Canada; however, there
was no consensus on exactly what the Royal Proclamation had granted
and to whom. Mr. Vic Savino, legal counsel for the Native Council of
Canada, described it as "the source document from which aboriginal
title in this country stems."[5] The government acknowledged that First
Nations' rights stemmed from the Proclamation but not Inuit or Métis
rights.[6] Yet one Inuit group said the Proclamation gave them status as
a nation.[7] Many groups wanted the Proclamation to be included in the
Schedule to the Constitution and thus "constitutionalized" to protect
the rights flowing from it.[8] The government refused this request on the
grounds that only documents created after 1867 could be included in
the Constitution of Canada.[9] However, a reference to the Proclamation
was included in the final version of section 25.

Many Aboriginal groups were distrustful of judicial interpretations
of their rights[10] – especially given that the judiciary was, and continues
to be, overwhelming composed of non-Aboriginal judges.[11] For those
wary of the courts, the threat of judicial interpretation was amplified by
the lack of definition of Aboriginal rights or Aboriginal title – the 1973

*Calder* case had revealed that the Supreme Court was not prepared to be a staunch enforcer of Aboriginal title.[12] A member of the Algonquin Council was offended that "we must prove indigenous title in courts of an alien system which by its very nature constitutes a subterfuge of justice to our people."[13] Other groups thought judicial interpretation was an acceptable part of enshrining rights.[14]

In discussing Aboriginal rights, there was much questioning from committee members about the definition of such terms as *Aboriginal, Indian, Métis,* and *Inuit.* Most commentators thought Aboriginal groups should be able to decide this themselves (as opposed to the courts), and the government ultimately agreed. Aboriginal women's groups made their presence felt at the Joint Committee and articulated the concerns of Aboriginal women, despite the fact that male-dominated Aboriginal groups had received government funding to participate in the patriation process while they had not.[15] Métis groups played an important role as well.

The territories played a strong and vocal role in advocating for Aboriginal rights. The proposal to divide the Northwest Territories into two territories, creating Nunavut for better representation of the Inuit people, was already under way.[16]

### Explanation for Non-entrenchment of Aboriginal Rights

**Senator Paul Lucier (LIB, Yukon):** ... Section 24 [which became section 25] ... seems to me a rather negative statement. It really says that the rights that they now have will not be jeopardized. I am just wondering if there could not be something more positive than that to protect the native people. There really seems to be nothing in there that would protect what they feel are very genuine concerns of theirs. I wonder if anything can be done to make it more positive than to just say that we will not do anything to hurt you.

**The Hon. Jean Chrétien (Minister of Justice and Attorney General of Canada):** What we are trying to do in, I think it is Section 24 we want to protect all the rights of the natives. The problem is, some are arguing at this time it is in a negative way rather than in a positive way. Exactly the reason why we are doing that is to make sure that all the rights be protected because in Canada we still need some clarification to come to an agreement about native rights.

I have been working on that problem myself for many years and there is the right based on the treaty, the right that was given to the natives at the time of the royal proclamation of 1762 or 1763 by King George II and the instruction he gave to his colonies at this time to settle the rights of the natives, there is the question of the rights that have been either abandoned by some of them or have been taken away by different actions of governments in the past. It is a very complex issue, and in having this Clause drafted that way we wanted to make sure that we were not creating any prejudice to their rights, so we say all the rights they have today will not be changed by this bill.

If we were to move into an affirmative declaration of the rights at this moment, if the Committee wants to make the change, it could be that in affirming the rights we could make an error. Now, negatively, we are telling them there is no way we want to take any rights away from you, but if you start to affirm them you might leave some rights outside of the affirmation and that is why the drafter decided to proceed by the negative route. ... This has been going on with the Indians for a long time and to incorporate that type of problem in one of the clauses could be very dangerous, to try to solve it in six lines; so in having a negative presentation like this we are trying to protect and keep their rights as they are without prejudicing them in any way. (3: 32–4)

## Historical Context and the Royal Proclamation

**Mr. Eric Tagoona (Co-Chairman, Inuit Committee on National Issues)**: ... In order to trace our history to the modern day, it is essential to have some appreciation of the relationship which existed between the aboriginal peoples and the Imperial Crown. Our status as a nation is given some legal confirmation and protection in the Royal Proclamation of October 7, 1763. This constitutional document, which states our special and unique historical relationship with the Imperial Crown, has been called both an Indian bill of rights, and a charter of Indian rights, due to its fundamental importance to aboriginal peoples in Canada. While the Royal Proclamation, by nature, is not a law of the Imperial Parliament, it does have the same legal effect as a statute. Furthermore, its provisions relating to aboriginal lands still have the full force of law in Canada.

As indicated in our brief to the Foreign and Commonwealth Affairs Committee of the British House of Commons, the Royal Proclamation clearly reflects several basic principles that underline the relationship existing between the aboriginal peoples of Canada and the Imperial Crown. These principles:

1. recognize the aboriginal peoples as nations;
2. imply the necessity of mutual consent to alterations in the relationship;
3. confirm and protect the aboriginal rights in and to lands in Canada covered by the Royal Proclamation;
4. imply a right of aboriginal self-government in those areas not ceded to the Crown.

As evidenced by the Royal Proclamation, the aboriginal peoples of Canada interacted with Imperial representatives very much like nations in the international sense. This status as nations within Canada vests in us rights not held by others who later immigrated to Canada. As original inhabitants, such rights flowed as a natural consequence from our historical status and position. (16: 5–6)

**Mr. Jack Woodward (Legal Counsel, Nuu-Chah-Nulth Tribal Council):** I want to say a word about the Royal Proclamation and its historical significance which will perhaps make clear the reason we reached the conclusion that you, your Committee, the Parliament of Canada is bound to include it and its principle in the definition of the constitution, section 52.

The Proclamation – and I recommend that you all obtain a copy and read it – it can be found in the Constitutional Appendix to the Revised Statutes of Canada, in your office. It was issued as a result of the Treaty of Paris of 1763, at the conclusion of the Seven Years' War.

In the United States, that same Seven Years' War called the French and Indian War, the British had two allied enemies on this continent during that war, the French and the Indians, and when it came time to make peace in the vast new territories acquired by the British, the British Government – and I say the British Government, not just the King because this Proclamation was issued by advice and consent – it required a royal guarantee for both the former enemies if they were to avoid interminable guerrilla warfare in the territories. To the French was granted the self-governing colony of Quebec; to the Indians, an explicit recognition of and guarantee of their aboriginal title, explicit protection of minority interest, as the foundation of a new peace in the expanding British Dominion. That is what the Royal Proclamation of 1763 was all about.

The process which began in 1763 has evolved dramatically for Quebec. All of the fundamentals of a self-governing minority are preserved in each successive constitutional document: in the Quebec Act of 1774, in the BNA Act of 1867. For the Indians, there have been a series of treaties, according to the terms of the Proclamation whereby aboriginal title is purchased from the Indians. For those Indians who have not signed treaties, the Proclamation most surely applies as their continuing royal guarantee. In any case, we wish to make clear and we support the principle enunciated this afternoon by the National Indian Brotherhood that the doctrine of aboriginal title existed as a constitutional principle of the common law prior to 1763. The Proclamation merely reiterates the principle and provides some machinery for giving it effect. (27: 128–31)

**Mr. George Watts (Chairman, Nuu-Chah-Nulth Tribal Council):** ... I would first of all like to talk about who we are. The Nuu-Chah-Nulth people are the people of the West Coast of Vancouver Island. Today, we have 15 bands and we have some 4,200 people that belong to our Tribal Council. The Constitution can only set the stage for us to exist as Indian people. We do not want any kind of programs, cultural programs to guarantee that we exist as Indian people. My people still have our way of life. We still have our own laws. We still have our own culture. We have our own language. We have our own societies.

The time has come for the government of this country to now recognize that and to quit attempting to try to change us, to make us better Canadians. We are prepared to be Canadians. We want to be Canadians but we can only be Canadians and good Canadians if we are allowed to be Indians and the only way that we can be allowed to be Indians is if you allow us to have our land and our sea and our resources because that is where our history as Indian people lies. (27: 126–7)

...

**Chief Stanley Johnson (President, Union of Nova Scotia Indians):** ... We have two questions which we would like the Committee to ponder and answer for us. First, will the Canada Act freeze the notions of a superior European race and culture into constitutional law or is it an attempt to break the history of colonialism and racism in Canada? Second, does Canada still believe that tribal society is an evolutionary cul-de-sac in political development which is preordained to vanish by the will of racial genes and scientific racism or that it is entitled to the same protections as the French people in Canada? These are dangling questions in the debate over the Canada Act. The answer to these questions would help our society address the Canada Act in a more rational manner. (32: 84–7)

## On Aboriginal Rights

**Mr. George Braden, MLA (Leader of the Elected Members of the Executive Committee, Government of the Northwest Territories):** There is even a lot of controversy about the use of the term "aboriginal rights." Well, Mr. Chairman, we are not hung up on that and we think that the rights of the native people can be negotiated and defined between the native organizations and the Government of Canada – a process which is taking place right now. (12: 85–6)

**Miss Mary Simon (Member, Inuit Committee on National Issues):** ...

Conclusions and Recommendations

Inuit have, and must continue to have, a homeland within Canada. This is our birthright. It is also our right in law, as reflected in the terms of the Royal Proclamation of 1763.

Our status as Inuit within Canada must not be altered without our consent.

Aboriginal rights are an inseparable part of our identity as Inuit.

The right to our identity is enshrined in international law, and this principle has been accepted by the Government of Canada.

There are constant pressures of assimilation in the existing political, legal and economic make-up of Canada which seriously threaten to erode our identity.

The proposed resolution further compromises Inuit status by refusing to recognize our status within Canada. The proposed resolution compromises Inuit status by ignoring the necessity of obtaining our consent in relation to further changes in our status.

The proposed resolution leaves little real opportunity for obtaining constitutional amendments in our favour in the postpatriation period.

It is therefore critical that prepatriation amendments in favour of aboriginal peoples be obtained which give some indication of our relationship with governments in Canada.

In this regard we therefore propose:

That our right to Inuit identity be enshrined as a principle in the proposed resolution.

That, in accordance with this principle, the future of Inuit in Canada be premised upon the principle of self-determination within the Canadian federation.

12. That within this context, the Government of Canada commit itself to negotiate a framework of constitutional rights and protections for aboriginal peoples.

That our aboriginal rights, as an inseparable part of our individual and collective identities, must not be subject to extinguishment by Parliament.

That the participation of the aboriginal peoples of Canada in future constitutional conferences as promised by the Government of Canada be formalized in the proposed resolution in a manner similar to the commitment made to the provinces.

That any further amendments to the constitution that make specific reference to the aboriginal peoples of Canada should not be permitted without the consent of those aboriginal peoples so affected.

That the Royal Proclamation of 1763 and the Order-in-Council respecting Rupert's Land be included in Schedule 1 of the proposed resolution so as to be clearly recognized as part of the constitution of Canada.

That mobility rights in the Charter be further limited so as to protect the cultural, economic, social and environmental interests of the aboriginal peoples, particularly in light of special needs and conditions in the northern regions of Canada. (16: 16–17)

## Definition of Aboriginal Rights

**Mr. Peter Ittinuar (NDP, NWT):** One more brief question. I would like to ask you about the definition of aboriginal rights, whether you have one or whether it is something you can state to people on an equal basis and, again to allay the fears of people generally, whether these proposed amendments you have take away anything from the people of Canada.

**Mr. Gordon (Inuit Committee on National Issues):** To define aboriginal rights in this brief time that we have is almost impossible, to try and encompass all the concepts involved in what we call aboriginal rights, but basically what it means to us is the right to live as a distinct society within Canada, with the right to go within Canada and the rights to our lands and to our heritage. These rights encompass areas of our culture which would include even areas of family law or our particular notion of collective property rights in and to the lands. There is not enough time to try to include everything that could possibly be included in this but aboriginal rights are not an outright claim on the entire territory, so we can exclude everyone else. We are only asking the right to be able to exist in dignity and as an organized society with the opportunity to grow with other societies in Canada. (16: 24)

**The Hon. Warren Allmand, MP (LIB, PQ):** Some members of Parliament have said to us that they do not know what you mean by aboriginal rights. You should define it. I have asked other witnesses before the Committee if they have a definition or whether they think it should be left to the courts to define. What is your position?

**Mr. Harry Daniels (Native Council of Canada):** Oh well, I must draw on the strength of the Oxford dictionary, which states in respect to aboriginal rights: "Any rights that the people held before the colonists arrived." That implies to me, linguistic rights, land rights, the right of access to resources; cultural rights, social rights, political rights, religious rights. Those are the aboriginal rights; those are the rights of people.

Those statements or responses by government people to the effect that they do not know what aboriginal rights are, are an indication of either a great deal of ignorance of the English language or their unwillingness to accept that these people, who were a nation of people, rich in culture with linguistic differences, with a social system, with a very definite political system with dealings with each other, and a way of holding land – that is the aboriginal right; before the arrival of Europeans on these shores, whoever got here first, whether it was the Vikings or Jacques Cartier, the people operating within a set mode and in different geographical areas, and these people are now saying, "We want to continue that." And that is our aboriginal right to do so. (17: 128–9)

**Mr. Warren Allmand, MP (LIB, PQ):** Some people have said that we cannot put the term aboriginal rights in the constitution now because it is not well defined, and if it is not well defined, putting it in just like that, let us say confirm your aboriginal rights, your land rights, to put it in simple terms like that might go against you in the future, but there are many other people that say: look, just put it in like that and you will define it in the future, it will be defined if you have to go to court to do it or if you have to negotiate to do it, but you would like it in just very simple terms right now? ...

**Mr. Rob Milen (Legal Counsel, Association of Métis and Non-Status Indians of Saskatchewan):** Mr. Allmand, we believe that by putting the word "aboriginal" there it sufficiently opens the door for us to go and do our homework, to prove to the government of Canada, or if necessary to the courts, what rights we have. We feel that would sufficiently open the door for the Indian, Inuit, Métis or nonstatus peoples, whatever, to then convince the government to go sit down with their people community by community, provide all the historical research.

We ask you, we believe, a very simple thing, by putting the word "aboriginal" there. Then we have got to do our homework. It is not good enough to put the word "aboriginal" in there, then we have got to go back and it may take years to get all that evidence, we are trying to get that evidence now, but then our homework really begins because we are prepared to take our case to the Canadian government, the Canadian people, or failing that, to the courts. (22: 48–9)

...

**Mr. Jim Hawkes, MP (PC, AB):** Are you not concerned, though, Mr. Sinclair, that once you put a clause like this in the Charter that in effect you have turned jurisdiction over to the courts and they will in fact define. I wonder about a situation, for instance, if you buy some of that land, if you negotiate an agreement, then people sue to be included within the definition of Métis because you have found a lot of oil or some other kind of resource on that land, and that the courts might uphold those claims, is that a concern at all or not?

**Mr. Jim Sinclair (Association of Métis and Non-Status Indians of Saskatchewan):** The concern that we have, it is like going from the fox to the wolf, who is going to be tougher on us, the courts or the politicians. Like I say, that is going to be another road but I would personally feel that something should be enshrined in the constitution that we could at least take to the court because if we leave it to the whims of the politicians who will change it because the majority says so, and you get elected by the majority, we are in trouble. Again, the other thing that is wrong with the democratic system, and I see it wrong in Canada today, is the fact that in a democracy the majority seems to trample on the rights of the minority groups and it leaves us out.

**Mr. Nelson Riis, MP (NDP, BC):** Does the Chamber of Commerce recognize the concept of aboriginal rights?

**Mr. Duncan McKillop (Chairman of Task Force on Constitutional Change, Alberta Chamber of Commerce):** Well, we have not directed our attention to it, we have not discussed it. It is hard to deny, though, that the natives, all natives perhaps including the Métis, have aboriginal rights and that they should be dealt with. (27: 52)

...

**Mr. Paul Williams (Union of Ontario Indians, as the agent for Anishinabek):** We also want to explain that we do not have what you call Indian rights. The rights of each of these nations, in relation to the Crown, are different; because the treaties of each of these nations with the Crowns contained different terms. Thus the Ojibways do not have Indian rights; they have Ojibway rights. The Micmacs do not have Indian rights; they have Micmac rights. Canada's Indian Act has been an attempt to take a diversity of nations, with a diversity of relationships with the Crown, and to generalize, and then in the process of this generalization to lose sight of certain rights, certain specific relationships, because each of these is different.

I should also like to point out that we are not discussing the kind of rights that are described in the proposed Charter of Rights and the resolution. Canada, with its European heritage, understands things in terms of relations between the individual and his government. The rights we are talking about are not individual rights. They are the rights of groups. There is nothing in the proposed Charter of Rights that deals in any way with collective rights. What we are discussing here are collective rights and not individual rights.

**Ms. Delia Opekokew (Legal Counsel, Federation of Saskatchewan Indians):** Aboriginal rights relates to the right for the Indian people to have their ownership to the lands and people to control those resources and lands, so it is a two aspect answer. Presently in the court system in Canada aboriginal title only recognizes the right to occupancy without recognizing the right to self-determination and the right to control, so it is a two aspect answer, and for that reason also because of how much control you want, et cetera, an indefinite type of statement, it is very difficult to answer the second aspect of it, except to say that is where the right to self-determination comes in. ...

**Mr. Ron Irwin, MP (LIB, ON):** ... What you are saying is your definition of aboriginal is not [what] the courts, at least in a minority position, have decided what is the definition of aboriginal, and you want these amplified to fit what you feel are your traditional aboriginal rights. (31: 86–7)

**Mr. Graydon Nicholas (Chairman of the Board, Union of New Brunswick Indians):** ... Aboriginal rights include our right to exist as Indians, to govern ourselves and to determine our livelihood, political, cultural, economic, social and legal units. We have these rights and much more, because we have never been conquered, never released or extinguished our aboriginal rights in New Brunswick. In fact, our very essence of belief is that we cannot sign our rights away.

How can we, as descendants, sign away aboriginal rights that have existed since time immemorial for our past, present and future generations of Indians? We would not – and there is evidence to support the fact that up to now our past and present Indian leaders would not – sign our Indianness away and would not break away from our traditional aboriginal rights. Aboriginal rights are much more than a slogan, more than a people, because they include our spiritual, cultural, physical and emotional needs. We hope that you, as honourable representatives of Canada, will act with due faith and freedom of thought to accept the principle that aboriginal rights do exist today in New Brunswick. (32: 77–8)

...

### Definition of Aboriginal Peoples

**Senator Duff Roblin (PC, Manitoba):** ... I wonder if you could give me some idea of who you think about when you refer to "every person of aboriginal descent." Now we have a definition in the Indian Act which, I am sure, would not be a completely satisfactory definition from your point of view; and we do know that Indian people are very widely spread in our community; we also know that there are various categories of status, nonstatus Indians, Métis and other descriptions. How do you look at this expression "every person of aboriginal descent"? Where is the cut-off line? How far would you go? Can you help us to define this idea?

**Ms. Marlee Pierre-Aggamaway (Native Women's Association of Canada):** To be of aboriginal descent is to be born of at least one parent who two generations before descended from the first people. Now, that is a first kind of description we are giving you in answer to that. That is not an acceptable definition at this point in time and has not been thoroughly discussed and agreed to by our own nations. But those are some of the offerings. (17: 76)

...

**Mrs. Nellie Carlson (Western Vice President, Indian Rights for Indian Women):** My definition of an Indian across Canada is that an Indian who had been born and raised in this country, who had never come from across the ocean to immigrate into this country, but was born and raised, had lived through the hardships but yet, at the same time, as Indian people we have our own highly spiritual belief which we transmit to our children, an Indian language, which a non-Indian woman cannot do to give that kind of transmission of an Indian belief or an Indian language which we have. We have these traditions for thousands and thousands and thousands of years. Indian people have been here and they have their certain spiritual beliefs, that is my definition of an Indian and that is something that no other race of people could transmit. (17: 97)

**Senator Duff Roblin (PC, Manitoba):** One last question, which has to do with the definition you have [of] aboriginal peoples in Canada. I take it you are certainly not satisfied with the definition which appears in the Indian Act these days. I take it that you are also supporting the appeal of Indian women to be treated in all respects equally with Indian men in connection with the definition of aboriginal peoples. I am glad to hear that. But I would press you to consider a further definition, because the question of where the Metis status begins and takes off, and where the non-status Indian begins and takes off is always a very perplexing problem.

I suppose that the real answer is to say that anyone who says, "I am an aboriginal" thinks himself to be one and living in that society probably is one way of approaching it, so that it becomes a self-defining term. But I can assure you it is going to cause a lot of trouble in defining that expression in any advance we make to improve this measure; and any help you can give us in clarifying the matter will be most helpful to me.

**Mr. Harry Daniels (President, Native Council of Canada):** We, Senator Roblin, have stated time and time again that we will decide who aboriginal people are.

We have been suffering with artificial definitions for so long and forced to play a silly game of who is an aboriginal person, who is an Indian, who is not an Indian, who is a Metis, a non-status and franchised

Indian, a treaty Indian, a non-treaty Indian, a registered Indian or a non-registered Indian. There are about 14 definitions of who we are.

Now, in the context of identifying who the native people are, there is a simple process and I think it is one that the Maori's have used and the aboriginal people of Australia are using, that they will decide for themselves. If you are Maori and the Maori's accept you and you have ancestry to the Maori people, however limited your blood and the Maori people accept you, then you are a Maori. If you are an aboriginal with blue eyes and black curly hair, it does not matter to them as long as you accept the lifestyle, the culture, you are accepted by the people, you have ancestry there and you are part of the community, they will decide who the aboriginal people are, rather than have someone alien to our culture decide for us. Does anybody tell the Israelis who is an Israeli, does anybody tell the Quebecois what a Quebecois is, does anybody tell a Basque what a Basque is, does anybody try and tell the Walloons who the Walloons are, does anybody try to tell a Welshman who a Welshman is, does anybody try to tell an Irishman or a Scotsman; no, it is a white concept that they will tell the Indians who they are. Why us? Why tell the blacks who they are, why tell the Maori's. We know who we are. It does not matter the pigment of the skin if there is white blood in you. I am half white and half Indian, I have never been called white in my life. Why does not someone say, Harry, you are a white man. I have been an Indian all my life. I have chosen to be an Indian. I have been labelled as a Metis, as part of the Metis nation, but I am a Metis Indian.

My mother and I grew up, we spoke three languages at home, French, English and Cree. We had to be able to do those kinds of things. Talk about bilingualism, many of our people speak four and five languages by association of alienation cultures. We will decide who a native person is, we do not want anybody or anybody should not suggest that they have the right to decide for us who we are. We will not decide for the Quebecois, we will not decide for the English, we will not decide for anybody in this country, the Ukrainians, the Romanians, anybody. We let them decide for themselves. (17: 132–3)

**Senator Paul Lucier (LIB, NWT):** ... I would like to have a definition of some kind, if it is possible, how can we deal with aboriginal peoples without knowing what "aboriginal peoples" means? I have heard the words "nonstatus," "status," "Indian," "native": I do not think the people know what it means and if you know, could you tell us, and if you do not know, how are we going to find out?

**Mr. Delbert Riley (National Indian Brotherhood):** One of the things we have been attempting to do with the present and past governments is to sit down and negotiate this. We have been attempting this since the early 1960's and early 1970's, but to no avail.

**Senator Lucier:** How about if you were to go somewhere, and in fact why would you not just appear as one group, why do you call yourselves status and nonstatus and metis, why would you not be just one group and present yourselves to the government as one group, they would have no alternative but to accept you as such?

**Mr. Riley:** Well, we are Indians, and probably for some of the same basic reasons that: why do you need three parties to run Canada?

**Senator Lucier:** We do not. We need one to run it and two to oppose.

**Mr. Riley:** Why do you not all get together?

**Senator Lucier:** We keep trying. I am just really confused, Mr. Riley, and I am not trying to be difficult about this, I really am confused because I keep reading the words "aboriginal people" and I really do not know what it means, and I would think before you continue to talk about aboriginal peoples in all the sections you might outline, that we should know what aboriginal peoples are, know what we are dealing with?

**Mr. Riley:** There are three basic peoples: Indian, Inuit and you have the Metis and nonstatus. That is the three, the only three that I can see, and well, I have a tough time understanding what a Canadian is. I do not know, you tell me. (27: 103–4)

## Métis Rights

**Mr. Harry Daniels (President, Native Council of Canada):** Canadian history records a legal and political tradition of recognition of the aboriginal rights of mixed blood people. ... In the 19th Century the most prominent recognition of our rights was on the prairies where the Metis had emerged as a distinct national group and had asserted national rights against the Selkirk Colony, against the Hudson's Bay Company and, in the Provisional Government of 1869, against the Government of Canada. The Government of Canada met with negotiators representing the Provisional Government and the terms of the Manitoba Act were drafted and agreed to. The Manitoba Act was passed by the Provisional Government, by the Canadian Parliament and confirmed by Imperial legislation.

It stands as part of the Constitution of Canada. The Manitoba Act recognized Metis land rights and provided, in addition to their holdings in 1870, for an additional Metis land base of 1.4 million acres. (17: 107–15)

**Mme Hervieux-Payette (LIB, Quebec):** I would like to ask Mr. Daniels, finally, why he is so suspicious concerning the provinces and the recognition of the Metis rights? Probably he is more competent than I am to give me and my colleagues a summary of the problems the Metis have with the provincial governments.

**Mr. Harry Daniels (President, Native Council of Canada):** Well, the provincial governments have not been that much of a problem. They would be a problem if the amending formula went through as it is. The problem that exists now and has existed is with the federal government and their denial and their unwillingness or incapability of dealing with the rights of the Metis and nonstatus Indian people of Canada. As Mr. Savino pointed out, that if the amending formula goes through as it exists, unilaterally or bilaterally, the federal government with the province at that time becoming a problem could abrogate all those rights we have. So at this point we have been shuffled from the federal government to the provincial carpet many times, and every time we get to the provinces, and in that respect they are a problem, they always say that you are a federal responsibility and are unwilling to verbalize that in public in any kind of way or support us. (17: 123)

...

**Mr. Douglas Anguish, MP (NDP, SK):** ... How do you in future propose to go about proving or identifying who the Metis people are?

**Mr. Jim Sinclair (President, Association of Métis and Non-Status Indians of Saskatchewan):** We will do that by setting up a process by which we will identify our own people. We are working on that now, and have been doing research of our own. We are doing it ourselves, and we will present that when the time is right.

**Mr. Anguish:** Do you think it is possible to find and identify who the Metis people are?

**Mr. Sinclair:** The organization will have to do it, because no one else can. (22: 138)

**Mr. Anguish:** ... What do you visualize, if your concerns are met, what do you visualize the Metis nation as being?

**Mr. Jim Sinclair (President, Association of Métis and Non-Status Indians of Saskatchewan):** Well, all right, the Metis nation of course is people and what we are saying again is that we are not looking at a separate system or separate government because the referendum in Quebec has shown there is not that desire. What we are saying is that we feel the Metis nation could extend from Northwestern Ontario into Northeastern British Columbia and the people that we talked to are prepared to sit down and negotiate pieces of land here and there, that we will say: look, this is ours and we will develop it the way we want to. We will meet on the basis of talking to each other, not on the basis that we want control or to form our own government, but we do have to have control over our own land and some economics of our own because that is the only way we are going to carry our fair share of the load. (22: 141–2)

## Aboriginal Title

**Mr. Frank Oberle, MP (PC, BC):** I would say this, that some of us have a better perception of what the term aboriginal title means. I would daresay if you go around the Committee here everyone would come up, likely, with a different version of what aboriginal title means. There is no jurisprudence, the courts have never decided what it means, what aboriginal title means, and I daresay it means different things to different Indian groups in different parts of the country as well. So the entrenchment of aboriginal title, there has got to be a definition to it, or are you relying on the Declaration of 1763 to define the term aboriginal title?

**Mr. Donald Rosenbloom (Legal Counsel, Nishga Tribal Council):** Clearly, once you enshrine the doctrine of aboriginal title, there will be judicial interpretation made on the meaning of that term. We concede that once there has been an entrenchment of the principle, that principle will require continuous interpretation by the judicial bodies of this nation, but that is no different, Mr. Oberle, from the requirement to continuously go through a definition process in terms of freedom of speech, freedom of assembly, freedom of religion, issues about whether under freedom of religion Jehovah's Witnesses can refuse to have their children take blood transfusions; issues about freedom of assembly, whether that freedom entitles a group to obstruct traffic through a roadway. Every day in this country the courts are being called upon with the present Bill of Rights to define what is meant by the principle as it is placed in the Bill of Rights. Indeed, if you look at the history of the United States with their Constitution and their rights enshrined in a document, the courts are being called upon to give an interpretation.

It is the essence of this country that the courts go through an interpretation process, a definition process to refine principles that are placed in documents and in legislation in a general way. We do not pretend that the courts will not be called upon to take your move one step further, but we say that it is false to say we cannot enshrine the principle of aboriginal title in the constitution because we are not completely sure of all its elements for definition, but you are willing to enshrine all the other freedoms as listed in your Charter that I suggest are equally vague, that equally will call upon the courts of this nation to interpret, and we say that we just want equal treatment in terms of aboriginal title with all the other freedoms that are in their present day form in the Charter as the Charter is before you. (26: 33–4)

...

**Mr. Jack Woodward (Legal Counsel, Nuu-Chah-Nulth Tribal Council):** ... With respect to the doctrine of aboriginal title and the Royal Proclamation of 1763, we submit that they are at the present time part of the constitution of Canada. The former is a common law principle of binding constitutional effect. The latter is a constitutional document which predates Confederation but which persists as part of the Canadian constitutional law. These two fundamental laws are explicitly intended to protect Native people from the abuse and displacement they could expect with the invasion of the Europeans. It is the protection of a minority, exactly the kind of purpose for which we have designed constitutional entrenchment, the concept of constitutional entrenchment. (27: 129–30)

## Treaties

**Mr. Graydon Nicholas (Chairman of the Board, Union of New Brunswick Indians):** We have not released our treaty rights; yet we continue to face prosecution in courts at the authority of the Attorney General who shows no respect for our solemn treaties. We have lived up to our end of the bargain, and yet we face harassment and persecution. Our people cannot afford to pay their fines. Why has Parliament sat silently and allowed our treaty rights to be abrogated by federal legislation, such as the Fisheries Act, the Migratory Birds Convention Act, the National Parks Act and the regulations enacted at the whim of conservation officers who advised the appropriate Minister? We have been denied the equitable and just exercise of our treaty rights without compensation, without consultation and without our consent. There were two parties represented in those treaties. How come we are now denied our right to participate and protect our treaties?

There is a solution to this dilemma. They are presented in the part touching on entrenchment. We will also never sign away our treaty rights. It is beyond our authority. Besides, treaties are not like contracts and agreements. They are solemn commitments and obligations on both sides, a sacred covenant.

... Our treaty and aboriginal rights have to be protected, have to be safeguarded, preserved. Our unique relationship with the Crown has to be manifested by entrenchment into this country's most sacred, solemn and honourable constitution. (32: 78–9)

**Dr. Sageth Henderson (Legal Advisor, Union of Nova Scotia Indians):** ... Basically treaty federalism preceded provincial federalism. Treaty federalism is where your original treaty between the Indian nations, the Micmac nation and the Crown, which allocated jurisdiction both to the Crown and reserve lands and jurisdiction in the tribal polity. That has remained untouched over all these years except for the lack of administration of the Crown's responsibility, first by provincial agents of the Crown and now the federal agents.

Provincial federalism is basically the same idea in a more elaborate form. It is the essence of the notion that the Quebec referendum, when it went to Great Britain and was introduced into the Imperial Parliament, it was introduced, the British North America Act, as a treaty of union between the peoples of those provinces to create a bigger and better form of responsible government. They are virtually identical in theory and origin. The only difference is that the Indian tribes were acknowledged as members of the law of nations whereas the British Parliament would not go so far as to acknowledge the provinces having any standing in the international community until quite recently, 1931. That is the major difference. (32: 92)

## Aboriginal Nationhood and Aboriginal Self-Government

**Ms. Marlee Pierre-Aggamaway (Native Women's Association of Canada):** ... We believe that the constitution of Canada, not the charter of rights, must state that the aboriginal people belong to sovereign nations and by putting this statement in the constitution we feel that the Government of Canada, by doing so, will ensure that the aboriginal people will be recognized as sovereign nations and as a third order of government.

The way it is now, rights can be denied by Parliament but if they are entrenched, they cannot be tampered with. We want to be recognized in the same way as it is being presented, there being two founding nations of English and French and also Indian government.

**The Hon. John Fraser, MP (PC):** Okay, let us see if I have got your point. Are you saying to me, and I think you are, that you represent the original peoples of this country and that as a consequence of that, that you have certain inherent and historical rights, some of which were confirmed by treaties and some of which have been granted by agreements since then, but that what you are really after is a recognition of your identity as a people within the total Canadian community and the people with whom the rest of us in our dealings with you must reach substantial agreement if the actions of the rest of the community impinge upon your identity and your rights as a people, as part of the Canadian family, but as a distinct people within that family. Is that what you are getting at?

**Ms. Pierre-Aggamaway:** Yes, nationhood within nation.

**Mr. Fraser:** All right. Now, let me understand the word "nation." As I take it, what you mean is nation in the sense of the people, not nation in the sense of necessarily a political entity. Can you help me on that?

**Ms. Pierre-Aggamaway:** I hope I said third order of government and 1 am not sure what you are getting at, but what we are stating is that we would act as a third order of government to make agreements with your government for certain kinds of whatever.

**Mr. Fraser:** Okay, when you talk about a third order of government, I gather, because your brief is very broad, you talk not, for instance, just as the Inuit did of their own people in a specific, but very large region of the country, you are speaking now of native peoples, aboriginal rights. Metis, status Indians, others, all of the native aboriginal family wherever they may be in Canada.

**Ms. Pierre-Aggamaway:** Yes.

**Mr. Fraser:** When you say that you wish that native family within the context of Canada to be treated as a third order of government. I have a little bit of difficulty here. I do not have any trouble understanding the concept of nation and the sense that members of your nation may be anywhere in the country at any given time and I do not have any difficulty in understanding the concept of government to some degree in certain regions where it is practical to have native or original peoples government; for instance, like Nunavut, which is the proposal of the Inuit. But I have a little difficulty understanding quite how you would govern for your people, where your people are scattered throughout an area in which there are already municipal and provincial and federal government levels. Could you address that?

**Ms. Pierre-Aggamaway:** I am not in a position at this point to share with you on divisions that we have of how our government would work. We are charging our people to do that for us and in that way I cannot be more specific.

**Mr. Fraser:** All right, that is fine, but am I right in assuming that however you mean the term "government" your fundamental concern is that you must be seen by the rest of us to be an entity, to be a group that recognizes itself as a group and that the actions that we take, or for that matter, the actions that you take, must be done on the basis of a partnership between yourselves and the rest of your fellow Canadians wherever they may be?

**Ms. Pierre-Aggamaway:** Correct. ... When we said that we believe that the aboriginal people have the right to negotiate as sovereign nations with governments of Canada to change, alter or amend aboriginal rights through treaties and agreements, we see this as a third order of government which would allow negotiations for changes in the distribution of powers and authority, or definition and exercising of rights through the setting out of mutually agreeable legal documents. That is what we interpret, from our standpoint, what that means. (16: 67–9)

...

**Senator Duff Roblin (PC, Manitoba):** ... You say that these people should have ... the right of self-government. ... Can you help me with that concept? Self-government usually implies not only people, but territory. That is the way it is usually related. Yet, we know that aboriginal people are very widely dispersed throughout the Canadian society. They are not all in one place, and are not easily isolated from the rest of the community. How far would you go in relation to this right of self-government in relation to the widespread dispersal of aboriginal people in the country?

**Mr. Harry Daniels (Native Council of Canada):** We are mainly concerned with our self-determination in this country within the political process. We have to support our brothers and sisters on these and other subjects which are of mutual concern. Self-government for us would have to come through negotiation with the federal government. At that time as I stated earlier, Mr. Senator, we are working on our definition of that, and we want to get that clear in our heads before making a truly definitive statement on self-government. But as you know the Metis and nonstatus people are still in the process of attempting to deal with the government for the resolution of all particular rights and freedoms as we see them in Canada and to enter into the negotiation stage for a settlement of land and/or compensation. At that time once we have agreed on the process we will get further into the self-government aspect.

**Mr. Roblin:** What you are telling me is that this is a negotiable item at the present time.

**Mr. Daniels:** At the present time. (17: 130–1)

...

**Mr. Eric Tagoona (Co-Chairman, Inuit Committee on National Issues):** Today we seek self-government within the Canadian federation. For instance, the Inuit of the Northwest Territories have proposed a Nunavut government in a detailed proposal, a copy of which is available. The main thrust of this proposal is to create a new territory above the treeline which would become a province after an orderly transition period. The Nunavut government would initially have powers similar to the existing government in Yellowknife. All residents could vote, the government would be for all those in Nunavut, and Nunavut would adhere to the highest standards of human rights. (16: 8–9)

...

**Chief Rod Robinson (Vice-President, Nishga Tribal Council):** Mr. Chairman, it sounds like we are a bunch of separatists, [but] we are not talking about separatism in any form. What we want is to be a part of Canada. We want local government but within a framework of the Canadian government. That is the reason why we want the aboriginal rights entrenched so that we can be recognized, not only the two founding nations as they call them, they completely forgot about the Indian. So if you can entrench our aboriginal rights in the constitution then we will be a legal entity, we will be able to have our own self-government but within the framework of the constitution, not as separatist. (26: 24)

### General: Protection under the Charter

**Mr. Jim Hawkes, MP (PC, AB):** You are a minority group, a charter of rights is supposed to protect minorities and you do not feel very well protected by this Charter, is that what you are saying?

**Mr. Mark Gordon (Inuit Committee on National Issues):** Well, I believe that the minority groups are protected quite well in this package as it now stands if your minority group is European in origin because this proposal endorses the European values and European systems. Since our culture and our system is completely different, we believe that there should be a way for us to integrate it into this package.

**Mr. Charlie Watt (Co-chair, Inuit Committee on National Issues):** Especially when you are aboriginal inhabitants of this country. (17: 18)

### General: Assimilation

**Mr. Charlie Watt (Inuit Committee on National Issues):** There is another area of concern to us. We are gradually being assimilated into the existing system, rather than contributing to the system. I do not think we should be looked at in that way, nor do I think that in the long run you are going to succeed in assimilating the native people. We are prepared to use all modern techniques, technologies, to our benefit, and, again, to the benefit of the rest of Canada. Instead of putting us into the welfare case, put us in a position where we can be productive. That is the point we are trying to put across.

For that reason we say – without political institutions, without an economic base – this does not mean anything at all to us, that is, if we are going to be wholly dependent upon government handouts. If we are not going to be able to rely on our own resources, on ourselves, which can be our economic base, then it is very difficult as an area to survive, not only because of being ethnic groups, such as the Inuit, or the Indians, but because of the lack of delivery of services which are to be provided to the native people, and because we are dependent upon government handouts. We are saying let us look at the whole thing and see if some adjustment can be made within the society. I think there is room for that. (17: 13–14)

## Aboriginal Women

**Mrs. Marlene Pierre-Aggamaway (President, Native Women's Association of Canada):** Thank you. ... We come to this historical event not to directly address the proposed amendment as it is inappropriate from the stand which we are taking. It is inappropriate for us to discuss it as it is written because it does not allow for native nations for self-determination and self-government on our behalf.

We, the aboriginal women of this land, are making representation to the Government of Canada to declare the sovereignty of our peoples and to serve notice that we intend to relate to Confederation as equal partners with the federal and provincial orders of government. As women we speak for ourselves, our children and the generations yet unborn, and join with the aboriginal peoples of this land in unity to declare that our rights, our nations and our sovereignty are ours to proclaim and ours to exercise. We want you to convey to the Government of Canada our willingness to negotiate and participate in such a partnership. ...

We believe that it is the fundamental right of every person of aboriginal descent to be recognized as such. We believe that the aboriginal people hold a special relationship with the British Crown that cannot be extinguished by any Canadian government. We believe that the aboriginal people of this land belong to sovereign nations that have the right of self-determination. We believe that the aboriginal rights, set out in the treaties, agreements and conventions and as based on our historical claim to this land, must be recognized. We believe that the Government of Canada must recognize that the aboriginal people have the right to determine their own form of government. We believe that it is the right of the aboriginal people to determine their own citizenship, and that it is the right of all people of aboriginal descent who so wish to be recognized as such. We believe that it is the right of the aboriginal people to retain the uniqueness and vitality of their cultures, customs, languages and heritages. We believe that no act of the governments of Canada may abrogate, expropriate or extinguish aboriginal rights, including treaty rights. We believe that the aboriginal people have the right to negotiate as sovereign nations with the governments of Canada to change, alter or amend aboriginal rights through treaties or agreements. We believe that it is the fundamental right of native women to have access and participation in any decision making process, and full protection of the law without discrimination based on sex or marital status. We believe that the rights of our children must be protected. (17: 63–5)

**Ms. Rose Charlie (Western Vice-President, Indian Rights for Indian Women):** ... The concerns we express concentrate on the injustices suffered for so long by Indian women in Canada. But we are not just Indian women. We are Indian, we are women, we are persons, and we are citizens of Canada and of the various provinces and territories. We are proud, not ashamed, that some of our remarks concern native men and nonnative women as well as ourselves. (17: 83–4)

Section 24, the only one that includes reference to the native peoples of this country, could be construed as supporting the defensibility and legality of section 12(1)(b) of the Indian Act. Under that section of that Act, Indian men have rights denied to Indian women. We are unequivocally opposed to this. (17: 86)

### General: Socio-economic

**Mr. Jim Sinclair (President, Association of Metis and Non-Status Indians of Saskatchewan):** You have wasted your dollars up to date. You have spent your dollars in keeping us in the jails and building the jails bigger to accommodate our people, which consists of maybe up to

80 per cent. Ninety per cent of us are unemployed. Eighty per cent of us are on welfare. Sixty per cent of us are affected by alcohol and those sixty per cent affect the other people who are sober and trying to make a go of it. We have family breakdowns. We have suicides, the highest suicide rate probably right now in the world. We do not have any future. We are kicked out of Northern Saskatchewan; we are kicked out of the urban centres. Where is it all going to end?

The other thing that I am going to have to say at this meeting which I know I will be shot down by some of the other Indian Leadership, but we have to talk about extinguishment of aboriginal rights because if you make a deal and you say, look, we are going to make a deal and we are going to settle this and I am giving up this for that, then we are going to have to stick by that. We cannot go back home and come back and say we sold you the land and we sold our rights but next week we want to send another delegation back to claim for some more land. No, we are going to have to make a settlement, but we are going to have to have political structured native organizations so that we do not sell the land for our own gain, so that land remains there for our people and for future generations, and it is protected. (22: 131–2)

## General: Disadvantaged Group

**Mr. James Manly, MP (NDP, BC):** I think all Canadians are concerned about our past record of relationships with you and your people. At the same time, it is very important for Canadians and members of Parliament to understand how you feel about some of these things. We often look on Indians as a disadvantaged group. I would like to ask you that question. Do you look upon yourselves and upon your people as members of a disadvantaged group?

**Mr. George Watts (Chairman, Nuu-chah-nulth Tribal Council):** I guess we look upon ourselves as a disadvantaged group in the sense that we are living with many things which are not ours. If you look back in our history, you will see that at one time we were a people who used to work seven months of the year and spend five months of the year feasting.

Now, many of our people spend 52 weeks of the year living on welfare, and the others who are fortunate enough to be employed spend 50 weeks of the year working and two weeks feasting.

Now, if you ask me if we feel disadvantaged, well, the answer is: yes we do, because you have replaced our world with a less satisfactory one.

We are saying to the government of this country that you can draw up all the solutions you want to our problems, they are not going to work, because the basic solution to the problems we have is to return to being Indian people, but within the 20th Century and living alongside Canadian people. But there are some basic things in our lives which we are going to have to return to. What we want is the opportunity to return to those things through the entrenchment of our rights to both the sea and the land resources. (27: 135–6)

### "This Is Our 1776"

**Mr. Douglas Anguish, MP (NDP, SK):** Legally, Mr. Milen, what do you see the Metis people or that association of Metis and nonstatus Indians of Saskatchewan, legally what are they asking for?

**Mr. Rob Milen (Legal Counsel, Association of Métis and Non-Status Indians of Saskatchewan):** I think it is very simple, Mr. Anguish. I think we are saying that we are looking for a Canada first constitution which will take us into the 21st century, a constitution for tomorrow's children, not yesterday's men. This is our 1776.

We are concerned that we see differences in our country, split along regional lines, east versus west; along linguistic lines, French versus English; and we do not want to add to this a split along racial lines, natives versus non natives. We perceive the constitutional process to be a constructive process, a healing process, a communal process in which we stress our similarities.

We have similarities with the logger in B.C., the oil rig worker in Alberta, the trapper in Saskatchewan and the farmer in Manitoba, the merchant in Montreal, the businessman in Ontario and the fisherman on the east coast. We want the constitution to stress our similarities, to take care of our physical and social need, to take care to provide [the] basis for which our country can deal with the problems of housing and food and so on. (22: 139)

...

### Minister of Justice Chrétien Presents Amended Text

[On 12 January 1981, Minister of Justice Jean Chrétien returned to the Joint Committee to present the government's amendments. At that time, the government was prepared to amend section 24 (what became section 25) of the Charter but not to actually entrench Aboriginal rights in the Constitution. Here is his explanation.]

**The Hon. Jean Chrétien (Minister of Justice and Attorney General of Canada):** There have been many groups representing native people who have appeared before you. I am pleased that they have had a full opportunity to be heard. As a government, we have been impressed by the testimony which has been presented to you. Of course, it is not possible to agree to everything that has been proposed. Most of the matters raised before the Committee remain subject to negotiation between governments and the native peoples. The Prime Minister has made a commitment that these negotiations will take place immediately after patriation. Yet it is possible to state in greater detail the kinds of native rights which are not to be adversely affected by the Charter and it is possible to set these rights apart from other undeclared rights and freedoms. Therefore, I am proposing somewhat along the lines suggested by Premier Blakeney that Section 24 be reworded to read as follows:

The guarantee in this Charter of certain rights and freedoms shall not be construed as denying the existence of:

any aboriginal, treaty or other rights or freedoms that may pertain to the aboriginal peoples of Canada including any right or freedom that may have been recognized by the Royal Proclamation of October 7, 1763;

or

any other rights or freedoms that may exist in Canada. ... (36: 18)

...

[As described in chapter 3, significant political pressure by Aboriginal groups and their supporters in January 1981 led the government to ultimately agree to the constitutional entrenchment of Aboriginal rights in a new part of the Constitution, Part II, in what was ultimately section 35 of the Constitution Act, 1982. Thus, on 30 January 1981, Minister Chrétien returned to the Joint Committee.]

**Mr. Chrétien:** Mr. Chairman, we have come to the conclusion on this issue of aboriginal rights that despite the difficulties surrounding this matter in terms of legal definition – difficulties that were being created for the government, after a series of negotiations and discussions involving a lot of people, we have come to accept a text which would entrench into the Canadian constitution the recognition and confirmation of the aboriginal rights of the original citizens of Canada. Due to the diligence of the deliberations – and I did not expect it to come today, but when we have a momentum we should try to maintain it; that is why I am pleased on behalf of the government to say that the aboriginal rights of the aboriginal people of Canada will be entrenched in the constitution. ... Before I proceed any further, I would like to thank the National Indian Brotherhood, the Inuit Tapirisat, the Métis and Nonstatus Federation of Canada for their work. (49: 83–4)

...

**Mr. Chrétien:** I would like to move on Clause 31, Clause 31 is the clause of entrenching the confirmation of the aboriginal rights in the constitution. ... So I will again ask Mr. Ittinuar to propose it and Warren Allmand to second it in French.

**The Joint Chairman (Mr. Joyal):** Mr. Ittinuar.

**Mr. Peter Ittinuar, MP (LIB, NWT):** Thank you, Mr. Chairman. I have the great honour to move that the proposed constitution act, 1980 be amended by (a) adding immediately after line 2 on page 9 the following headings and section:

Recognition of aboriginal and treaty rights

PART II

Rights of the Aboriginal Peoples of Canada

31. (1) The aboriginal and treaty rights of the aboriginal peoples of Canada are hereby recognized and affirmed.

Definition "aboriginal peoples of Canada"

(2) In this Act, "aboriginal peoples of Canada" include the Indian, Inuit and Métis peoples of Canada.

and (b) renumbering all subsequent parts and clauses accordingly.

...

**Mr. James Manly, MP (NDP, BC):** I believe that this amendment calls for a small celebration when it is finally included in our charter; and when the charter as part of a new Canadian constitution is brought home, then I believe it will call for a large celebration.

I would like to join others in commending the Minister for bringing this amendment forward, I believe that it marks a very significant day, not only for the aboriginal peoples of Canada, but for all peoples of Canada because it means that we are not only saying to Great Britain that we want to end any vestiges of colonial status that remain, but also that we are not interested in looking on the aboriginal peoples simply as subjects to be colonized, that we want them to take their full place and their full stature as members of Canadian society.

... I would like to commend my friend, Mr. Ittinuar, for moving this, and Mr. Broadbent, the leader of my party, who has done a great deal of work on behalf of our party, which has had for many years now on record our desire to have these rights recognized.

So, Mr. Minister, I simply hope that now we have taken this small step we will go on and take the final step.

One question: I presume that the phrase that this "includes Indian, Métis and Inuit peoples," that that leaves open the way for nonstatus Indians also to be included in having their rights recognized?

**Mr. Chrétien:** That is exactly why we have not fixed – we had a kind of open definition rather than a closed definition.

**Mr. Manly:** Would the word "Indian" include nonstatus Indians?

**Mr. Chrétien:** Yes, it is all aboriginal peoples. We have decided that we were not to use this generic term.

For me, when I started on that problem, I could not even use the word "aboriginal titles." It was something that was in legal jargon, if I can use that, was prohibited and I had so many problems with it because I could talk about the Royal Proclamation of 1763 but I could not refer to aboriginal rights and even if we were speaking about the same thing, and I had a lot of problems with it. I sweated in many, many meetings because this word was not part of the Canadian legal system. Now it is there, we are confirmed and I am waiting and I will make a comment after it is voted on. (49: 95–7)

...

**Mr. Lorne Nystrom, MP (NDP, SK):** I also want to associate myself with the tremendous accomplishment that has been made here at the Committee this afternoon of affirming the treaty and aboriginal rights of our aboriginal people, and I feel very strongly about this, as other people, and Senator Austin referred to when he was in law school and the tremendous discrimination or law against the aboriginal peoples. ... Mr. Chairman, this is a major first step in the new chapter of what I hope is a very exciting book in the new Canada of the 20th and 21st Centuries. (49: 99–100)

# Appendix A: The Special Joint Committee of the Senate and the House of Commons on the Constitution of Canada, 1980–81

*Joint Chairmen:*
Senator Harry Hays, P.C. (LIB)
Serge Joyal, MP (LIB)

*Representing the Senate:*
Martial Asselin (PC)
Jack Austin (LIB)
John J. Connolly (LIB)
H. Carl Goldenberg (LIB)
Maurice Lamontagne (LIB)
Paul Lucier (LIB)
William J. Petten (LIB)
Duff Roblin (PC)
Arthur Tremblay (PC)

*Representing the House of Commons:*
Perrin Beatty (PC)
Robert Bockstael (LIB)
Coline Campbell (LIB)
Eymard G. Corbin (LIB)
David Crombie (PC)
Jake Epp (PC)
John A. Fraser (PC)
George Henderson (LIB)
Ron Irwin (LIB)
Stanley Knowles (NDP) (participated in only one meeting; replaced
   by Svend Robinson)
Jean Lapierre (LIB)

Bryce Mackasey (LIB)
James A. McGrath (PC)
Lorne Nystrom (NDP)

*"Honorary Members" of the Joint Committee:*
Warren Allmand (LIB)
Jim Hawkes (PC)
Brian Tobin (LIB)

# Appendix B: Groups and Individuals Who Appeared and Gave Evidence before the Committee

*Advisory Council on the Status of Women:*
   Doris Anderson, President;
   Lucie Pépin, Vice-President for Eastern Canada;
   Mary Eberts, Legal Counsel;
   Nicole Duplé, Laval University;
   Beverly Baines.

*Afro-Asian Foundation of Canada:*
   Sebastian Alakatusery, Chairman;
   Carole Christinson.

*Aird, P. L., Professor, Faculty of Forestry, University of Toronto.*

*Alberta Chamber of Commerce:*
   Reinhold Lehr, President;
   Duncan McKillop, Chairman of Task Force on Constitutional Change;
   Maureen Mahoney, Public Affairs Manager.

*Alberta Social Credit Party:*
   Rod Sykes, Leader.

*Algonquin Council:*
   Lena Nottaway;
   William Commanda;
   Richard Kistabish;
   Salomon Wawatie;
   Major Kistabish;
   Louis Jerome;
   Kermot Moore;
   Pamela Kistabish.

*Alliance for Life:*
   Karen Murawsky, Past Vice-President;
   Paul de Bellefeuille, M.D., Associate Professor of Pediatrics (University of Ottawa);
   John J. H. Connors, LL.B., Consultant.

*Association canadienne-française de l'Ontario:*
   Yves St-Denis, President;
   Gérard Lévesque, Secretary General.

*Association culturelle franco-canadienne de la Saskatchewan:*
   Irène Chabot, President;
   Florent Bilodeau, Director General;
   Claire Doran, Political Adviser.

*Association of Iroquois and Allied Indians:*
   Charles Cornelius, President;
   Bill Tooshkenig;
   Gordon Peters.

*Association of Métis and Non-Status Indians of Saskatchewan:*
   Wayne McKenzie, Executive Director;
   Jim Sinclair, President;
   Jim Durocher, Provincial Treasurer;
   Frank Tomkins, Provincial Secretary;
   Rob Milen, Legal Counsel.

*Attikamek-Montagnais Council:*
   René Simon, Chairman;
   Aurélien Gill, Chief of Pointe-Bleue;
   Renée Dupuis, Legal Counsel.

*British Columbia Civil Liberties Association:*
   William Black, Member of Executive Committee;
   David Copp, Vice-President.

*Business Council on National Issues:*
   Peter Gordon, Chairman.

*Campaign Life-Canada:*
   Kathleen Toth, President;
   Gwen Landolt, Legal Counsel;
   Michael Barry, Psychiatrist.

*Canada West Foundation:*
  Stanley Roberts, President;
  David Elton, Research Director;
  Peter McCormick, Political Science, University of Lethbridge;
  Honourable J. V. Clyne, Counsel.

*Canadian Abortion Rights Action League:*
  J. Robert Kellermann, Legal Counsel;
  Eleanor Wright Pelrine, Honorary Director;
  Wendell W. Watters, M.D., Honorary Director.

*Canadian Association for the Prevention of Crime:*
  W. Frank Chafe, President of Association;
  Fred Sussman, Chairman of the Committee on Legislation;
  Tadeusz Grygier, Member of the Committee on Legislation.

*Canadian Association of Chiefs of Police:*
  John Ackroyd, Chief, Metro Toronto Police;
  Guy Lafrance, Legal Adviser, Montreal Urban Community Police.

*Canadian Association of Crown Counsels:*
  Roderick McLeod, Q.C., Assistant Deputy Attorney General of Ontario.

*Canadian Association of Lesbians and Gay Men:*
  Peter Maloney, Member of the Executive Committee;
  Christine Bearchell;
  George Hislop;
  Paul-François Sylvestre;
  Monique Bell.

*Canadian Association of the Mentally Retarded:*
  Paul Mercure, President;
  David Vickers, Vice-President;
  David Lincoln, President (People First – Ontario).

*Canadian Association of Social Workers:*
  Richard Splane, President;
  Gweneth Gowanlock, Executive Director.

*Canadian Bar Association:*
  A. William Cox, Q.C., President;
  John P. Nelligan, Q.C., Chairman, Special Committee on the Consti-
    tution of Canada;

Jacques Viau, Q.C., Bâtonnier, Past President;
L. Yves Fortier, Q.C., National Treasurer;
Victor Paisley, Chairman, Civil Liberties Section;
David Matas, Chairman, Constitutional and International Law
   Section.

*Canadian Bar Association, Newfoundland Branch:*
   Raymond J. Halley, Q.C., President;
   Ed Hearn, Member.

*Canadian Catholic School Trustees' Association:*
   Philip Hammel, President;
   Reverend Patrick Fogarty, Executive Secretary.

*Canadian Chamber of Commerce:*
   William F. Gunn, Chairman of the Executive Committee;
   Sam Hughes, President;
   Graeme T. Haig, Q.C., Chairman of the Constitution Reform Committee;
   André Bouchard, Member of the Constitution Reform Committee.

*Canadian Citizenship Federation:*
   Nicolas Zsolnay, President;
   J. B. Rudnyckyj;
   Eric L. Teed, Past President.

*Canadian Civil Liberties Association:*
   Alan Borovoy, General Counsel;
   Walter Tarnopolsky, President;
   J. S. Midanik, Q.C. (a past president).

*Canadian Committee on Learning Opportunities for Women:*
   Mary Corkery, Coordinator;
   Linda Ryan Nye;
   Monique Burchell.

*Canadian Connection:*
   Marion Dewar;
   Alan Clarke;
   Honourable David Macdonald;
   Mary Hegan;
   Lawrence Greenspon.

*Canadian Consultative Council on Multiculturalism:*
   Lawrence Decore, Chairman;

Errol Townshend, Chief Editor of "Cultures Canada."

*Canadian Council on Children and Youth:*
Andrew Cohen, Director General;
David Cruichshank, Vice-President;
Joseph Ryant, Member of Board of Directors.

*Canadian Council on Social Development:*
Ed Pennington, Board Member;
Nicole Dumouchel, Board Member;
Karen Hill.

*Canadian Federation of Civil Liberties and Human Rights Associations:*
Edwin Wedking, President;
Norman Whalen, Vice-President;
Gilles Tardif, Director.

*Canadians for Canada:*
Robert A. Willson, Chairman;
Donald Skagen;
John Crispo, Co-ordinator.

*Canadians for One Canada:*
Honourable James Richardson, P.C., National Chairman;
Pat Newbound, President;
Bill Scandrett, Executive Director.

*Canadian Human Rights Commission:*
Gordon Fairweather, Chief Commissioner;
Rita Cadieux, Deputy Chief Commissioner.

*Canadian Jewish Congress:*
Max Cohen, Chairman, Selected Committee on the Constitution of
    Canada of the Canadian Jewish Congress;
Martin Friedland;
Joseph Magnet, Special Adviser;
Irwin Cotler;
Frank Schlesinger.

*Canadian Life Insurance Association:*
P. D. Burns, Director;
C. T. P. Galloway;
Lise Bacon;
T. D. Kent.

*Canadian National Institute for the Blind:*
  Robert Mercer, National Managing Director;
  Dayton Foreman, National Vice-President;
  David Lepofsky, Member of the Ontario Board of Directors.

*Canadian Polish Congress:*
  Jan Kaszuba, President;
  Marek Malichi;
  Jan Federorowicz.

*Chrétien, Jean (The Honourable), Minister of Justice and Attorney General of Canada.*

*Church of Jesus Christ of Latter Day Saints:*
  Bruce Smith, President of Toronto Ontario East Stake;
  Regan Walker, Executive Secretary, Toronto Stake;
  Malcolm Warner, President Hamilton Stake.

*Coalition for the Protection of Human Life:*
  Barry DeVeber, M.D., Head of Pediatrics at University of Western
    Ontario;
  Elizabeth Callahan, M.D., Board Member;
  Philip Cooper, Vice-President;
  Don McPhee, Executive Director;
  Denyre Handler, Journalist.

*Coalition of Provincial Organizations of the Handicapped:*
  Monique Couillard, First Vice-President, Carrefour Adaptation, Quebec;
  Yvonne Peters, Member, Executive Committee;
  Ron Kanary, Vice-Chairman;
  Jim Derksen, National Co-ordinator.

*Cohen, Maxwell, McGill University.*

*Council for Yukon Indians:*
  Elijah Smith, Vice-Chairman;
  David Joe, Legal Counsel;
  Harry Allen, Chairman;
  Michael Smith, Legal Counsel.

*Council of National Ethnocultural Organizations of Canada:*
  Laureano Leone, President;
  Navin Parekh, First Vice-President;
  George Imai, Secretary;

Andriy Bandera;
Algis Juzukonis.

*Council of Quebec Minorities:*
Eric Maldoff, President;
Casper Bloom;
James Leavy.

*Denominational Educational Committees of Newfoundland:*
Archbishop A. L. Penney, Chairman;
Bishop M. Mate;
Reverend Boyd Hiscock;
Pastor Roy King;
James Greene.

*Department of Justice:*
Roger Tassé, Q.C., Deputy Minister;
B. L. Strayer, Q.C., Assistant Deputy Minister, Public Law;
F. Jordan, Senior Counsel, Public Law.

*la Fédération des francophones hors Québec:*
Jeannine Séguin, President;
Donald Cyr, Director General;
René-Marie Paiement, Assistant Director General (Policies).

*Federation of Canadian Municipalities:*
Dennis Flynn, President;
Glennis Perry.

*Federation of Independent Schools of Canada:*
Molly Boucher, President;
Patrick Whelan, Treasurer;
Gary Duthler, Director.

*Federation of Saskatchewan Indians:*
Sol Sanderson, Chief;
John B. Tootoosis, Senator;
Kirk Kickingbird, Legal Counsel;
Delia Opekokew, Legal Counsel;
Rodney Soonias, Legal Counsel;
Doug Cuthand, First Vice-President.

*German-Canadian Committee on the Constitution:*
Dietrich Kiesewalter, Coordinating Chairman;

Gunther Bauer, Vice-Chairman of German Speaking Alliance of Ottawa and Region;

Klaus Bongart, Chairman, German Canadian Council of Kitchener Waterloo;

Benno Knodel, Chairman, German Canadian Alliance of Alberta;

Arthur Grenke, Historian.

*Government of New Brunswick:*
Honourable Richard B. Hatfield, Premier of New Brunswick.

*Government of Nova Scotia:*
Honourable John Buchanan, Premier of Nova Scotia;
Honourable Edmond Morris, Minister of Intergovernmental Affairs.

*Government of Prince Edward Island:*
Honourable J. Angus MacLean, Premier of Prince Edward Island;
Fred Driscoll, Minister of Education.

*Government of Saskatchewan:*
Honourable Allan E. Blakeney, Premier of Saskatchewan.

*Government of the Northwest Territories:*
George Braden, MLA, Leader of the Elected Members of the Executive Committee;
Stien Lal, Legal Adviser to the Executive Committee.

*Government of the Yukon Territory:*
Honourable C. W. Pearson, Government Leader.

*Indian Association of Alberta:*
Eugene Steinhauer, President;
Charles Wood, Chief, Constitution Committee for Alberta;
John Snow, Chief from Treaty 7;
Willy Littlechild, Legal Counsel.

*Indian Rights for Indian Women:*
Nellie Carlson, Western Vice-President;
Rose Charlie, Board Member;
Barbara Wyss, Treasurer.

*Inuit Committee on National Issues:*
Charlie Watt, Co-Chairman;
Eric Tagoona, Co-Chairman;
Mark R. Gordon, Coordinator;

Mary Simon;
Zebedee Nungak;
Thomas Suluk.

*Italian-Canadians National Congress (Quebec Region):*
Rita Desantis, Spokeperson;
Giovanni Molina, President;
Antonio Sciascia, Legal Adviser.

*Kaplan, Robert (The Honourable), Acting Minister of Justice.*

*La Forest, Gérard V. J., University of Ottawa.*

*Love, D. V., Faculty of Forestry, University of Toronto.*

*Media Club of Canada:*
Esther Crandall, President;
Alison Hardy, Historian.

*Mennonite Central Committee (Canada):*
Ross Nigh, Vice-Chairman;
William Janzen, Director General of the Ottawa Office;
J. M. Klassen, Executive Secretary.

*National Action Committee on the Status of Women:*
Lynn McDonald, President;
Jill Porter, Member of Executive;
Betsy Carr, Member of Executive;
Marilou McPhedran, Member of the National Association of Women
and the Law.

*National Anti-Poverty Organization:*
J. Hartling, Executive Director.

*National Association of Japanese Canadians:*
Gordon Kadota, President;
Roger Obata;
Art Shimizu, Constitution Committee Chairman.

*National Association of Women and the Law:*
Deborah Acheson, Member of the Steering Committee;
Monique Charlebois, Member of the Steering Committee;
Tamra Thomson, Ottawa Caucus;
Pamela Medjuck, Member, National Steering Committee.

*National Black Coalition of Canada:*
  Wilson Head, President;
  J. A. Mercury, Executive Secretary.

*National Indian Brotherhood:*
  Del Riley, President;
  Sykes Powderface, Vice-President;
  Doug Saunders, Legal Counsel;
  William T. Badcock, Legal Counsel.

*Native Council of Canada:*
  Harry Daniel, President;
  Louis Bruyère, Vice-President;
  Gene Rhéaume, Honorary President;
  Vic Savino, Legal Counsel.

*Native Women's Association of Canada:*
  Marlene Pierre-Aggamaway, President;
  Donna Phillips, Treasurer.

*New Brunswick Human Rights Commission:*
  Noel A. Kinsella, Chairman;
  Francis Young, Legal Counsel;
  John Humphrey, President, Canadian Human Rights Foundation;
  Sandra Lovelace, Tobique Indian Reservation, New Brunswick.

*New Democratic Party of Alberta:*
  Grant Notley, Leader;
  M. McCreary, Co-Chairman, NDP Constitution Committee;
  Davis Swan, Chairman, NDP Energy Committee;
  Garth Stevenson, Professor.

*Nishga Tribal Council:*
  James Gosnell, President;
  Rod Robinson, Vice-President;
  Percy Tate, Executive Assistant to the President;
  Donald Rosenbloom, Legal Counsel;
  Stewart Leggatt, MLA, Legal Counsel.

*Nuu-Chah-Nulth Tribal Council:*
  George Watts, Chairman;
  Jack Woodward, Legal Counsel.

*Ontario Conference of Catholic Bishops:*
   Bishop Alexander Carter, President;
   Archbishop J. Aurèle Plourde, Vice-President;
   Father Raymond Durocher, Research Specialist;
   Father Angus Macdougall, General Secretary;
   Joseph Magnet, Legal Counsel.

*Parti de l'Union National du Québec:*
   Michel Le Moignan, Interim Leader;
   Claude Gélinas;
   Bertrand Goulet, Member of the Quebec National Assembly.

*Positive Action Committee:*
   S. McCall, Co-Chairman;
   Alex Paterson, Co-Chairman.

*Progressive Conservative Party of Saskatchewan:*
   Grant Devine, Leader;
   Robert Andrew, MLA.

*Protestant School Board of Greater Montreal:*
   Joan Dougherty, Chairman;
   L. P. Patterson, Chairman, Constitution Committee;
   Marcel Fox, Director General.

*Public Interest Advocacy Center:*
   Nick Schultz, Associate General Counsel.

*Rémillard, Gil, Laval University.*

*Russell, Peter, University of Toronto.*

*Saskatchewan Human Rights Commission:*
   Ken Norman, Chief Commissioner;
   Louise Simard, Deputy Chief Commissioner.

*Scott, Edward W. (Reverend), Primate, Anglican Church of Canada.*

*la Société Franco-manitobaine:*
   Gilberte Proteau, President;
   Lucille Roch, Director General;
   Joseph Elliott Magnet, Counsel.

*Ukrainian Canadian Committee:*
John Nowosad, President;
Manoly Lupul, Director, Institute of Ukrainian Studies.

*Union of New Brunswick Indians:*
Graydon Nicholas, Chairman of the Board;
Albert Levi.

*Union of Nova Scotia Indians:*
Stanley Johnson, President;
Stuart Killen, Research Director;
Sageth Henderson, Legal Adviser.

*Union of Ontario Indians:*
Patrick Madahbee, President;
Paul Williams;
James Mason.

*United Church of Canada:*
Clarke MacDonald, Senior Secretary – Office of Church in Society;
Reverend Robert Lindsey, Associate Secretary – Division of Mission in Canada;
Reverend Guy Deschamps, French-English Relations Officer.

*Vancouver People's Law School Society:*
Diana Davidson, President.

*World Federalists of Canada – Operation Dismantle:*
Francis Leddy, National President of World Federalists of Canada;
T. James Stark, Director, Operation Dismantle.

*Yalden, M. F., Commissioner of Official Languages.*

# Notes

## Introduction

1 Lois Harder and Steve Patten, "Looking Back on Patriation and Its Consequences," in *Patriation and Its Consequences: Constitution Making in Canada*, ed. Lois Harder and Steve Patten (Vancouver: UBC Press, 2015), 4.

2 See, e.g., P.E. Bryden, "The Rise of Spectator Constitutionalism, 1967–81," in *Patriation and Its Consequences: Constitution Making in Canada*, ed. Lois Harder and Steve Patten (Vancouver: UBC Press, 2015), 93.

3 Mary Eberts, "Women and Constitutional Renewal," in *Women and the Constitution in Canada*, ed. Audrey Doerr and Micheline Carrier (Ottawa: Canadian Advisory Council on the Status of Women, 1981), 3.

4 Edward McWhinney, *Canada and the Constitution 1979–1982* (Toronto: University of Toronto Press, 1982), 57.

5 See Lawrence Martin, *Chrétien*, vol. 1, *The Will to Win* (Toronto: Lester Publishing, 1995), 299.

6 Harder and Patten, "Looking Back on Patriation and its Consequences," 12.

7 McWhinney, *Canada and the Constitution 1979–1982*, 57.

8 See, e.g., the comments of Barry L. Strayer, "The Evolution of the Charter," in *Patriation and Its Consequences: Constitution Making in Canada*, ed. Lois Harder and Steve Patten (Vancouver: UBC Press, 2015), 81–7.

9 Polls during 1980–81 showed overwhelmingly strong support for the idea of a charter. See Peter H. Russell, *Constitutional Odyssey: Can Canadians Become a Sovereign People?*, 3rd ed. (Toronto: University of Toronto Press, 2004), 115–16; also cites sources.

10 Stephen Clarkson and Christina McCall, *Trudeau and Our Times*, vol. 1, *The Magnificent Obsession* (Toronto: McClelland and Stewart, 1990), 297.

11  Chaviva Hošek, "Women and the Constitutional Process," in *And No One Cheered: Federalism, Democracy and the Constitution Act*, ed. Keith Banting and Richard Simeon (Toronto: Methuen, 1983), 280, 286.

12  Harder and Patten, "Looking Back on Patriation and its Consequences," 13.

13  Ibid., 12.

14  Alan C. Cairns, *Charter versus Federalism: The Dilemmas of Constitutional Reform* (Montreal and Kingston: McGill-Queen's University Press, 1992), 67–8.

15  Russell, *Constitutional Odyssey*, 115. See also Janine Brodie, "Constituting Constitutions: The Patriation Moment," in *Patriation and Its Consequences: Constitution Making in Canada*, ed. Lois Harder and Steve Patten (Vancouver: UBC Press, 2015), 37–8.

16  Brodie, "Constituting Constitutions," 42.

17  Russell, *Constitutional Odyssey*, 115.

18  This ultimately became the Canada Act, 1982 (1982, c 11).

19  Hošek, "Women and the Constitutional Process," 286.

20  Canada, Parliament, Special Joint Committee on the Constitution of Canada, *Minutes of Proceedings and Evidence: Report to Parliament*, 32nd Parliament, 1st Session, issue 57 (13 February 1981): 40, 42.

21  Ibid., 5.

22  Ibid.

23  Martin, *The Will to Win*, 300.

24  Joint Committee, *Proceedings: Report to Parliament*, issue 57: 5.

25  Hošek, "Women and the Constitutional Process," 286.

26  See, generally, Louise Mandell and Leslie Hall Pinder, "Tracking Justice: The Constitution Express to Section 35 and Beyond," in *Patriation and Its Consequences: Constitution Making in Canada*, ed. Lois Harder and Steve Patten (Vancouver: UBC Press, 2015), 180.

27  But see the important role the committee's hearings play in the work of Lorraine Weinrib – e.g., Lorraine E. Weinrib, "Canada's Charter of Rights: Paradigm Lost?," *Review of Constitutional Studies* 6, no. 2 (2002): 119. See also Kerri Froc, "Is Originalism Bad for Women? The Curious Case of Canada's 'Equal Rights Amendment,'" *Review of Constitutional Studies* 19, no. 2 (2014): 237.

28  See the criticism of Marilou McPhedran, "A Truer Story: Constitutional Trialogue," in *A Living Tree: The Legacy of 1982 in Canada's Political Evolution*, ed. Graeme Mitchell, Ian Peach, David E. Smith, and John D. Whyte (Toronto: LexisNexis, 2007), 101, 103; also notes keynote speakers at a series of conferences in 2007 on the 25th anniversary of patriation and the Charter.

29  *Reference re Motor Vehicle Act (British Columbia), s. 94*, [1985] 2 S.C.R. 486
    [*B.C. Motor Vehicle Reference*].
30  Ibid., para. 52.
31  See J.L. Granatstein, *Who Killed Canadian History?* (Toronto: HarperCollins,
    1998; repr. 2007).
32  Adam M. Dodek, "The Dutiful Conscript: An Originalist View of Justice
    Wilson's Conception of Charter Rights and Their Limits," *Supreme Court
    Law Review: Osgoode's Annual Constitutional Cases Conference* 41, article 331
    (2008): 333, 334. For notable exceptions to my comments, see John Bor-
    rows, "(Ab)Originalism and Canada's Constitution," *Supreme Court Law
    Review* 58 (2d) (2012): 351; Peter Martin Jaworski, "Originalism All the Way
    Down. Or: The Explosion of Progressivism," *Canadian Journal of Law and
    Jurisprudence* 26 (2013): 313; Daniel C. Santoro, "The Unprincipled Use of
    Originalism and Section 24(2) of the Charter," *Alberta Law Review* 45, no.
    1 (2007); Froc, "Is Originalism Bad for Women?," 237; Bradley W. Miller,
    "Origin Myth: The Persons Case, the Living Tree, and the New Original-
    ism," in *The Challenge of Originalism: Theories of Constitutional Interpretation*,
    ed. Grant Huscroft and Bradley W. Miller (Cambridge: Cambridge Univer-
    sity Press, 2011), 120; and Grégoire C.N. Webber, "Originalism's Constitu-
    tionalism," in Huscroft and Miller, eds., *The Challenge of Originalism*, 147.
33  See, e.g., Ian Binnie, "Interpreting the Constitution: The Living Tree vs.
    Original Meaning," *Policy Options*, 1 October 2007, http://policyoptions.
    irpp.org/magazines/free-trade-20/interpreting-the-constitution-the-
    living-tree-vs-original-meaning/; and Justice Ian Binnie, "Constitutional
    Interpretation and Original Intent," in *Constitutionalism in the Charter Era*,
    ed. Grant Huscroft and Ian Brodie (Toronto: LexisNexis, 2004), 345. For my
    criticisms, see Dodek, "The Dutiful Conscript," 334.
34  S.C. 1960, c. 44.
35  Binnie, "Interpreting the Constitution."
36  John Borrows has argued – critically – that in the area of Aboriginal rights,
    the Supreme Court has adopted a very restrictive originalist approach; see
    Borrows, "(Ab)Originalism and Canada's Constitution." However, as seen
    in chapter 15, the possibilities regarding the meaning of Aboriginal rights
    under section 35 of the Constitution Act, 1982 were far broader than the
    restrictive interpretations preferred by the Supreme Court of Canada to date.
37  See *Hunter et al. v. Southam Inc.*, [1984] 2 S.C.R. 145.
38  [1985] 1 S.C.R. 295.
39  See Shalin M. Sugunasiri, "Contextualism: The Supreme Court's New
    Standard of Judicial Analysis and Accountability," *Dalhousie Law Journal* 22
    (1999): 126.

40 See Peter W. Hogg and Allison A. Bushell, "The Charter Dialogue between Courts and Legislatures (or Perhaps the Charter of Rights Isn't Such a Bad Thing After All)," *Osgoode Hall Law Journal* 35, no. 1 (1997): 75. Hogg and Bushell updated their theory in 2007; see Peter W. Hogg, Allison A. Bushell Thornton, and Wade K. Wright, "Charter Dialogue Revisited – or 'Much Ado about Metaphors,'" *Osgoode Hall Law Journal* 45, no. 1 (2007).

41 See, e.g., *Vriend v. Alberta*, [1998] 1 S.C.R. 493, paras. 137–9, 178; *M. v. H.*, [1999] 2 S.C.R. 3, para. 328; *Corbiere v. Canada (Minister of Indian and Northern Affairs)*, [1999] 2 S.C.R. 203, para. 116; *R. v. Mills*, [1999] 3 S.C.R. 668, paras. 20, 57, 125; *Little Sisters Book and Art Emporium v. Canada (Minister of Justice)*, [2000] 2 S.C.R. 1120, para. 268; *Bell ExpressVu Limited Partnership v. Rex*, [2002] 2 S.C.R. 559, 2002 SCC 42, paras. 65–6; *Harper v. Canada (Attorney General)*, [2004] 1 S.C.R. 827, 2004 SCC 33, para. 37.

42 See *Vriend v. Alberta*, [1998] 1 S.C.R. 493, paras. 137–9, 178.

43 See also Grant Huscroft, "'Thank God We're Here': Judicial Exclusivity in Charter Interpretation and Its Consequences," *Supreme Court Law Review* 25, no. 2 (2004): 241.

## Chapter 1

1 G.E.D. Martin, "Introduction to the 2006 Edition," in *The Confederation Debates in the Province of Canada, 1865*, ed. P.B. Waite (Montreal and Kingston: McGill-University Press, 2006), xxvii.

2 James Ross Hurley, *Amending Canada's Constitution: History, Processes, Problems and Prospects* (Ottawa: Minister of Supply and Services, 1996), 24.

3 Ibid., 25.

4 Ibid., 25–6.

5 These are documented wonderfully, ibid.

6 Peter H. Russell, *Constitutional Odyssey: Can Canadians Become a Sovereign People?*, 3rd ed. (Toronto: University of Toronto Press, 2004), 106.

7 See Richard Simeon, *Federal-Provincial Diplomacy: The Making of Recent Policy in Canada* (Toronto: University of Toronto Press, 1972), 88.

8 *Montreal Star*, 2 December 1966, quoted in Simeon, ibid.

9 Lorraine Eisenstat Weinrib, "Trudeau and the Canadian Charter of Rights and Freedoms: A Question of Constitutional Maturation," in *Trudeau's Shadow: The Life and Legacy of Pierre Elliott Trudeau*, ed. Andrew Cohen and J.L. Granatstein (Toronto: Random House, 1998), 267.

10 Ibid.

11 Stephen Clarkson and Christina McCall, *Trudeau and Our Times*, vol. 1, *The Magnificent Obsession* (Toronto: McClelland and Stewart, 1990).

12  Barry L. Strayer, "The Evolution of the Charter," in *Patriation and Its Consequences: Constitution Making in Canada*, ed. Lois Harder and Steve Patten (Vancouver: UBC Press, 2015), 77.

13  In August 2014, Minister of Justice Peter MacKay became the first justice minister in recent memory to skip the CBA's annual conference; see Catherine Cullen, "Peter MacKay Skipping Canadian Bar Association's Annual Conference," *CBC News*, 1 August 2014, http://www.cbc.ca/news/politics/peter-mackay-skipping-canadian-bar-association-s-annual-conference-1.2724995.

14  *Ottawa Journal*, "Government Ready to Discuss Constitutional Change," 5 September 1967, 22.

15  Pierre Elliott Trudeau, "A Constitutional Declaration of Rights," in *Federalism and the French Canadians* (Toronto: Macmillan, 1968), 57.

16  Pierre E. Trudeau, *A Canadian Charter of Human Rights* (Ottawa: Queen's Printer, 1968).

17  Strayer, "The Evolution of the Charter," 78.

18  See, generally, ibid., 78–9.

19  Trudeau, *A Canadian Charter of Human Rights*.

20  Roy Romanow, John Whyte, and Howard Leeson, *Canada ... Notwithstanding: The Making of the Constitution, 1976–1982* (Toronto: Carswell, 2007), 228–9.

21  Clarkson and McCall, *The Magnificent Obsession*, 264.

22  In Richard Simeon's *Federal-Provincial Diplomacy: The Making of Recent Policy in Canada* (Toronto: University of Toronto Press, 1972), quoted in Russell, *Constitutional Odyssey*, 81.

23  See Russell, *Constitutional Odyssey*, 80–1. See also Nancy Fraser, "Social Justice in the Age of Identity Politics: Redistribution, Recognition and Participation" (Tanner Lectures on Human Values, Stanford University, Stanford, CA, 30 April–2 May 1996), quoted in Marilou McPhedran, Judith Erola, and Loren Braul, "'28 – Helluva Lot to Lose in 27 Days': The Ad Hoc Committee and Women's Constitutional Activism in the Era of Patriation," in *Patriation and Its Consequences: Constitution Making in Canada*, ed. Lois Harder and Steve Patten (Vancouver: UBC Press, 2015), 203: "The executive federalism that characterized over fifty years of constitutional negotiations in Canada is not consistent with participatory parity – that is, with the idea that individuals and groups can participate 'on a par with others in social interaction.'"

24  Russell, *Constitutional Odyssey*, 81.

25  See Simeon, *Federal-Provincial Diplomacy*, xvii.

26  Russell, *Constitutional Odyssey*, 92.

27  Ibid., 82.

28  Ibid., 88

29  See "Canadian Constitutional Charter, 1971 (the Victoria Charter)," in *Canada's Constitution Act 1982 and Amendments: A Documentary History*, ed. Anne F. Bayefsky (Toronto: McGraw-Hill Ryerson, 1989), 214.

30  Romanow, Whyte, and Leeson, *Canada … Notwithstanding*, 252.

31  Barry L. Strayer, *Canada's Constitutional Revolution* (Edmonton: University of Alberta Press, 2013), 87.

32  See Romanow, Whyte, and Leeson, *Canada … Notwithstanding*, 1–20 ("The Quest Begins Anew 1976–1979").

33  On public interest generally in constitution making in Canada, see P.E. Bryden, "The Rise of Spectator Constitutionalism, 1967–81," in *Patriation and Its Consequences: Constitution Making in Canada*, ed. Lois Harder and Steve Patten (Vancouver: UBC Press, 2015), 93.

34  Russell, *Constitutional Odyssey*, 99.

35  Ibid.

36  Ibid., 98.

37  Strayer, *Canada's Constitutional Revolution*, 90.

38  See Romanow, Whyte, and Leeson, *Canada … Notwithstanding*, 8.

39  For discussion about Bill C-60 and reaction to it, see Strayer, "The Evolution of the Charter," 78–9.

40  See "The Constitutional Amendment Bill (Bill C-60), First Reading, June 20, 1978, Text and Explanatory Notes," in Bayefsky, *Canada's Constitution Act 1982 and Amendments*, 340.

41  Russell, *Constitutional Odyssey*, 101.

42  Romanow, Whyte, and Leeson, *Canada … Notwithstanding*, 12.

43  *Re: Authority of Parliament in relation to the Upper House*, [1980] 1 S.C.R. 54.

44  Clarkson and McCall, *The Magnificent Obsession*, 273.

45  Ibid., 275.

46  Graham Fraser, *PQ: René Lévesque and the Parti Québécois in Power* (Toronto: Macmillan, 1984), 179.

47  *Re: Authority of Parliament in relation to the Upper House*, [1980] 1 S.C.R. 54.

48  Romanow, Whyte, and Leeson, *Canada … Notwithstanding*, 43.

49  Ibid., 106.

50  See Bayefsky, *Canada's Constitution Act 1982 and Amendments*, 598.

51  See Canada, Parliament, Cabinet, *Minutes*, 3 June 1980, CBM 63-80.

52  Clarkson and McCall, *The Magnificent Obsession*, 285.

53  On 3 July 1980, Chrétien briefed the Cabinet on "The Federal Government's Approach to Constitutional Reform and its Initial Negotiating Position on the Twelve Items," Committee Report 453-80CR (NSD). Cabinet met all through July. See Canada, Parliament, Cabinet, *Minutes*, 10 July 1980, No. 67-80 CBM; 16 July 1980, No. 68-80 CBM; 17 July 1980, No. 69-80

CBM; 24 July 1980, No. 70-80 CBM; 31 July 1980, No. 71-80 CBM; 1 August 1980, No. 72-80 CBM.

54  Romanow, Whyte, and Leeson, *Canada … Notwithstanding*, 240.
55  See ibid.
56  "Report to Cabinet on Constitutional Discussions, Summer, 1980 and the Outlook for the First Ministers Conference and Beyond," August 30, 1980 (Kirby Memorandum)," excerpted in David Milne, *The New Canadian Constitution* (Toronto: Lorimer, 1982), 219*ff*.
57  Cabinet, *Minutes*, 5 September 1980, No. 73-80 CBM.
58  Russell, *Constitutional Odyssey*, 110. The September 1980 first ministers' meeting is discussed in Romanow, Whyte, and Leeson, *Canada … Notwithstanding*, 94–6.
59  Robert Sheppard and Michael Valpy, *The National Deal: The Fight for a Canadian Constitution* (Toronto: Fleet Books, 1982), 1.
60  Jean Chrétien, *Straight from the Heart*, rev. ed. (Toronto: Key Porter, 1994), 175.
61  Sheppard and Valpy, *The National Deal*, 4–5.
62  Chrétien, *Straight from the Heart*, 175–6.
63  Milne, "Kirby Memorandum," *The New Canadian Constitution*, 223.
64  Ibid., 225.
65  See, e.g., Sheppard and Valpy, *The National Deal*, 65–6.
66  Cabinet, *Minutes*, 18 September 1980, No. 74-80 CBM.
67  Sheppard and Valpy, *The National Deal*, 65–6.
68  Cabinet, *Minutes*, 18 September 1980, No. 74-80 CBM.
69  Ibid., 66.
70  Ibid., 68.
71  Canada, Parliament, Special Joint Committee on the Constitution of Canada, *Minutes of Proceedings and Evidence*, 32nd Parliament, 1st Session, issue 2: 45.
72  See, e.g., Cabinet, *Minutes*, summer 1980, in note 53 above.
73  Nathan Nurgitz and Hugh Segal, *No Small Measure: The Progressive Conservatives and the Constitution* (Ottawa: Deneau, 1983), 81.
74  See, e.g., Noel Lyon, "The Teleological Mandate of the Fundamental Freedoms Guarantee: What to Do with Vague but Meaningful Generalities," *Supreme Court Law Review* 4 (1982): 57, 67; Alan D. Gold, "The Legal Rights Provisions – A New Vision or Déjà Vu?," *Supreme Court Law Review* 4 (1982): 107.
75  Cabinet, *Minutes*, 2 October 1980, No 76-80 CBM.
76  Trudeau's speech was broadcast at 8:00 p.m. According to network schedules, these were the other shows televised at that time; see https://en.wikipedia.org/wiki/1980%E2%80%9381_United_States_network_television_schedule.

77  John English, *Just Watch Me: The Life of Pierre Elliott Trudeau, 1968–2000* (Toronto: Vintage Canada, 2010), 480–1.
78  Joint Committee, *Proceedings*, issue 1 (6 November 1980): 5.

**Chapter 2**

1  Stephen Clarkson and Christina McCall, *Trudeau and Our Times*, vol. 1, *The Magnificent Obsession* (Toronto: McClelland and Stewart, 1990), 296.
2  Hubert Bauch, "Serge Joyal: The Black Sheep Returns to the Fold," *Montreal Gazette*, 23 September 1981.
3  Clarkson and McCall, *The Magnificent Obsession*, 296.
4  Robert Sheppard and Michael Valpy, *The National Deal: The Fight for a Canadian Constitution* (Toronto: Fleet Books, 1982), 138.
5  Ibid., 139.
6  *Canadian Encyclopedia*, s.v. "Harry William Hays, http://www.thecanadianencyclopedia.ca/en/article/harry-william-hays/.
7  Ibid.
8  Sheppard and Valpy, *The National Deal*, 139.
9  Ibid.
10  Clarkson and McCall, *The Magnificent Obsession*, 296.
11  "Un entretien avec l'honorable sénateur Serge Joyal," *Ottawa Law Review* 44, no. 3 (2013): 595, 614.
12  Sheppard and Valpy, *The National Deal*, 139.
13  Ibid.
14  Clarkson and McCall, *The Magnificent Obsession*, 296.
15  Canada, Parliament, Special Joint Committee on the Constitution of Canada, *Minutes of Proceedings and Evidence*, 32nd Parliament, 1st Session, issue 50: 86.
16  See, e.g., Serge Joyal, ed., *Protecting Canadian Democracy: The Senate You Never Knew* (Montreal: McGill-Queen's University Press, 2003).
17  Sheppard and Valpy, *The National Deal*, 136.
18  Ibid., note.
19  Pierre Elliott Trudeau, "A Constitutional Declaration of Rights," in *Federalism and the French Canadians* (Toronto: Macmillan, 1968), 52, 55.
20  Clarkson and McCall, *The Magnificent Obsession*, 261.
21  Graham Fraser, *PQ: René Lévesque and the Parti Québécois in Power* (Toronto: Macmillan, 1984), 192.
22  See Constitution Act (No. 2), 1975, S.C. 1974-75-76, c. 53.
23  *CBC News* online, "Yukon's First Senator, Paul Lucier, Dies," 25 July 1999, http://www.cbc.ca/news/canada/yukon-s-first-senator-paul-lucier-dies-1.183579.

24  Sheppard and Valpy, *The National Deal*, 8.
25  See http://www.parl.gc.ca/Parlinfo/Files/Parliamentarian.aspx?Item=
    1b2d233e-dfb8-493e-ad47-1cce8ffc73b3&Language=E&Section=
    FederalExperience.
26  See http://www.parl.gc.ca/parlinfo/Files/Parliamentarian.aspx?
    Item=b2bac502-7edd-43fc-b68a-1edd076606f4&Language=E&Section=
    ALL.
27  Sheppard and Valpy, *The National Deal*, 140.
28  Ibid., 136.
29  *Globe and Mail*, "Off-the Record Chats Can Go off the Rails," 16 December
    2005, A9.
30  Joint Committee, *Proceedings: Report to Parliament*, issue 57 (13 February
    1981): 2–3.
31  Brian Tobin, *All in Good Time* (Toronto: Penguin, 2002), 46.
32  Ibid.
33  Sheppard and Valpy, *The National Deal*, 139.
34  See ibid., 88.
35  Ibid., 140.
36  Nathan Nurgitz and Hugh Segal, *No Small Measure: The Progressive Con-
    servatives and the Constitution* (Ottawa: Deneau Publishers, 1983), 44.
37  Sheppard and Valpy, *The National Deal*, 140.
38  See ibid., 88.
39  See Nurgitz and Segal, *No Small Measure*, 4, 44.
40  Sheppard and Valpy, *The National Deal*, 140.
41  On the occasion of the Charter's 30th anniversary in 2012, senior public
    servants in the Department of Justice wanted to celebrate the event, but
    the minister vetoed the idea, and all the government could do was issue a
    press release. See Mark Bourrie, *Kill the Messengers: Stephen Harper's Assault
    on Your Right to Know* (Toronto: HarperCollins, 2015), 157.
42  Sheppard and Valpy, *The National Deal*, 85.
43  Ibid., 86.
44  Sandra Martin, "Duff Roblin, Former Manitoba Premier, Dies at 92," *Globe
    and Mail*, 31 May 2010.
45  Tremblay was deputy minister of intergovernmental relations when the
    Parti Québécois was elected in 1976. He was considered the "dean" of
    deputy ministers. See Fraser, *PQ*, 80.
46  Sheppard and Valpy, *The National Deal*, 87.
47  Cynthia Ramsay, "Longtime Community Friend: John Fraser Supports
    Several Causes, Including Camp Miriam," *Jewish Independent*, 1 Novem-
    ber 2013, http://www.jewishindependent.ca/oldsite/archives/nov13/
    archives13nov01-10.html.

48  Joint Committee, *Proceedings*, issue 13: 11–12.
49  "The Speakers of the House of Commons – Hon. John Allen Fraser," Parliament of Canada website, http://www.parl.gc.ca/About/Parliament/Speakers/Hoc/sp-32Fraser-e.htm.
50  Graeme Truelove, *Svend Robinson: A Life in Politics* (Vancouver: New Star Books, 2013), 73.
51  Sheppard and Valpy, *The National Deal*, 119.
52  Truelove, *Svend Robinson*, 73.
53  Michael Valpy, "A Charter of Equivocal Rights," *Vancouver Sun*, 3 November 1980.
54  Joint Committee, *Proceedings: Report to Parliament*, issue 57: 6.
55  Sheppard and Valpy, *The National Deal*, 119.
56  Joint Committee, *Proceedings: Report to Parliament*, issue 57: 5.
57  Lawrence Martin, *Chrétien*, vol. 1, *The Will to Win* (Toronto: Lester Publishing, 1995), 277; Sheppard and Valpy, *The National Deal*, 21–2.
58  Martin, *The Will to Win*, 279.
59  Ibid.
60  Jean Chrétien, *Straight from the Heart*, rev. ed. (Toronto: Key Porter, 1994), 125.
61  Martin, *The Will to Win*, 299–300.
62  Ibid., 306.
63  Barry L. Strayer, *Canada's Constitutional Revolution* (Edmonton: University of Alberta Press, 2013), 154–5.
64  Roger Tassé, *A Life in the Law – The Constitution and Much More: Memoirs of a Federal Deputy Minister of Justice* (Toronto: Thomson Reuters, 2013), 189.
65  Ibid., 140.
66  Radio-Canada.ca, "Le père de la Charte des droits et libertés en faveur de celle des valeurs," 29 December 2013, http://ici.radio-canada.ca/nouvelles/societe/2013/12/28/002-pere-charte-canadienne-droits-libertes-charte-valeur-quebecoise-laicite-roger-tasse.shtml.
67  Sheppard and Valpy, *The National Deal*, 149.
68  Chrétien, *Straight from the Heart*, 219–20.
69  Strayer, *Canada's Constitutional Revolution*, 25.
70  Ibid., 156.
71  Ibid., 157.
72  Ibid., 156–7.
73  *Reference re Motor Vehicle Act (British Columbia), s. 94*, [1985] 2 S.C.R. 486 [*B.C. Motor Vehicle Reference*].
74  Ibid., para. 52.

75  See *Canada (Attorney General) v. Hislop*, [2007] 1 S.C.R. 429, 2007 SCC 10.

76  Sheppard and Valpy, *The National Deal*, 161; Joint Committee, *Proceedings*, issue 31: 6–7.

77  Joint Committee, *Proceedings*, issue 32: 5–28.

78  Joint Committee, *Proceedings*, issue 24: 7–9, 19–20.

79  Victor Rabinovitch, email message to author, 24 November 2016.

80  Joint Committee, *Proceedings*, issue 22: 7–9.

81  Joint Committee, *Proceedings*, issue 26: 11.

82  *Calder et al. v. Attorney-General of British Columbia*, [1973] S.C.R. 313.

83  Douglas E. Sanders, "The Indian Lobby," in *And No One Cheered: Federalism, Democracy and the Constitution Act*, ed. Keith Banting and Richard Simeon (Toronto: Methuen, 1983), 310.

84  Ibid., 313.

85  Joint Committee, "Report to Parliament and Proposed Resolution for a Joint Address to Her Majesty the Queen Respecting the Constitution of Canada, as Amended by the Committee," *Proceedings*, 57: 2–37, 13 February 1981 (proposed section 35).

86  See Constitution Act, 1982, s. 37 repealed by Constitution Act, 1982, s. 54 on 17 April 1983; Constitution Act, 1982, s. 37.1 repealed by Constitution Act, 1982, s. 54. See also Constitution Act, 1982, s. 35.1.

87  *Reference re meaning of the word "Persons" in s. 24 of British North America Act*, [1928] S.C.R. 276, 290.

88  Henrietta Muir Edwards and others (Appeal No. 121 of 1928) v the Attorney-General of Canada (Canada), [1929] UKPC 86, [1930] A.C. 124, 136. See, generally, Robert J. Sharpe and Patricia I. McMahon, *The Persons Case: The Origins and Legacy of the Fight for Legal Personhood* (Toronto: Osgoode Society for Canadian Legal History, 2007).

89  Mary Eberts, "Women and Constitutional Renewal," in *Women and the Constitution in Canada*, ed. Audrey Doerr and Micheline Carrier (Ottawa: Canadian Advisory Council on the Status of Women, 1981), 3.

90  Ibid., 6.

91  *Attorney General of Canada v. Lavell*, [1974] S.C.R. 1349.

92  *Bliss v. Attorney General of Canada*, [1979] 1 S.C.R. 183.

93  Joint Committee, *Proceedings*, issue 11: 26–8.

94  Chaviva Hošek, "Women and the Constitutional Process," in *And No One Cheered: Federalism, Democracy and the Constitution Act*, ed. Keith Banting and Richard Simeon (Toronto: Methuen, 1983), 280, 285–6.

95  Ibid., 280, 286–8.

96  Ibid., 280, 286.

## Chapter 3

1   "Room 200 West Block, The Confederation Room, The House of Commons Heritage Collection," Parliament of Canada website, http://www.parl.gc.ca/About/House/collections/collection_profiles/CP_room200-e.htm.
2   Ibid.
3   Canada, Parliament, Special Joint Committee on the Constitution of Canada, *Minutes of Proceedings and Evidence*, 32nd Parliament, 1st Session, issue 1 (6 November 1980): 27.
4   Ibid., 34–5.
5   Ibid., 7–8.
6   Canada, Parliament, Cabinet, *Minutes*, 30 September 1980, No. 75-80 CBM.
7   Joint Committee, *Proceedings*, issue 1: 48–75.
8   Cabinet, *Minutes*, 13 November 1980, No. 82-80 CBM.
9   Joint Committee, *Proceedings: Report to Parliament*, issue 57 (13 February 1981): 4.
10  Joint Committee, *Proceedings*, issue 1: 12.
11  Joint Committee, *Proceedings: Report to Parliament*, issue 57: 5.
12  Joint Committee, *Proceedings*, issue 2: 23–6.
13  Ibid., 23–45.
14  Joint Committee, *Proceedings*, issue 5 (14 November 1980): 6.
15  Ibid., 20.
16  Ibid.
17  Ibid., 9.
18  Ibid.
19  Ibid., 15–16.
20  Ibid., 16.
21  Ibid., 9.
22  On the evolution of s. 1, see Barry L. Strayer, "The Evolution of the Charter," in *Patriation and Its Consequences: Constitution Making in Canada*, ed. Lois Harder and Steve Patten (Vancouver: UBC Press, 2015), 82–4.
23  Joint Committee, *Proceedings*, issue 7 (18 November 1980): 7.
24  Canada, Parliament, Cabinet Committee on Priorities and Planning, *Minutes*, 26 November 1980, 26-80 CMPP.
25  Cabinet, *Minutes*, 27 November 1980, No. 84-80 CRM.
26  Joint Committee, *Proceedings*, issue 7: 7.
27  Joint Committee, *Proceedings*, issue 22: 32.
28  Joint Committee, *Proceedings*, issue 21: 17.
29  Cabinet Committee on Priorities and Planning, *Minutes*, 26 November 1980, 26-80 CMPP.

30  Joint Committee, *Proceedings*, issue 7: 80.
31  Ibid., 81.
32  Ibid., 82.
33  Joint Committee, *Proceedings*, issue 9 (20 November 1980): 57.
34  Ibid., 75.
35  Ibid.
36  Ibid.
37  Marilou McPhedran, "A Truer Story: Constitutional Trialogue," in *A Living Tree: The Legacy of 1982 in Canada's Political Evolution*, ed. Graeme Mitchell, Ian Peach, David E. Smith, and John D. Whyte (Toronto: LexisNexis, 2007), 101, 118.
38  See Alexandra Dobrowolsky, *The Politics of Pragmatism: Women, Representation, and Constitutionalism in Canada* (Toronto: Oxford University Press, 2000), 48.
39  International Women's Rights Project, *Constitute!* 33:13, http://constitute.ca/the-film/.
40  *Ottawa Citizen*, 5 May 1982, 11.
41  Joint Committee, *Proceedings*, Index, 51.
42  Joint Committee, *Proceedings*, issue 13: 5.
43  Ibid.
44  Ibid., 6–7.
45  Ibid., 9, 25.
46  Ibid., 6.
47  Ibid., 11.
48  Robert Sheppard and Michael Valpy, *The National Deal: The Fight for a Canadian Constitution* (Toronto: Fleet Books, 1982), 136 note.
49  Joint Committee, *Proceedings*, issue 41: 101.
50  See *R. v. Morgentaler*, [1988] 1 S.C.R. 30 (which struck down the Criminal Code prohibition on abortion as unconstitutional) and *United States v. Burns*, [2001] 1 S.C.R. 283, 2001 SCC 27 (which held that the Charter prohibited the extradition of persons to face the death penalty in all but exceptional cases).
51  See Cabinet, *Minutes*, 17 November 1980, No. 84-80 CBM; 11 December 1980, No. 86-80 CBM; 19 December 1980, No. 87-80 CBM.
52  Joint Committee, *Proceedings*, issue 23: 8–9, 11.
53  Joint Committee, *Proceedings*, issue 30: 39.
54  An example of this minimal discussion can be found in Cabinet, *Minutes*, 30 September 1980, No. 75-80 CBM, which stated that Aboriginal rights would not be satisfied with the provision to the effect that whatever rights they might have would be unaffected. They would want protection of

treaty and Aboriginal rights. While protection of treaty rights might be acceptable to the government, protection of Aboriginal rights, which were vague and which Aboriginal peoples were reluctant ever to give up, even for full compensation, was not. Aboriginal groups might create political problems in London, but this problem might be mitigated if the prime minister met with their leaders at an early date.

55  Cabinet, *Minutes*, 27 November 1980, No. 84-80 CBM (the Constitution and Native Peoples).

56  See Louise Mandell and Leslie Hall Pinder, "Tracking Justice: The Constitution Express to Section 35 and Beyond," in *Patriation and Its Consequences: Constitution Making in Canada*, ed. Lois Harder and Steve Patten (Vancouver: UBC Press, 2015), 180.

57  Joint Committee, *Proceedings*, issue 31: 91.

58  Joint Committee, *Proceedings: Report to Parliament*, issue 57 (appendix B): 44–53.

59  Ibid., 5.

60  Joint Committee, *Proceedings*, issue 35: 78–9.

61  Ibid., 80–1.

62  Joint Committee, *Proceedings: Report to Parliament*, issue 57: 6.

63  Joint Committee, *Proceedings*, issue 43: 7–8.

64  Joint Committee, *Proceedings*, issue 36: 10.

65  Cabinet Committee on Priorities and Planning, *Minutes*, 26 November 1980, 26-80 CMPP.

66  Joint Committee, *Proceedings*, issue 36: 10.

67  Sheppard and Valpy, *The National Deal*, 143.

68  Cabinet Committee on Priorities and Planning, *Minutes*, 16 December 1980, 29-80 CMPP.

69  Lawrence Martin, *Chrétien*, vol. 1, *The Will to Win* (Toronto: Lester Publishing, 1995), 300.

70  Joint Committee, *Proceedings*, issue 43: 59.

71  Graeme Truelove, *Svend Robinson: A Political Life* (Vancouver: New Star Books, 1983), 82–4. See also Dwight Newman and Lorelle Binnion, "The Exclusion of Property Rights from the *Charter*: Correcting the Historical Record," *Alberta Law Review* 52, no. 3 (2015): 543.

72  Joint Committee, *Proceedings*, issue 45: 4–5.

73  Joint Committee, *Proceedings*, issue 41: 96–101.

74  Joint Committee, *Proceedings*, issue 46: 127.

75  Joint Committee, *Proceedings*, issue 50: 86.

76  Cabinet, *Minutes*, 29 January 1981, No. 3-81 CBM.

77  Joint Committee, *Proceedings*, issue 56: 13.

78  Ibid., 63–5.
79  Ibid., 65.
80  Joint Committee, *Proceedings*, issue 30 (19 December 1980): 39.

**Chapter 4**

1  David Milne, *The New Canadian Constitution* (Toronto: Lorimer, 1982), 88.
2  Peter H. Russell, *Constitutional Odyssey: Can Canadians Become a Sovereign People?*, 3rd ed. (Toronto: University of Toronto Press, 2004), 115–16; also cites sources.
3  Barry L. Strayer, *Canada's Constitutional Revolution* (Edmonton: University of Alberta Press, 2013), 165.
4  Milne, *The New Canadian Constitution*, 97–8.
5  Canada, Parliament, Cabinet, *Minutes*, 12 February 1981, No. 5-81 CBM.
6  Cabinet, *Minutes*, 5 March 1981, No. 8-81 CBM.
7  Cabinet, *Minutes*, 12 March 1981, No. 9-81 CBM.
8  Milne, *The New Canadian Constitution*, 98.
9  Robert Sheppard and Michael Valpy, *The National Deal: The Fight for a Canadian Constitution* (Toronto: Fleet Books, 1982), 143; Milne, *The New Canadian Constitution*, 99–100.
10  Canada, Parliament, House of Commons, *Debates*, 32nd Parliament, 1st Session, 23 April 1981, 9470–2.
11  See Penney Kome, *The Taking of Twenty-Eight: Women Challenge the Constitution* (Toronto: Women's Press, 1983).
12  House of Commons, *Debates*, 32nd Parliament, 1st Session, 23 April 1981; Charter, preamble. According to Barry Strayer, Cabinet agreed to add the preamble, long sought by the Tories, on 16 April 1981; see Strayer, *Canada's Constitutional Revolution*, 162–3, which cites the Cabinet minutes of that date.
13  House of Commons, *Debates*, 32nd Parliament, 1st Session, 23 April 1981, 9471–3.
14  Ibid., 9474.
15  Sheppard and Valpy, *The National Deal*, 143.
16  "Constitutional Accord: Canadian Patriation Plan, April 16, 1981, Document 850-19/002," in *Canada's Constitution Act 1982 and Amendments: A Documentary History*, ed. Anne F. Bayefsky (Toronto: McGraw-Hill Ryerson, 1989), 805.
17  "News Release, April 16, 1981, Document 850-19/001," in Bayefsky, *Canada's Constitution Act 1982 and Amendments*, 804.
18  Cabinet, *Minutes*, 2 July 1981, No. 25-81 CBM.

19  Cabinet, *Minutes*, 16 July 1981, No. 27-81 CBM.

20  Cabinet, *Minutes*, 24 September 1981, No. 32-81 CBM.

21  See Philip Girard, *Bora Laskin: Bringing Law to Life* (Toronto: Osgoode Society for Legal History, 2005), 509.

22  See *Resolution to Amend the Constitution*, [1981] 1 S.C.R. 753 [*Patriation Reference*].

23  For contemporary accounts, see, e.g., Milne, *The New Canadian Constitution*, 104–34; William Lederman, "The Supreme Court of Canada and Basic Constitutional Amendment," in *And No One Cheered: Federalism, Democracy and the Constitution Act*, ed. Keith Banting and Richard Simeon (Toronto: Methuen, 1983), 176; Gil Rémillard, "Legality, Legitimacy and the Supreme Court," in Banting and Simeon, eds., *And No One Cheered*, 189; Peter Russell, "Bold Statecraft, Questionable Jurisprudence," in Banting and Simeon, eds., *And No One Cheered*, 210; and Edward McWhinney, *Canada and the Constitution 1979–1982* (Toronto: University of Toronto Press, 1982), 80–9. For more recent evaluation, see Philip Girard, "Law, Politics, and the *Patriation Reference* of 1981," in *Patriation and Its Consequences: Constitution Making in Canada*, ed. Lois Harder and Steve Patten (Vancouver: UBC Press, 2015), 115.

24  See, e.g., Russell, "Bold Statecraft, Questionable Jurisprudence," 210.

25  Strayer, *Canada's Constitutional Revolution*, 195.

26  For the text of the 5 November 1981 accord, see Howard Leeson, *The Patriation Minutes* (Edmonton: Centre for Constitutional Studies, Faculty of Law, University of Alberta, 2011), 101–3. On the November Accord, see Roy Romanow, Howard Leeson, and John Whyte, *Canada … Notwithstanding: The Making of the Constitution 1976–1982* (Toronto: Carswell, 2007); Ron Graham, *The Last Act: Pierre Trudeau, the Gang of Eight and the Fight for Canada* (Toronto: Allen Lane Canada, 2011), 357–86; McWhinney, *Canada and the Constitution 1979–1982*, 90–101; Milne, *The New Canadian Constitution*, 135–64; Stephen Clarkson and Christina McCall, *Trudeau and Our Times*, vol. 1, *The Magnificent Obsession* (Toronto: McClelland and Stewart, 1990), 357–87; Sheppard and Valpy, *The National Deal*, 263–302; Brian Peckford, *Some Day the Sun Will Shine and Have Not Will Be No More* (St. John's, NL: Flanker Press, 2012), 176–7, 251–89.

27  Milne, *The New Canadian Constitution*, 141.

28  Sheppard and Valpy, *The National Deal*, 263.

29  Milne, *The New Canadian Constitution*, 156–8; Romanow, Leeson, and Whyte, *Canada … Notwithstanding*, 209–11.

30  "Fact Sheet: The Notwithstanding or Override Clause as Applied to the Charter of Rights and Freedoms, Document 800-15/022," in *Canada's Constitution Act 1982 and Amendments: A Documentary History*, ed. Anne F. Bayefsky (Toronto: McGraw-Hill Ryerson, 1989), 905.

31 Canada, Parliament, Special Joint Committee on the Constitution of Canada, *Minutes of Proceedings and Evidence*, 32nd Parliament, 1st Session, issue 30: 39.
32 Sheppard and Valpy, *The National Deal*, 144.
33 See Adam M. Dodek, "The Canadian Override: Constitutional Model or *Bête Noire* of Canadian Constitutional Politics?," *Israel Law Review* 48, no. 3 (2015): 45.
34 Russell, *Constitutional Odyssey*, 120.
35 Chaviva Hošek, "Women and the Constitutional Process," in *And No One Cheered: Federalism, Democracy and the Constitution Act*, ed. Keith Banting and Richard Simeon (Toronto: Methuen, 1983), 280, 291.
36 Sheppard and Valpy, *The National Deal*, 307.
37 House of Commons, *Debates*, 32nd Parliament, 1st Session, 6 November 1981, 12594.
38 Ibid., 9 November 1981, 12634.
39 Cabinet, *Minutes*, 6 November 1981, No. 39-81 CBM.
40 House of Commons, *Debates*, 32nd Parliament, 1st Session, 20 November 1981, 12992–3.
41 Hošek, "Women and the Constitutional Process," 292–5.
42 Sheppard and Valpy, *The National Deal*, 307.
43 Ibid.
44 House of Commons, *Debates*, 32nd Parliament, 1st Session, 24 November 1981, 13345.
45 House of Commons, *Debates*, 32nd Parliament, 1st Session, 26 November 1981, 13200.
46 McWhinney, *Canada and the Constitution 1979–1982*, 112.
47 House of Commons, *Debates*, 32nd Parliament, 1st Session, 2 December 1981, 13663.
48 Sheppard and Valpy, *The National Deal*, 144.
49 Ibid., 311.
50 Cabinet, *Minutes*, 3 December 1981, No. 45-81 CBM.
51 House of Commons, *Debates*, 32nd Parliament, 1st Session, 2 December 1981, 13663.
52 See Nathan Nurgitz and Hugh Segal, *No Small Measure: The Progressive Conservatives and the Constitution* (Ottawa: Deneau Publishers, 1983), 70; Graeme Truelove, *Svend Robinson: A Life in Politics* (Vancouver: New Star Books, 2013), 79.
53 Canada, Parliament, Senate, *Debates*, 32nd Parliament, 1st Session, 8 December 1981, 3428.
54 Sheppard and Valpy, *The National Deal*, 312.
55 Ibid., 159.

56 Senator Serge Joyal, who co-chaired the Joint Committee, was sworn in as a member of the Privy Council for Canada on 22 September 1981, when Pierre Trudeau made him a minister of state (without portfolio).

## Chapter 5

1 Canada, Parliament, Cabinet, *Minutes*, 11 December 1980, No. 87-80 CBM.

## Chapter 6

1 See *Health Services and Support – Facilities Subsector Bargaining Assn. v. British Columbia*, [2007] 2 S.C.R. 391.

## Chapter 7

1 Access to Information Act, RSC 1985, c. A-1.

## Chapter 10

1 Canada, Parliament, Special Joint Committee on the Constitution of Canada, *Minutes of Proceedings and Evidence*, 32nd Parliament, 1st Session, issue 25: 6–14 (Statement of Canadian National Institute for the Blind).
2 Joint Committee, *Proceedings*, issue 29: 8–10 (Statement of Church of Jesus Christ of Latter Day Saints); see also issue 29: 11–14, 16–17 (Questions to Church of Jesus Christ of Latter Day Saints).
3 Joint Committee, *Proceedings*, issue 33: 71–3 (Questions to Ontario Conference of Catholic Bishops).
4 Ibid., 87–92 (Statement of Canadian Life and Health Insurance Association; ibid., 93, 95–7 (Questions to Canadian Life and Health Insurance Association).
5 Joint Committee, *Proceedings*, issue 5: 8–9 (Statement of Canadian Human Rights Commission); issue 7: 93–4 (Statement of Canadian Jewish Congress); issue 21: 8 (Statement of Canadian Federation of Civil Liberties and Human Rights Associations); issue 21: 11–12, 21–2, 25–6 (Questions to Canadian Federation of Civil Liberties and Human Rights Associations).
6 Joint Committee, *Proceedings*, issue 47: 88–92 (Amendment G-20 and subamendments N-21 and CP-8(1)).
7 Joint Committee, *Proceedings*, issue 36: 13–15 (Statement of Minister of Justice); see also issue 41: 17–24 (Questions to Department of Justice).
8 See *Canadian Foundation for Children, Youth and the Law v. Canada (Attorney General)*, [2004] SCC 4.

Chapter 11

1 Canada, Parliament, Special Joint Committee on the Constitution of
  Canada, *Minutes of Proceedings and Evidence*, 32nd Parliament, 1st Session,
  issue 2: 26–7, 28–30 (Questions to Minister of Justice); issue 2: 40 (Comment of Mr. Lapierre on section 133); issue 2: 43–4 (Questions to Minister
  of Justice on provincial bilingualism); issue 3: 17–18 (Exchange between
  Minister Chrétien and Mr. Corbin on provincial bilingualism); issue 3:
  60–1 (Comment of Minister Chrétien on section 133); 4: 20–3 (Questions to
  Minister Chrétien on section 133); issue 4: 137–41 (Questions to Minister
  of Justice regarding institutional bilingualism); issue 6: 27 (Comment of
  Commissioner of Official Languages on BNA Act section 133); issue 7: 61–2
  (Questions to Positive Action Committee on provincial bilingualism); issue
  7: 75–6, 77–9 (Questions to Positive Action Committee on provincial bilingualism); issue 8: 36–7, 39–40 (Questions to linguistic minority groups);
  issue 12: 20–1 (Questions to Association culturelle franco-canadienne de
  la Saskatchewan on Section 133); issue 27: 15–16 (Statement of Canadians
  for One Canada); issue 27: 20–3 (Questions to Canadians for One Canada);
  issue 33: 84–5 (Comment of Mr Irwin on section 133); issue 35: 33–4 (Question to Professor Rémillard on section 133); issue 51: 75–6 (Comments of
  Mr Fraser on section 133); issue 51: 81 (Comments of Mr Mackasey on
  section 133).
2 Joint Committee, *Proceedings*, issue 3: 57 (Comment of Minister of Justice
  responding to Senator Asselin).
3 S. 16.1 was added by the Constitution Amendment, 1993 (New Brunswick);
  see SI/93-54.
4 Joint Committee, *Proceedings*, issue 14: 99–100 (Questions to premier of PEI
  on provincial bilingualism); issue 17: 43 (Comment of premier of Nova
  Scotia).
5 Joint Committee, *Proceedings*, issue 30: 51–2 (Comments of Mr Corbin to
  premier of Saskatchewan); see also issue 32: 139–42 (Question to PC Party of
  Saskatchewan regarding French in Saskatchewan).
6 Joint Committee, *Proceedings*, issue 33: 104 (Statement of Alberta NDP);
  issue 33: 179 (Comment of Social Credit Party of Alberta).
7 Joint Committee, *Proceedings*, issue 4: 60–1 (Question to Minister of Justice on section 20); (n1), issue 12: 8–12 (Statement of Association culturelle
  franco-canadienne de la Saskatchewan); issue 33: 69–71 (Questions to
  Ontario Conference of Catholic Bishops).
8 Joint Committee, *Proceedings*, issue 15: 9–10 (Statement of CBA Special
  Committee on Constitution of Canada).

Chapter 12

1  *R. v. Drybones,* [1970] S.C.R. 282.

Chapter 15

1  Canada, Parliament, Special Joint Committee on the Constitution of Canada, *Minutes of Proceedings and Evidence,* 32nd Parliament, 1st Session, issue
26: 19 (Statement of Nishga Tribal Council); issue 33: 19–20 (Questions to
Anglican Church of Canada); issue 37: 27 (Comment of Minister Chrétien
re post-patriation negotiations).
2  Joint Committee, *Proceedings,* issue 26: 19.
3  Joint Committee, *Proceedings,* issue 30: 55–6 (Statement of Saskatchewan
Premier Allan Blakeney).
4  Joint Committee, *Proceedings,* issue 49: 90 (Mr. Allmand).
5  Joint Committee, *Proceedings,* issue 17: 121.
6  Joint Committee, *Proceedings,* issue 3: 76 (Minister Chrétien).
7  Joint Committee, *Proceedings,* issue 16: 5–18 (Statement of Inuit Committee
on National Issues).
8  Ibid., 28–9 (Question to Inuit Committee on National Issues re Royal Proclamation); issue 17: 8–11 (Questions to Inuit Committee on National Issues
re Aboriginal rights); issue 17: 128–30 (Further questions to Native Council
of Canada); issue 22: 138–46, 48–9 (Questions to Association of Métis and
Non-Status Indians of Saskatchewan); issue 27: 83 (Statement of National
Indian Brotherhood); issue 27: 145 (Further questions to Nuu-chah-nulth
Tribal Council); issue 28: 22 (Questions to Attikamek-Montagnais Council);
issue 31: 35–42 (Question to Union of Ontario Indians); issue 32: 95–6 (Joint
questions to Union of New Brunswick Indians and the Union of Nova
Scotia Indians).
9  Joint Committee, *Proceedings,* issue 38: 66–72 (Further questions to government re new draft text); issue 54: 103 (Comments re [non]inclusion of
Royal Proclamation in Constitution).
10 Joint Committee, *Proceedings,* issue 33: 116 (Question re gender and
Aboriginal culture); issue 54: 20–1 (Aboriginal rights and jurisdiction
over land); 27: issue 108–9, 110–11; issue 26: 24, 27–8 (Statement of Nishga
Council); issue 26: 33–4 (Questions to Nishga Tribal Council re Aboriginal
title); issue 27: 103–12 (Further questions to National Indian Brotherhood),
including issue 31: 54 (Questions to Association of Iroquois and Allied
Indians); issue 31: 74 (Joint questions to Federation of Saskatchewan Indians and Indian Association of Alberta).

11  Joint Committee, *Proceedings*, issue 26: 15 (Statement of Nishga Tribal Council); issue 26: 21–8 (Questions to Nishga Tribal Council); issue 33: 116 (Questions to Alberta NDP); issue 27: 141 (Further questions to Nuu-chah-nulth Tribal Council).
12  *Calder et al. v. Attorney-General of British Columbia*, [1973] S.C.R. 313.
13  Joint Committee, *Proceedings*, issue 31: 12 (Excerpts from statement of Algonquin Council).
14  Joint Committee, *Proceedings*, issue 26: 31–4 (Questions to Nishga Tribal Council re Aboriginal title); issue 27: 141–4, 149 (Further Questions to Nuu-chah-nulth Tribal Council); issue 33: 120–2 (Questions to Alberta NDP).
15  Joint Committee, *Proceedings*, issue 17: 66, 98–9.
16  Joint Committee, *Proceedings*, issue 12: 57–8, 67–8, 73; issue 16: 9–10; issue 17: 21–4.

# Index

126–7; on rights of minorities, 376; on selective hiring practices, 382–3; on separation of church and state, 385
handicapped people, 87–8, 233, 257, 258, 260, 261–2
Hardy, Alison, 129–30, 147
Harper, Stephen, 40, 42
hate propaganda, 132, 140
Hatfield, Richard, 260, 294, 296, 307, 310, 312, 317–18
Hawkes, Jim: on access to social services, 181, 183; on authority of the courts, 363, 364; on continuation of Parliament, 154; debates about judicial review, 339, 349; on definition of bad legislation, 251; on definition of Métis, 409; as member of the Joint Committee, 42, 63; on mobility rights, 163, 167; on protection of minority groups, 387, 421; on protection of rights by the Charter, 345; on remedies clause, 363; on rights of the fetus, 125
Hays, Harry, 30, 31, 33, 34, 60, 64, 69–70
Head, Wilson: on affirmative actions, 280–1; on apprehended emergency, 151; on definition of "fundamental justice," 192; on discrimination, 270–1; on freedom of expression, 131; on Ku Klux Klan, 133, 134–5, 136–7; on limits of freedom of speech, 136; member of National Black Coalition, 8, 48; on power of courts to judicial review, 350–1; on rights of the native people, 273; on right to vote, 150

Henderson, George, 33, 34, 37, 168–9
Henderson, Sageth, 418
Hervieux-Payette, Céline, 415
Hislop, George, 47
*Hogan* case *(Hogan v. R.)*, 91, 354
Hošek, Chaviva, 5, 6, 51
Huffington, Arianna, 20
Hughes, Charles Evans, 345–6
Hughes, Sam, 170, 174
Humphrey, John, 47

Indian Act, 274
individual rights: *vs.* collective rights, 379–86, 382, 383–4, 385
institutional bilingualism, 293, 294, 308–16
International Bill of Human Rights, 140
International Covenant on Civil and Political Rights, 94, 98, 223, 228, 229, 231, 239, 254
Inuit people, 166
Irwin, Ron: on amendment to clause on ex post facto laws, 230; on amendment to denomination rights, 395–6; career of, 37; on cultural intrusion into the North, 166–7; on equality rights, 248; on language in legal proceedings, 325; limitation clause debate, 91; as member of the Joint Committee, 33, 34; on mobility rights, 166, 167; on non-discrimination before the law, 252–3; on protection from vandalism and defamation, 118–19
Ittinuar, Peter, 407, 427

Janzen, William, 122–3, 124, 142–3
Japanese Canadians, 89, 90, 99, 100
Jewett, Pauline, 241, 242–3, 272, 284–5